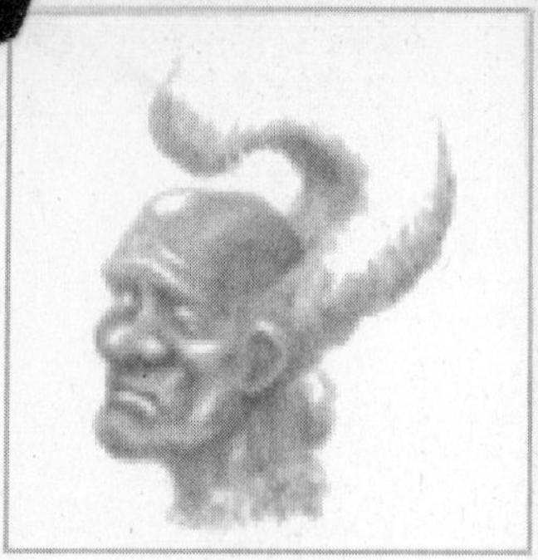

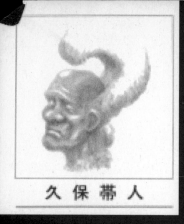

久保帯人

Hello there. You are now holding the very first volume of *BLEACH*. I worked really hard writing it. Please treat it kindly.
Sincerely,
Tite Kubo

BLEACH is author Tite Kubo's second title. Kubo made his debut with *ZOMBIE POWDER*, a four-volume series for Japan's *WEEKLY SHONEN JUMP*. To date, *BLEACH* has sold nearly 7 million volumes and has been translated into seven different languages. Beginning its serialization in 2001, *BLEACH* is still a mainstay in the pages of *WEEKLY SHONEN JUMP*.

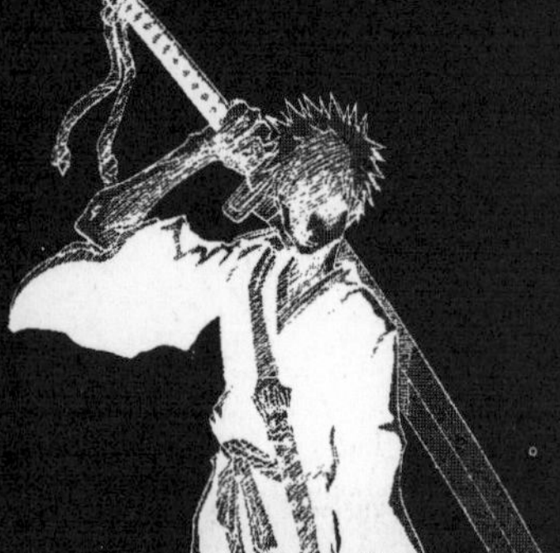

BLEACH VOL. 1
The SHONEN JUMP Graphic Novel Edition

STORY AND ART BY TITE KUBO

English Adaptation/Lance Caselman
Translation/Joe Yamazaki
Touch-up & Lettering/Andy Ristaino
Cover, Graphics & Design/Sean Lee
Editor/Kit Fox

Managing Editor/Annette Roman
Production Manager/Noboru Watanabe
Executive V.P./Editor in Chief/Hyoe Narita
Sr. Director of Licensing & Acquisitions/Rika Inouye
V.P. of Marketing/Liza Coppola
V.P. of Strategic Development/Yumi Hoashi
Publisher/Seiji Horibuchi

PARENTAL ADVISORY
BLEACH is rated "T" for teens. It contains fantasy violence and tobacco use.

Printed in the U.S.A.

Published by VIZ, LLC
P.O. Box 77010
San Francisco, CA 94107

SHONEN JUMP Graphic Novel Edition
10 9 8 7 6 5 4 3 2 1
First printing, May 2004

THE WORLD'S MOST
POPULAR MANGA

www.viz.com

www.shonenjump.com

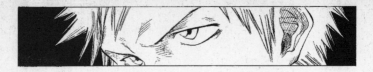

We fear that which we cannot see

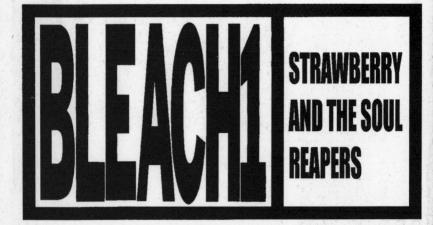

BLEACH 1

STRAWBERRY AND THE SOUL REAPERS

Shonen Jump Graphic Novel

BLEACH1

STRAWBERRY AND THE SOUL REAPERS

Contents

READ THIS WAY

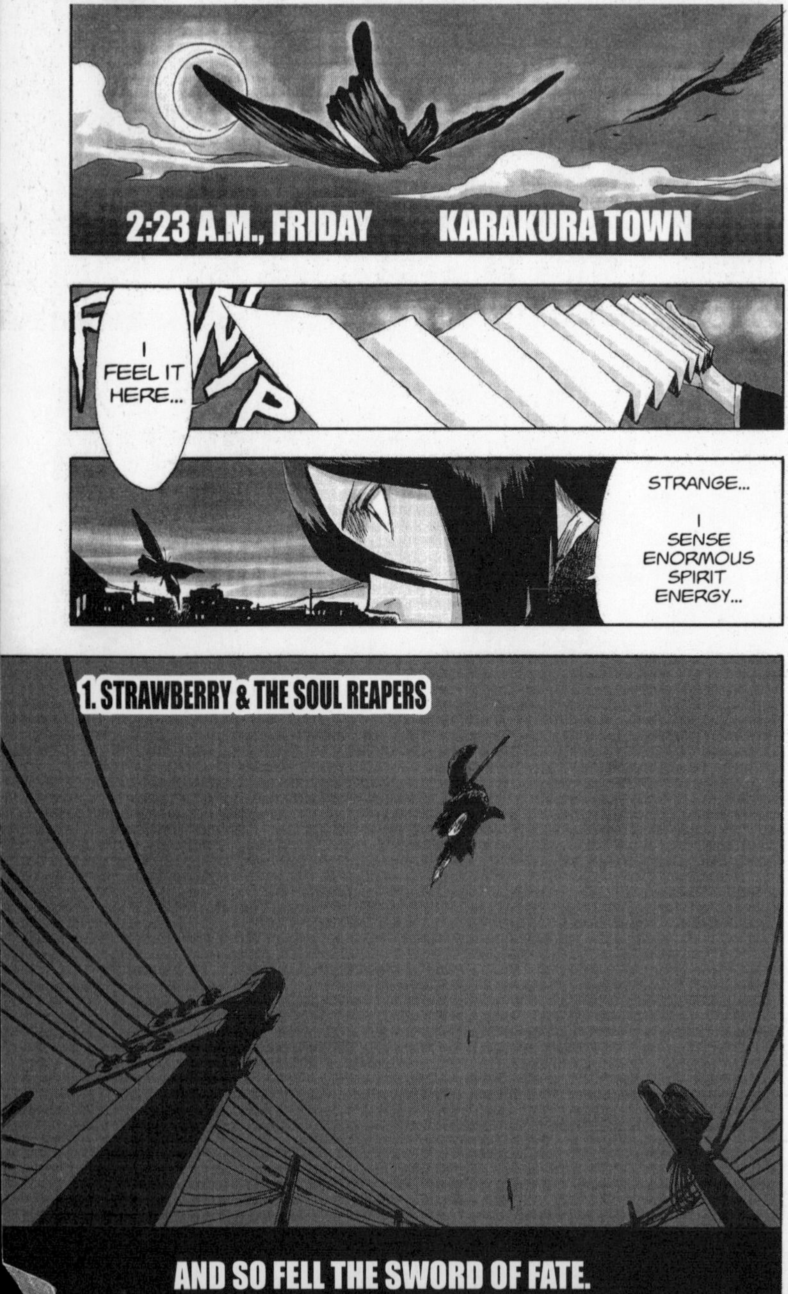
KARAKURA TOWN
2:23 A.M., FRIDAY
FWIP
I FEEL IT HERE...
STRANGE...
I SENSE ENORMOUS SPIRIT ENERGY...
1. STRAWBERRY & THE SOUL REAPERS
AND SO FELL THE SWORD OF FATE.

1. STRAWBERRY & THE SOUL REAPERS

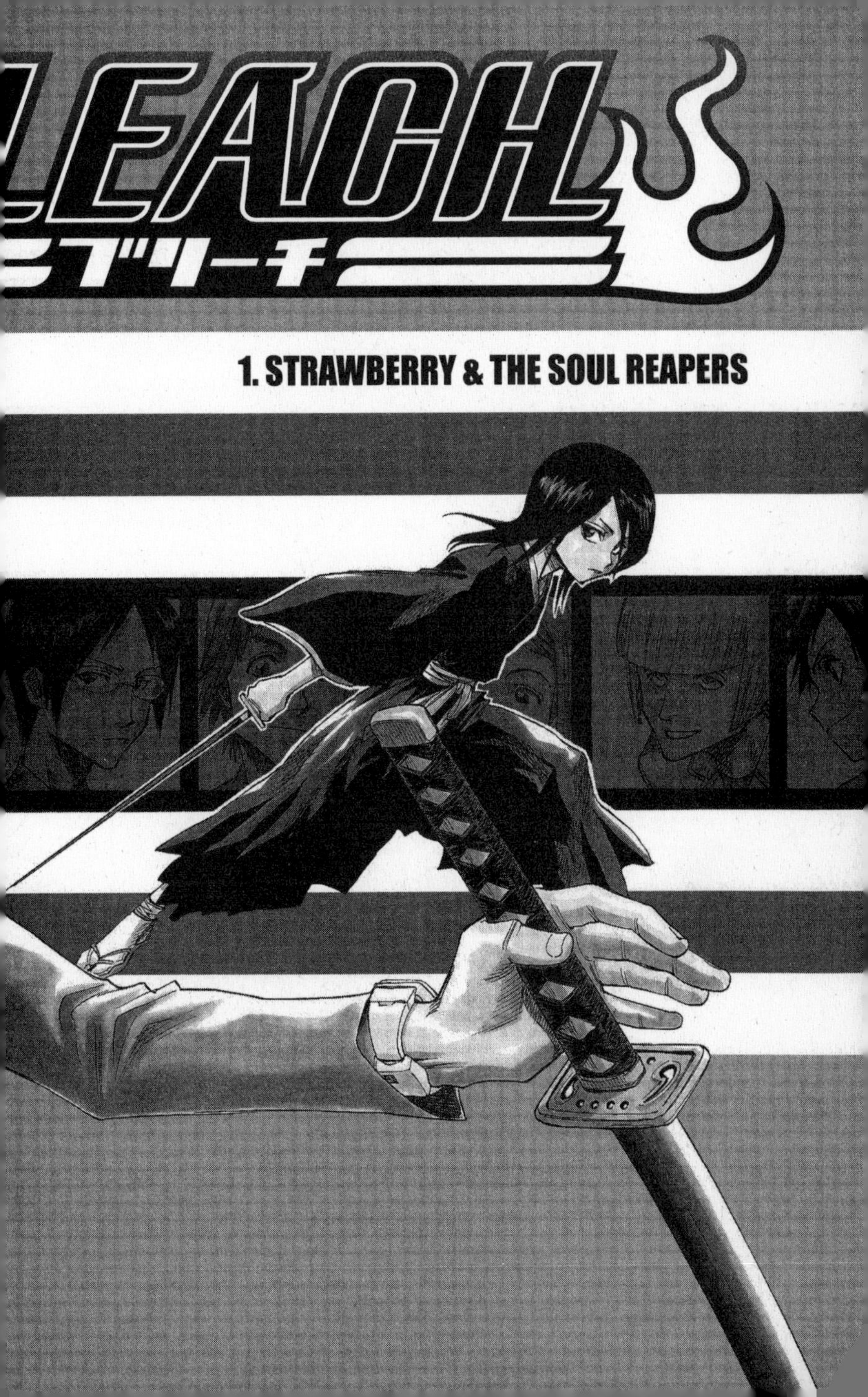

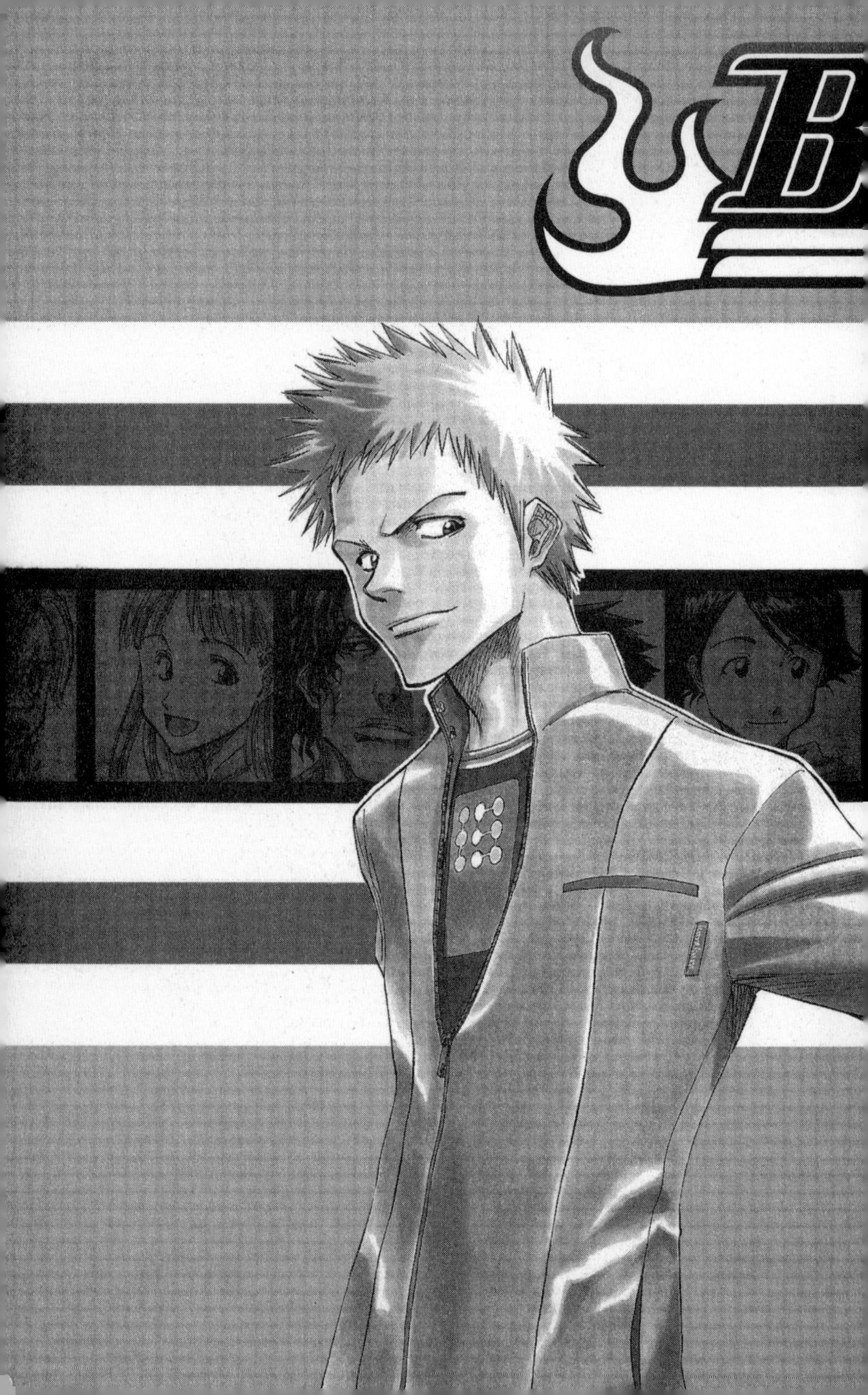

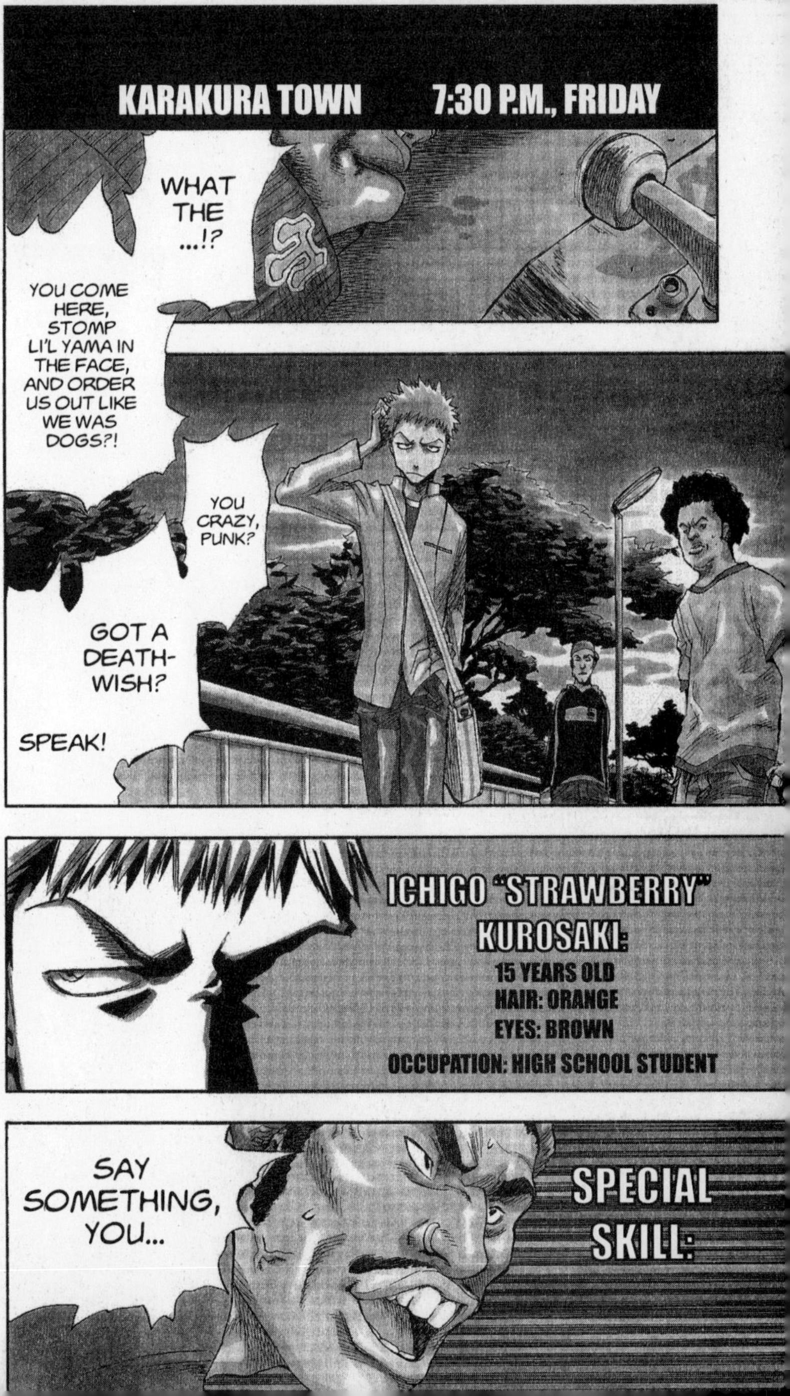
KARAKURA TOWN 7:30 P.M., FRIDAY
WHAT THE ...!?
YOU CRAZY, PUNK?
YOU COME HERE, STOMP LI'L YAMA IN THE FACE, AND ORDER US OUT LIKE WE WAS DOGS?!
GOT A DEATH-WISH?
SPEAK!
ICHIGO "STRAWBERRY" KUROSAKI:
15 YEARS OLD
HAIR: ORANGE
EYES: BROWN
OCCUPATION: HIGH SCHOOL STUDENT
SPECIAL SKILL:
SAY SOMETHING, YOU...

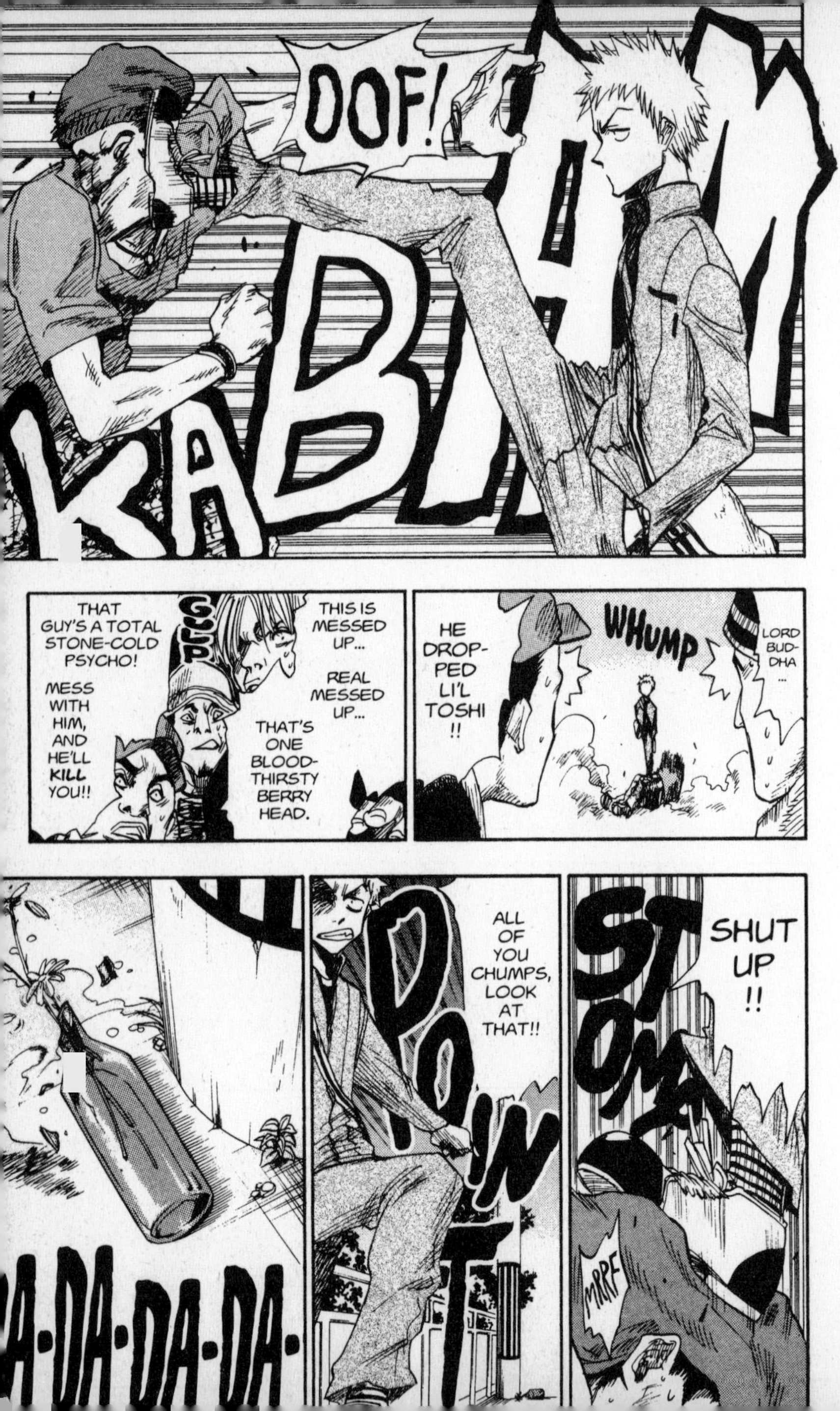

OOF!
KABL
HE DROP-PED LI'L TOSHI !!
WHUMP
LORD BUD-DHA ...
THIS IS MESSED UP...
REAL MESSED UP...
GULP
THAT GUY'S A TOTAL STONE-COLD PSYCHO!
MESS WITH HIM, AND HE'LL **KILL** YOU!!
THAT'S ONE BLOOD-THIRSTY BERRY HEAD.
SHUT UP !!
STOM
MRRF
ALL OF YOU CHUMPS, LOOK AT THAT!!
POINT
DA-DA-DA-DA-

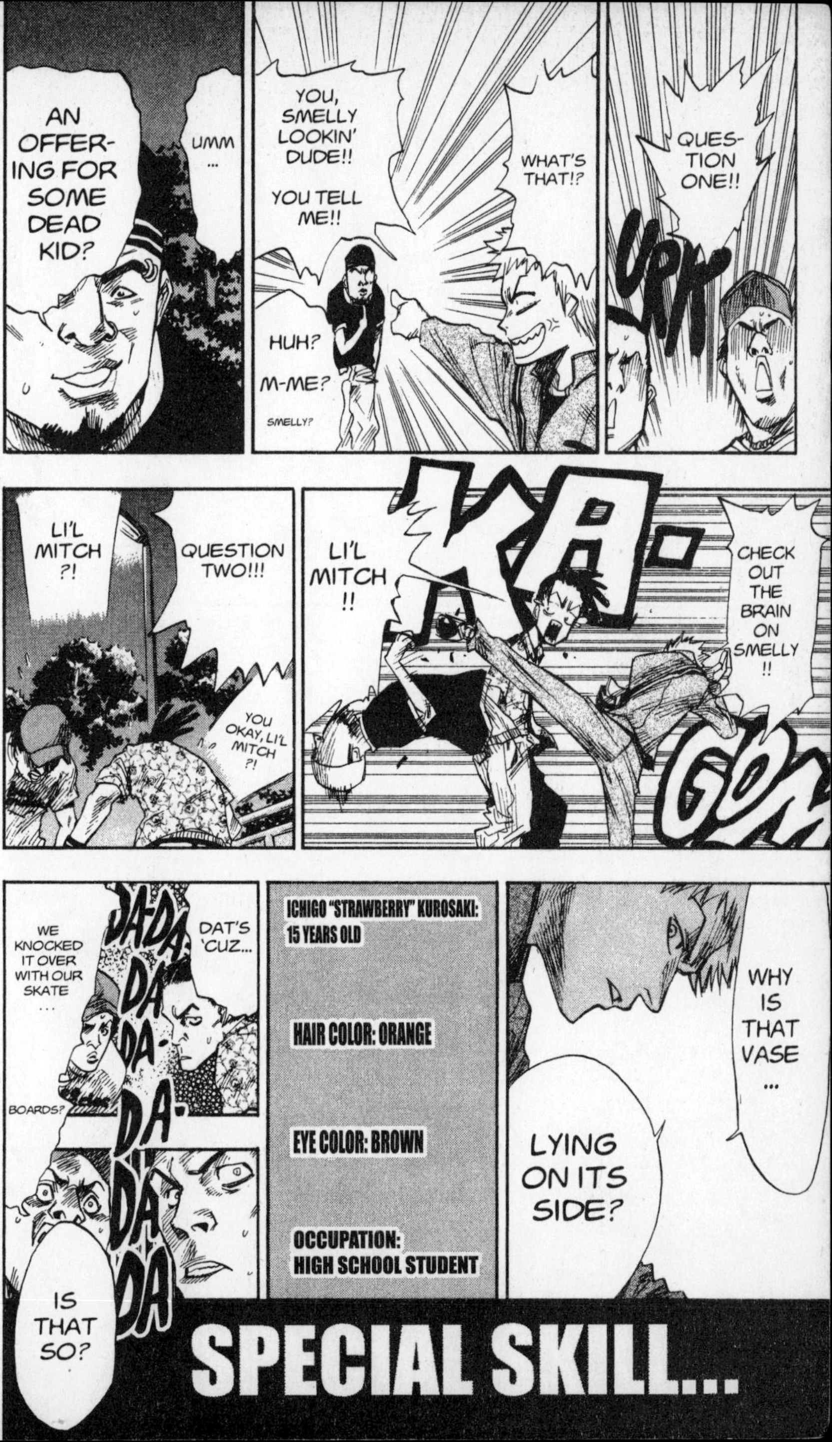
QUESTION ONE!!
URK
WHAT'S THAT!?
YOU, SMELLY LOOKIN' DUDE!!
YOU TELL ME!!
HUH?
M-ME?
SMELLY?
UMM ...
AN OFFERING FOR SOME DEAD KID?
KA-
CHECK OUT THE BRAIN ON SMELLY!!
LI'L MITCH!!
GO
QUESTION TWO!!!
LI'L MITCH ?!
YOU OKAY, LI'L MITCH ?!
WHY IS THAT VASE ...
LYING ON ITS SIDE?
ICHIGO "STRAWBERRY" KUROSAKI: 15 YEARS OLD
HAIR COLOR: ORANGE
EYE COLOR: BROWN
OCCUPATION: HIGH SCHOOL STUDENT
DAT'S 'CUZ...
WE KNOCKED IT OVER WITH OUR SKATE ...
BOARDS?
DA-DA DA DA DA- DA DA DA DA
IS THAT SO?
SPECIAL SKILL...

"HE CAN SEE GHOSTS"

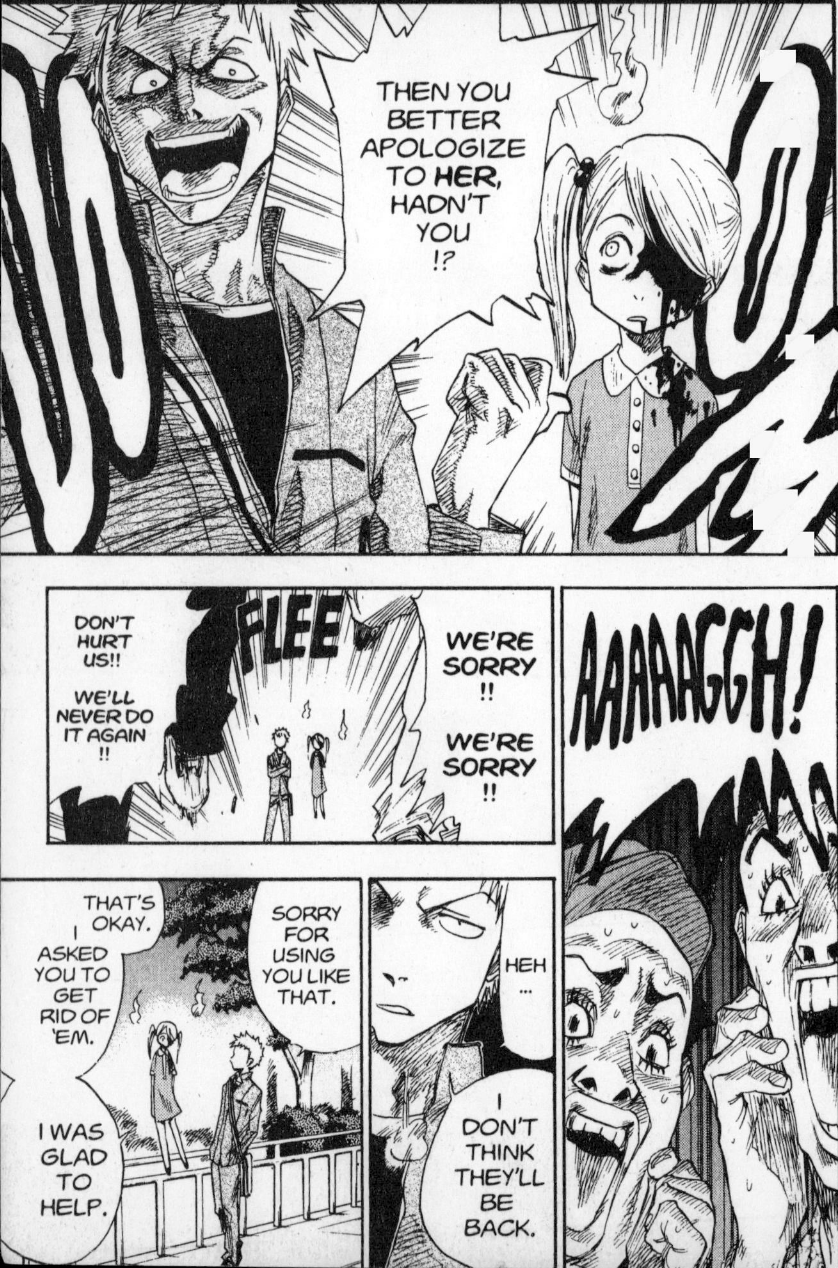
THEN YOU BETTER APOLOGIZE TO HER, HADN'T YOU !?
AAAAGGH!
WE'RE SORRY !!
WE'RE SORRY !!
FLEE
DON'T HURT US!!
WE'LL NEVER DO IT AGAIN !!
HEH ...
I DON'T THINK THEY'LL BE BACK.
SORRY FOR USING YOU LIKE THAT.
THAT'S OKAY.
I ASKED YOU TO GET RID OF 'EM.
I WAS GLAD TO HELP.

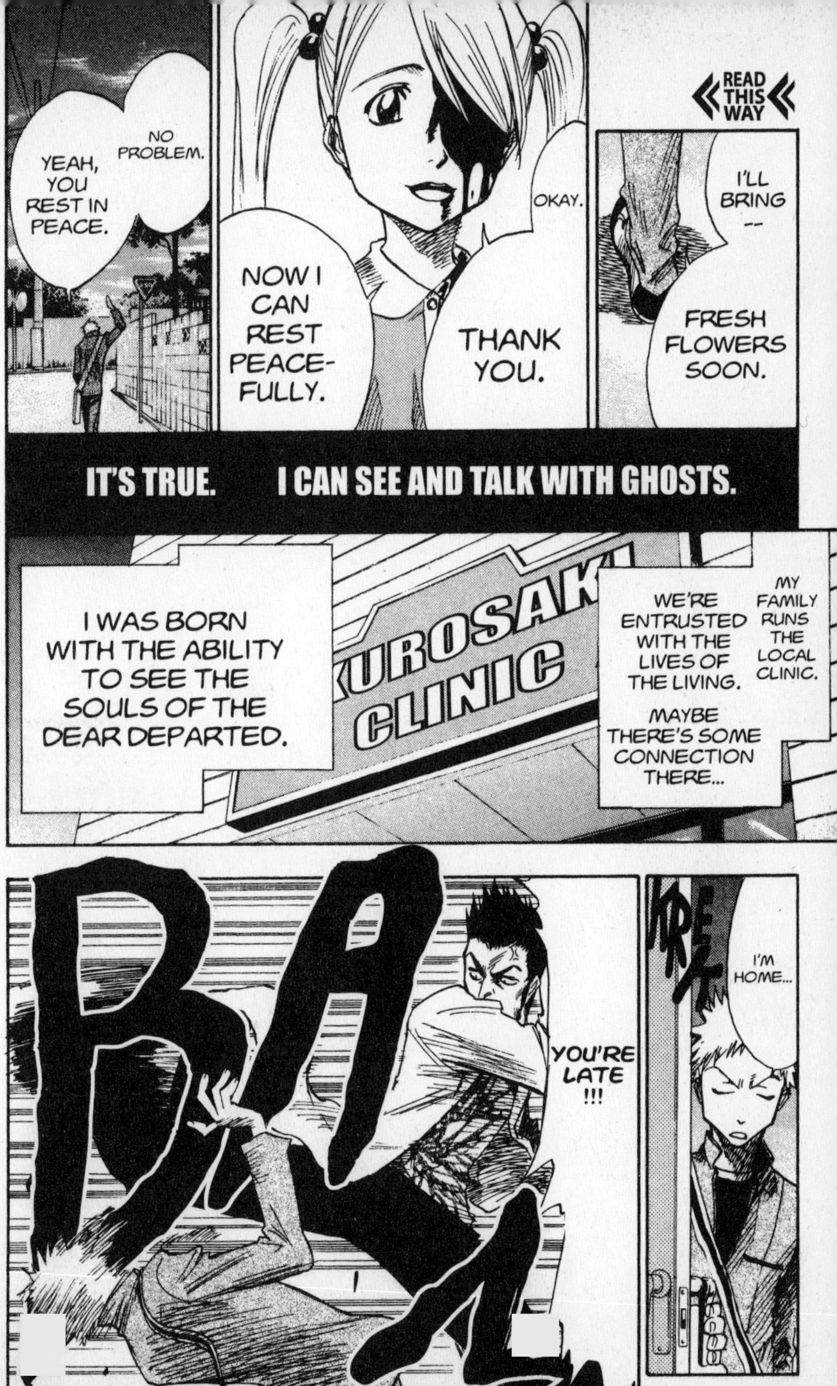
READ THIS WAY
I'LL BRING --
FRESH FLOWERS SOON.
OKAY.
THANK YOU.
NOW I CAN REST PEACE-FULLY.
NO PROBLEM.
YEAH, YOU REST IN PEACE.
IT'S TRUE. I CAN SEE AND TALK WITH GHOSTS.
MY FAMILY RUNS THE LOCAL CLINIC.
WE'RE ENTRUSTED WITH THE LIVES OF THE LIVING.
MAYBE THERE'S SOME CONNECTION THERE...
CLINIC
I WAS BORN WITH THE ABILITY TO SEE THE SOULS OF THE DEAR DEPARTED.
I'M HOME...
YOU'RE LATE!!!

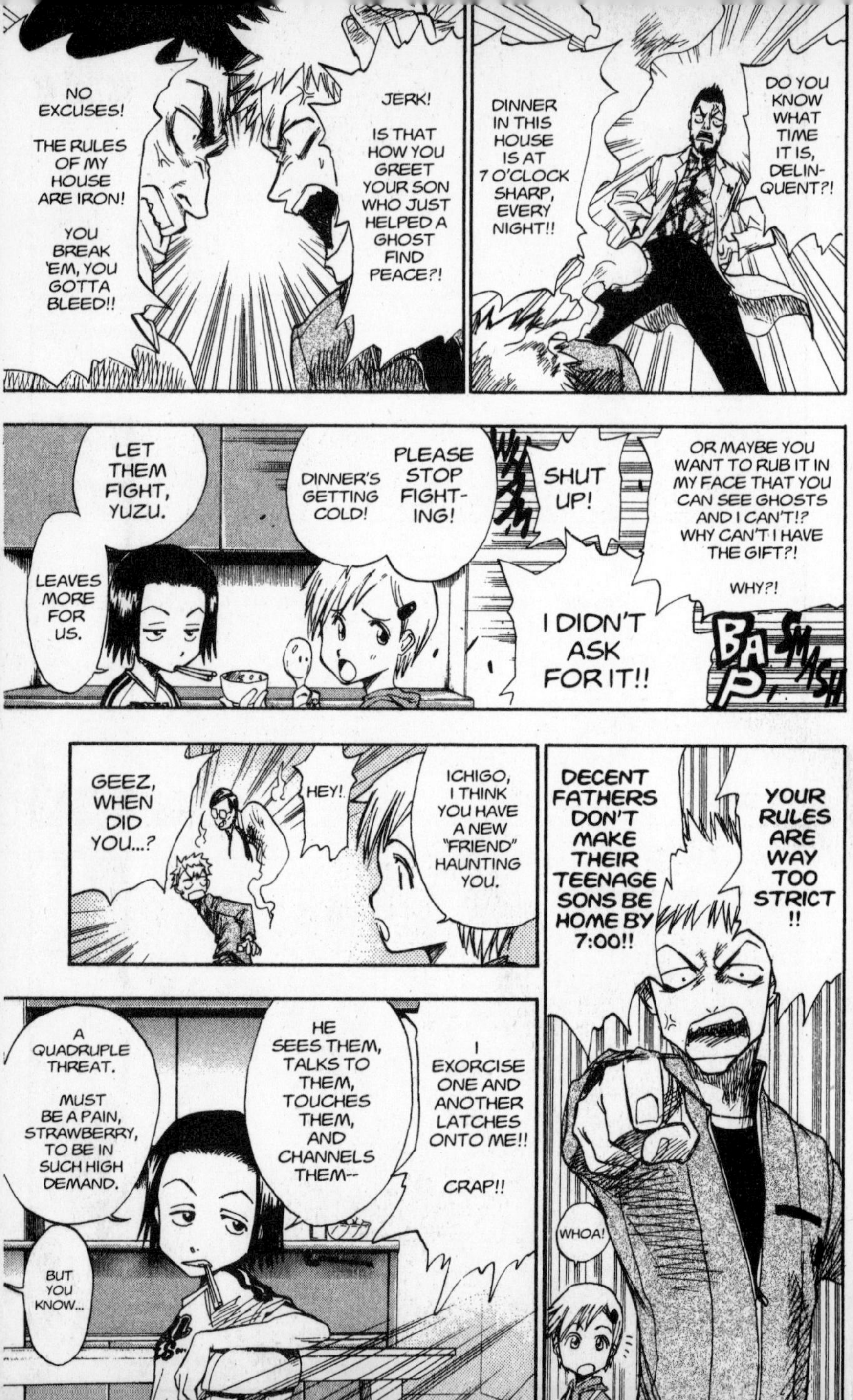
DO YOU KNOW WHAT TIME IT IS, DELINQUENT?!
DINNER IN THIS HOUSE IS AT 7 O'CLOCK SHARP, EVERY NIGHT!!
JERK! IS THAT HOW YOU GREET YOUR SON WHO JUST HELPED A GHOST FIND PEACE?!
NO EXCUSES! THE RULES OF MY HOUSE ARE IRON! YOU BREAK 'EM, YOU GOTTA BLEED!!
OR MAYBE YOU WANT TO RUB IT IN MY FACE THAT YOU CAN SEE GHOSTS AND I CAN'T!? WHY CAN'T I HAVE THE GIFT?! WHY?!
BAP, SMASH
I DIDN'T ASK FOR IT!!
SHUT UP!
WHAM
PLEASE STOP FIGHT-ING!
DINNER'S GETTING COLD!
LET THEM FIGHT, YUZU.
LEAVES MORE FOR US.
YOUR RULES ARE WAY TOO STRICT!!
DECENT FATHERS DON'T MAKE THEIR TEENAGE SONS BE HOME BY 7:00!!
WHOA!
ICHIGO, I THINK YOU HAVE A NEW "FRIEND" HAUNTING YOU.
HEY!
GEEZ, WHEN DID YOU...?
I EXORCISE ONE AND ANOTHER LATCHES ONTO ME!! CRAP!!
HE SEES THEM, TALKS TO THEM, TOUCHES THEM, AND CHANNELS THEM--
A QUADRUPLE THREAT. MUST BE A PAIN, STRAWBERRY, TO BE IN SUCH HIGH DEMAND.
BUT YOU KNOW...

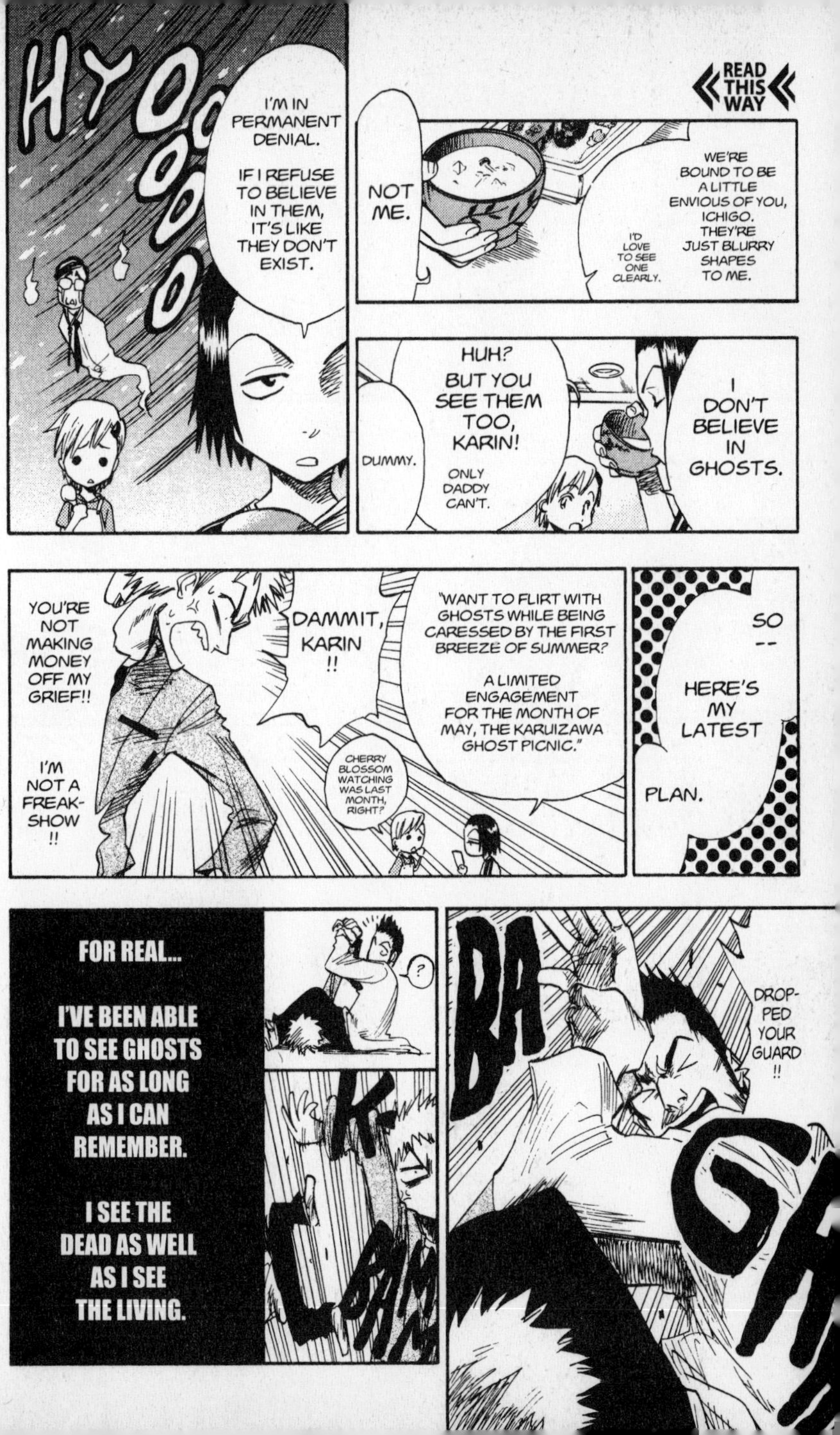
READ THIS WAY
WE'RE BOUND TO BE A LITTLE ENVIOUS OF YOU, ICHIGO. THEY'RE JUST BLURRY SHAPES TO ME.
I'D LOVE TO SEE ONE CLEARLY.
NOT ME.
I DON'T BELIEVE IN GHOSTS.
HUH? BUT YOU SEE THEM TOO, KARIN!
ONLY DADDY CAN'T.
DUMMY.
I'M IN PERMANENT DENIAL.
IF I REFUSE TO BELIEVE IN THEM, IT'S LIKE THEY DON'T EXIST.
HYOOOOOOO
SO -- HERE'S MY LATEST PLAN.
"WANT TO FLIRT WITH GHOSTS WHILE BEING CARESSED BY THE FIRST BREEZE OF SUMMER?
A LIMITED ENGAGEMENT FOR THE MONTH OF MAY, THE KARUIZAWA GHOST PICNIC."
CHERRY BLOSSOM WATCHING WAS LAST MONTH, RIGHT?
DAMMIT, KARIN!!
YOU'RE NOT MAKING MONEY OFF MY GRIEF!!
I'M NOT A FREAK-SHOW!!
BA
DROP-PED YOUR GUARD!!
?
FOR REAL...
I'VE BEEN ABLE TO SEE GHOSTS FOR AS LONG AS I CAN REMEMBER.
I SEE THE DEAD AS WELL AS I SEE THE LIVING.

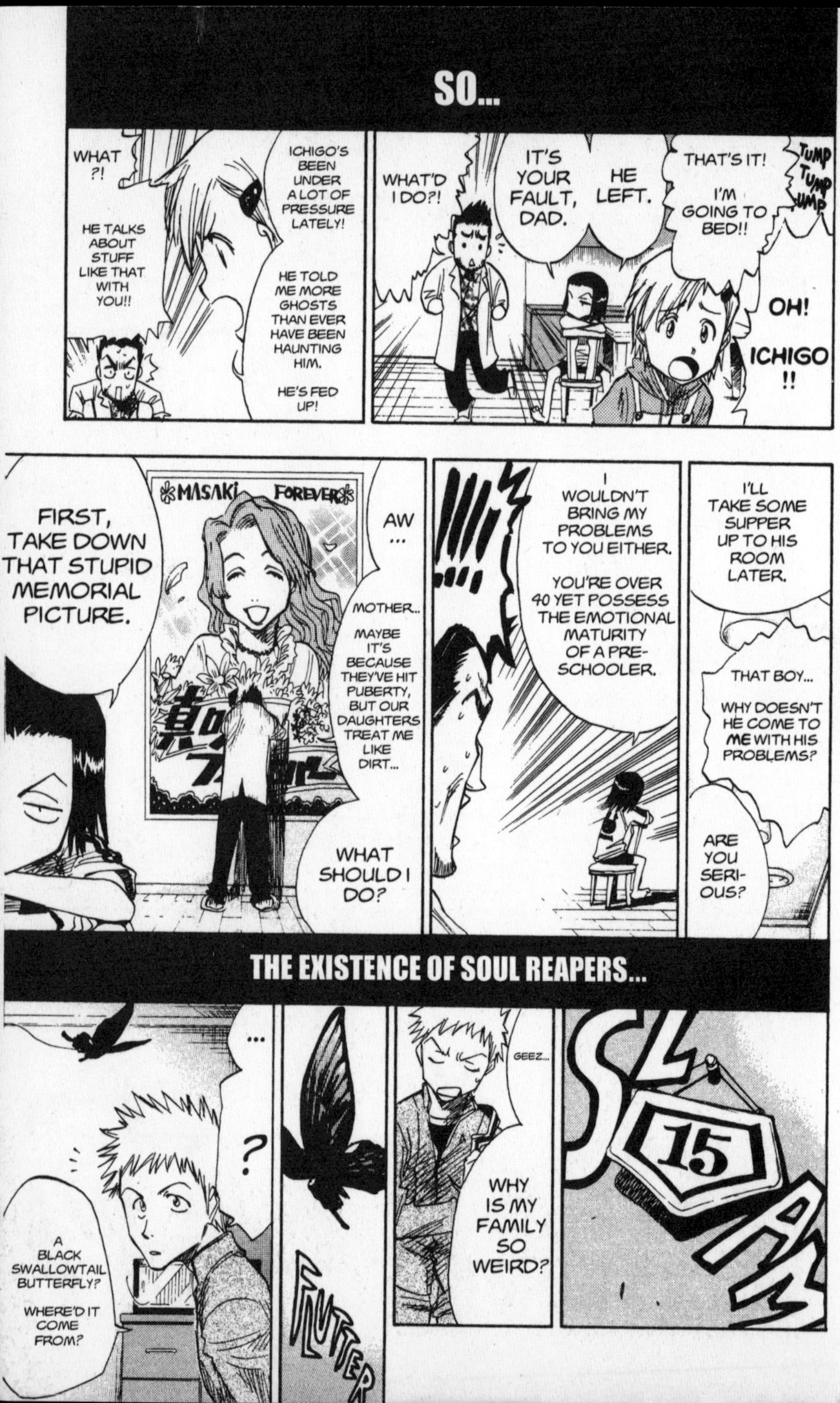
SO...
TUMP TUMP UMP
THAT'S IT! I'M GOING TO BED!!
OH! ICHIGO!!
HE LEFT.
IT'S YOUR FAULT, DAD.
WHAT'D I DO?!
ICHIGO'S BEEN UNDER A LOT OF PRESSURE LATELY!
HE TOLD ME MORE GHOSTS THAN EVER HAVE BEEN HAUNTING HIM.
HE'S FED UP!
WHAT?!
HE TALKS ABOUT STUFF LIKE THAT WITH YOU!!
I'LL TAKE SOME SUPPER UP TO HIS ROOM LATER.
THAT BOY... WHY DOESN'T HE COME TO ME WITH HIS PROBLEMS?
ARE YOU SERIOUS?
I WOULDN'T BRING MY PROBLEMS TO YOU EITHER.
YOU'RE OVER 40 YET POSSESS THE EMOTIONAL MATURITY OF A PRE-SCHOOLER.
AW...
MOTHER... MAYBE IT'S BECAUSE THEY'VE HIT PUBERTY, BUT OUR DAUGHTERS TREAT ME LIKE DIRT...
WHAT SHOULD I DO?
MASAKI FOREVER
FIRST, TAKE DOWN THAT STUPID MEMORIAL PICTURE.
THE EXISTENCE OF SOUL REAPERS...
SLAM
15
GEEZ...
WHY IS MY FAMILY SO WEIRD?
FLUTTER
...
?
A BLACK SWALLOWTAIL BUTTERFLY?
WHERE'D IT COME FROM?

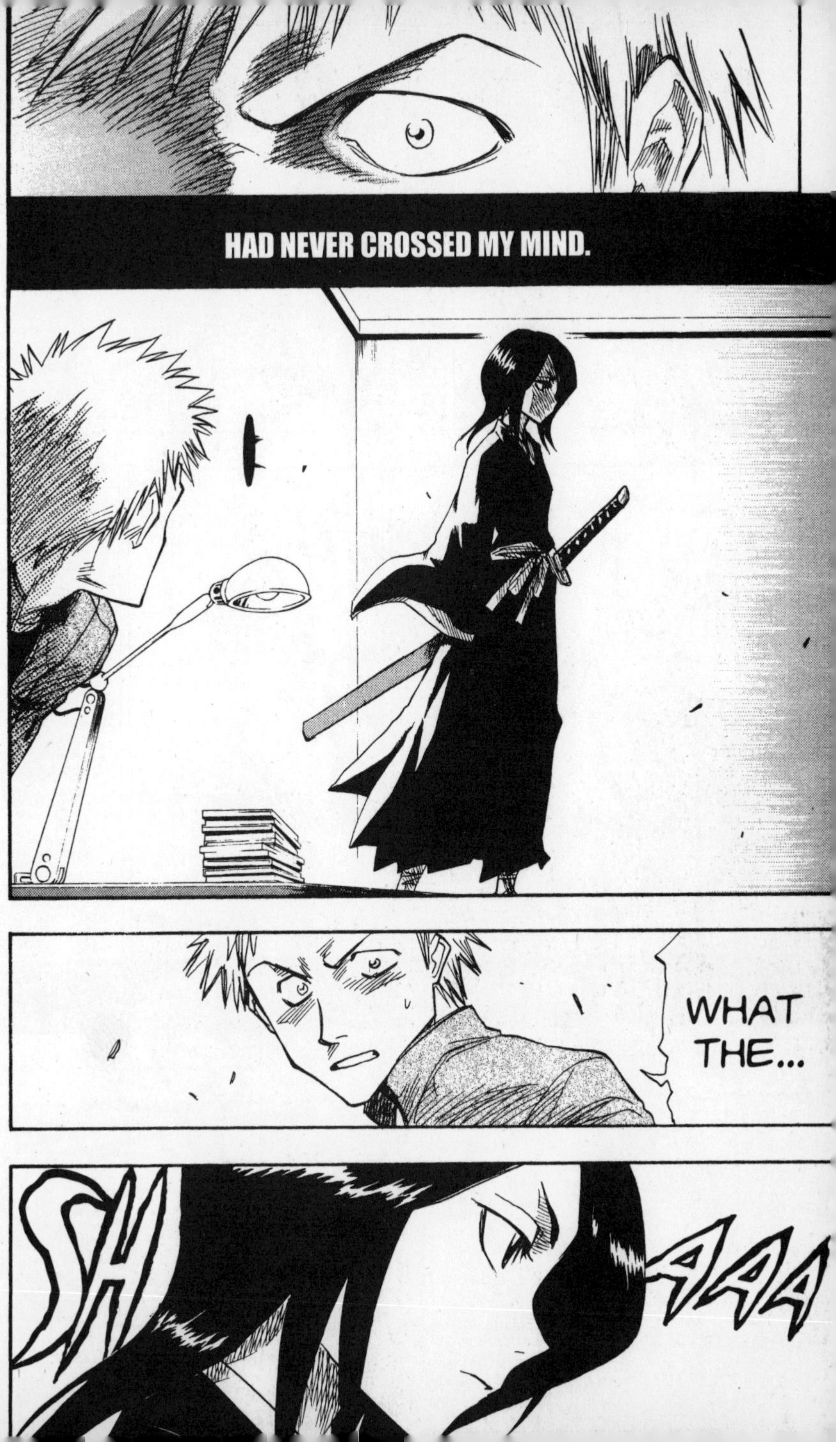
HAD NEVER CROSSED MY MIND.
WHAT THE...
SHAAA

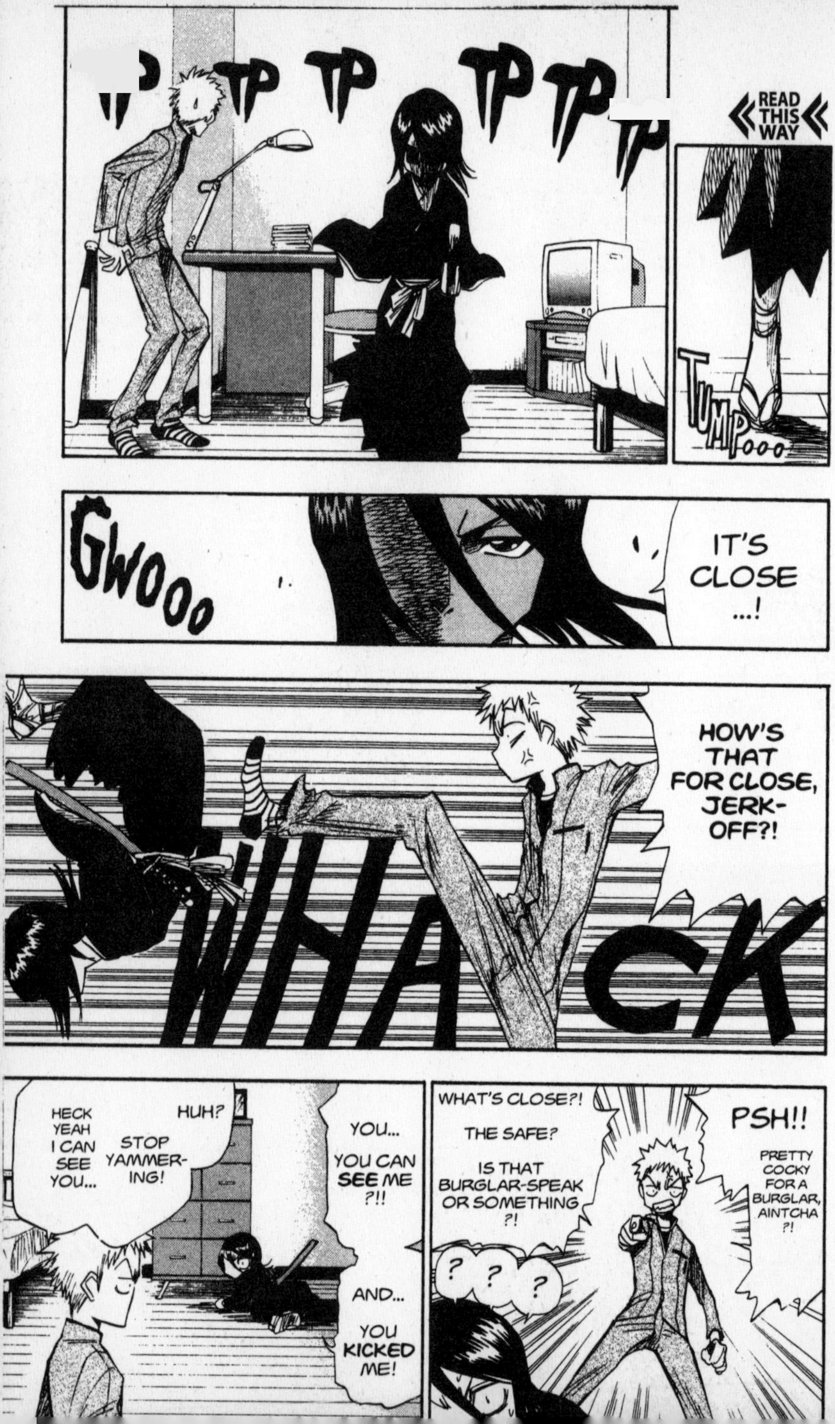
READ THIS WAY
TUMPooo
TP TP TP TP TP
IT'S CLOSE ...!
GWOOO
HOW'S THAT FOR CLOSE, JERK-OFF?!
WHACK
PSH!!
PRETTY COCKY FOR A BURGLAR, AINTCHA?!
WHAT'S CLOSE?!
THE SAFE?
IS THAT BURGLAR-SPEAK OR SOMETHING?!
? ? ?
YOU...
YOU CAN SEE ME?!!
AND... YOU KICKED ME!
HUH?
STOP YAMMERING!
HECK YEAH I CAN SEE YOU...

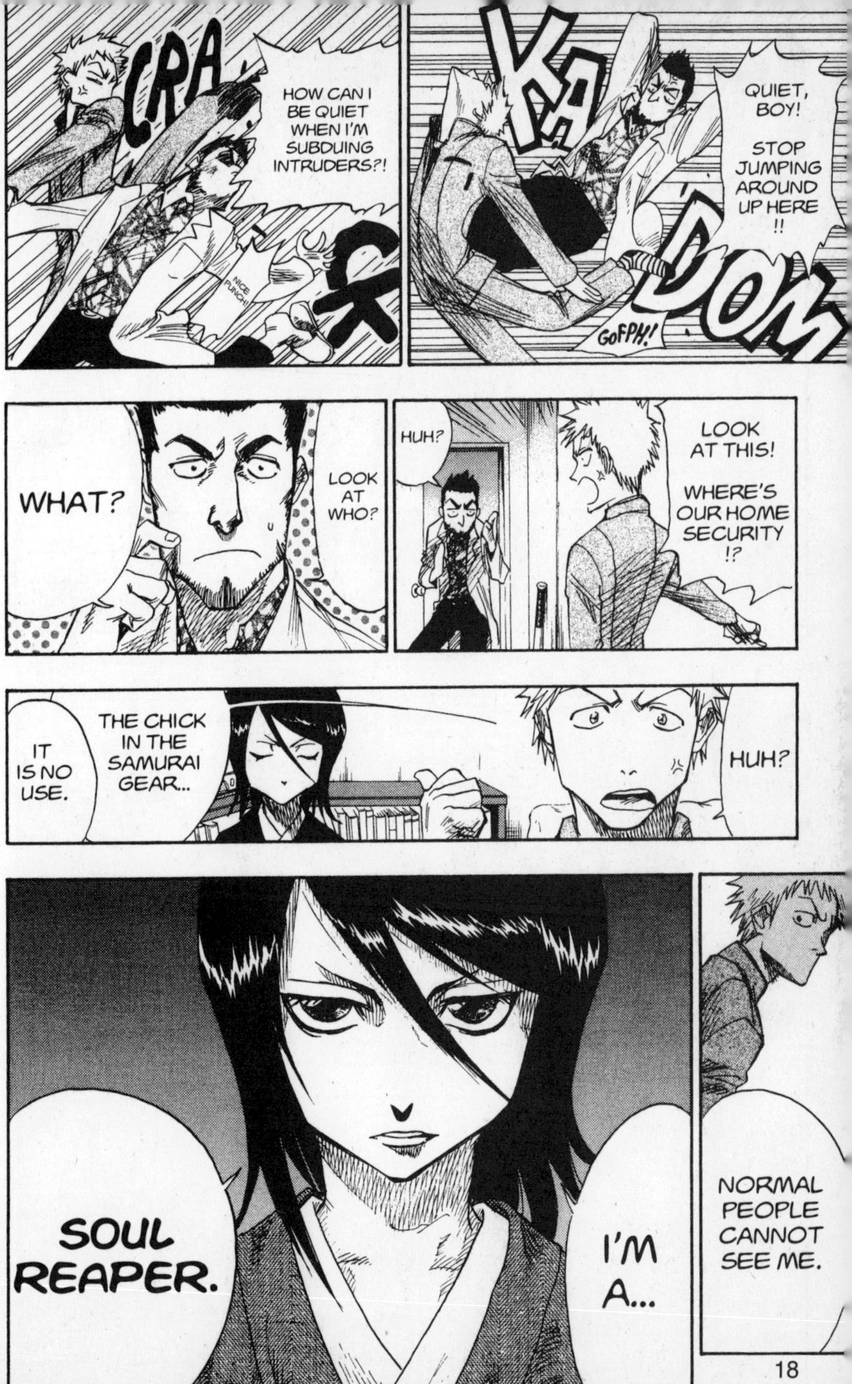
KA
QUIET, BOY!
STOP JUMPING AROUND UP HERE !!
DOM
GOFPH!
CRA
CK
HOW CAN I BE QUIET WHEN I'M SUBDUING INTRUDERS?!
NICE PUNCH!
HUH?
LOOK AT THIS!
WHERE'S OUR HOME SECURITY !?
LOOK AT WHO?
WHAT?
HUH?
THE CHICK IN THE SAMURAI GEAR...
IT IS NO USE.
NORMAL PEOPLE CANNOT SEE ME.
I'M A...
SOUL REAPER.

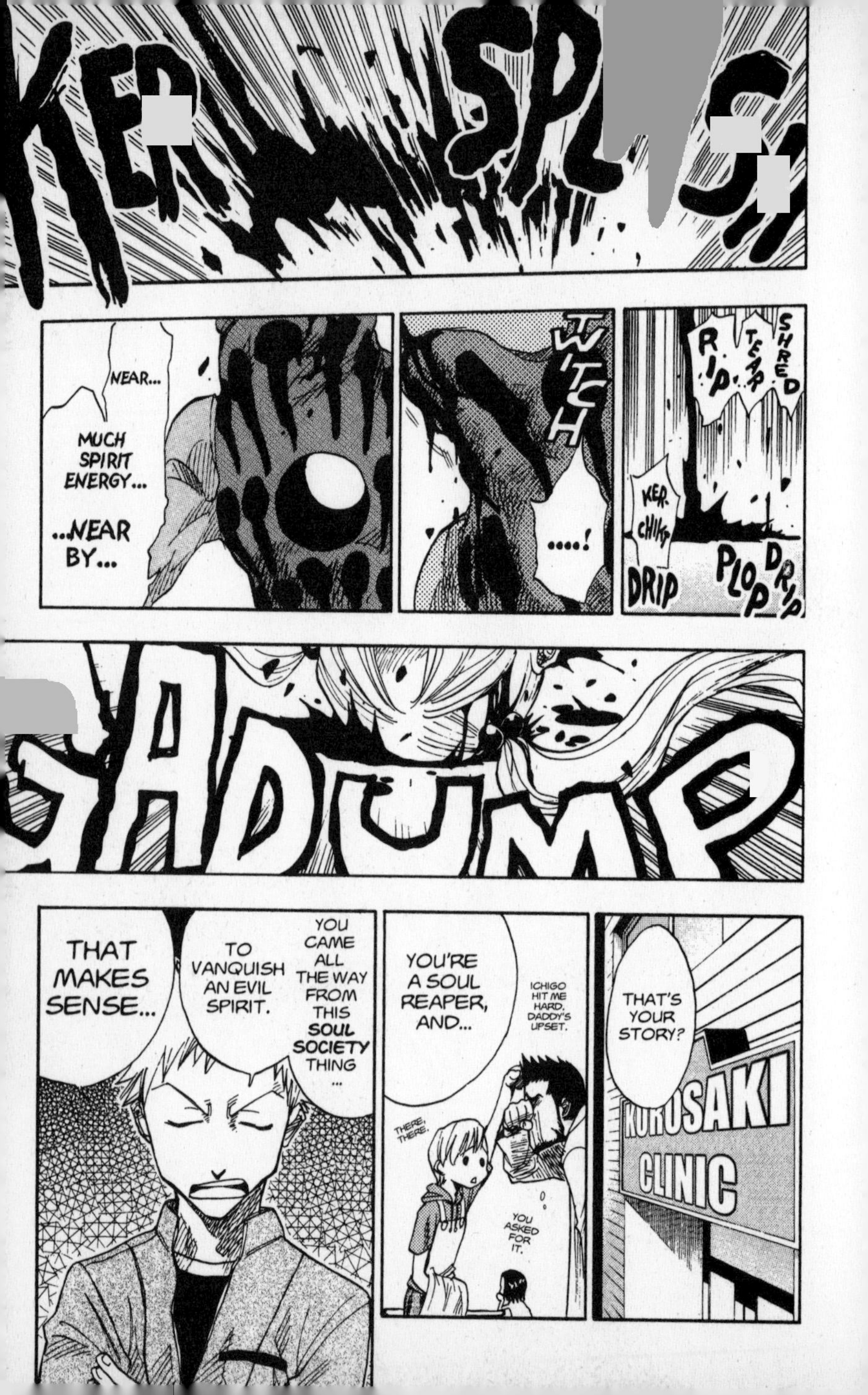
KER SPL
SHRED
TEAR
RIP
KER-CHIK
DRIP PLOP DRIP
TWITCH
.....!
NEAR...
MUCH SPIRIT ENERGY...
...NEAR BY...
GADUMP
THAT'S YOUR STORY?
KUROSAKI CLINIC
YOU'RE A SOUL REAPER, AND...
ICHIGO HIT ME HARD. DADDY'S UPSET.
THERE, THERE.
YOU ASKED FOR IT.
YOU CAME ALL THE WAY FROM THIS SOUL SOCIETY THING...
TO VANQUISH AN EVIL SPIRIT.
THAT MAKES SENSE...

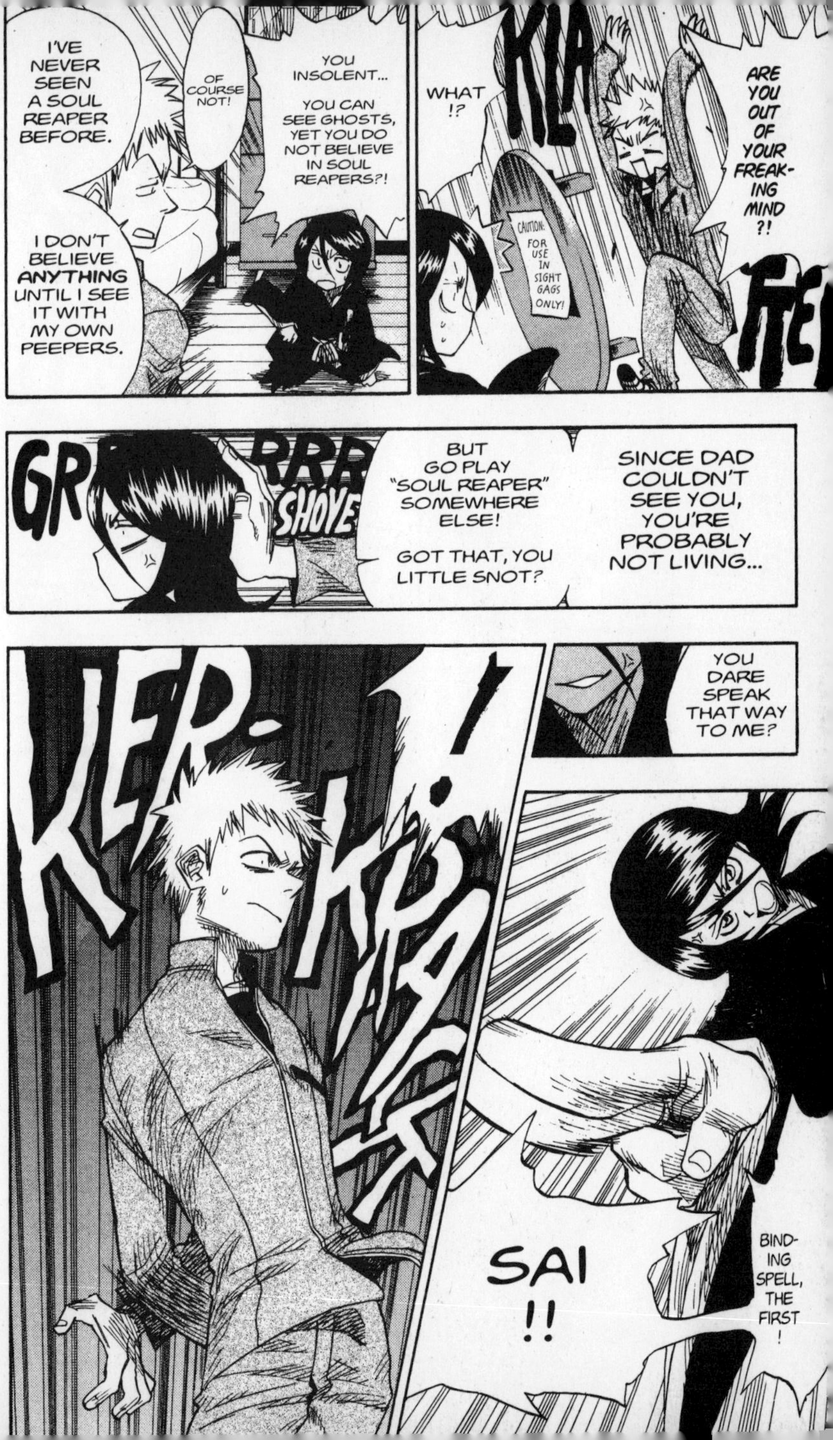
ARE YOU OUT OF YOUR FREAKING MIND?!
KLA
WHAT!?
CAUTION: FOR USE IN SIGHT GAGS ONLY!
YOU INSOLENT... YOU CAN SEE GHOSTS, YET YOU DO NOT BELIEVE IN SOUL REAPERS?!
OF COURSE NOT!
I'VE NEVER SEEN A SOUL REAPER BEFORE.
I DON'T BELIEVE **ANYTHING** UNTIL I SEE IT WITH MY OWN PEEPERS.
SINCE DAD COULDN'T SEE YOU, YOU'RE PROBABLY NOT LIVING...
BUT GO PLAY "SOUL REAPER" SOMEWHERE ELSE!
GOT THAT, YOU LITTLE SNOT?
SHOVE
GRRRR
YOU DARE SPEAK THAT WAY TO ME?
BINDING SPELL, THE FIRST!
SAI!!
KLER-

READ THIS WAY

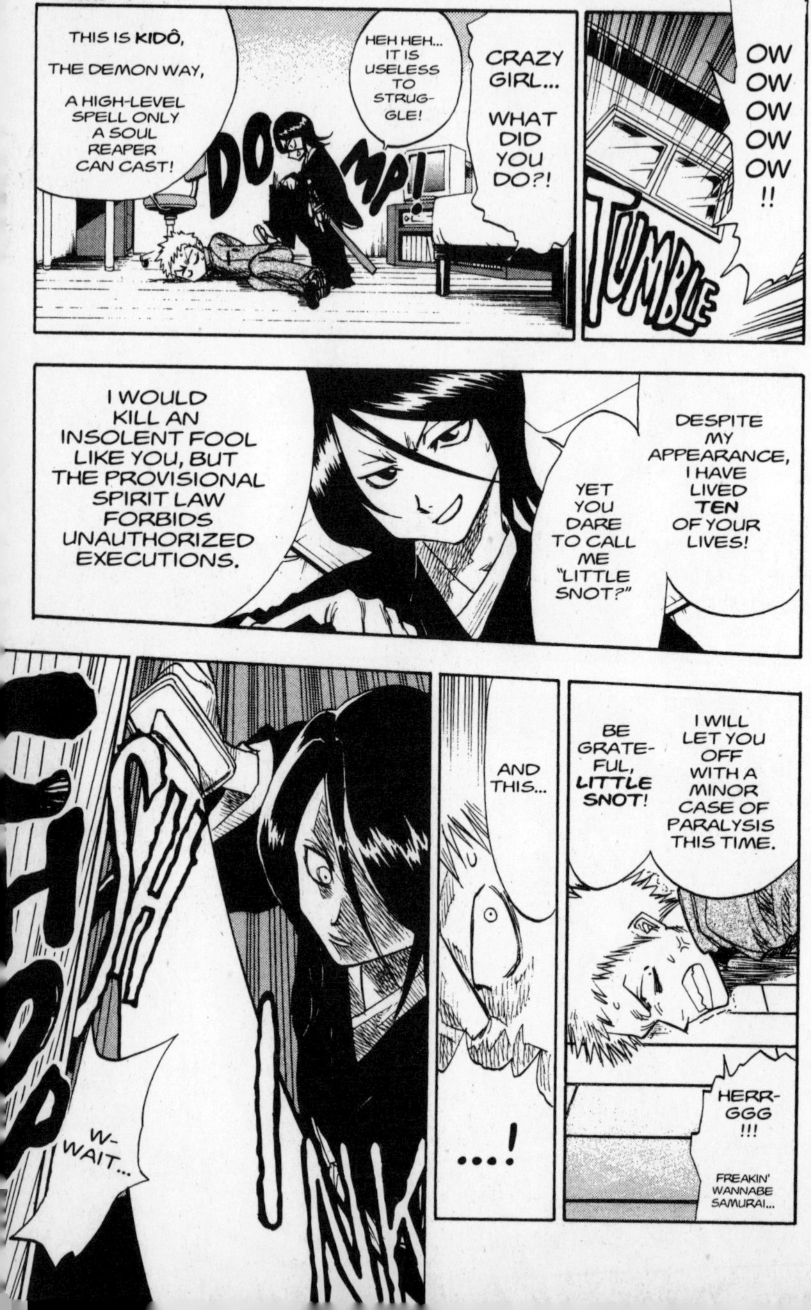

OW OW OW OW OW !!
TUMBLE
CRAZY GIRL... WHAT DID YOU DO?!
HEH HEH... IT IS USELESS TO STRUG-GLE!
THIS IS KIDÔ, THE DEMON WAY, A HIGH-LEVEL SPELL ONLY A SOUL REAPER CAN CAST!
DOOMP!
DESPITE MY APPEARANCE, I HAVE LIVED TEN OF YOUR LIVES!
YET YOU DARE TO CALL ME "LITTLE SNOT?"
I WOULD KILL AN INSOLENT FOOL LIKE YOU, BUT THE PROVISIONAL SPIRIT LAW FORBIDS UNAUTHORIZED EXECUTIONS.
I WILL LET YOU OFF WITH A MINOR CASE OF PARALYSIS THIS TIME.
BE GRATE-FUL, LITTLE SNOT!
HERR-GGG !!!
FREAKIN' WANNABE SAMURAI...
AND THIS...
...!
W-WAIT...

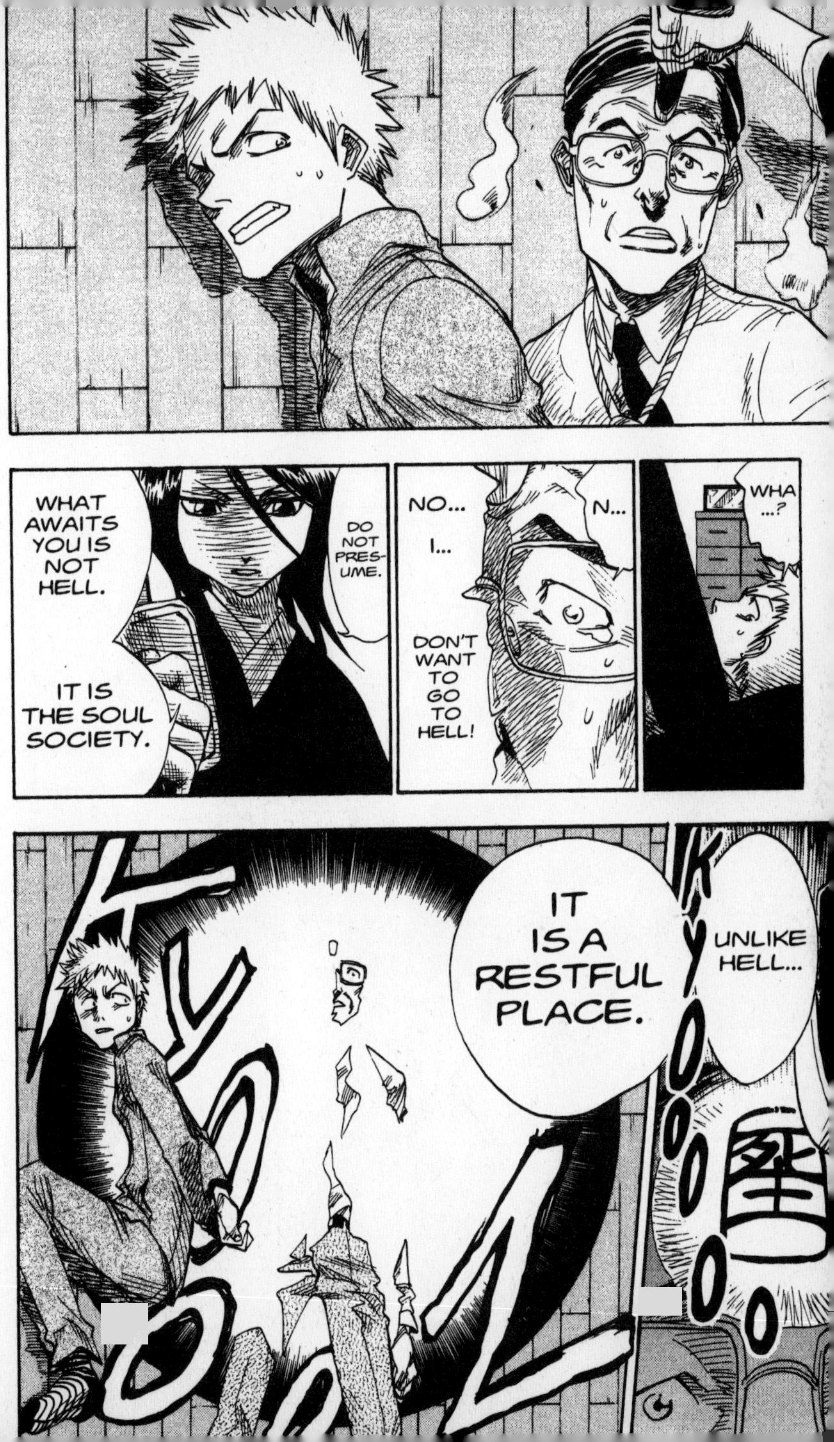
WHA ...?
N...
NO...
I...
DON'T WANT TO GO TO HELL!
DO NOT PRESUME.
WHAT AWAITS YOU IS NOT HELL.
IT IS THE SOUL SOCIETY.
UNLIKE HELL...
IT IS A RESTFUL PLACE.

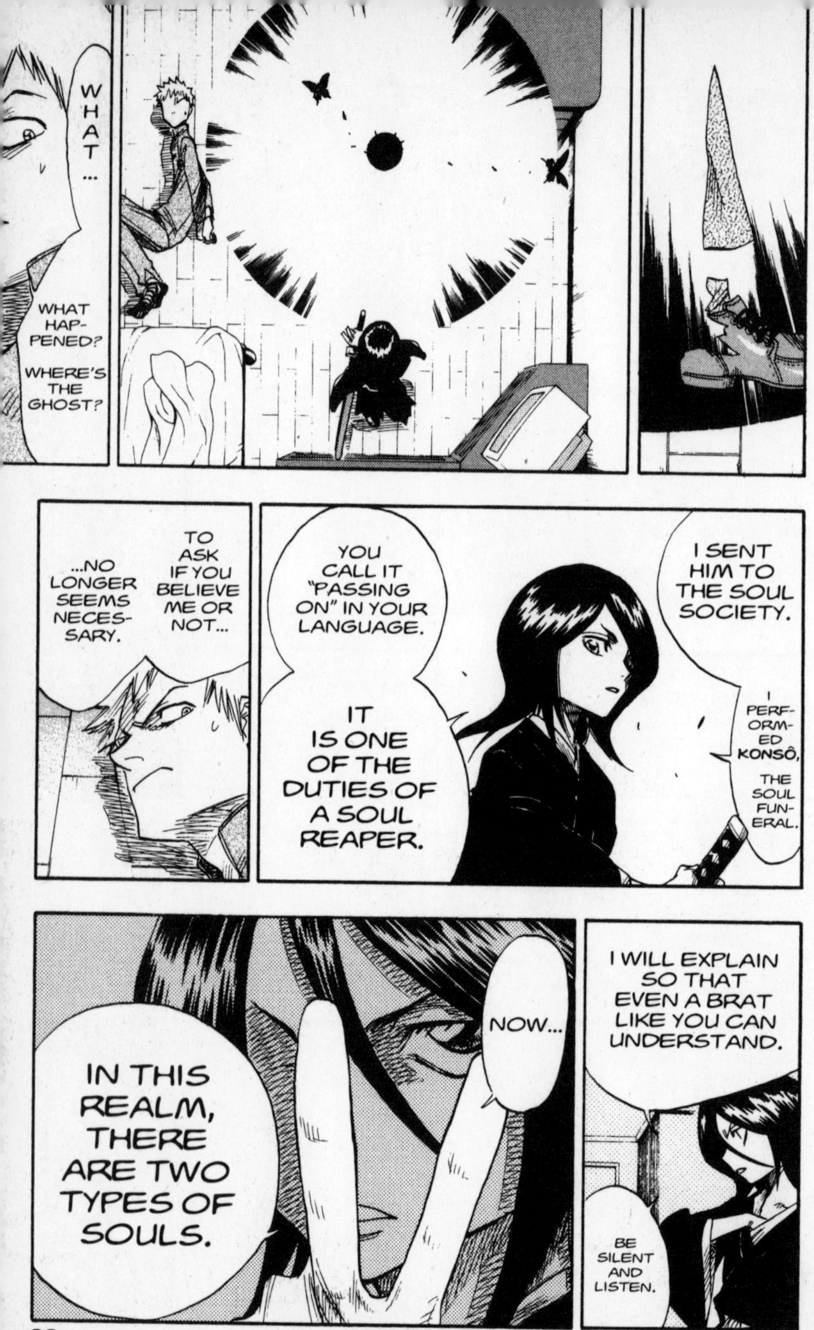
WHAT...
WHAT HAPPENED? WHERE'S THE GHOST?
I SENT HIM TO THE SOUL SOCIETY.
I PERFORMED KONSÔ, THE SOUL FUNERAL.
YOU CALL IT "PASSING ON" IN YOUR LANGUAGE.
IT IS ONE OF THE DUTIES OF A SOUL REAPER.
TO ASK IF YOU BELIEVE ME OR NOT...
...NO LONGER SEEMS NECESSARY.
I WILL EXPLAIN SO THAT EVEN A BRAT LIKE YOU CAN UNDERSTAND.
BE SILENT AND LISTEN.
NOW...
IN THIS REALM, THERE ARE TWO TYPES OF SOULS.

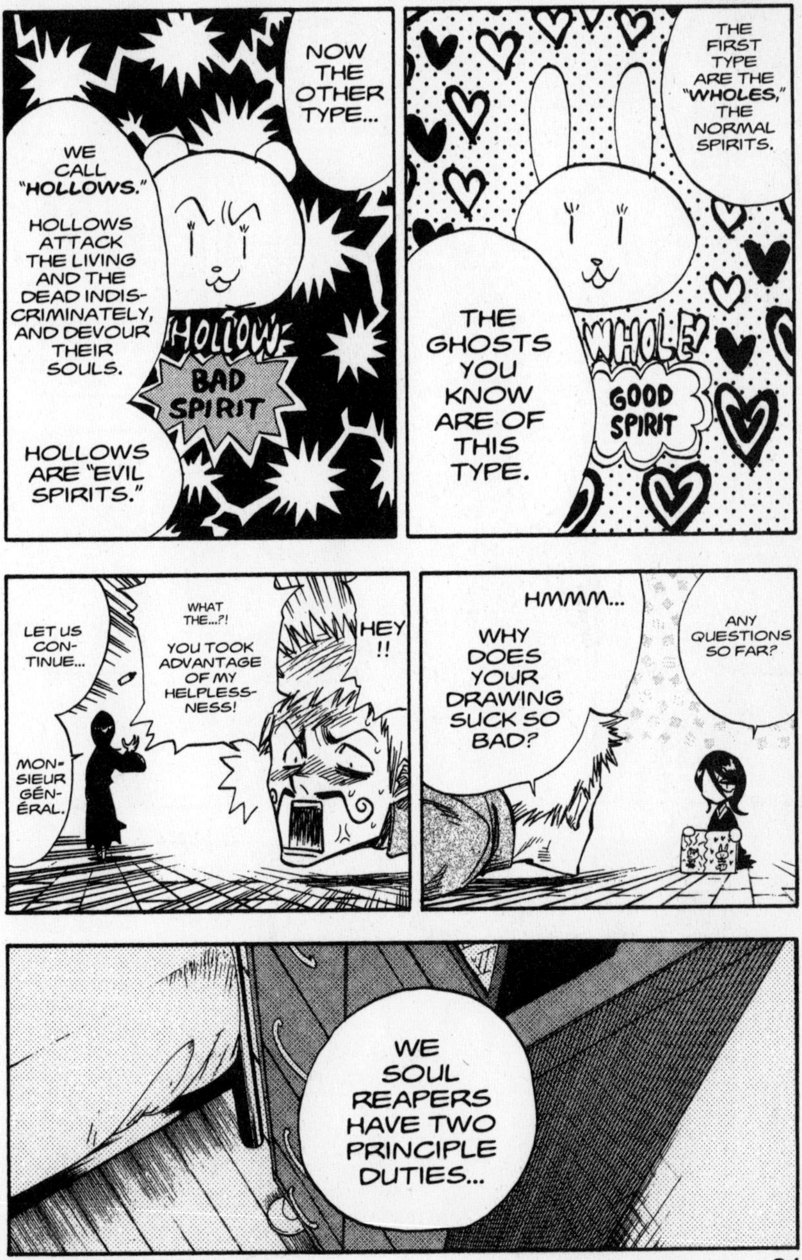
THE FIRST TYPE ARE THE "**WHOLES**," THE NORMAL SPIRITS.
THE GHOSTS YOU KNOW ARE OF THIS TYPE.
WHOLE!
GOOD SPIRIT
NOW THE OTHER TYPE...
WE CALL "**HOLLOWS**."
HOLLOWS ATTACK THE LIVING AND THE DEAD INDISCRIMINATELY, AND DEVOUR THEIR SOULS.
HOLLOW!
BAD SPIRIT
HOLLOWS ARE "EVIL SPIRITS."
ANY QUESTIONS SO FAR?
HMMM...
WHY DOES YOUR DRAWING SUCK SO BAD?
HEY !!
WHAT THE...?!
YOU TOOK ADVANTAGE OF MY HELPLESSNESS!
LET US CONTINUE...
MONSIEUR GÉNÉRAL.
WE SOUL REAPERS HAVE TWO PRINCIPLE DUTIES...

READ THIS WAY

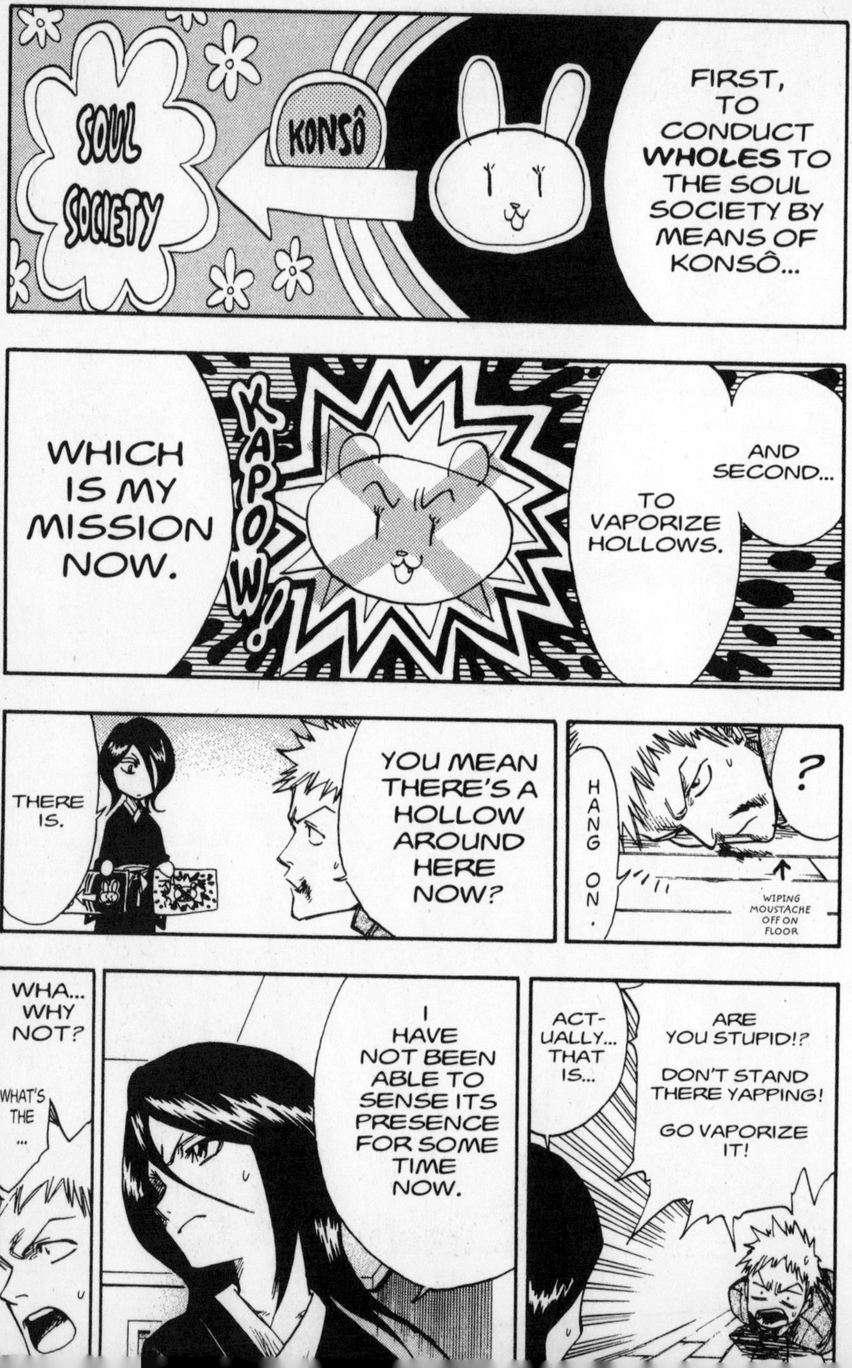
FIRST, TO CONDUCT WHOLES TO THE SOUL SOCIETY BY MEANS OF KONSÔ...
KONSÔ
SOUL SOCIETY
AND SECOND...
TO VAPORIZE HOLLOWS.
KAPOW!
WHICH IS MY MISSION NOW.
?
HANG ON.
WIPING MOUSTACHE OFF ON FLOOR
YOU MEAN THERE'S A HOLLOW AROUND HERE NOW?
THERE IS.
ARE YOU STUPID!? DON'T STAND THERE YAPPING! GO VAPORIZE IT!
ACT-UALLY... THAT IS...
I HAVE NOT BEEN ABLE TO SENSE ITS PRESENCE FOR SOME TIME NOW.
WHA... WHY NOT?
WHAT'S THE ...

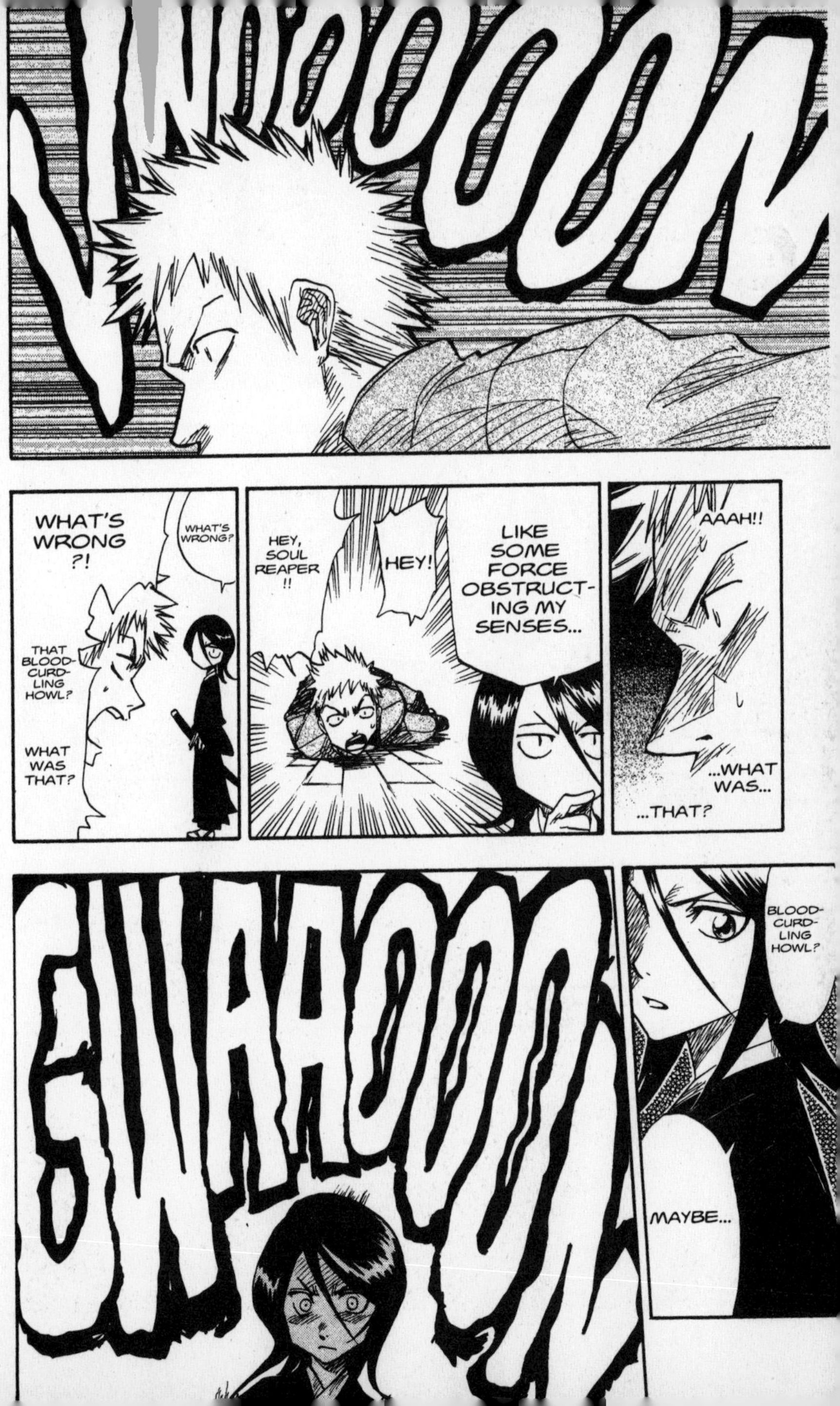
AAAH!!
...WHAT WAS...
...THAT?
LIKE SOME FORCE OBSTRUCTING MY SENSES...
HEY!
HEY, SOUL REAPER !!
WHAT'S WRONG?
WHAT'S WRONG ?!
THAT BLOOD-CURDLING HOWL?
WHAT WAS THAT?
BLOOD-CURDLING HOWL?
MAYBE...

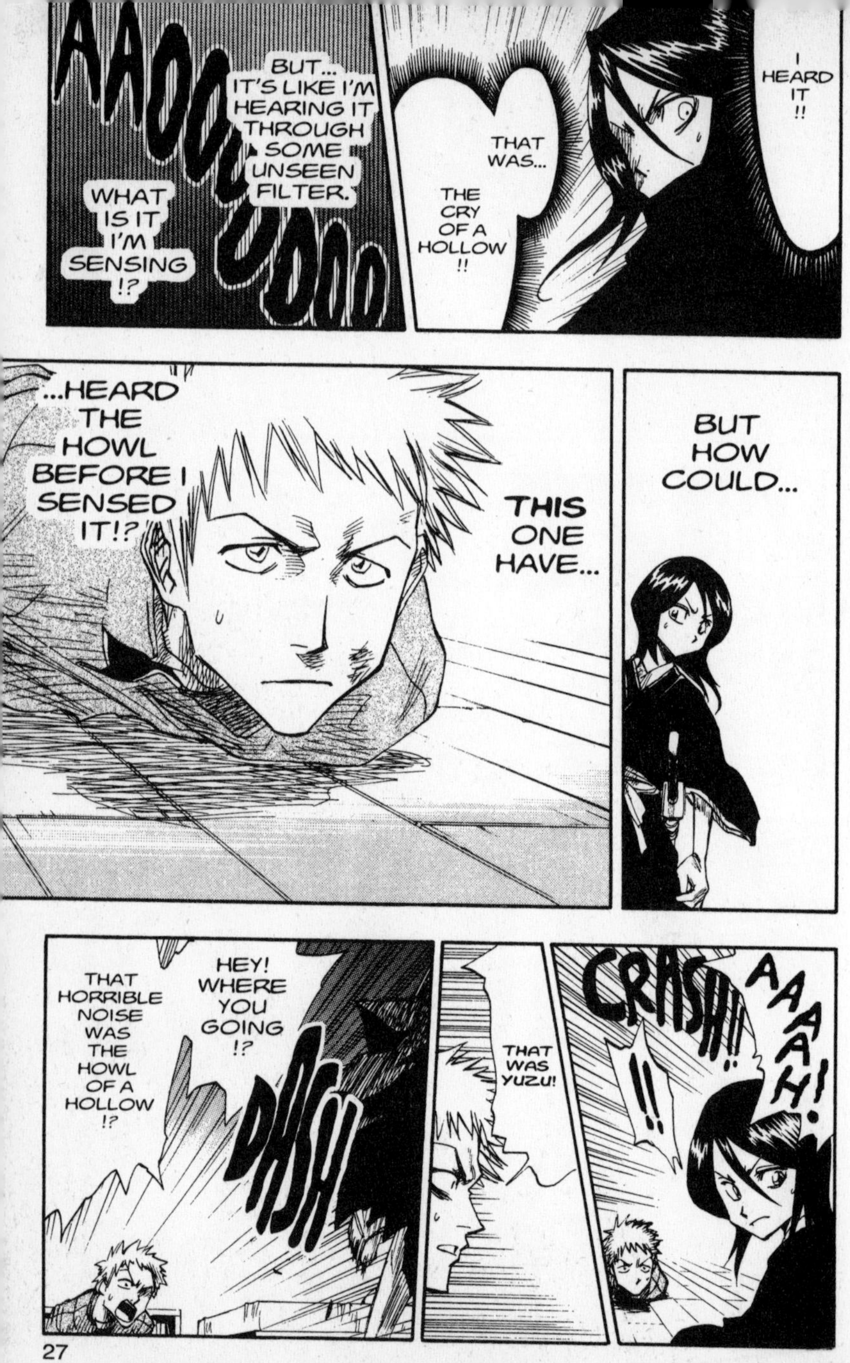
I HEARD IT !!
THAT WAS...
THE CRY OF A HOLLOW !!
AAOOUOOO
BUT... IT'S LIKE I'M HEARING IT THROUGH SOME UNSEEN FILTER.
WHAT IS IT I'M SENSING !?
BUT HOW COULD...
THIS ONE HAVE...
...HEARD THE HOWL BEFORE I SENSED IT!?
CRASH!!
AAAAH!
!!
THAT WAS YUZU!
HEY! WHERE YOU GOING !?
DASH
THAT HORRIBLE NOISE WAS THE HOWL OF A HOLLOW !?

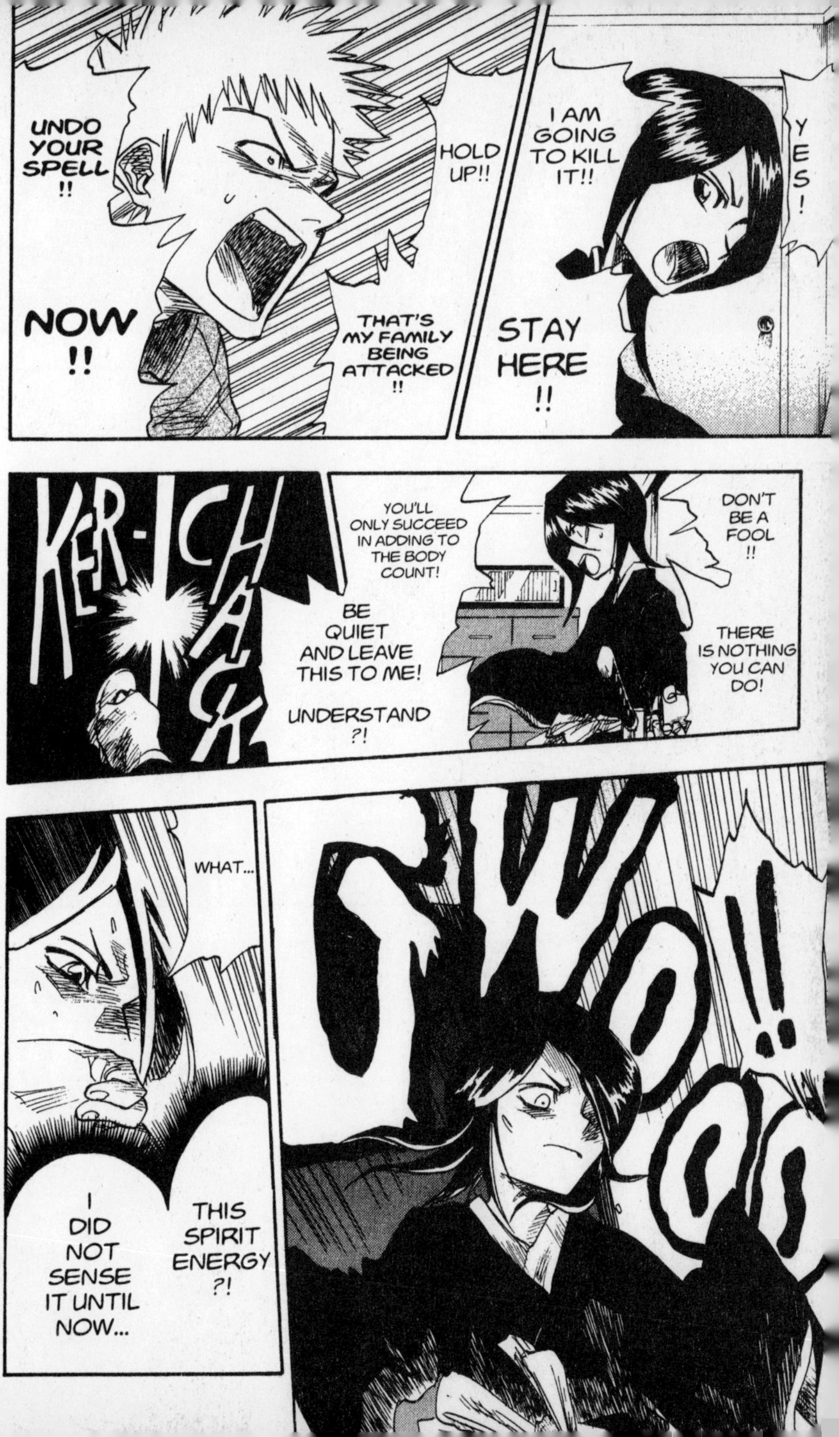
YES!
I AM GOING TO KILL IT!!
STAY HERE !!
HOLD UP!!
THAT'S MY FAMILY BEING ATTACKED !!
UNDO YOUR SPELL !!
NOW !!
DON'T BE A FOOL !!
THERE IS NOTHING YOU CAN DO!
YOU'LL ONLY SUCCEED IN ADDING TO THE BODY COUNT!
BE QUIET AND LEAVE THIS TO ME!
UNDERSTAND ?!
KER-ICHACK
OWOOO!!
WHAT...
THIS SPIRIT ENERGY ?!
I DID NOT SENSE IT UNTIL NOW...

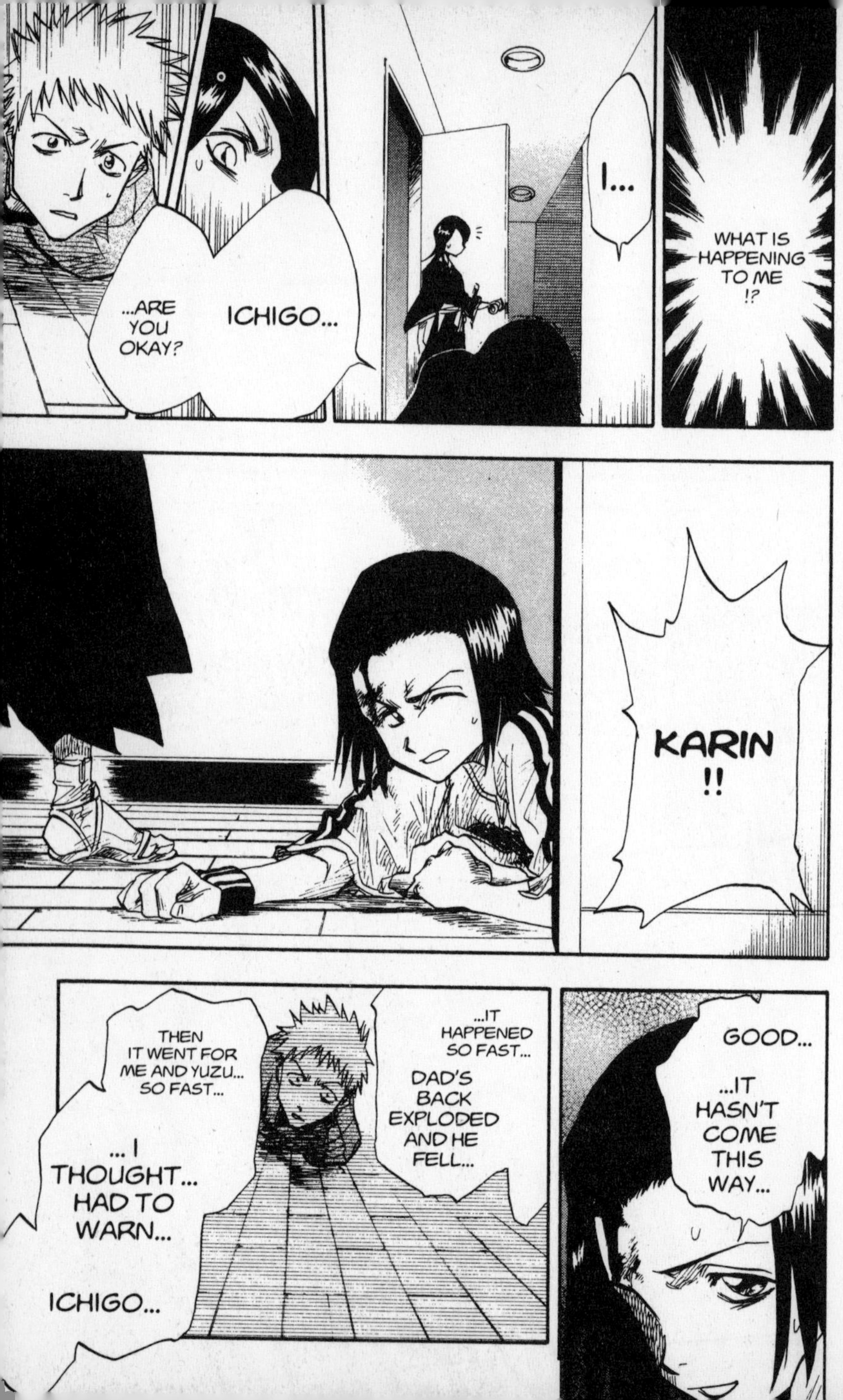
WHAT IS HAPPENING TO ME !?
I...
ICHIGO...
...ARE YOU OKAY?
KARIN !!
GOOD...
...IT HASN'T COME THIS WAY...
...IT HAPPENED SO FAST...
DAD'S BACK EXPLODED AND HE FELL...
THEN IT WENT FOR ME AND YUZU... SO FAST...
... I THOUGHT... HAD TO WARN...
ICHIGO...

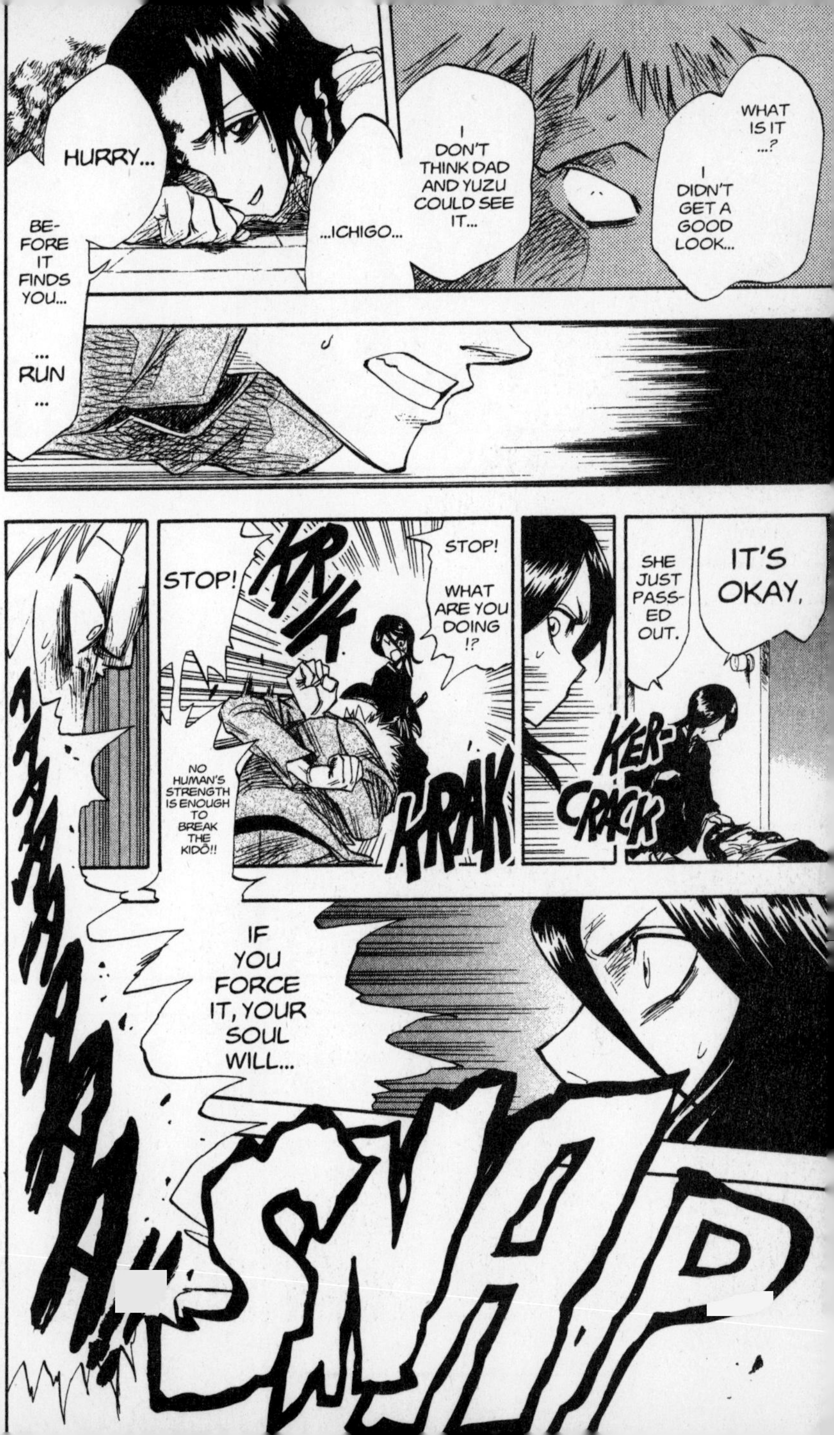
WHAT IS IT ...?
I DIDN'T GET A GOOD LOOK...
I DON'T THINK DAD AND YUZU COULD SEE IT...
...ICHIGO...
HURRY...
BEFORE IT FINDS YOU...
... RUN ...
IT'S OKAY,
SHE JUST PASSED OUT.
KER-CRACK
STOP!
WHAT ARE YOU DOING !?
KRIK
STOP!
KRAK
NO HUMAN'S STRENGTH IS ENOUGH TO BREAK THE KIDŌ!!
IF YOU FORCE IT, YOUR SOUL WILL...
SNAP

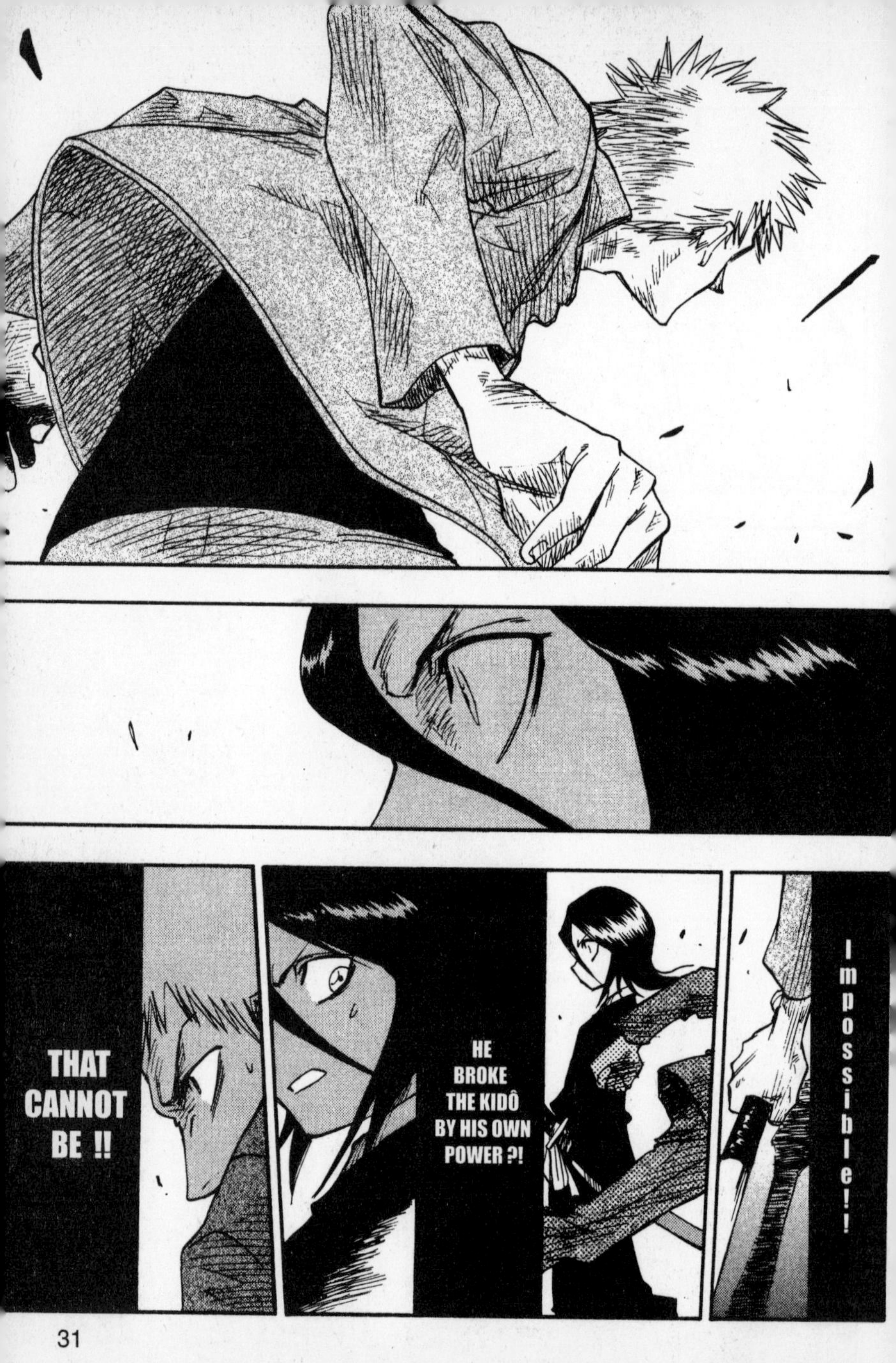
Impossible!!
HE BROKE THE KIDÔ BY HIS OWN POWER ?!
THAT CANNOT BE !!

READ THIS WAY

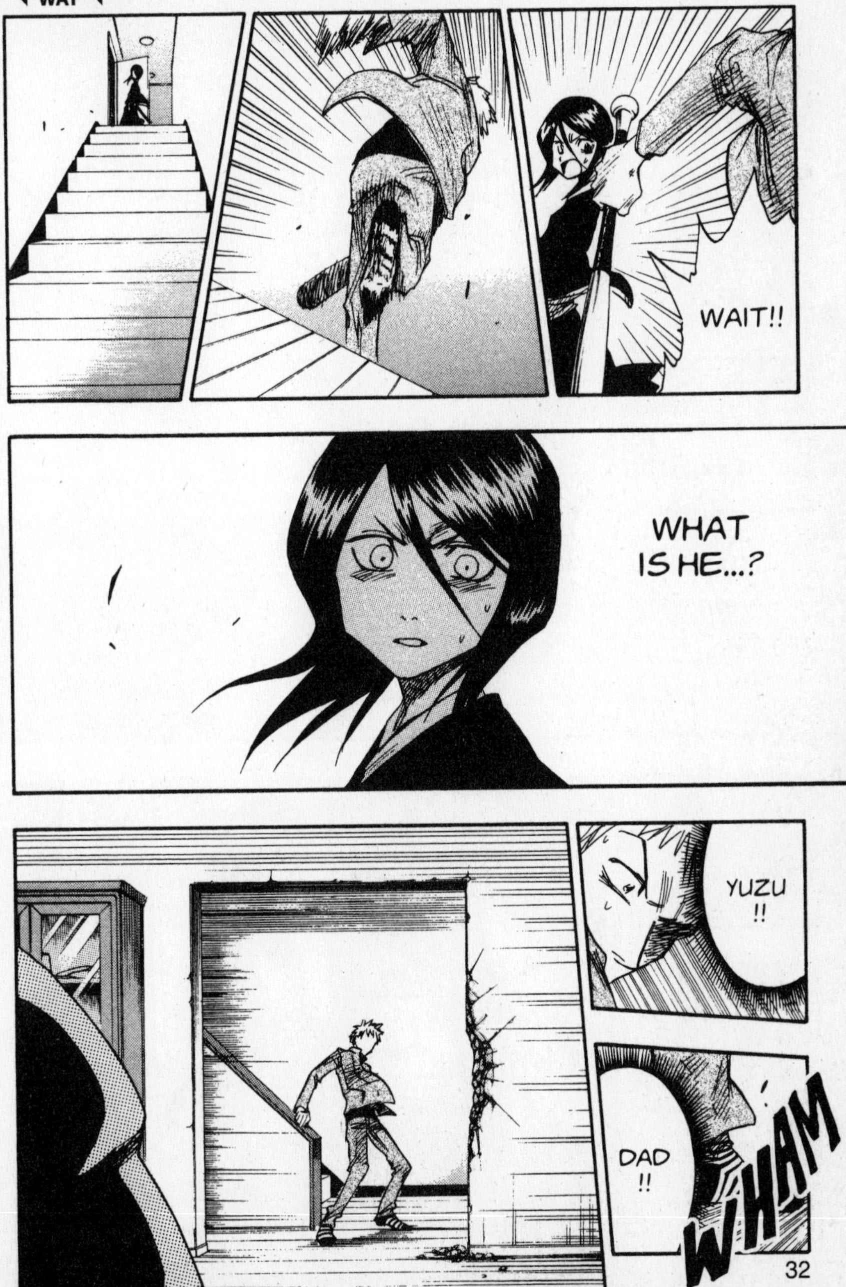
WAIT!!
WHAT IS HE...?
YUZU !!
DAD !!
WHAM

READ THIS WAY

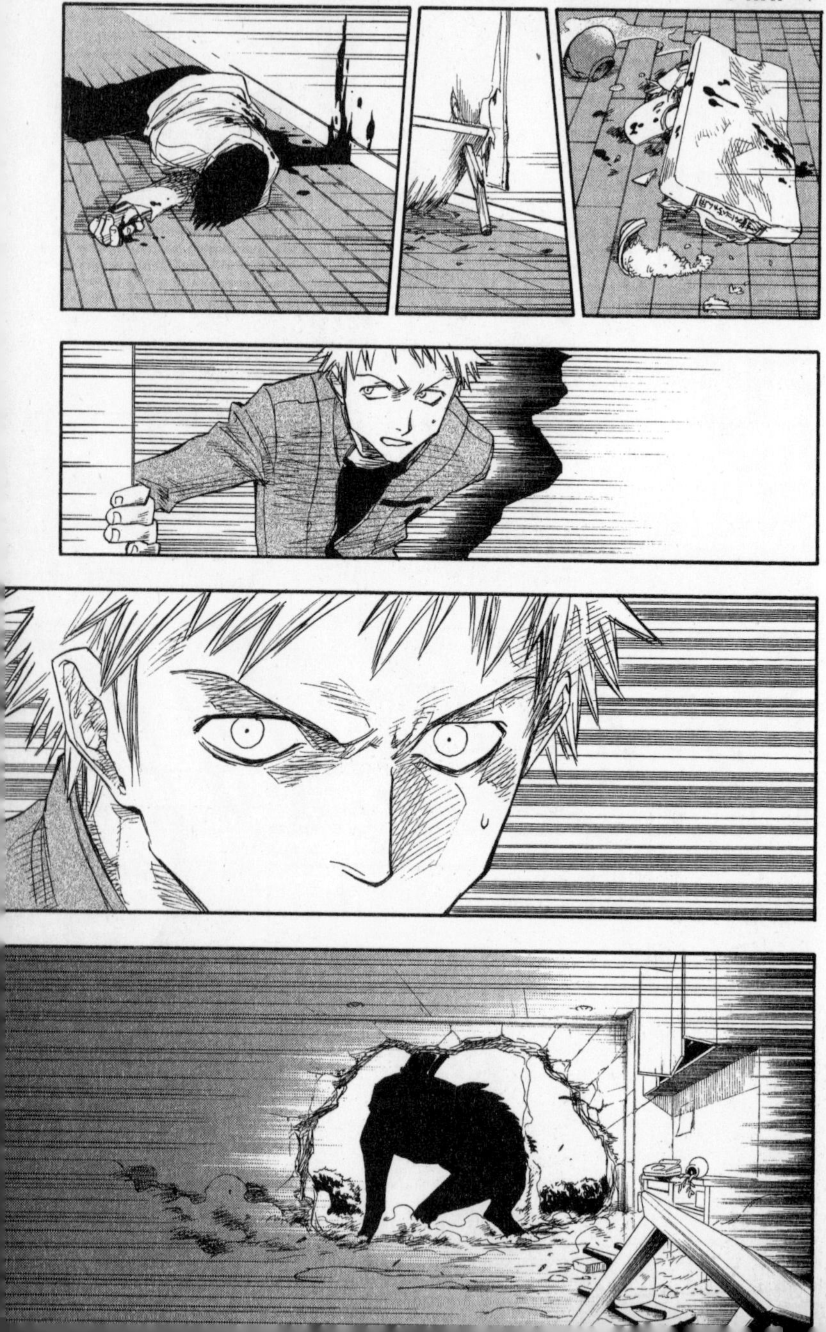

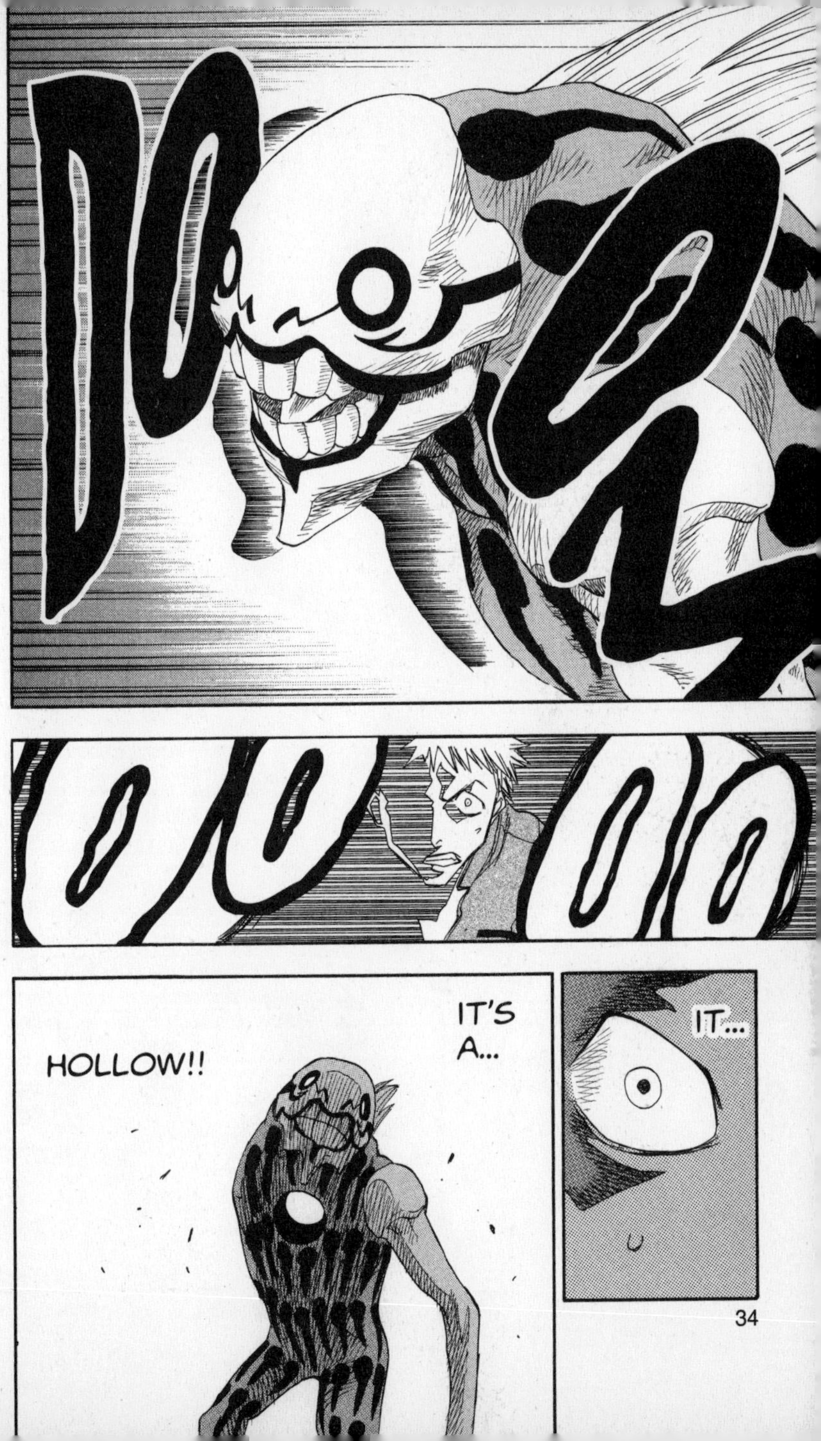
IT...
IT'S A...
HOLLOW!!

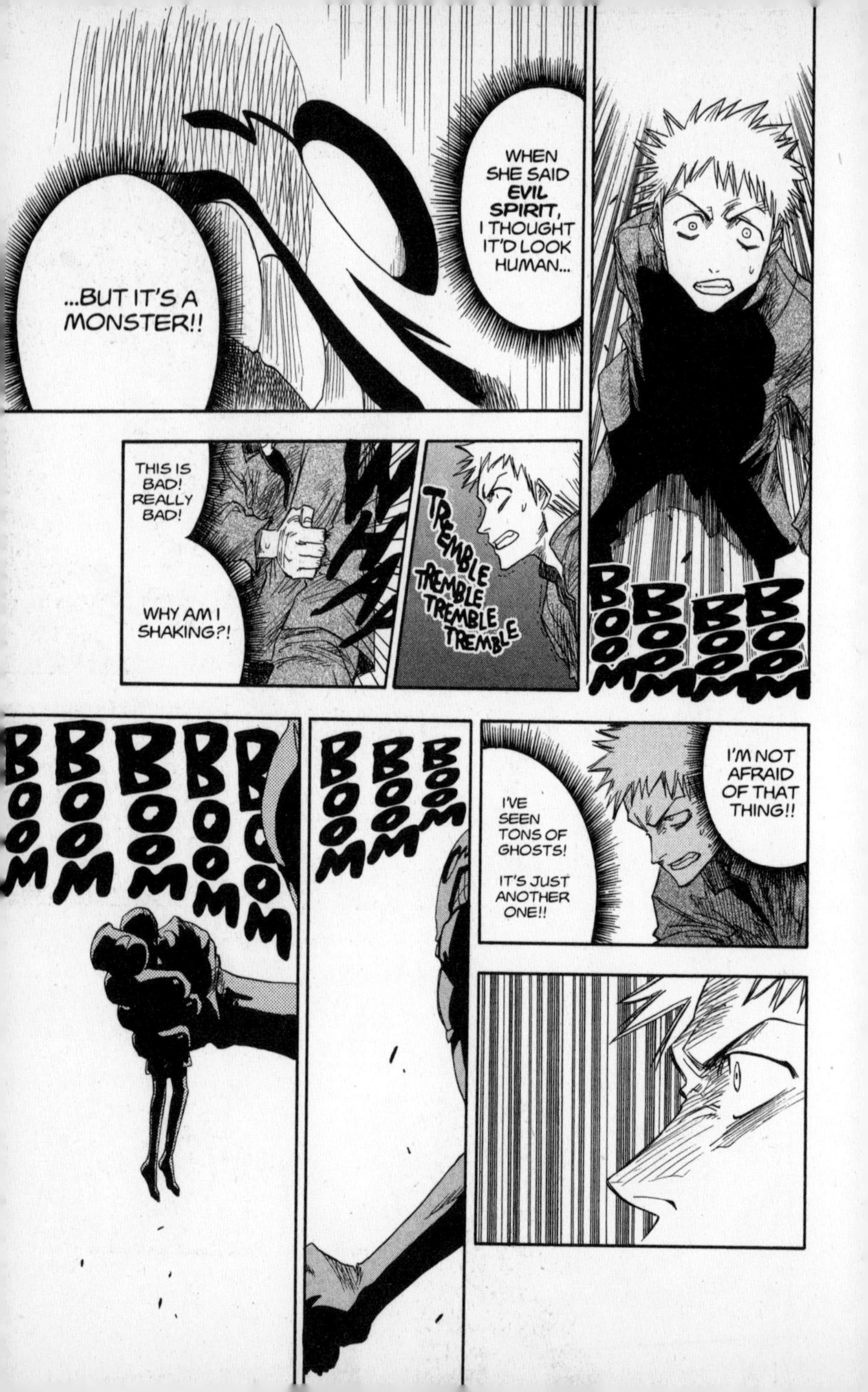
BOOOM BOOOM BOOOM BOOOM
WHEN SHE SAID EVIL SPIRIT, I THOUGHT IT'D LOOK HUMAN...
...BUT IT'S A MONSTER!!
TREMBLE TREMBLE TREMBLE TREMBLE
THIS IS BAD! REALLY BAD!
WHY AM I SHAKING?!
I'M NOT AFRAID OF THAT THING!!
I'VE SEEN TONS OF GHOSTS!
IT'S JUST ANOTHER ONE!!
BOOOM BOOOM BOOOM
BOOOM BOOOM BOOOM BOOOM BOOOM

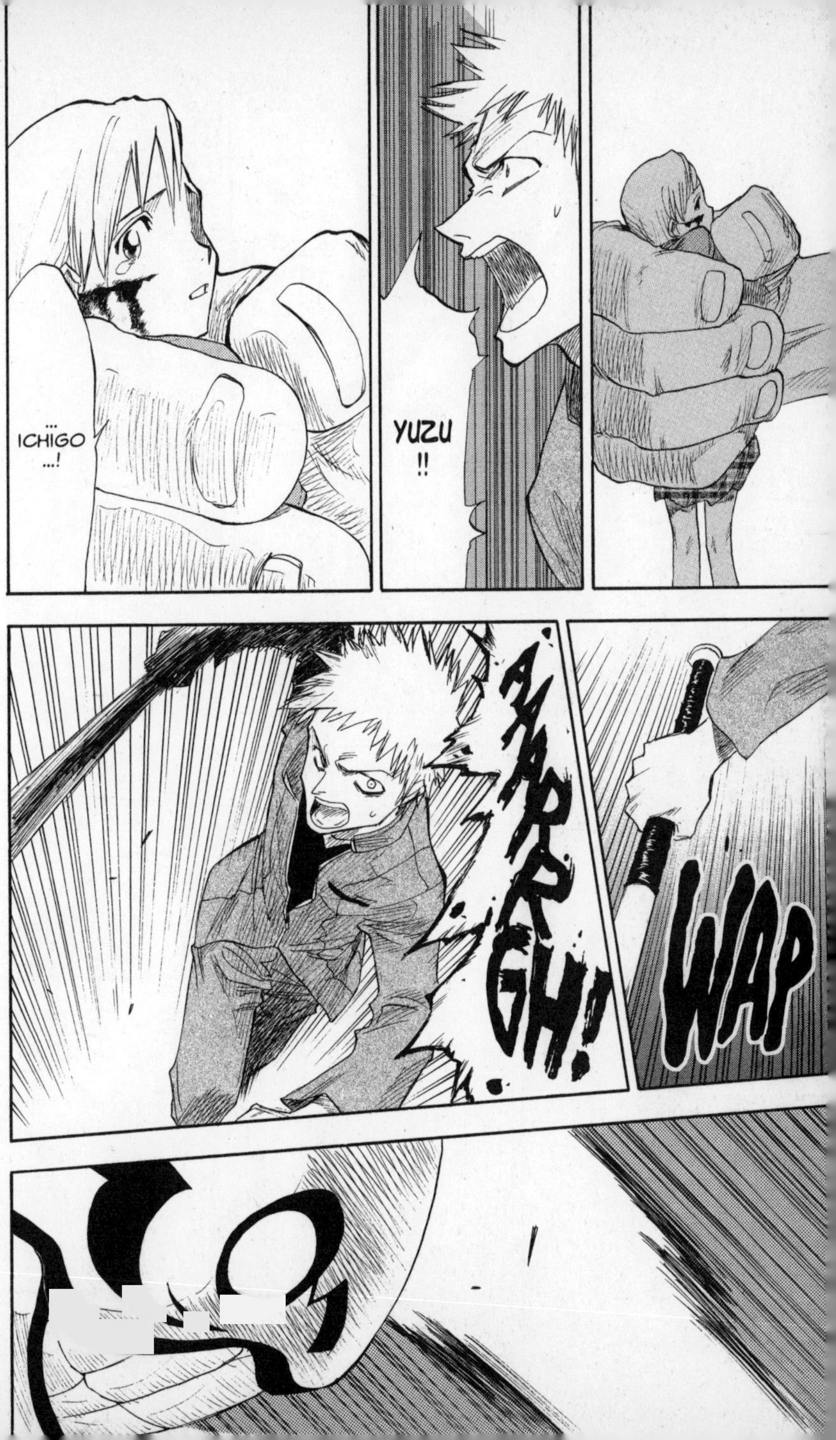
YUZU !!
... ICHIGO ...!
WAP
AARRGH!

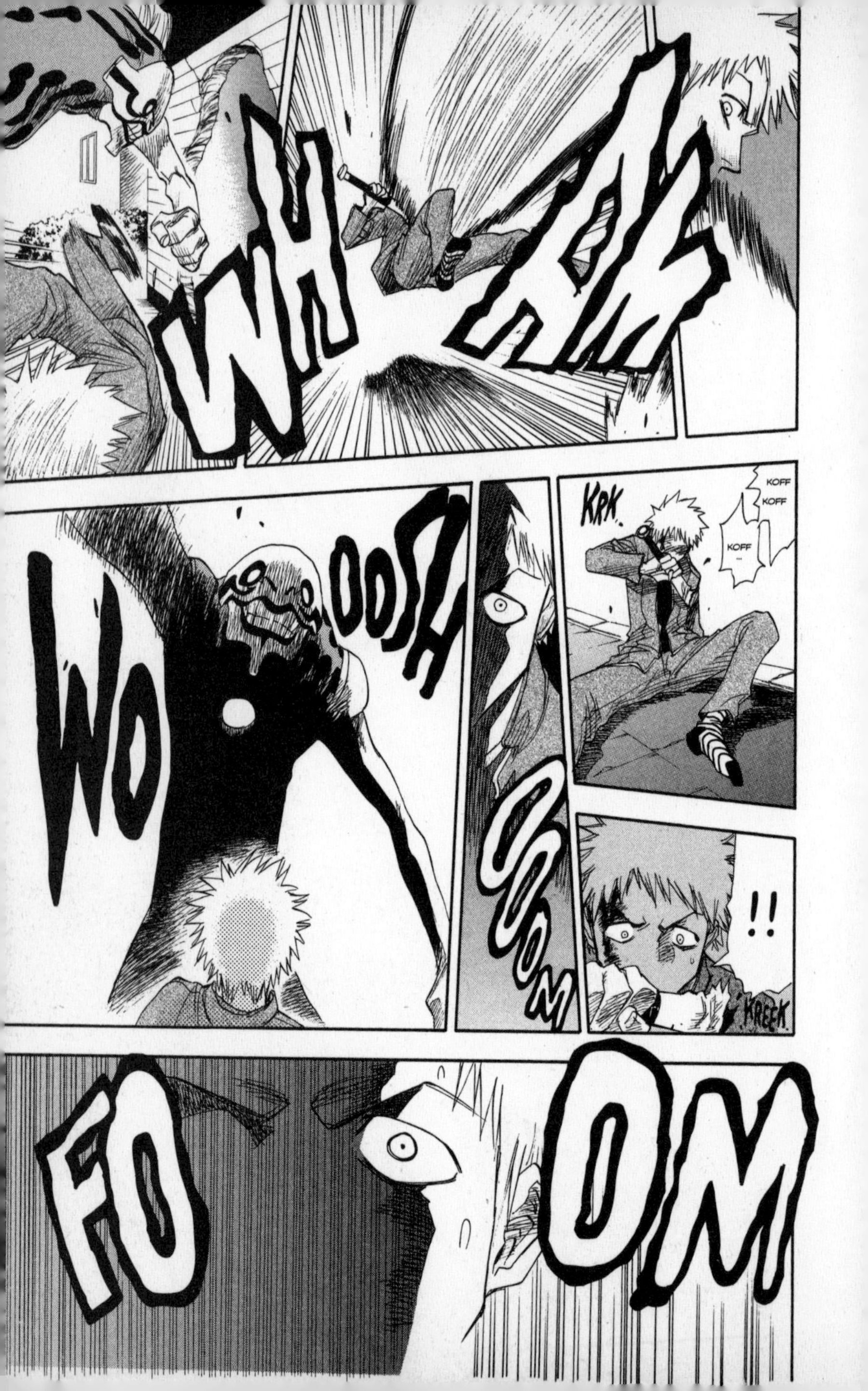
WHAM
KRK...
KOFF
KOFF
KOFF...
!!
KREEK
OOOOOM
WOOOSH
FOOM

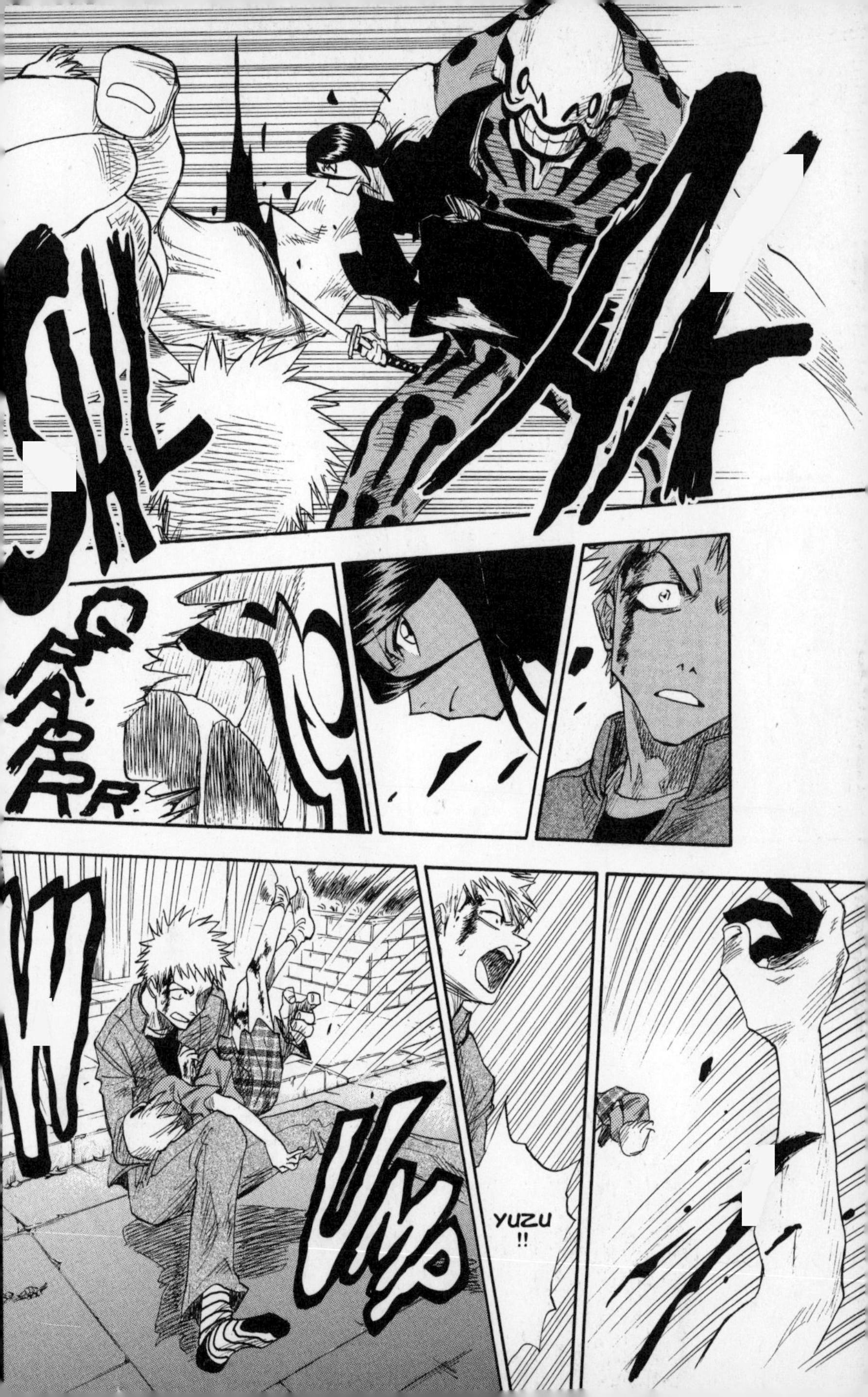
YUZU !!

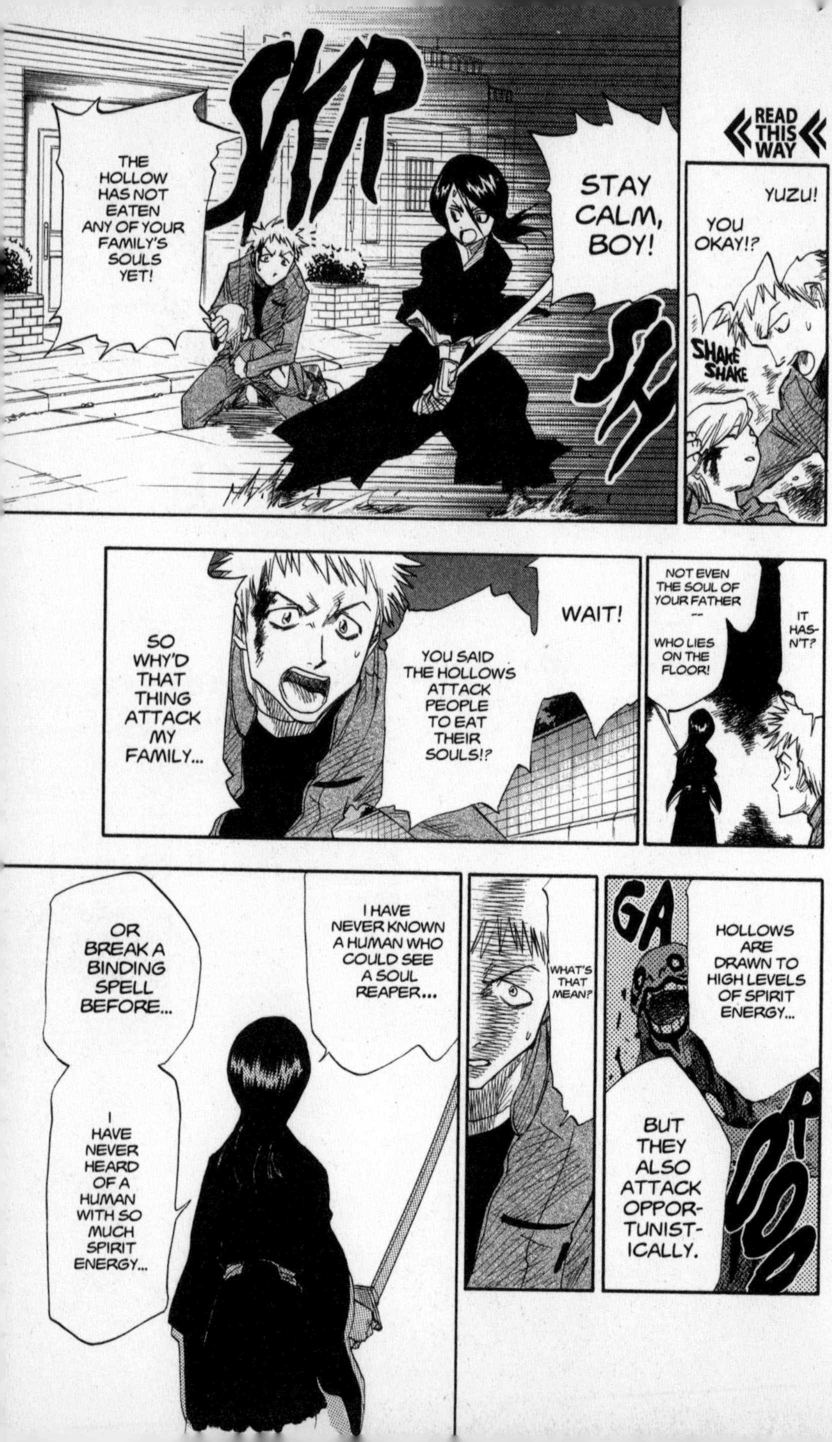
READ THIS WAY
YUZU!
YOU OKAY!?
SHAKE SHAKE
STAY CALM, BOY!
SKR
THE HOLLOW HAS NOT EATEN ANY OF YOUR FAMILY'S SOULS YET!
SH
IT HAS-N'T?
NOT EVEN THE SOUL OF YOUR FATHER --
WHO LIES ON THE FLOOR!
WAIT!
YOU SAID THE HOLLOWS ATTACK PEOPLE TO EAT THEIR SOULS!?
SO WHY'D THAT THING ATTACK MY FAMILY...
GA
HOLLOWS ARE DRAWN TO HIGH LEVELS OF SPIRIT ENERGY...
BUT THEY ALSO ATTACK OPPOR-TUNIST-ICALLY.
WHAT'S THAT MEAN?
I HAVE NEVER KNOWN A HUMAN WHO COULD SEE A SOUL REAPER...
OR BREAK A BINDING SPELL BEFORE...
I HAVE NEVER HEARD OF A HUMAN WITH SO MUCH SPIRIT ENERGY...

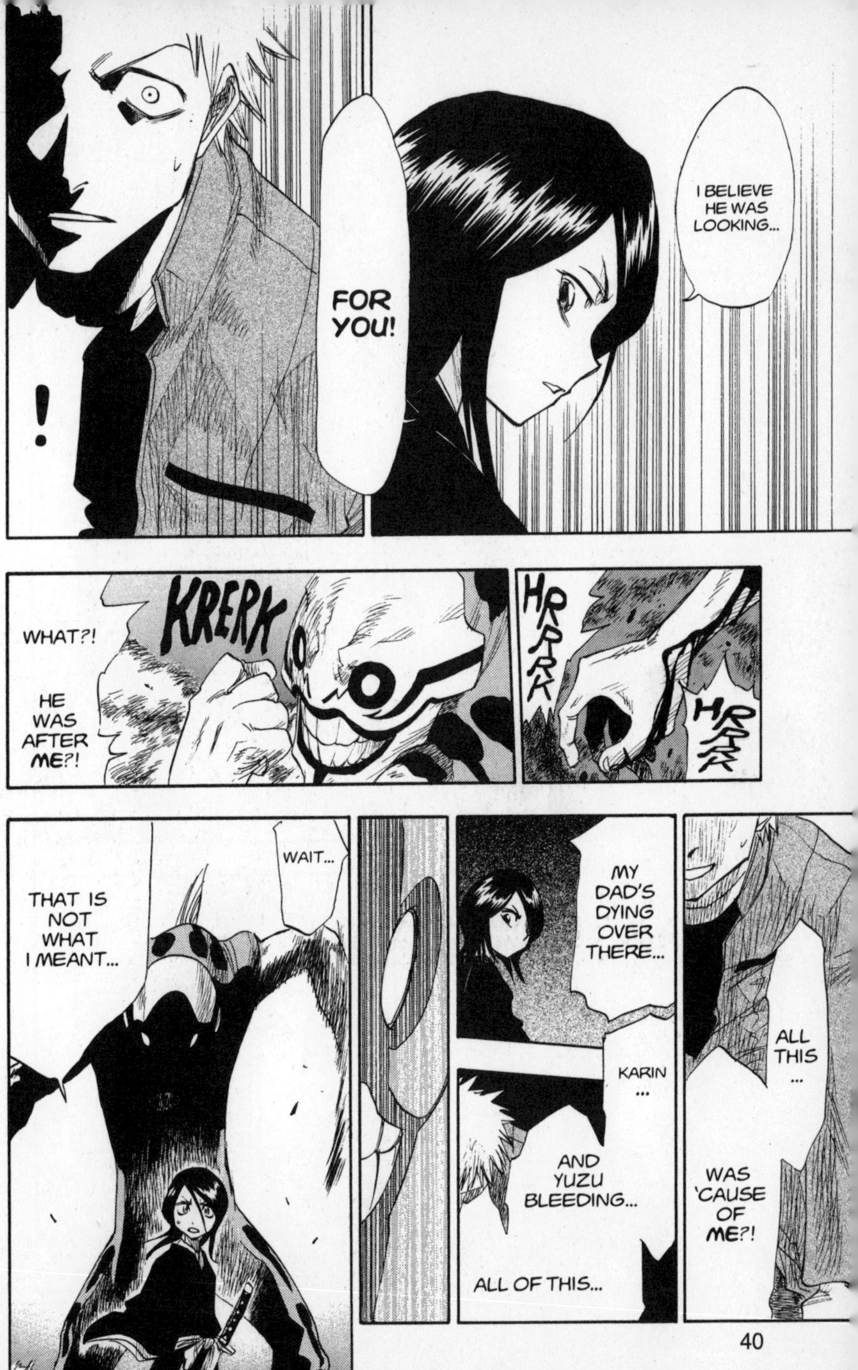
I BELIEVE HE WAS LOOKING...
FOR YOU!
!
HRRRK
HRRRK
KRERK
WHAT?!
HE WAS AFTER ME?!
ALL THIS...
WAS 'CAUSE OF ME?!
MY DAD'S DYING OVER THERE...
KARIN...
AND YUZU BLEEDING...
ALL OF THIS...
WAIT...
THAT IS NOT WHAT I MEANT...

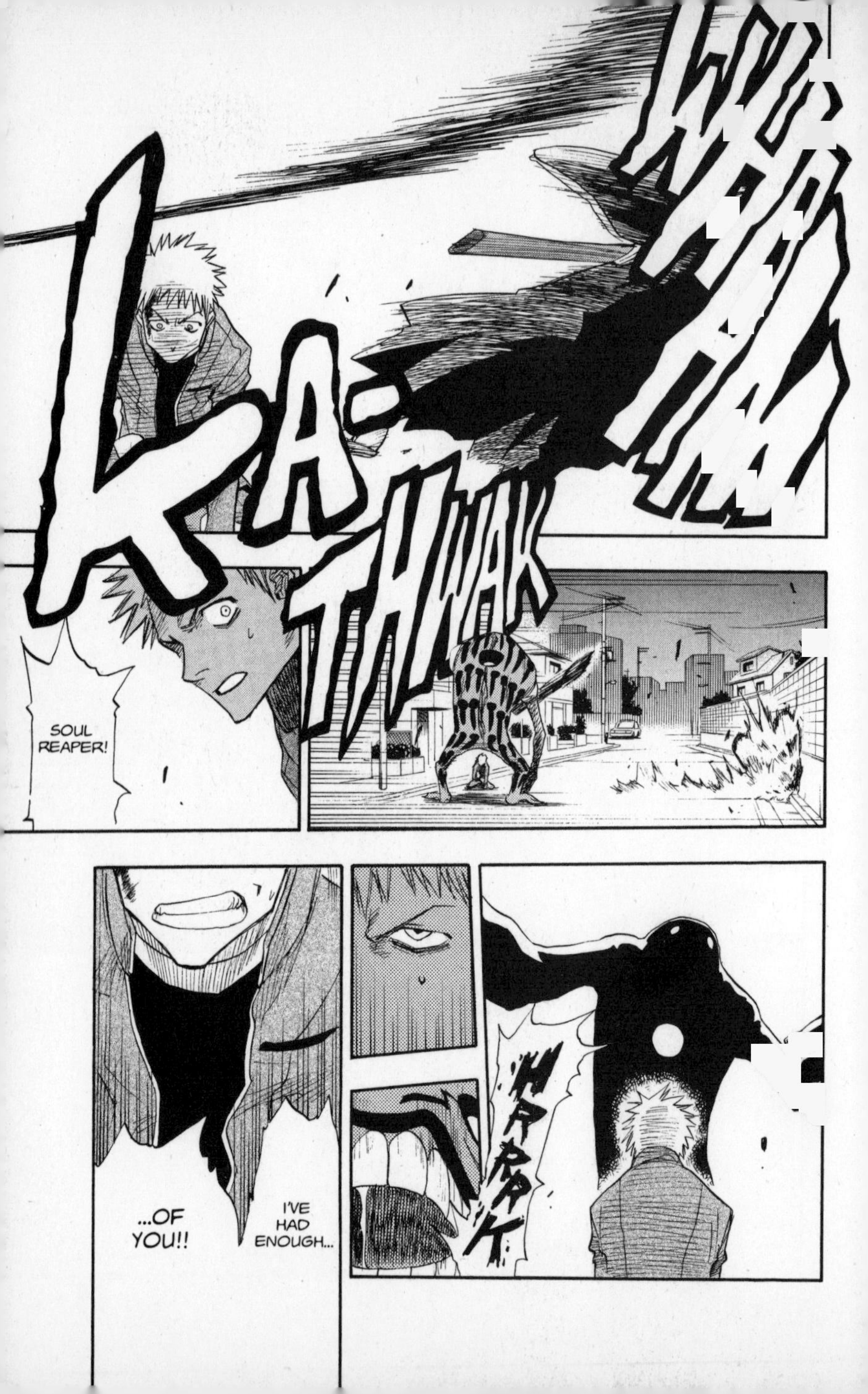
KA-THWAK
SOUL REAPER!
HRRRRK
I'VE HAD ENOUGH...
...OF YOU!!

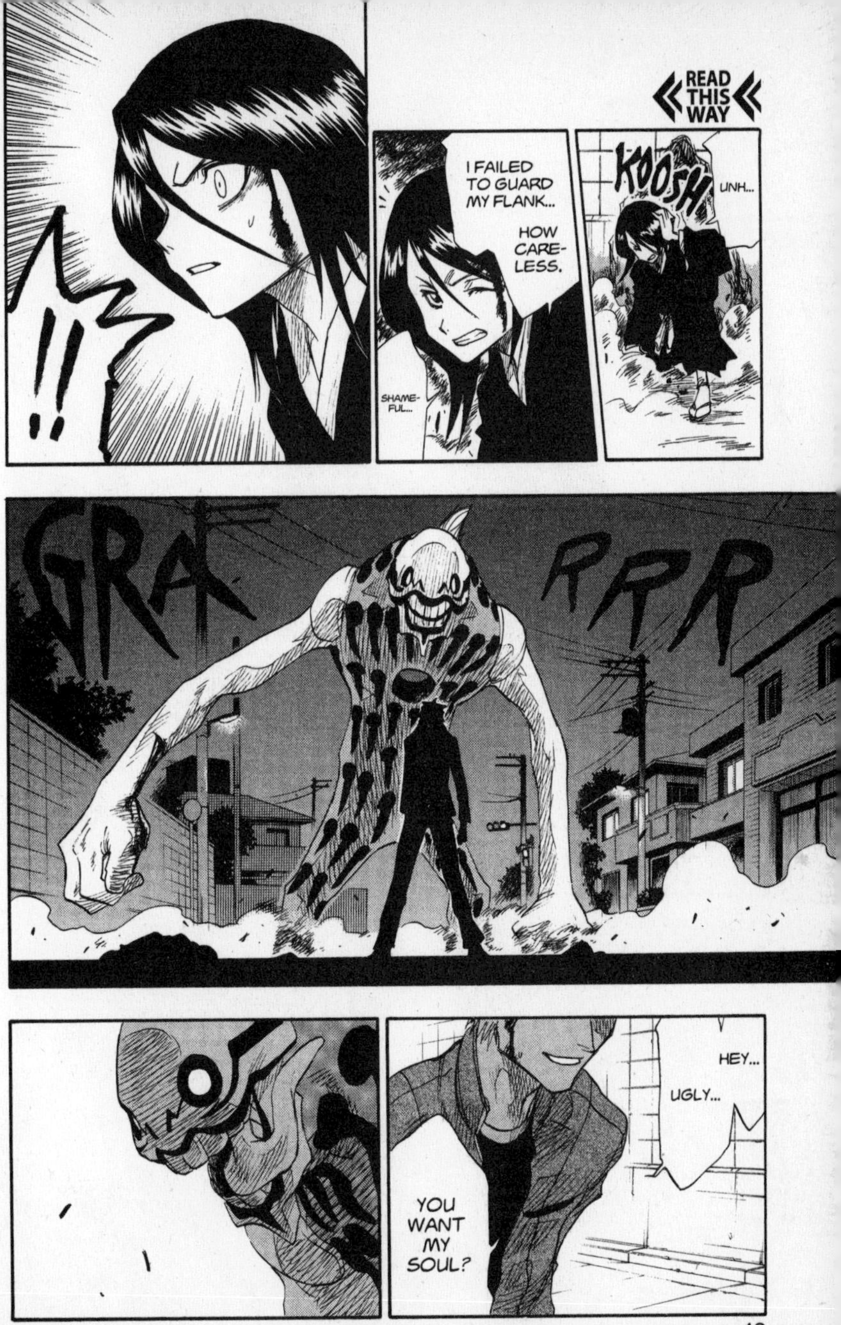
READ THIS WAY
KOOSH
UNH...
I FAILED TO GUARD MY FLANK...
HOW CARE-LESS.
SHAME-FUL...
!!
GRA RRR
HEY...
UGLY...
YOU WANT MY SOUL?

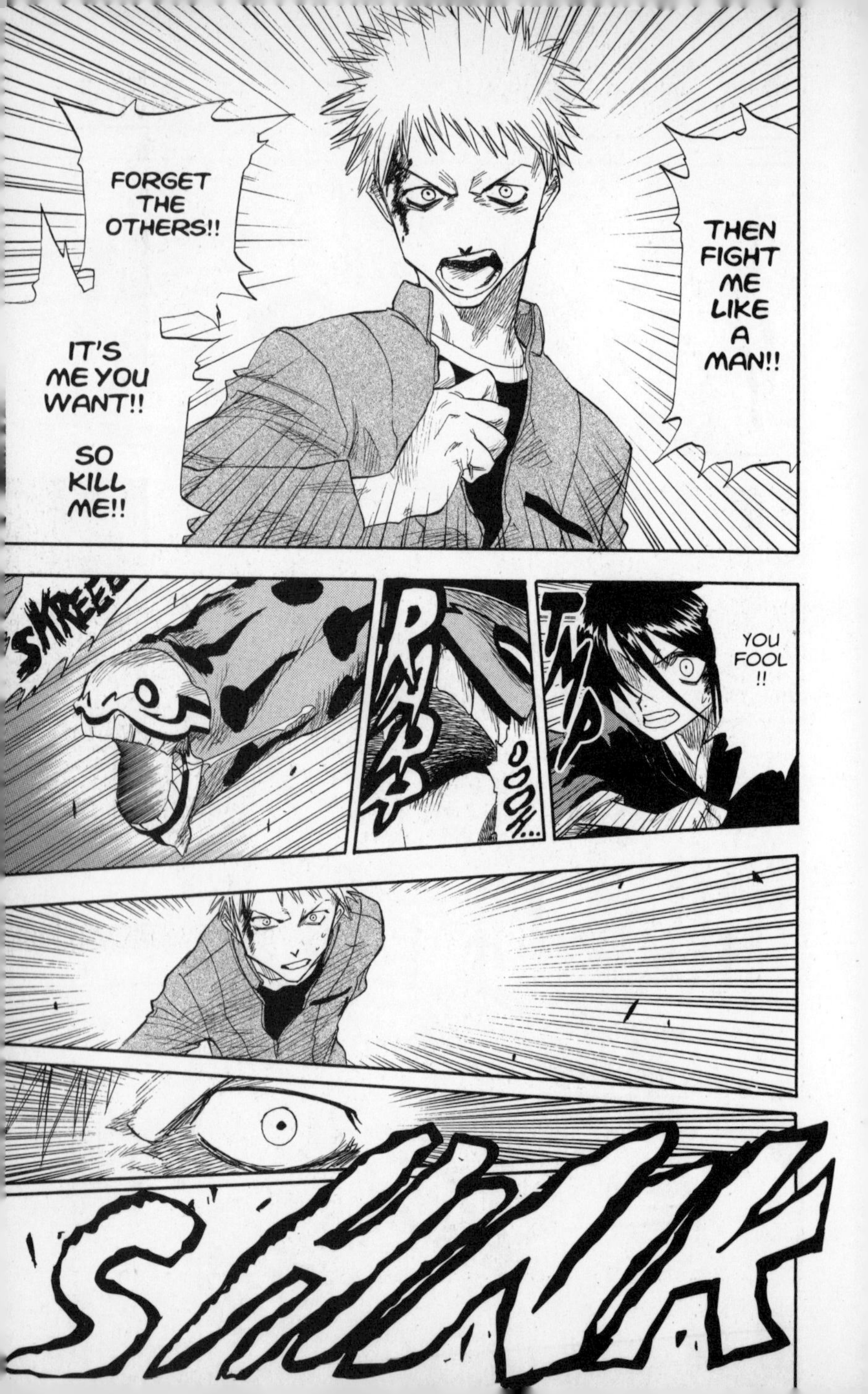
FORGET THE OTHERS!!
IT'S ME YOU WANT!!
SO KILL ME!!
THEN FIGHT ME LIKE A MAN!!
TMP
YOU FOOL!!
OOOOH...
SKREEE

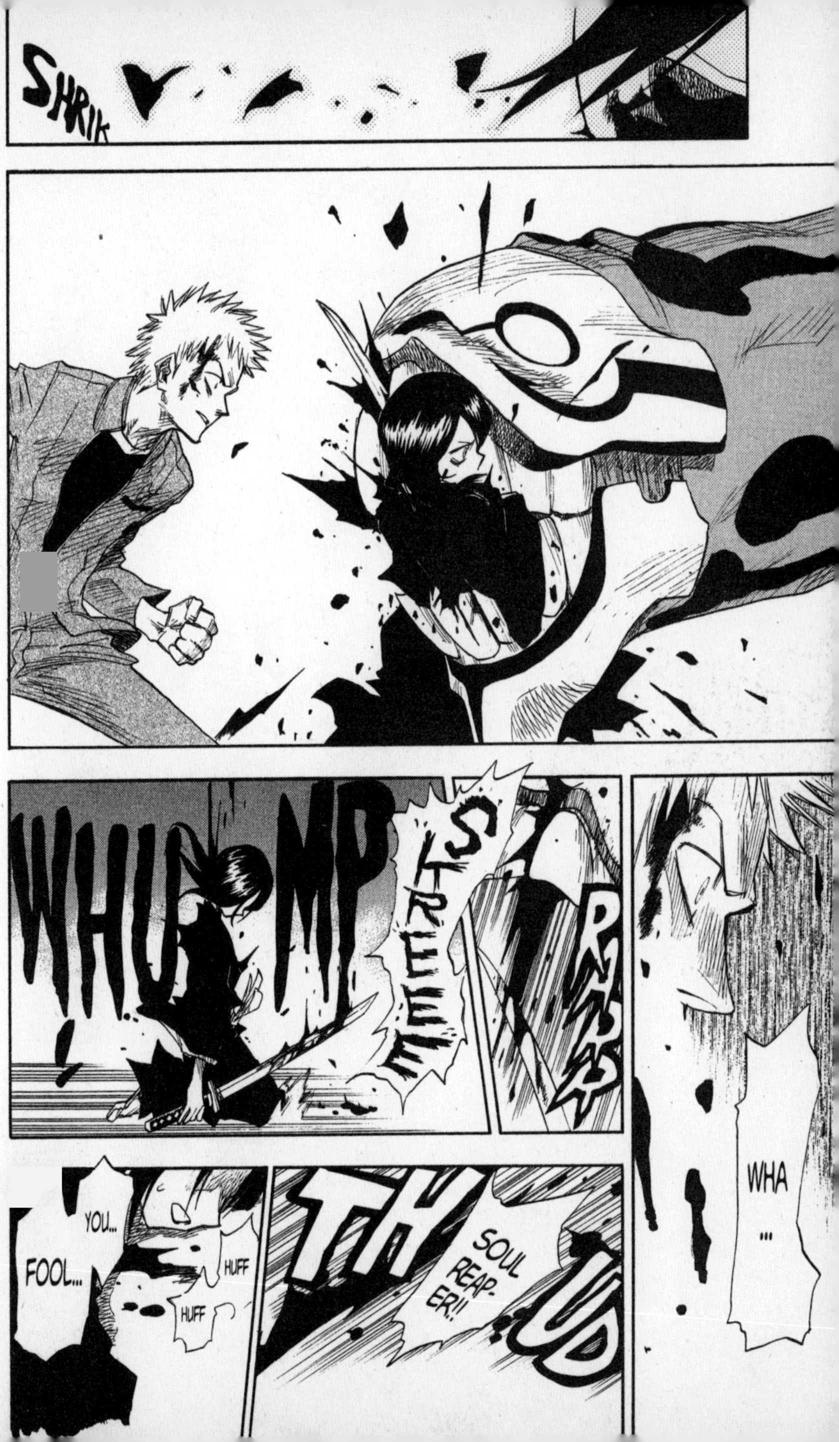
SHRIK
WHA
...
STREEEEE
WHUMP
THUD
SOUL REAP-ER!!
YOU...
FOOL...
HUFF
HUFF

READ THIS WAY

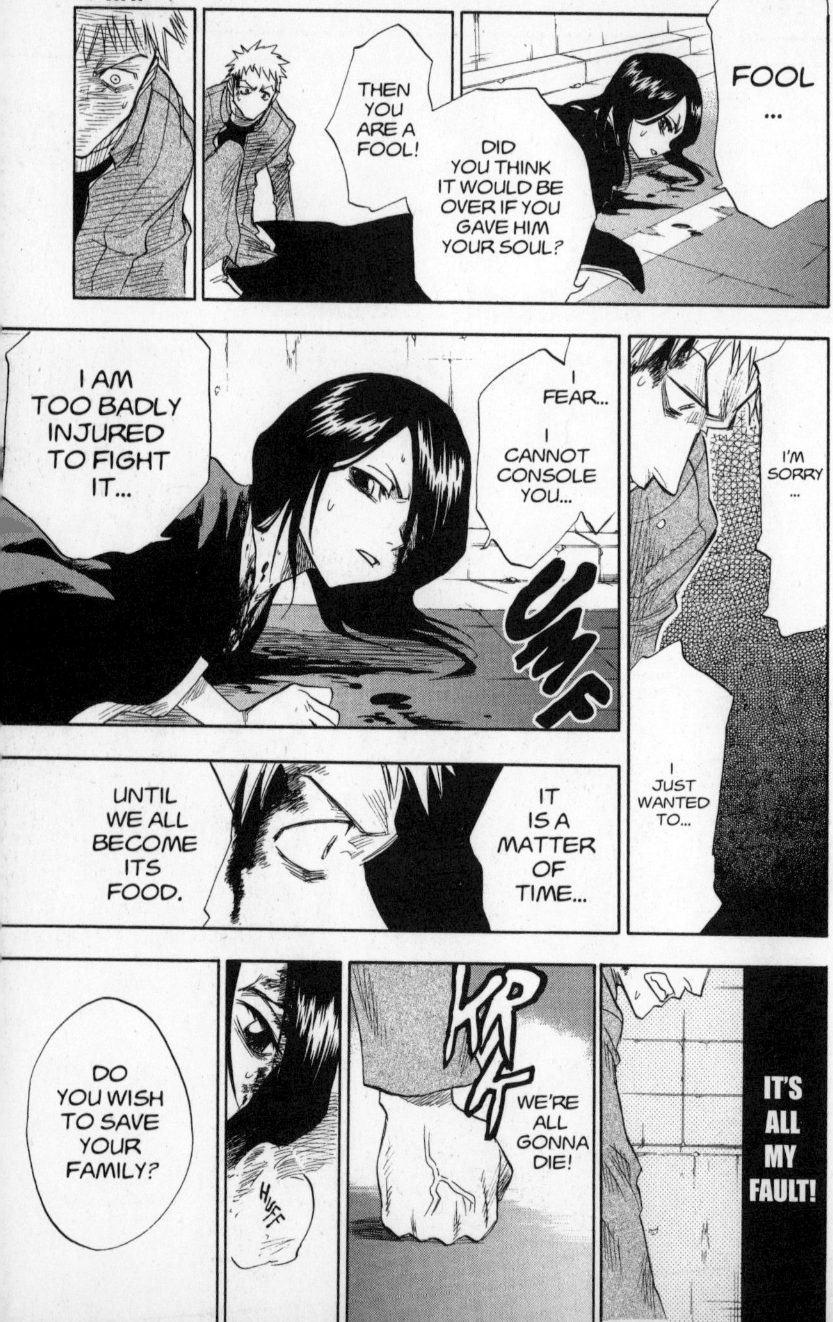
FOOL ...
DID YOU THINK IT WOULD BE OVER IF YOU GAVE HIM YOUR SOUL?
THEN YOU ARE A FOOL!
I'M SORRY ...
I JUST WANTED TO...
I FEAR... I CANNOT CONSOLE YOU...
UMF
I AM TOO BADLY INJURED TO FIGHT IT...
IT IS A MATTER OF TIME...
UNTIL WE ALL BECOME ITS FOOD.
IT'S ALL MY FAULT!
KRK
WE'RE ALL GONNA DIE!
HUFF
DO YOU WISH TO SAVE YOUR FAMILY?

READ THIS WAY

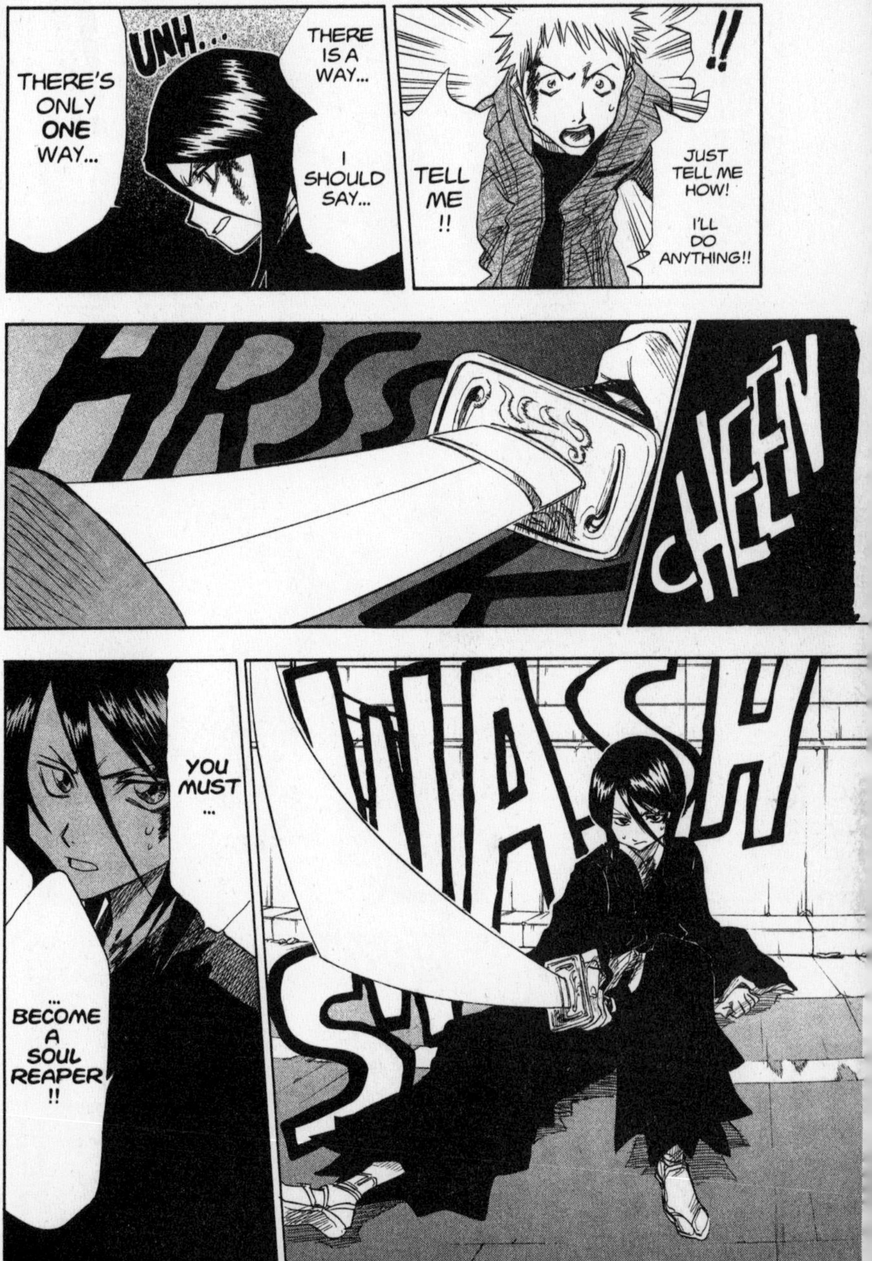

!!
JUST TELL ME HOW!
I'LL DO ANYTHING!!
TELL ME !!
THERE IS A WAY...
I SHOULD SAY...
UNH...
THERE'S ONLY ONE WAY...
CHEEN
HRSSK
SWASH
YOU MUST ...
... BECOME A SOUL REAPER !!

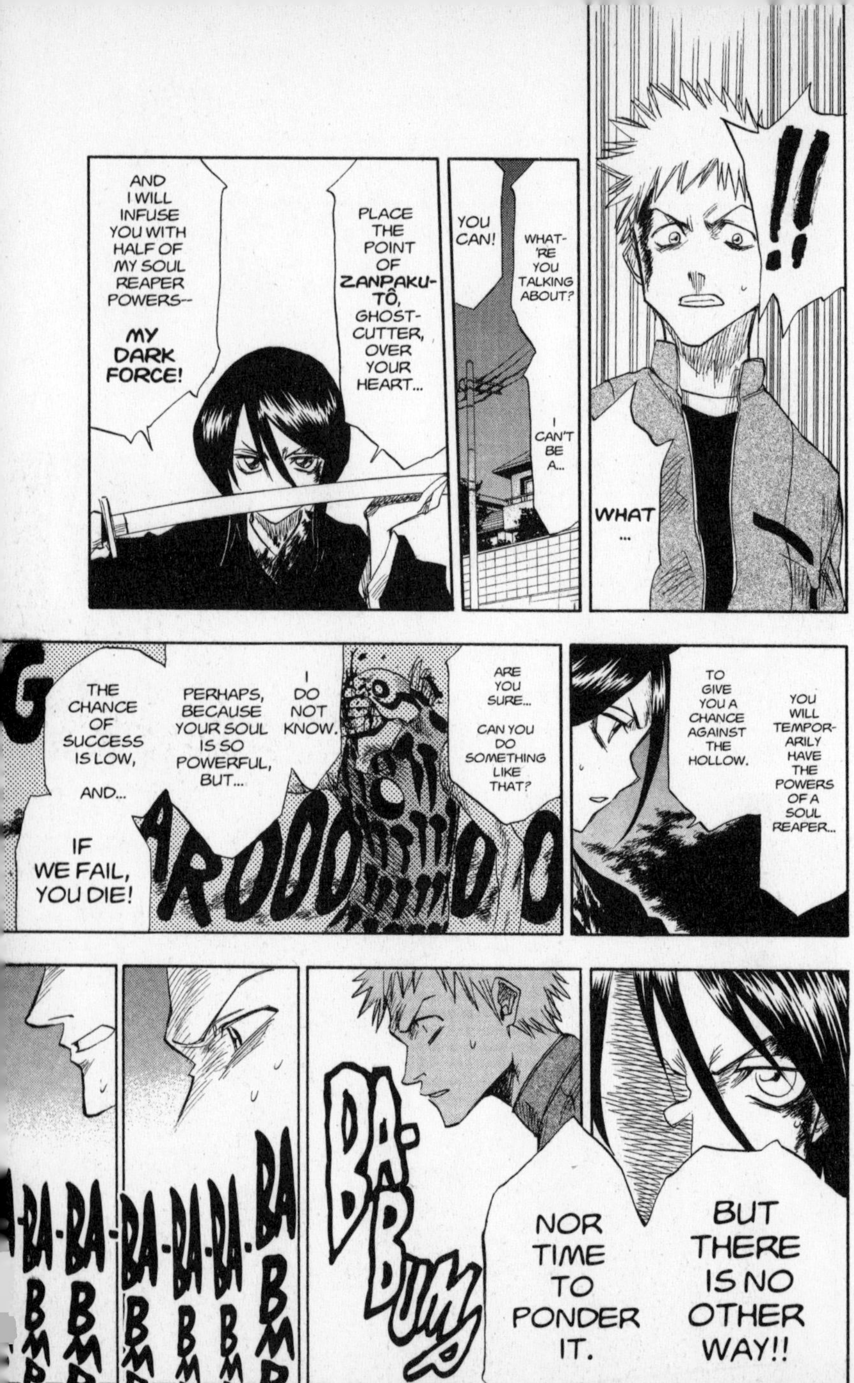
!!
WHAT...
WHAT'RE YOU TALKING ABOUT?
I CAN'T BE A...
YOU CAN!
PLACE THE POINT OF **ZANPAKU-TÔ**, GHOST-CUTTER, OVER YOUR HEART...
AND I WILL INFUSE YOU WITH HALF OF MY SOUL REAPER POWERS--
MY DARK FORCE!
YOU WILL TEMPORARILY HAVE THE POWERS OF A SOUL REAPER...
TO GIVE YOU A CHANCE AGAINST THE HOLLOW.
ARE YOU SURE...
CAN YOU DO SOMETHING LIKE THAT?
AROOOOOO
I DO NOT KNOW.
PERHAPS, BECAUSE YOUR SOUL IS SO POWERFUL, BUT...
THE CHANCE OF SUCCESS IS LOW,
AND...
IF WE FAIL, YOU DIE!
BUT THERE IS NO OTHER WAY!!
NOR TIME TO PONDER IT.
DA-BUMP
BA-BMP
BA-BMP
BA-BMP
BA-BMP
BA-BMP

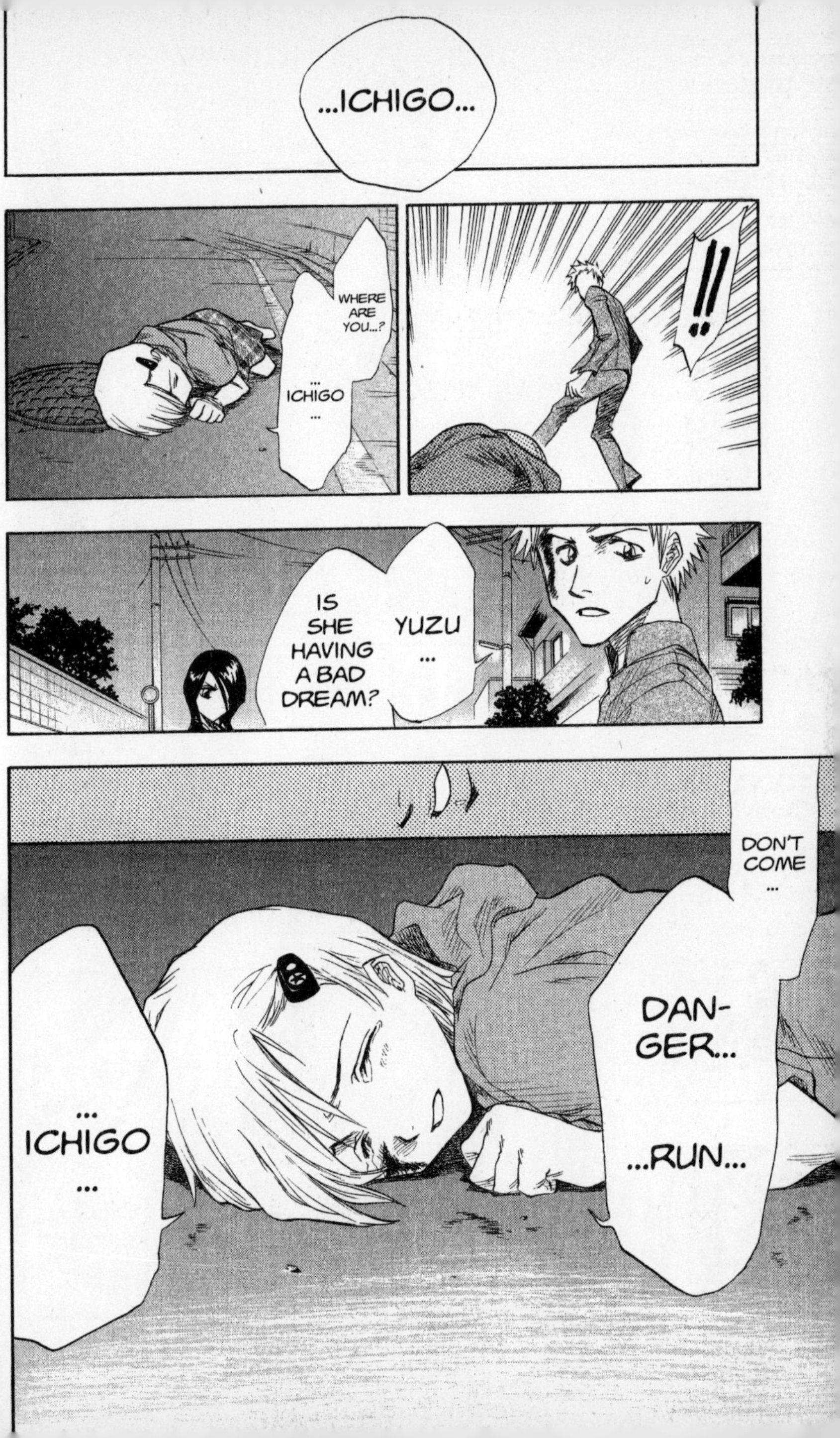
...ICHIGO...
!!
WHERE ARE YOU...?
...ICHIGO...
YUZU...
IS SHE HAVING A BAD DREAM?
DON'T COME...
DAN-GER...
...RUN...
...ICHIGO...

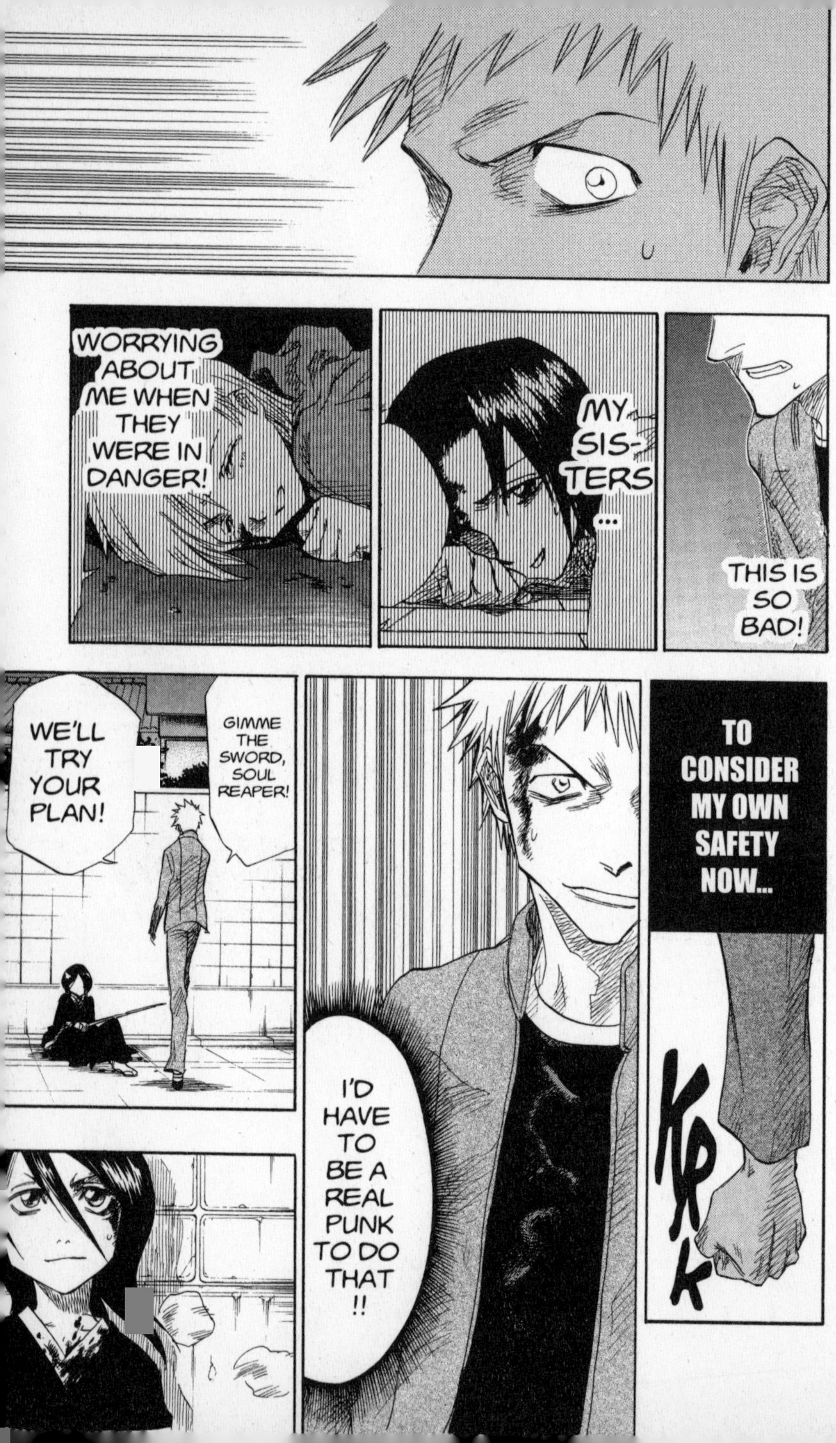
THIS IS SO BAD!
MY SISTERS...
WORRYING ABOUT ME WHEN THEY WERE IN DANGER!
TO CONSIDER MY OWN SAFETY NOW...
KRK
I'D HAVE TO BE A REAL PUNK TO DO THAT!!
GIMME THE SWORD, SOUL REAPER!
WE'LL TRY YOUR PLAN!

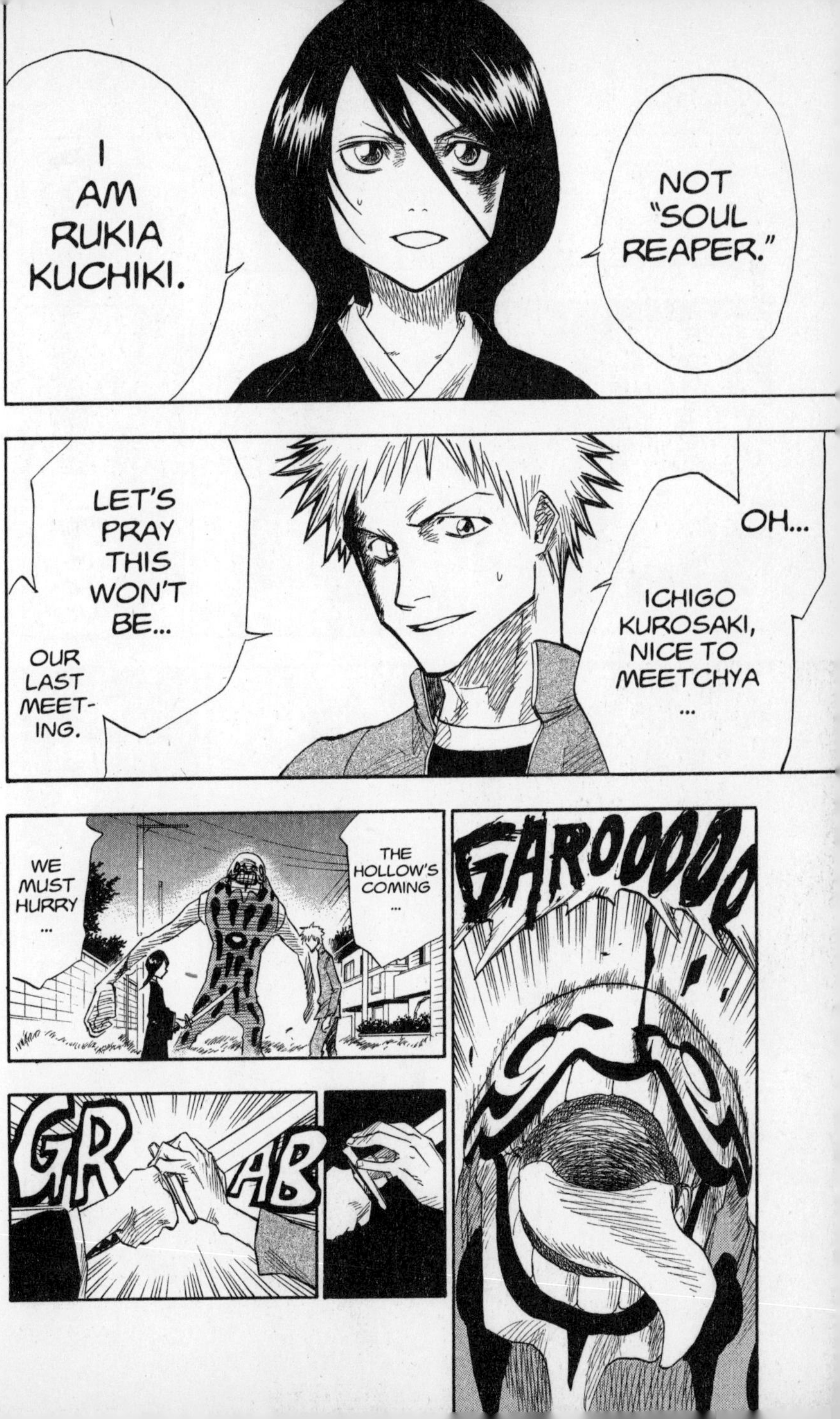
NOT "SOUL REAPER."
I AM RUKIA KUCHIKI.
OH...
ICHIGO KUROSAKI, NICE TO MEETCHYA ...
LET'S PRAY THIS WON'T BE...
OUR LAST MEET-ING.
GAROOOOO
THE HOLLOW'S COMING ...
WE MUST HURRY ...
GRAB

READ THIS WAY

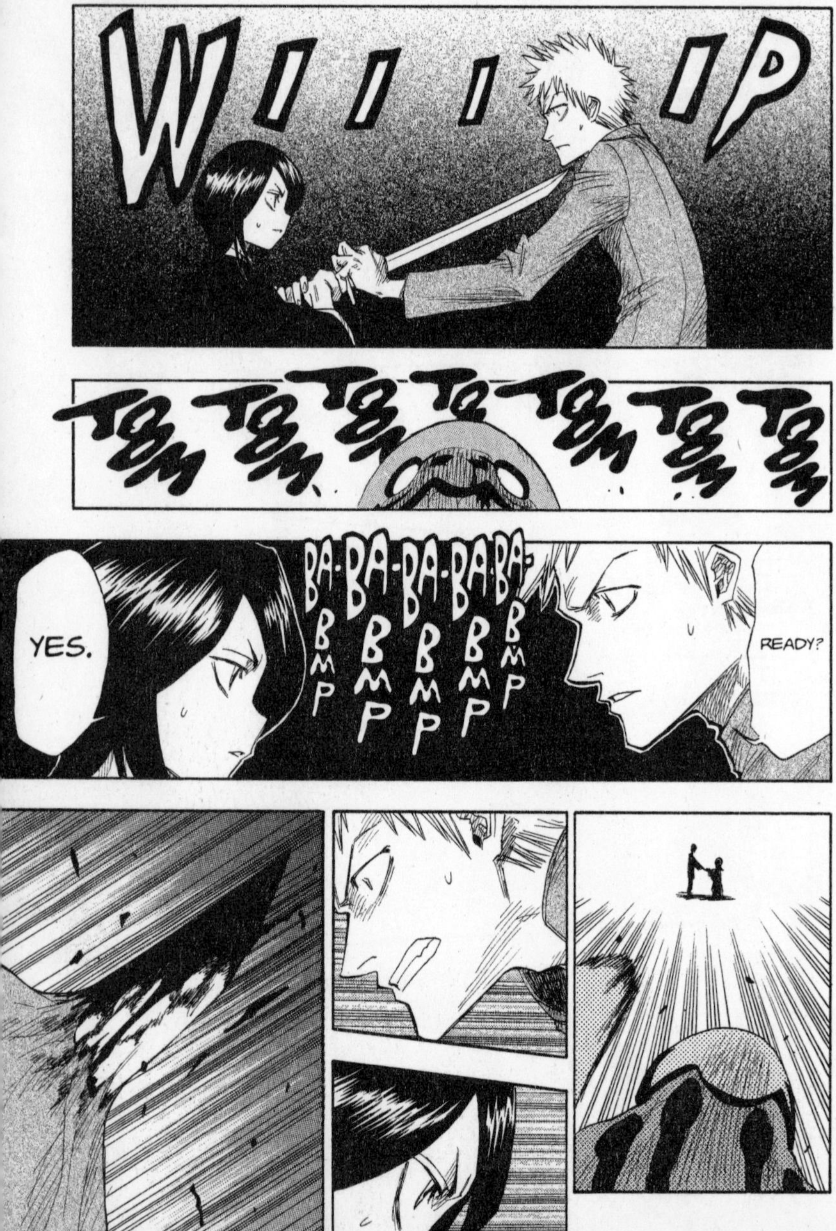
WIIIIP
TOM TOM TOM TOM TOM TOM TOM
READY?
BA-BA-BA-BA-BA-
BMP BMP BMP BMP BMP
YES.

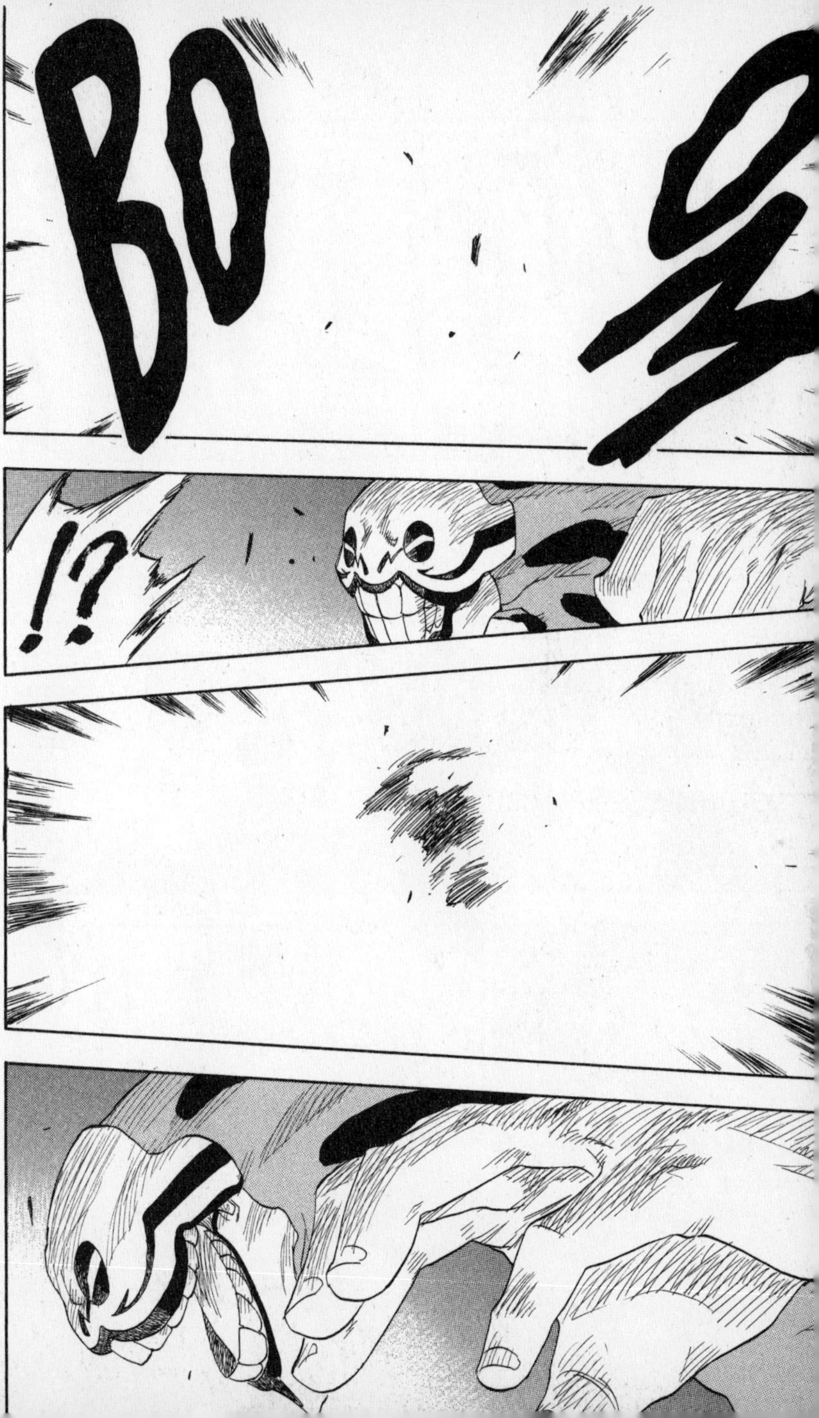
BO
!?

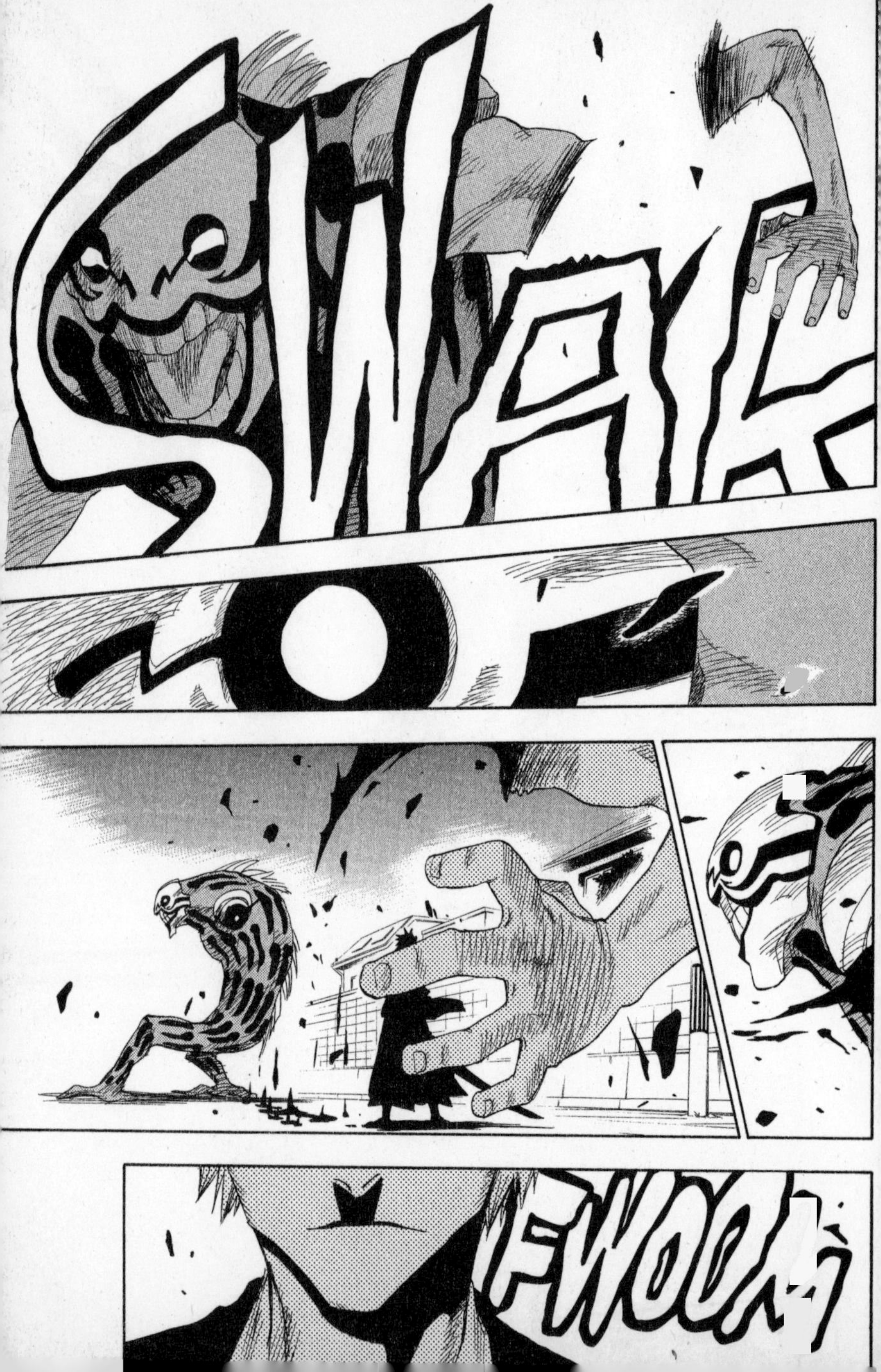
SWAK
FWOO

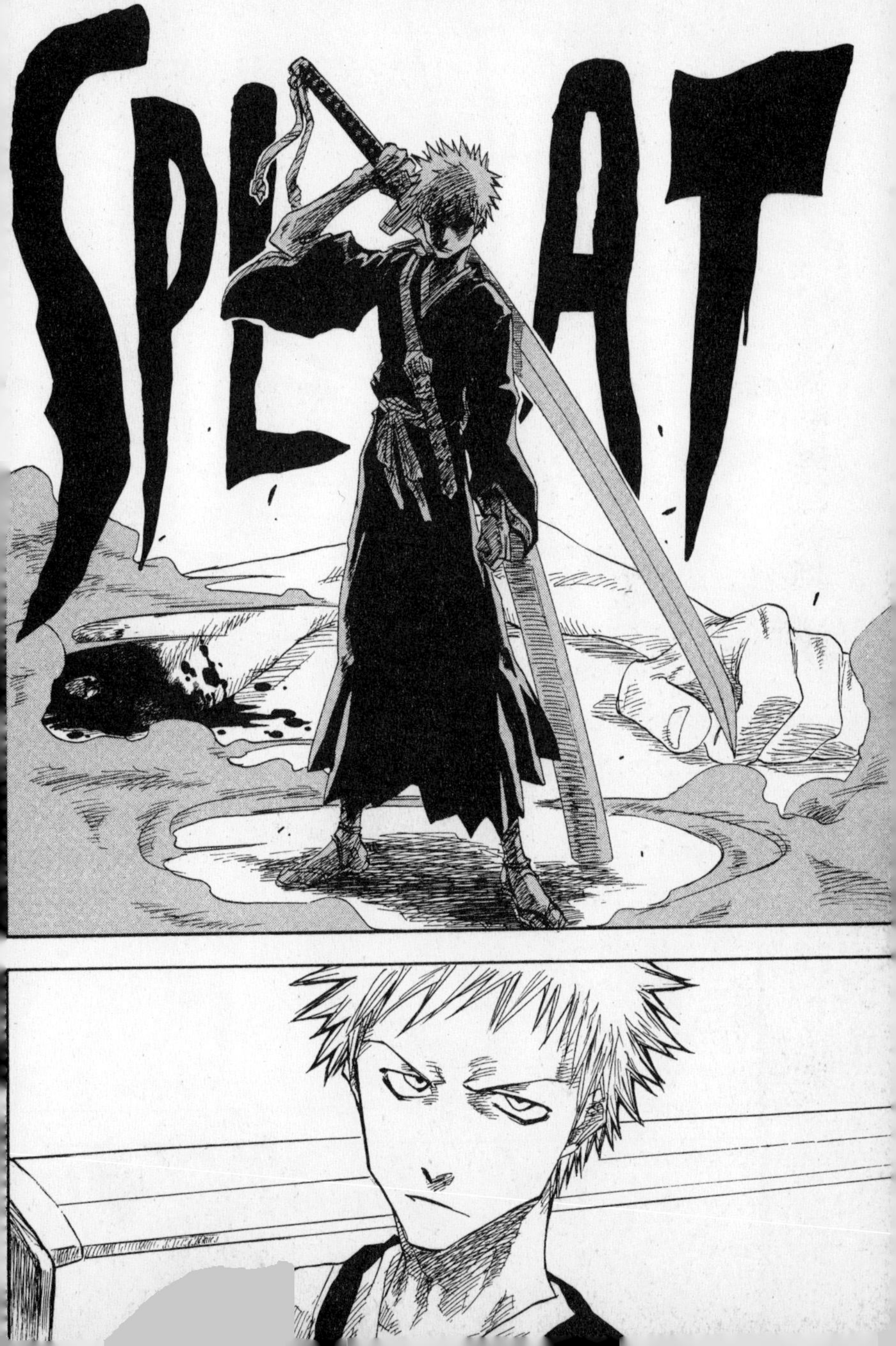
SPLAT

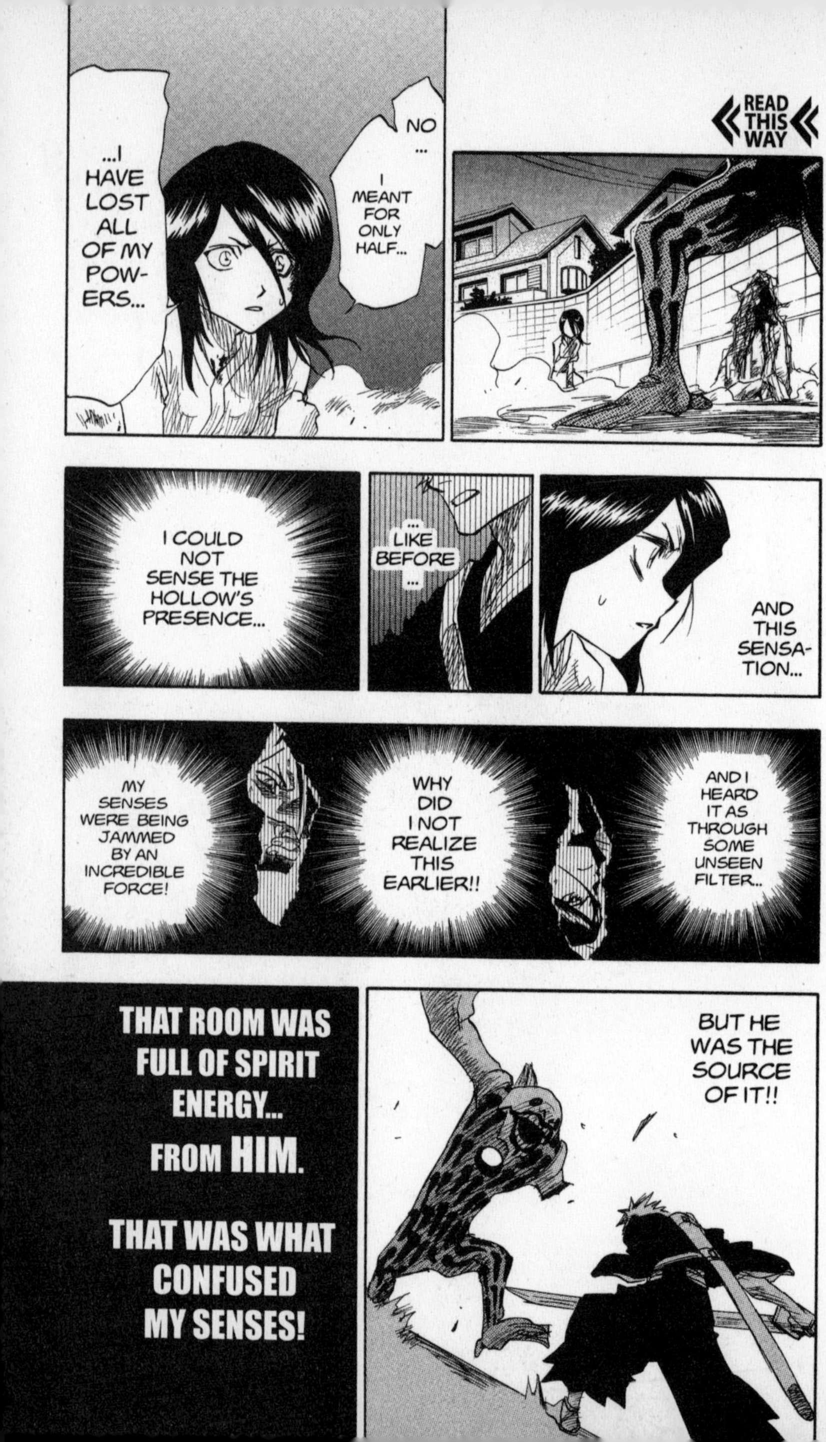
READ THIS WAY
NO ... I MEANT FOR ONLY HALF...
...I HAVE LOST ALL OF MY POWERS...
AND THIS SENSATION...
...LIKE BEFORE...
I COULD NOT SENSE THE HOLLOW'S PRESENCE...
AND I HEARD IT AS THROUGH SOME UNSEEN FILTER..
WHY DID I NOT REALIZE THIS EARLIER!!
MY SENSES WERE BEING JAMMED BY AN INCREDIBLE FORCE!
BUT HE WAS THE SOURCE OF IT!!
THAT ROOM WAS FULL OF SPIRIT ENERGY... FROM HIM.
THAT WAS WHAT CONFUSED MY SENSES!

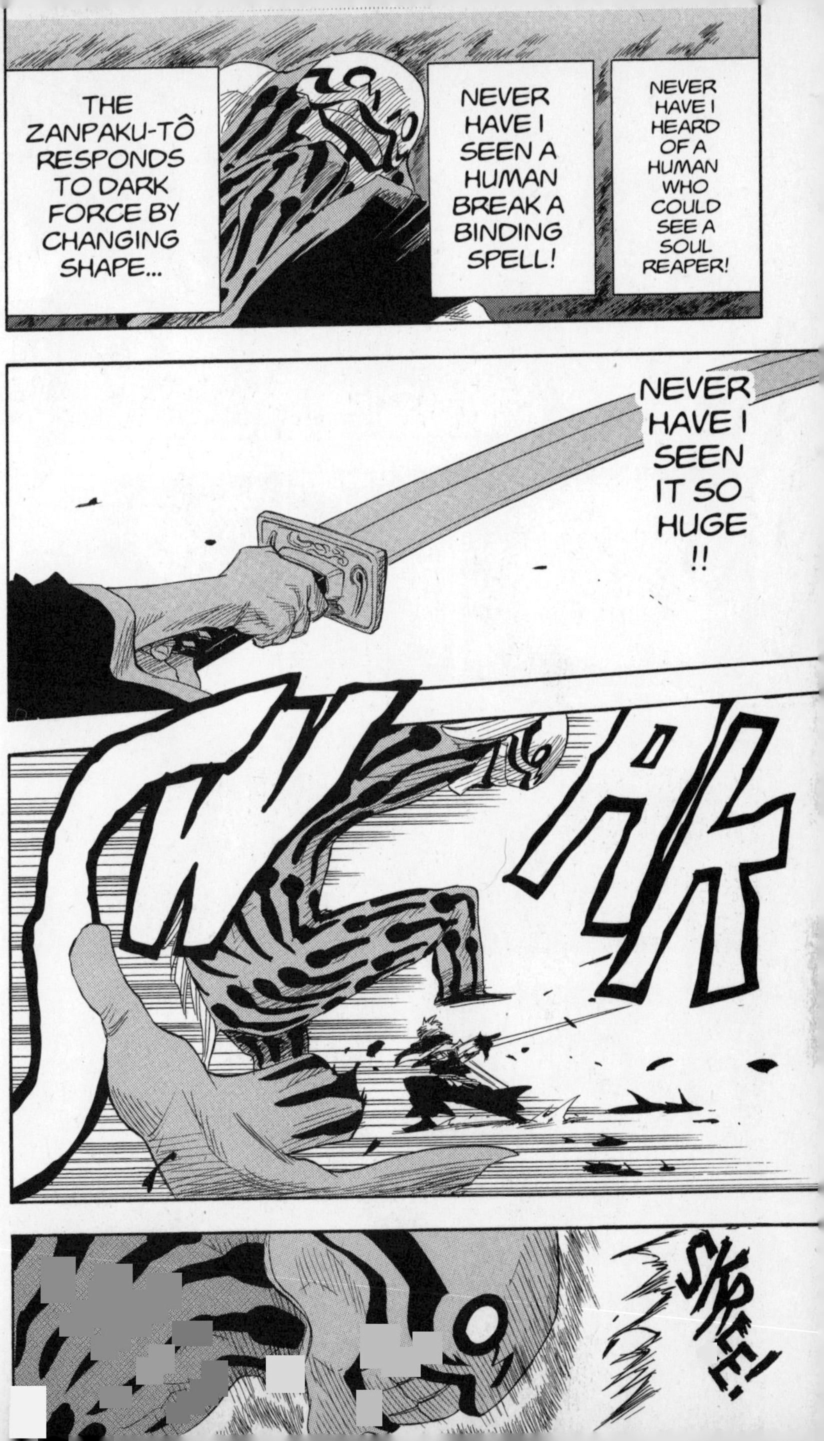
NEVER HAVE I HEARD OF A HUMAN WHO COULD SEE A SOUL REAPER!
NEVER HAVE I SEEN A HUMAN BREAK A BINDING SPELL!
THE ZANPAKU-TÔ RESPONDS TO DARK FORCE BY CHANGING SHAPE...
NEVER HAVE I SEEN IT SO HUGE !!
CHIK
SKREE!

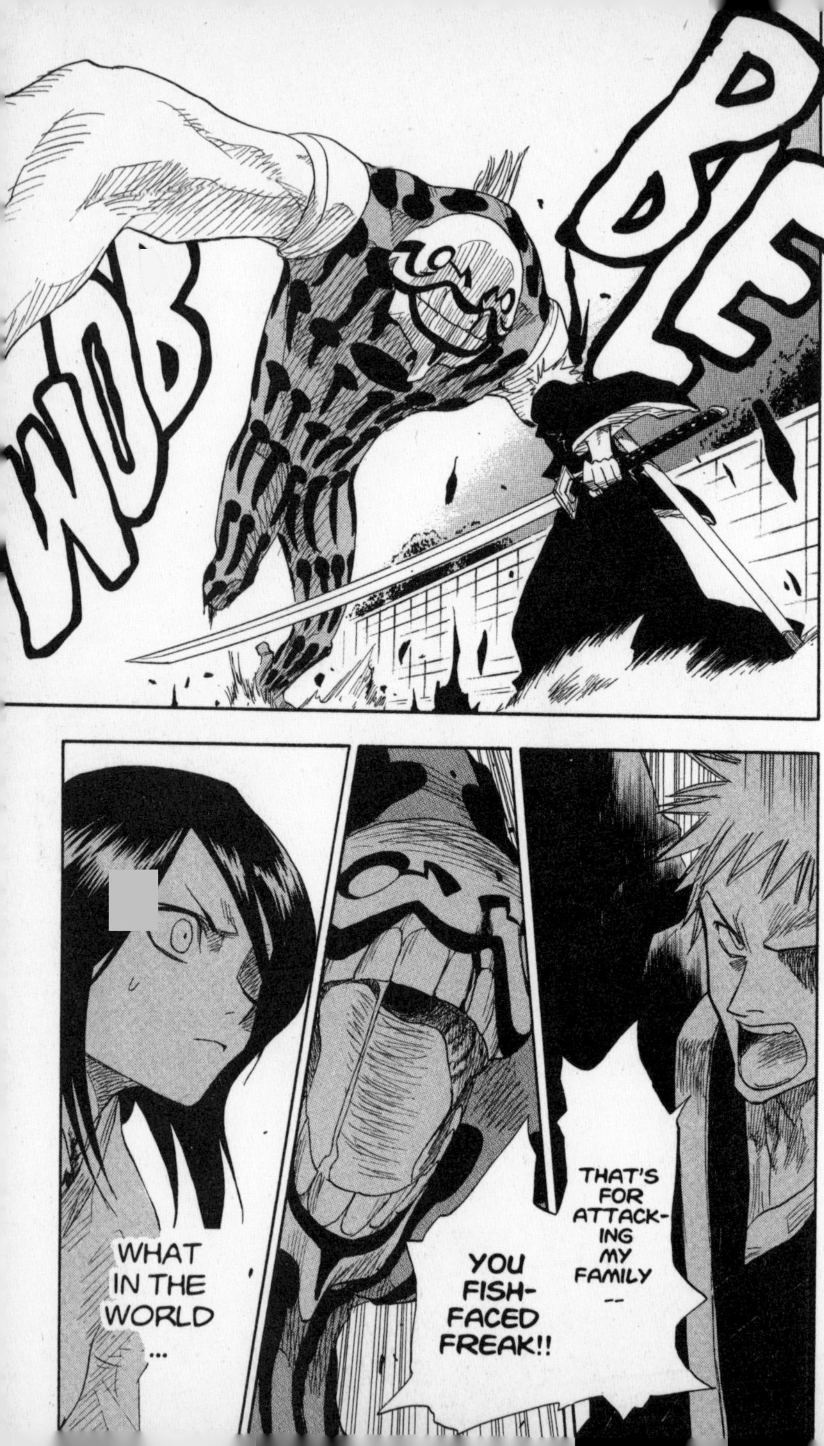
THAT'S FOR ATTACK-ING MY FAMILY --
YOU FISH-FACED FREAK!!
WHAT IN THE WORLD ...

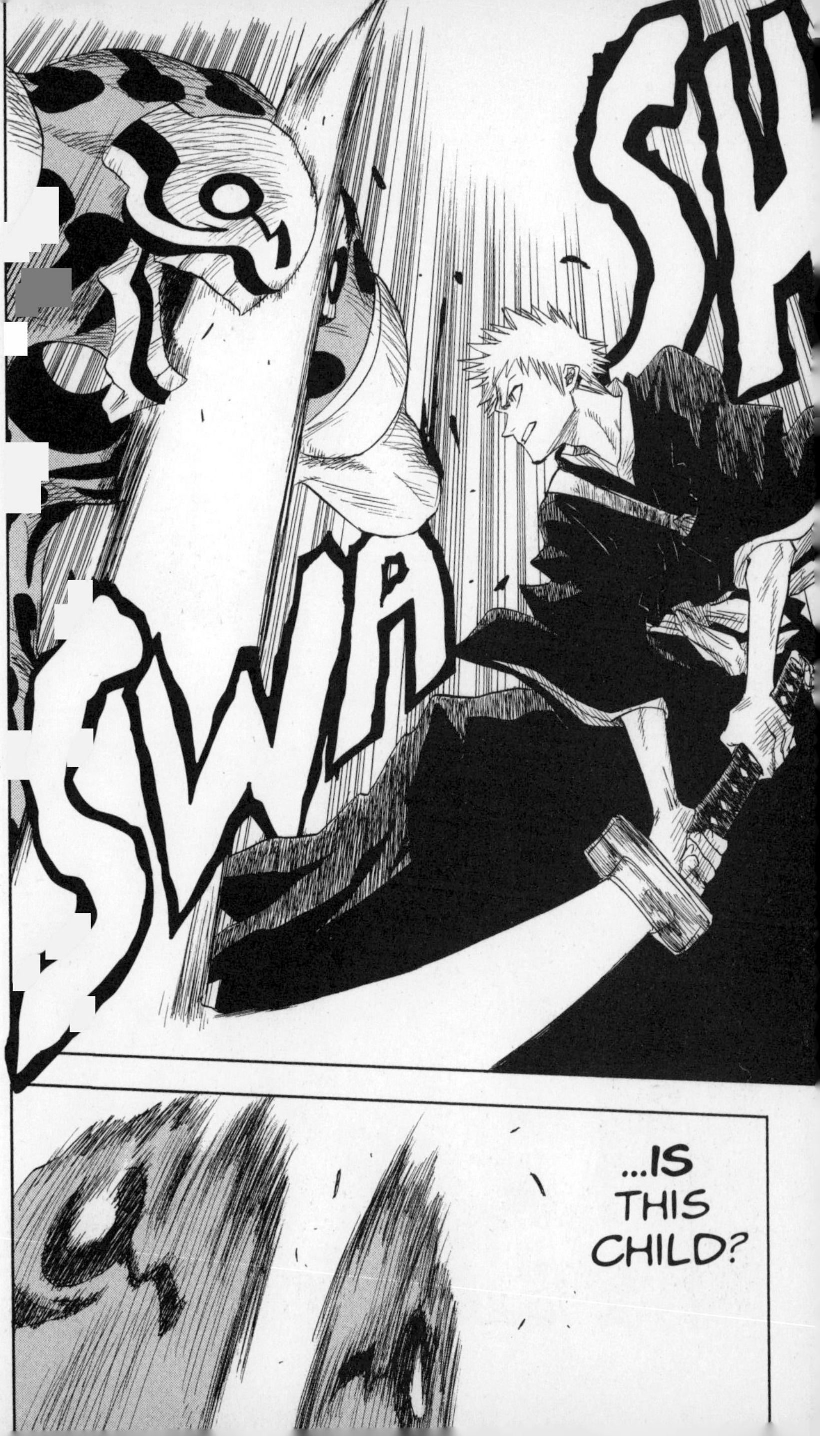
...IS THIS CHILD?

READ THIS WAY

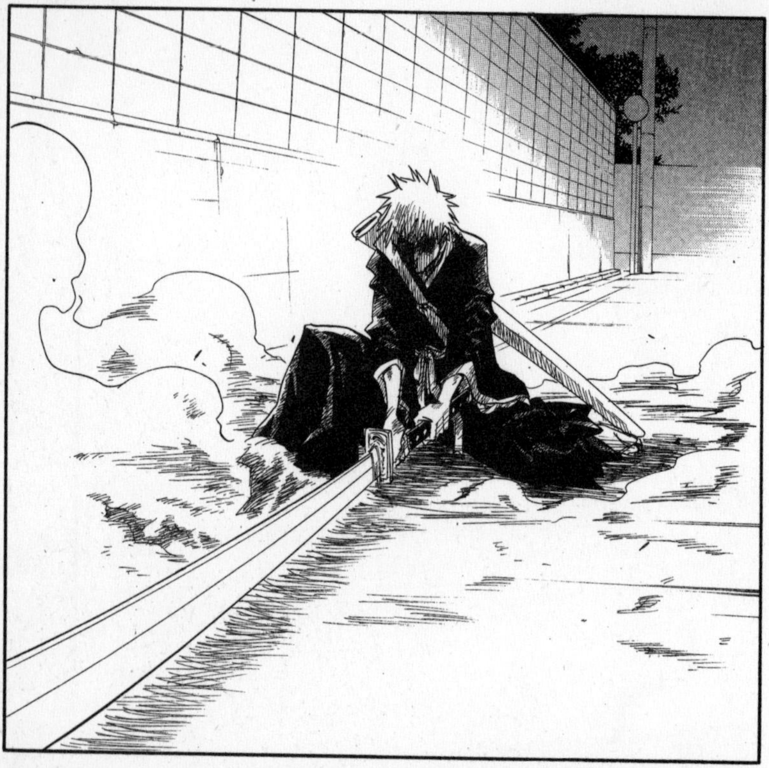

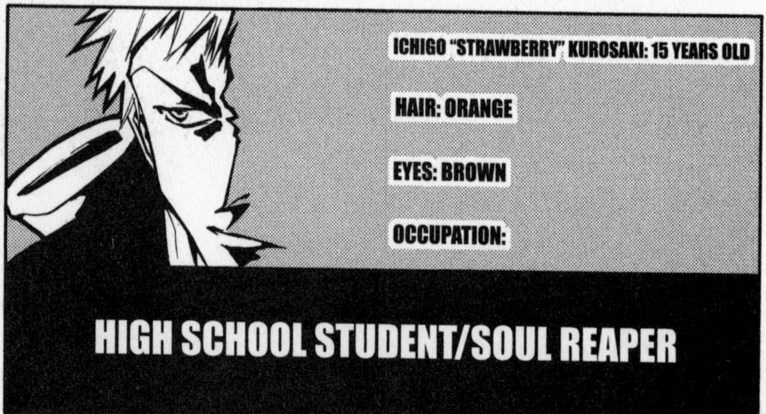
ICHIGO "STRAWBERRY" KUROSAKI: 15 YEARS OLD
HAIR: ORANGE
EYES: BROWN
OCCUPATION:
HIGH SCHOOL STUDENT/SOUL REAPER

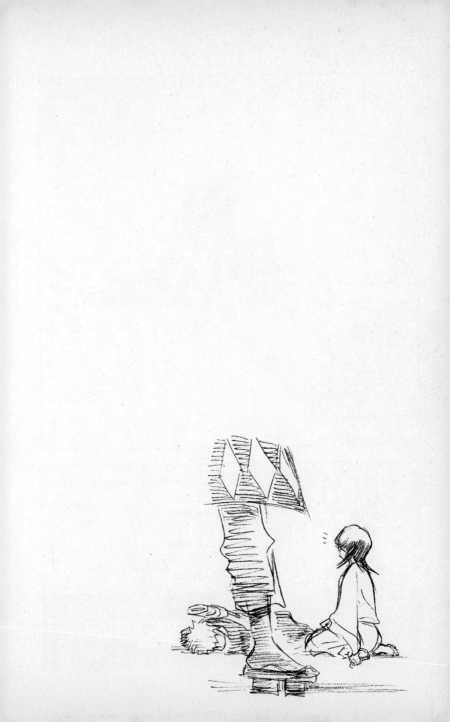

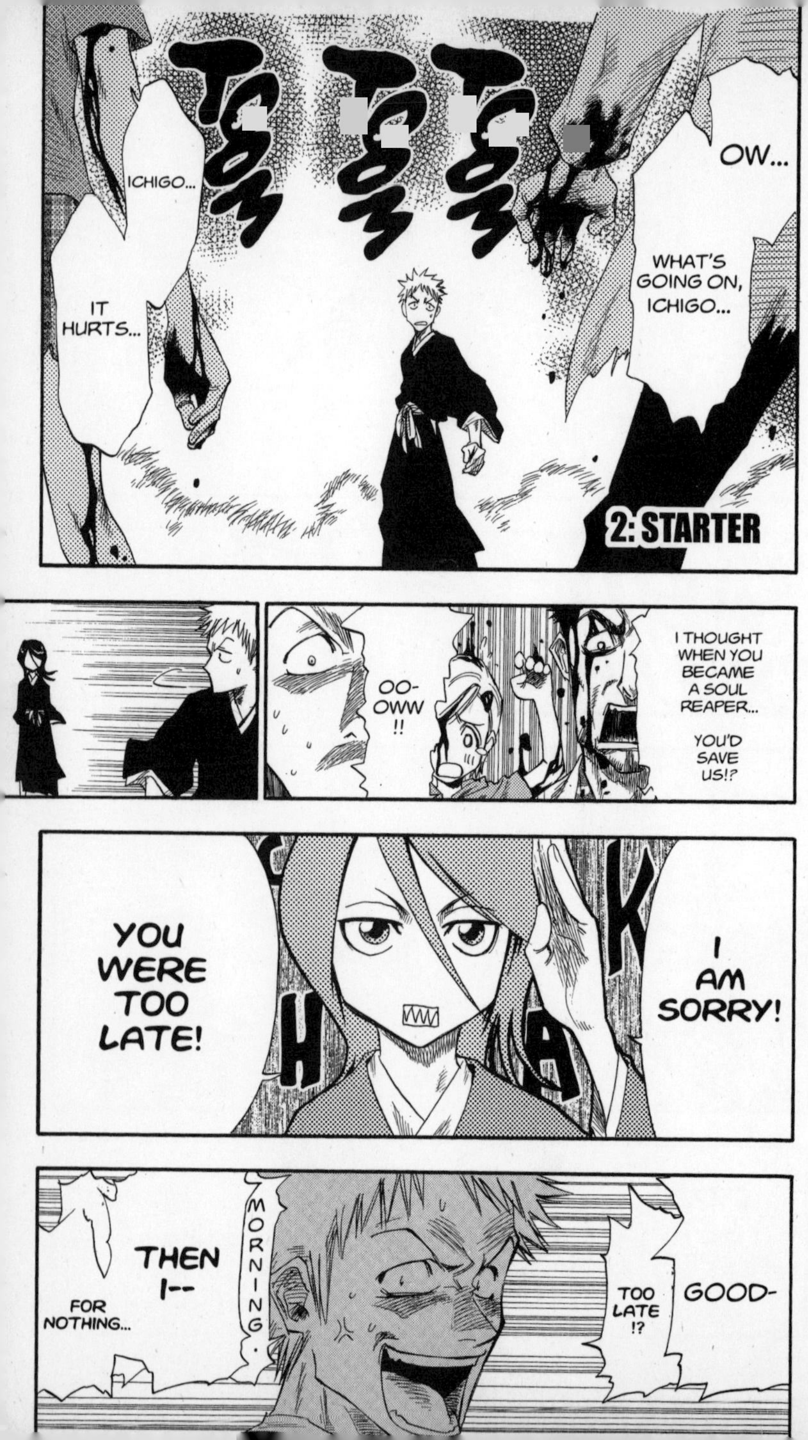

OW...
WHAT'S GOING ON, ICHIGO...
2: STARTER
ICHIGO...
IT HURTS...
I THOUGHT WHEN YOU BECAME A SOUL REAPER...
YOU'D SAVE US!?
OO-OWW!!
I AM SORRY!
YOU WERE TOO LATE!
GOOD-
TOO LATE!?
MORNING.
THEN I--
FOR NOTHING...

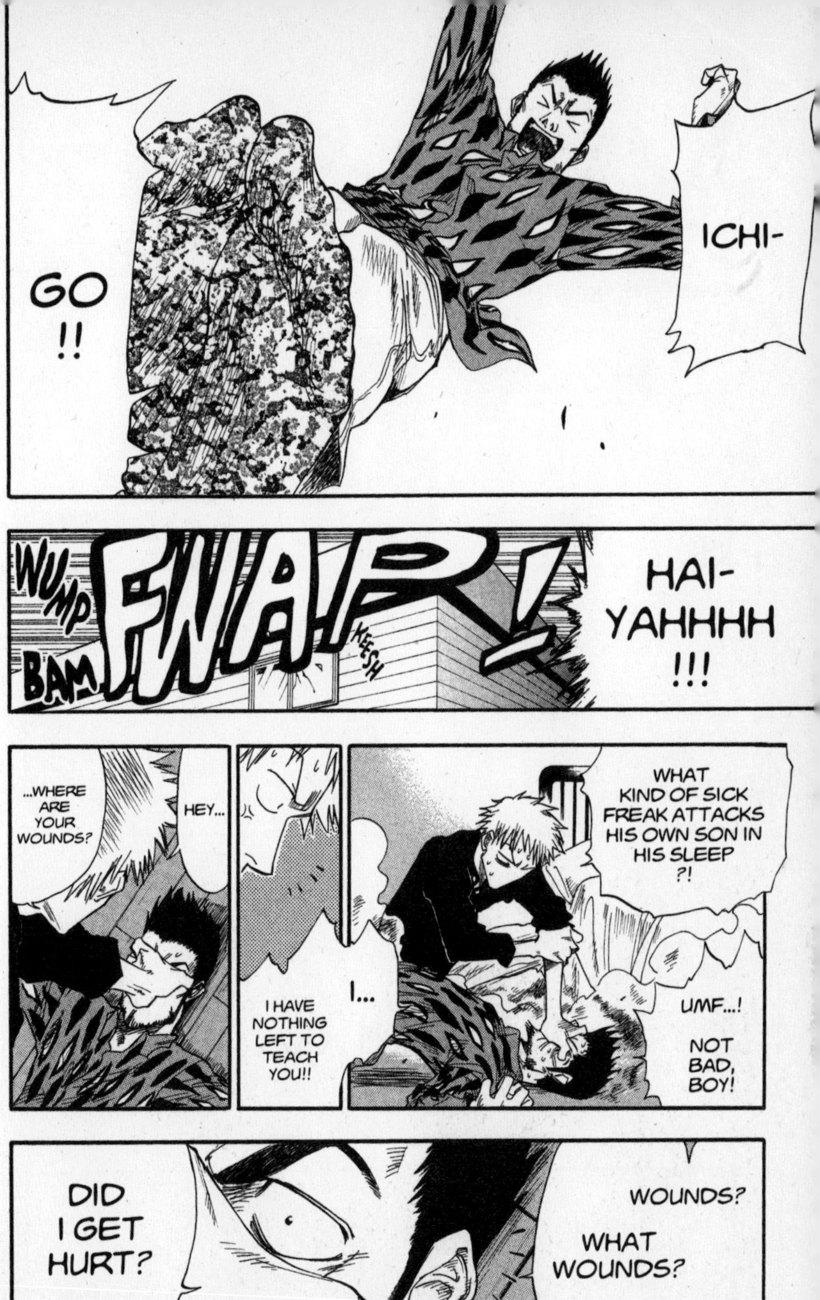
ICHI-
GO !!
HAI-YAHHHH !!!
FWAP!
WUMP
BAM
KEESH
WHAT KIND OF SICK FREAK ATTACKS HIS OWN SON IN HIS SLEEP ?!
UMF...!
NOT BAD, BOY!
I...
I HAVE NOTHING LEFT TO TEACH YOU!!
HEY...
...WHERE ARE YOUR WOUNDS?
WOUNDS?
WHAT WOUNDS?
DID I GET HURT?

2: STARTER

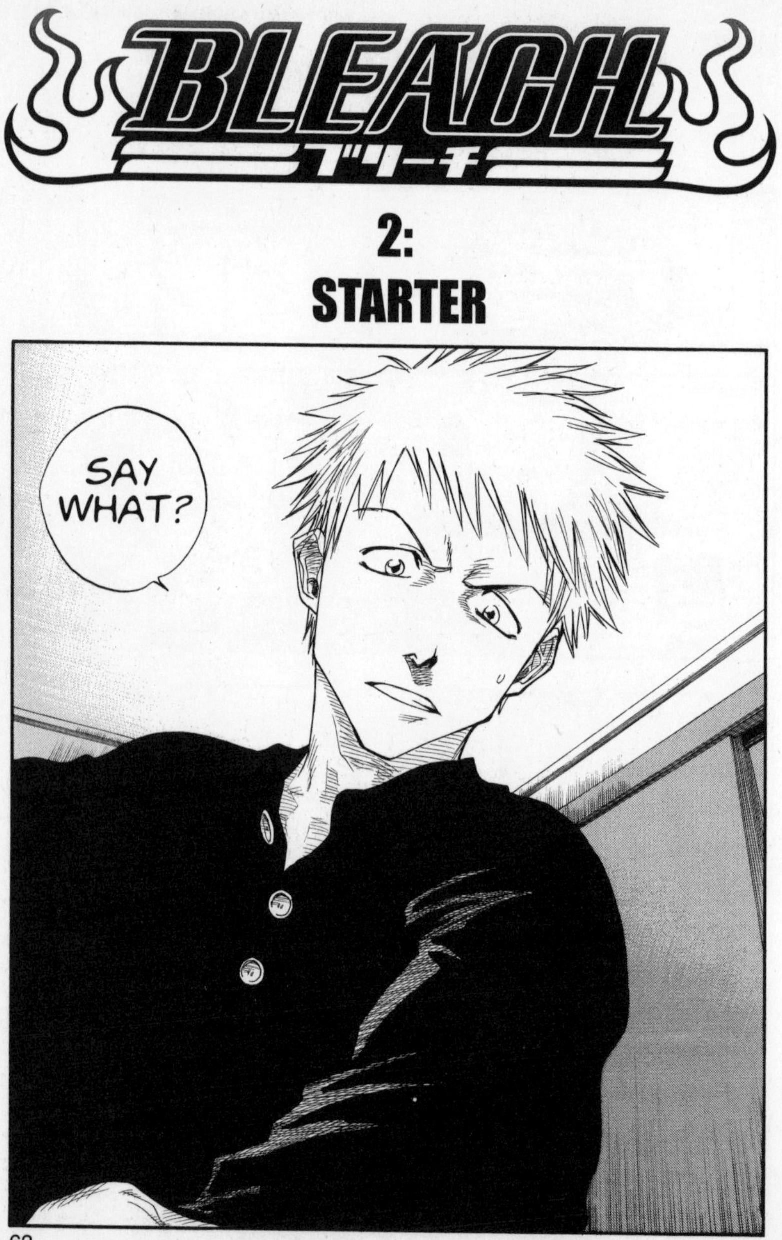
SAY WHAT?

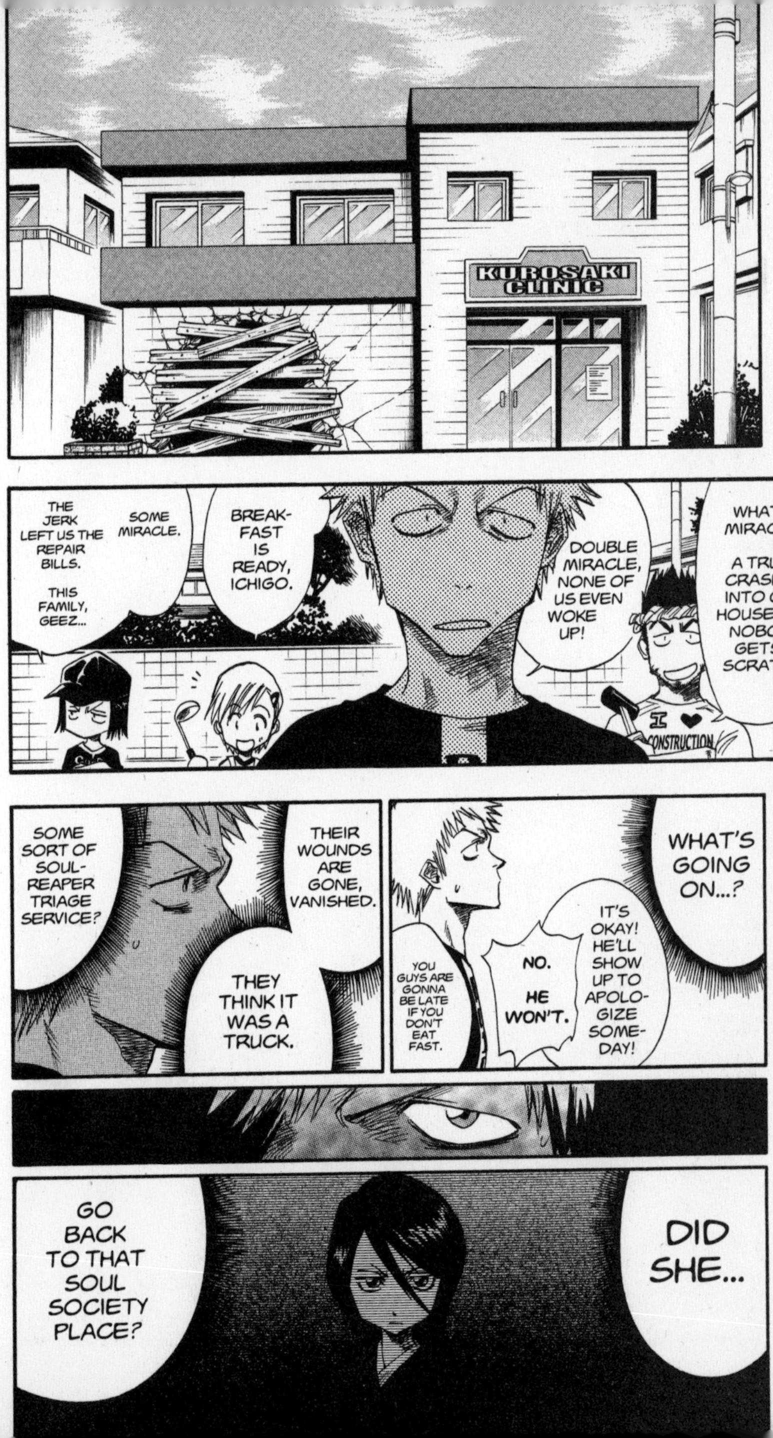
KUROSAKI CLINIC
WHAT A MIRACLE! A TRUCK CRASHES INTO OUR HOUSE AND NOBODY GETS A SCRATCH!
DOUBLE MIRACLE, NONE OF US EVEN WOKE UP!
I ♥ CONSTRUCTION
BREAK-FAST IS READY, ICHIGO.
SOME MIRACLE.
THE JERK LEFT US THE REPAIR BILLS. THIS FAMILY, GEEZ...
WHAT'S GOING ON...?
IT'S OKAY! HE'LL SHOW UP TO APOLO-GIZE SOME-DAY!
NO. HE WON'T.
YOU GUYS ARE GONNA BE LATE IF YOU DON'T EAT FAST.
THEIR WOUNDS ARE GONE, VANISHED.
SOME SORT OF SOUL-REAPER TRIAGE SERVICE?
THEY THINK IT WAS A TRUCK.
DID SHE...
GO BACK TO THAT SOUL SOCIETY PLACE?

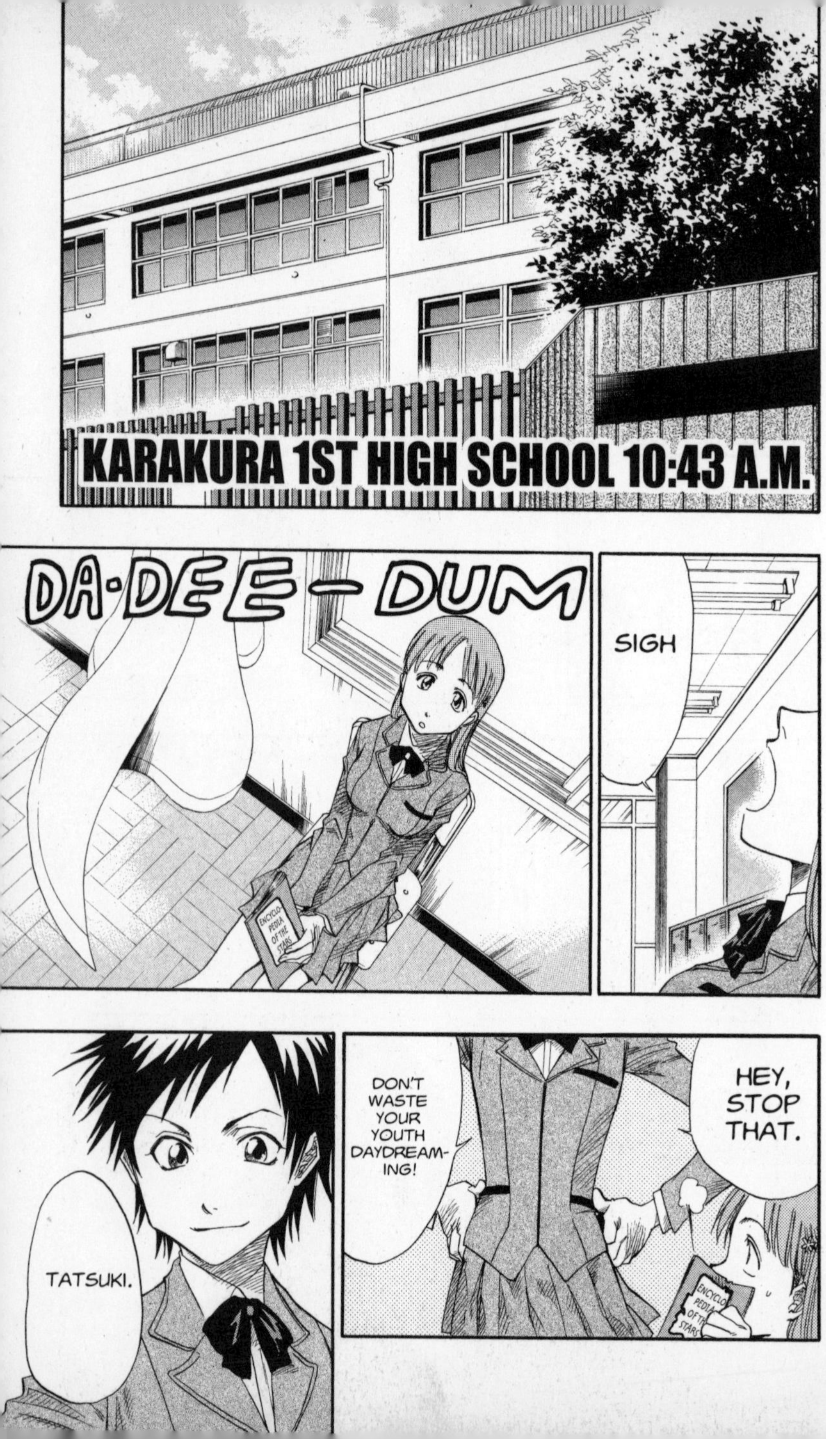
KARAKURA 1ST HIGH SCHOOL 10:43 A.M.
SIGH
DA-DEE-DUM
ENCYCLOPEDIA OF THE STARS
HEY, STOP THAT.
DON'T WASTE YOUR YOUTH DAYDREAMING!
TATSUKI.

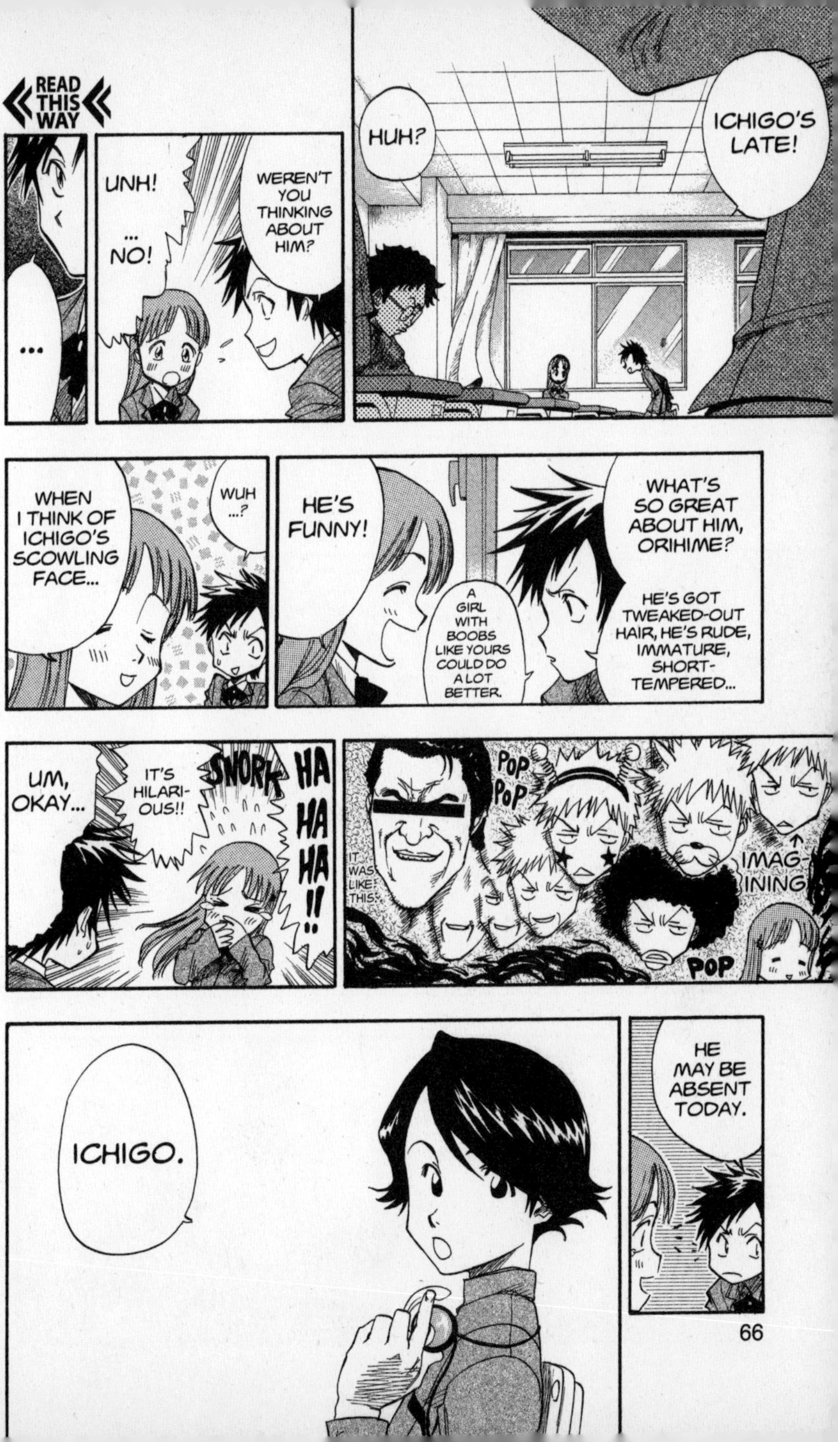
READ THIS WAY
ICHIGO'S LATE!
HUH?
WEREN'T YOU THINKING ABOUT HIM?
UNH!
... NO!
...
WHAT'S SO GREAT ABOUT HIM, ORIHIME?
HE'S GOT TWEAKED-OUT HAIR, HE'S RUDE, IMMATURE, SHORT-TEMPERED...
A GIRL WITH BOOBS LIKE YOURS COULD DO A LOT BETTER.
HE'S FUNNY!
WUH ...?
WHEN I THINK OF ICHIGO'S SCOWLING FACE...
POP POP
IMAG-INING
IT WAS LIKE THIS.
POP
HA HA HA HA!!
SNORK
IT'S HILARI-OUS!!
UM, OKAY...
HE MAY BE ABSENT TODAY.
ICHIGO.

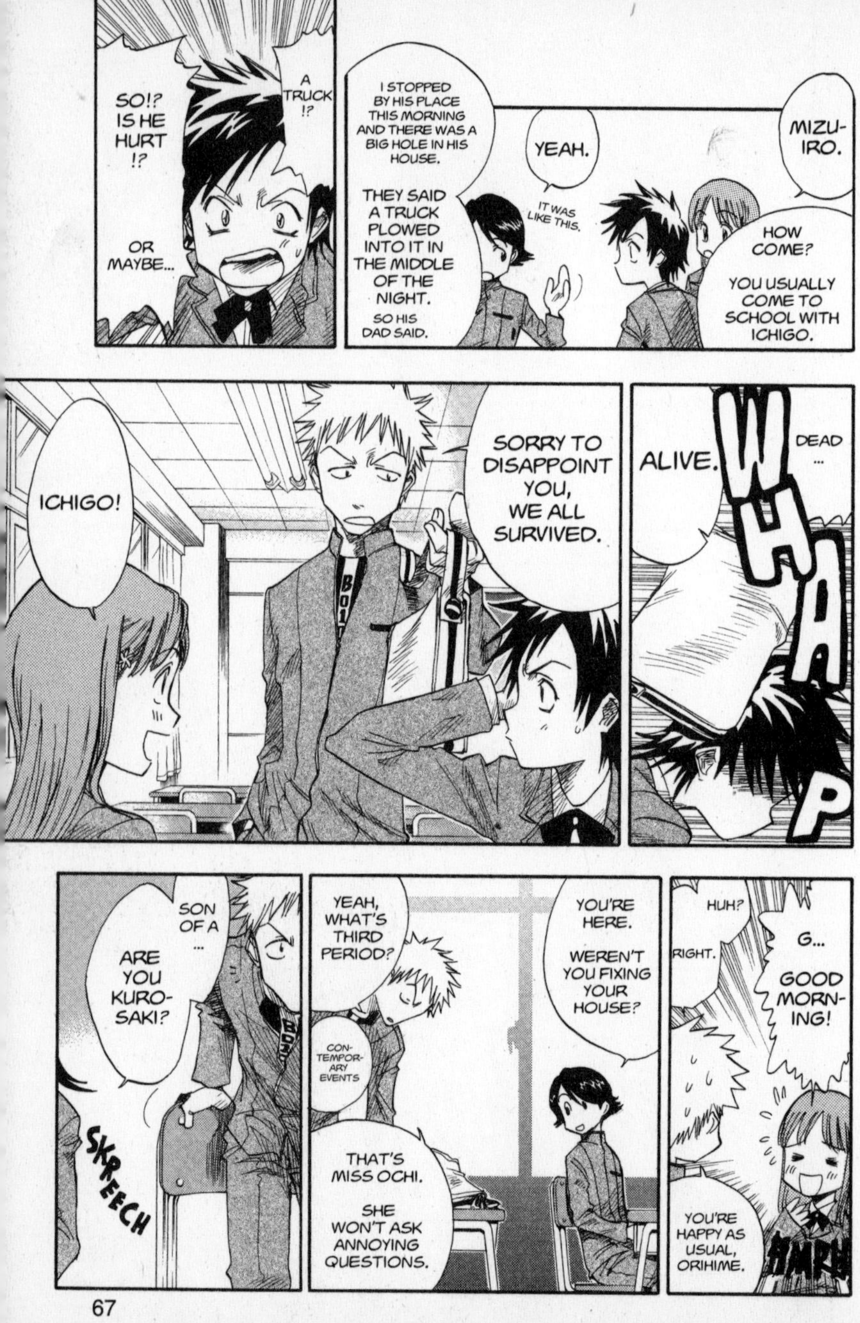
MIZU-IRO.
HOW COME?
YOU USUALLY COME TO SCHOOL WITH ICHIGO.
YEAH.
IT WAS LIKE THIS.
I STOPPED BY HIS PLACE THIS MORNING AND THERE WAS A BIG HOLE IN HIS HOUSE.
THEY SAID A TRUCK PLOWED INTO IT IN THE MIDDLE OF THE NIGHT.
SO HIS DAD SAID.
A TRUCK !?
SO!? IS HE HURT !?
OR MAYBE...
DEAD ...
WHAP
ALIVE.
SORRY TO DISAPPOINT YOU, WE ALL SURVIVED.
ICHIGO!
HUH?
G... GOOD MORNING!
RIGHT.
YOU'RE HAPPY AS USUAL, ORIHIME.
YOU'RE HERE.
WEREN'T YOU FIXING YOUR HOUSE?
YEAH, WHAT'S THIRD PERIOD?
CON-TEMPOR-ARY EVENTS
THAT'S MISS OCHI.
SHE WON'T ASK ANNOYING QUESTIONS.
SON OF A ...
ARE YOU KURO-SAKI?
SKREECH

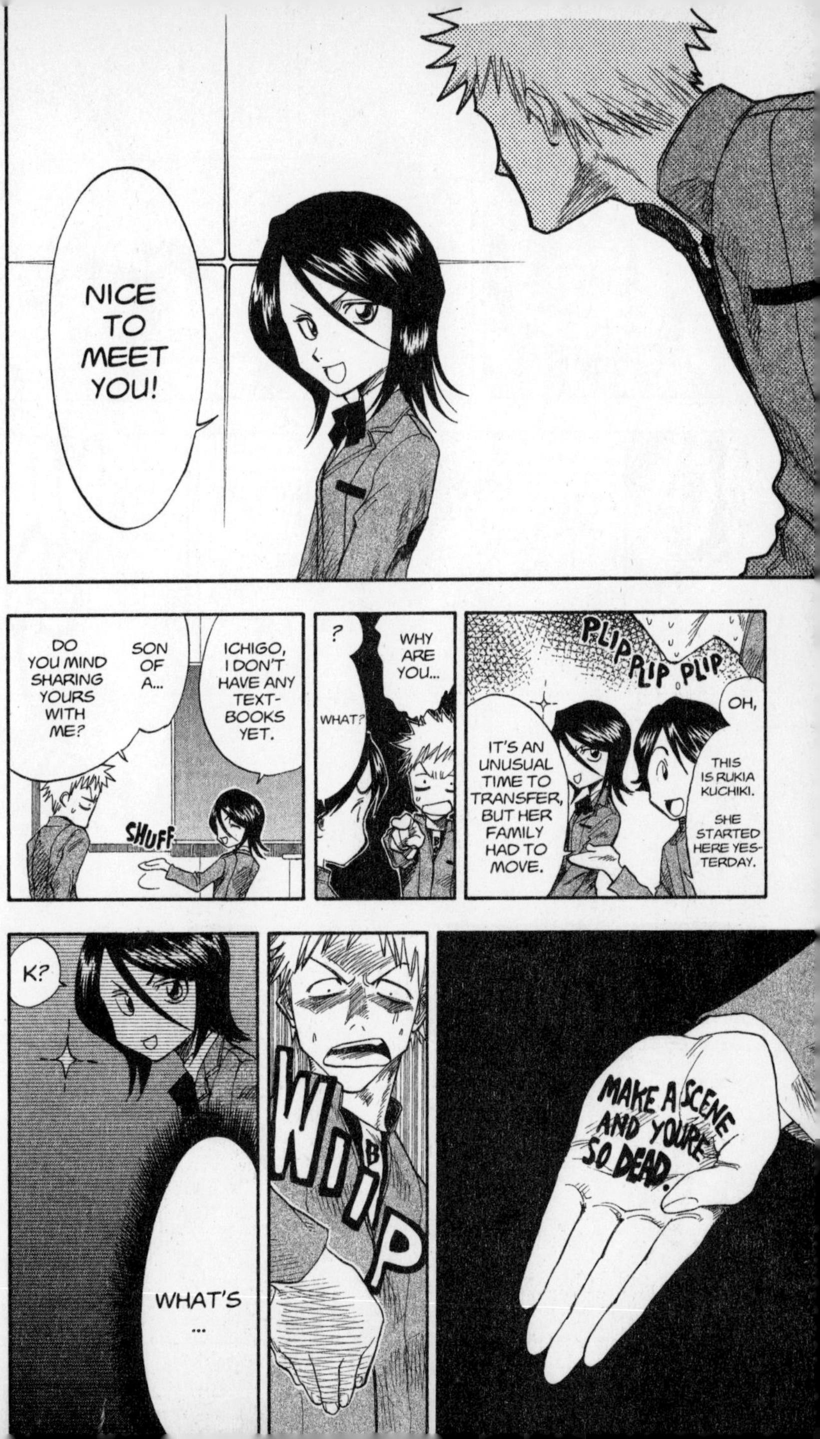
NICE TO MEET YOU!
PLIP PLIP PLIP
OH,
THIS IS RUKIA KUCHIKI.
SHE STARTED HERE YESTERDAY.
IT'S AN UNUSUAL TIME TO TRANSFER, BUT HER FAMILY HAD TO MOVE.
WHY ARE YOU...
?
WHAT?
ICHIGO, I DON'T HAVE ANY TEXT-BOOKS YET.
SON OF A...
DO YOU MIND SHARING YOURS WITH ME?
SHUFF
MAKE A SCENE AND YOURE SO DEAD.
WHIP
WHAT'S ...
K?

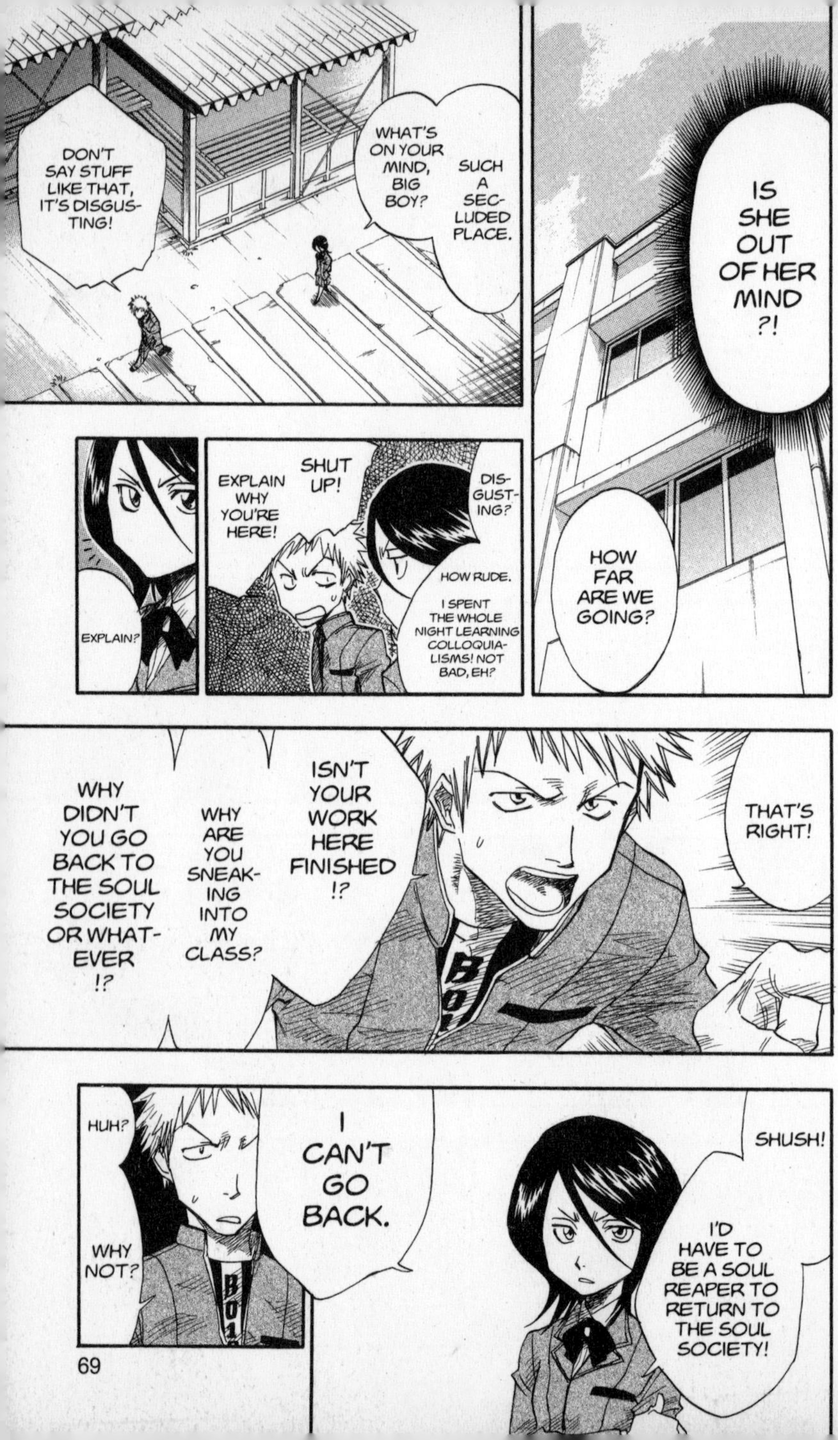
IS SHE OUT OF HER MIND?!
HOW FAR ARE WE GOING?
SUCH A SEC-LUDED PLACE.
WHAT'S ON YOUR MIND, BIG BOY?
DON'T SAY STUFF LIKE THAT, IT'S DISGUS-TING!
DIS-GUST-ING?
HOW RUDE.
I SPENT THE WHOLE NIGHT LEARNING COLLOQUIA-LISMS! NOT BAD, EH?
SHUT UP!
EXPLAIN WHY YOU'RE HERE!
EXPLAIN?
THAT'S RIGHT!
ISN'T YOUR WORK HERE FINISHED!?
WHY ARE YOU SNEAK-ING INTO MY CLASS?
WHY DIDN'T YOU GO BACK TO THE SOUL SOCIETY OR WHAT-EVER!?
SHUSH!
I'D HAVE TO BE A SOUL REAPER TO RETURN TO THE SOUL SOCIETY!
I CAN'T GO BACK.
HUH?
WHY NOT?

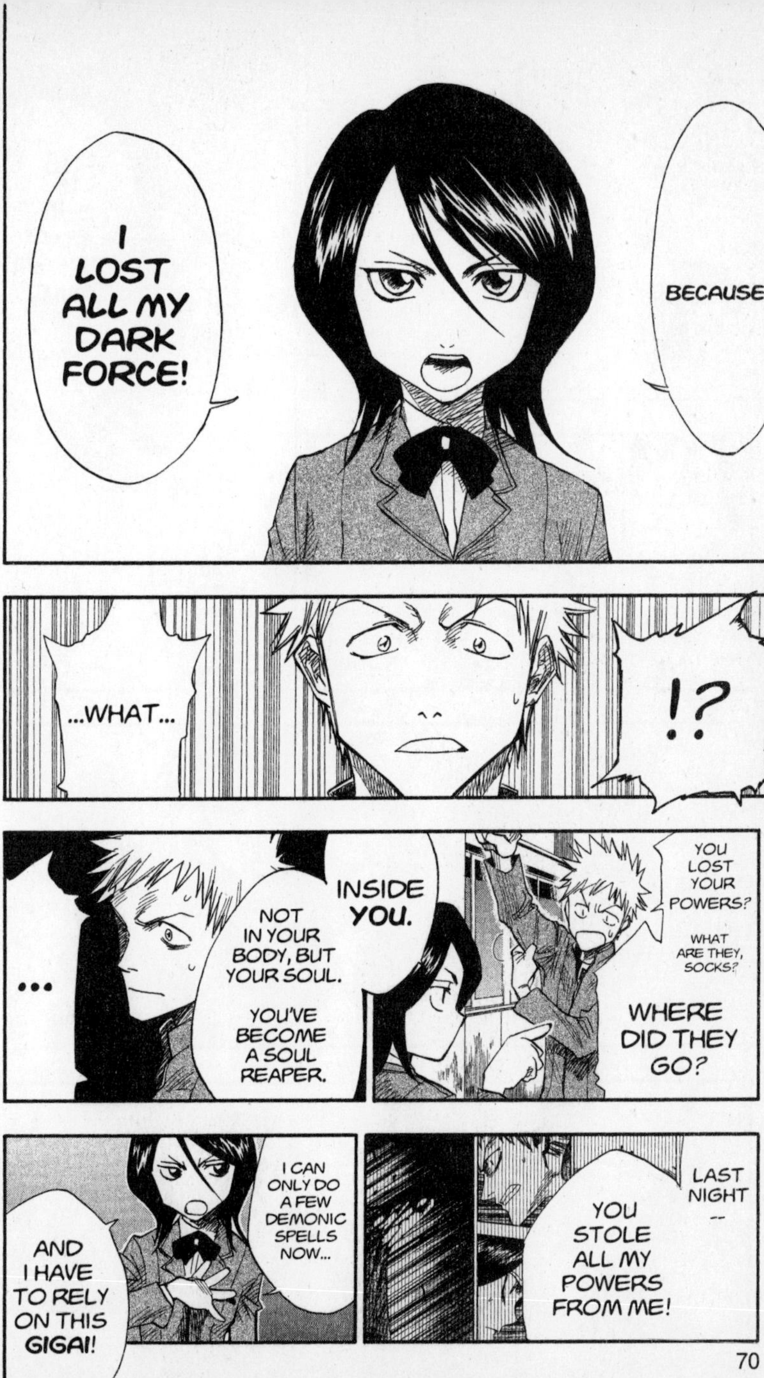
BECAUSE...
I LOST ALL MY DARK FORCE!
!?
...WHAT...
YOU LOST YOUR POWERS?
WHAT ARE THEY, SOCKS?
WHERE DID THEY GO?
INSIDE YOU.
NOT IN YOUR BODY, BUT YOUR SOUL.
YOU'VE BECOME A SOUL REAPER.
...
LAST NIGHT --
YOU STOLE ALL MY POWERS FROM ME!
I CAN ONLY DO A FEW DEMONIC SPELLS NOW...
AND I HAVE TO RELY ON THIS GIGAI!

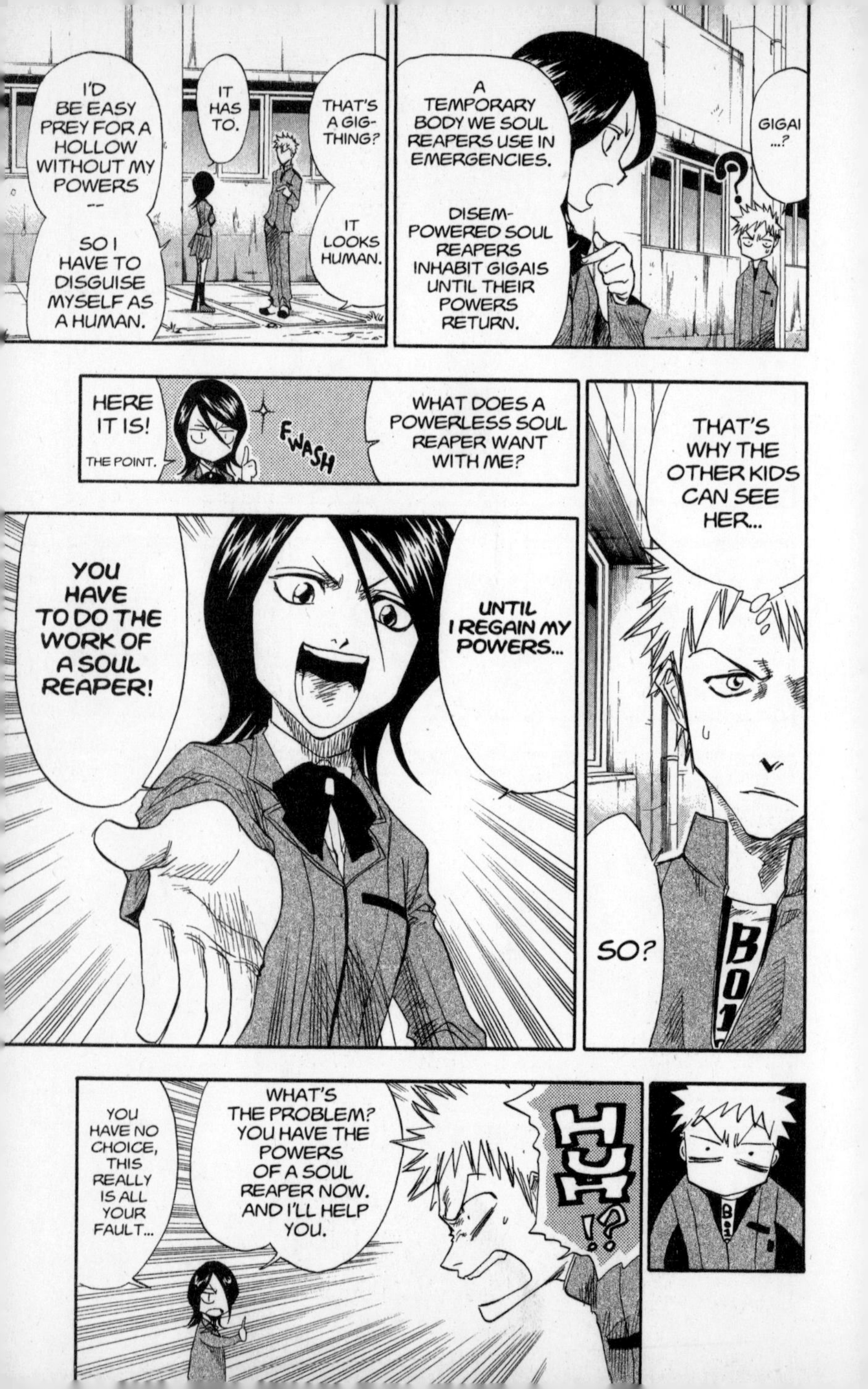
GIGAI ...?
A TEMPORARY BODY WE SOUL REAPERS USE IN EMERGENCIES.
DISEMPOWERED SOUL REAPERS INHABIT GIGAIS UNTIL THEIR POWERS RETURN.
THAT'S A GIG-THING?
IT LOOKS HUMAN.
IT HAS TO.
I'D BE EASY PREY FOR A HOLLOW WITHOUT MY POWERS --
SO I HAVE TO DISGUISE MYSELF AS A HUMAN.
THAT'S WHY THE OTHER KIDS CAN SEE HER...
SO?
WHAT DOES A POWERLESS SOUL REAPER WANT WITH ME?
FWASH
HERE IT IS!
THE POINT.
UNTIL I REGAIN MY POWERS...
YOU HAVE TO DO THE WORK OF A SOUL REAPER!
HUH!?
WHAT'S THE PROBLEM? YOU HAVE THE POWERS OF A SOUL REAPER NOW. AND I'LL HELP YOU.
YOU HAVE NO CHOICE, THIS REALLY IS ALL YOUR FAULT...

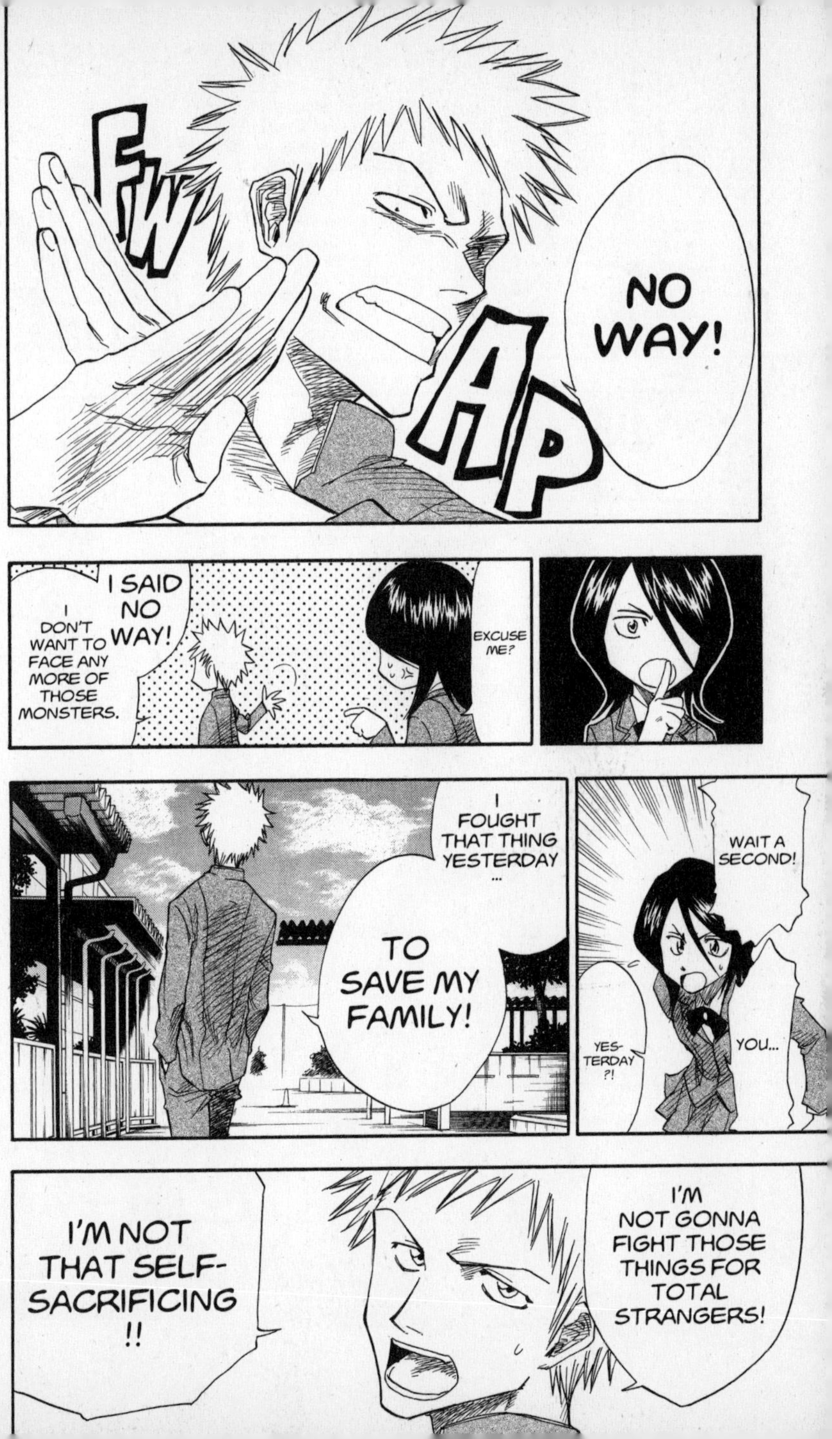
NO WAY!
FWAP
EXCUSE ME?
I SAID NO WAY!
I DON'T WANT TO FACE ANY MORE OF THOSE MONSTERS.
WAIT A SECOND!
YOU...
YES-TERDAY?!
I FOUGHT THAT THING YESTERDAY...
TO SAVE MY FAMILY!
I'M NOT GONNA FIGHT THOSE THINGS FOR TOTAL STRANGERS!
I'M NOT THAT SELF-SACRIFICING!!

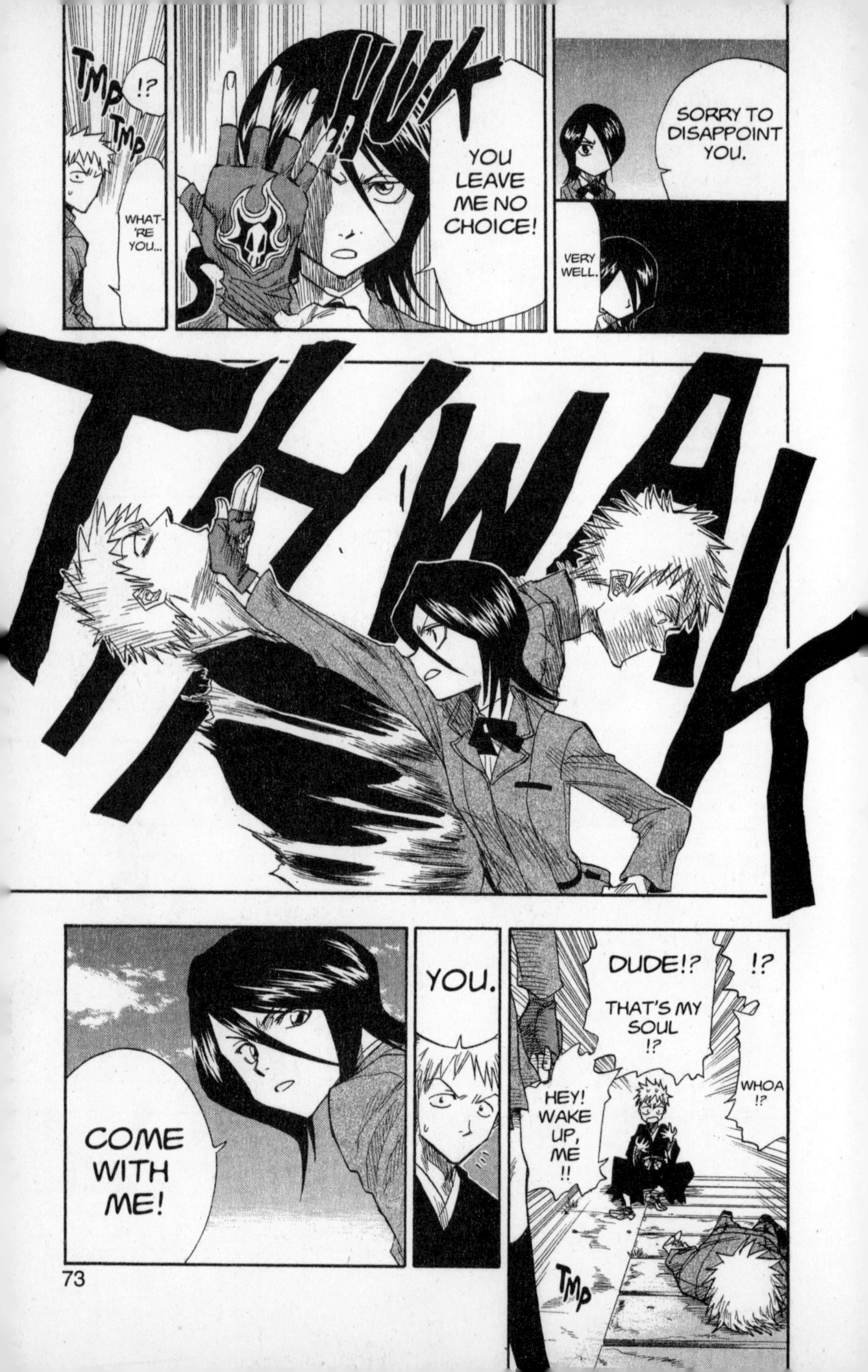
SORRY TO DISAPPOINT YOU.
VERY WELL.
HUK
YOU LEAVE ME NO CHOICE!
!?
TMP TMP TMP
WHAT-'RE YOU...
THWAK
!?
DUDE!?
THAT'S MY SOUL !?
WHOA !?
HEY! WAKE UP, ME !!
TMP
YOU.
COME WITH ME!

READ THIS WAY

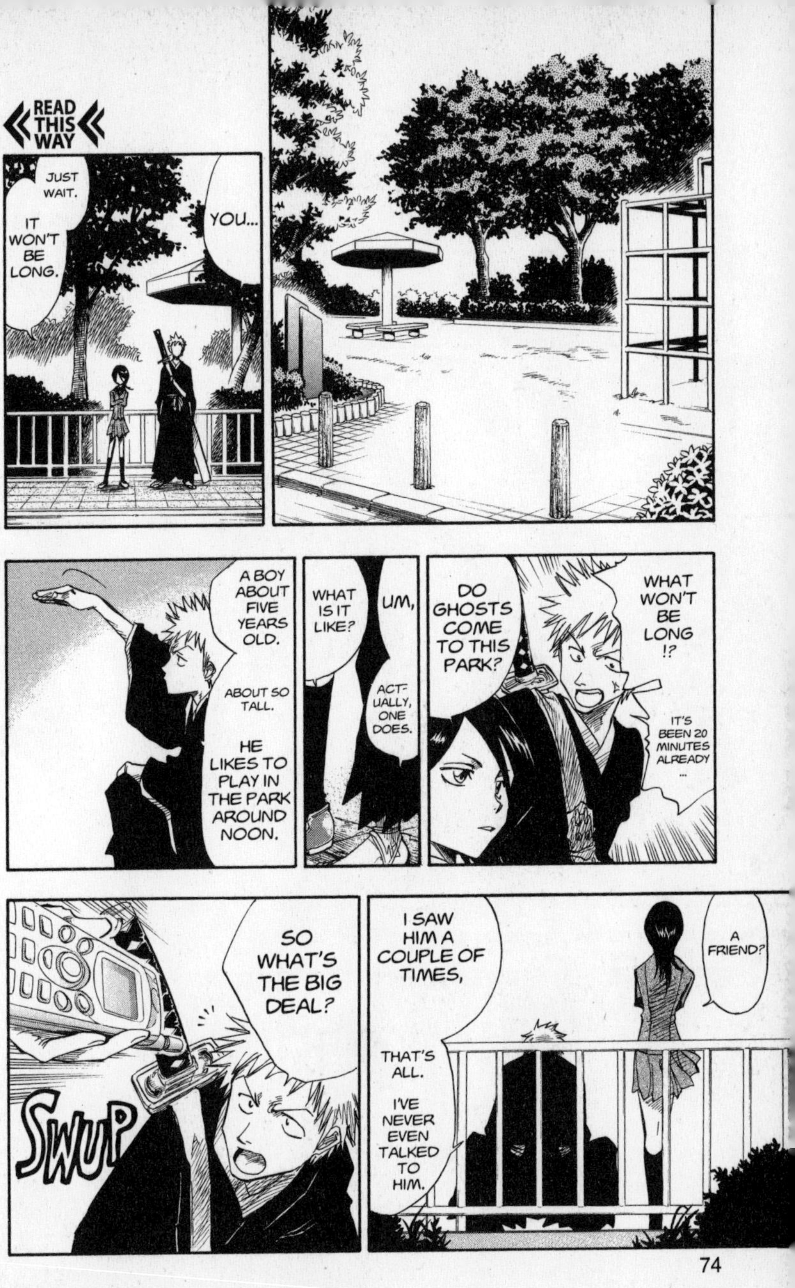

YOU...
JUST WAIT.
IT WON'T BE LONG.
WHAT WON'T BE LONG!?
IT'S BEEN 20 MINUTES ALREADY...
DO GHOSTS COME TO THIS PARK?
UM,
ACT-UALLY, ONE DOES.
WHAT IS IT LIKE?
A BOY ABOUT FIVE YEARS OLD.
ABOUT SO TALL.
HE LIKES TO PLAY IN THE PARK AROUND NOON.
A FRIEND?
I SAW HIM A COUPLE OF TIMES,
THAT'S ALL.
I'VE NEVER EVEN TALKED TO HIM.
SO WHAT'S THE BIG DEAL?
SWUP

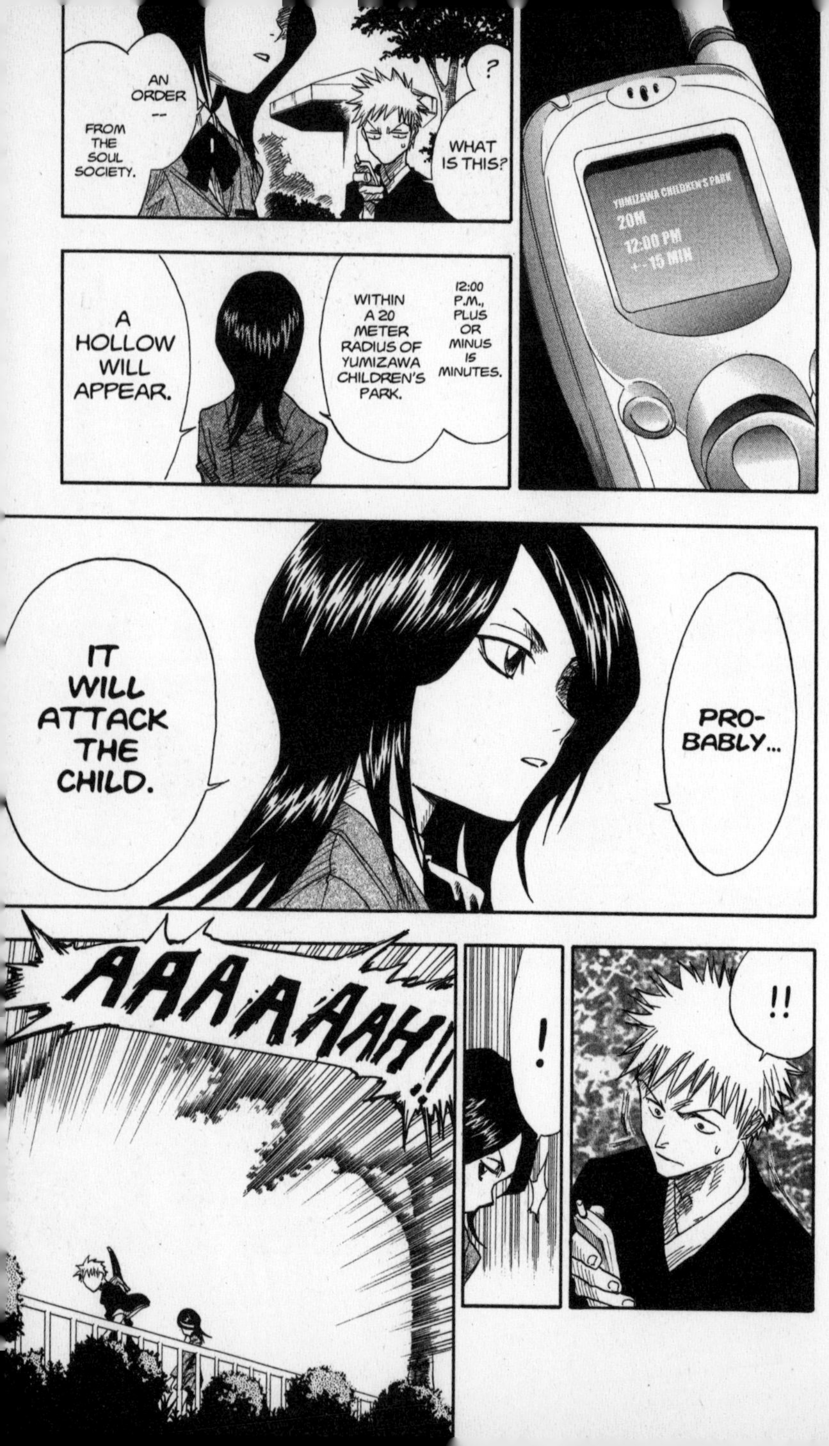
YUMIZAWA CHILDREN'S PARK
20M
12:00 PM
+- 15 MIN
?
WHAT IS THIS?
AN ORDER --
FROM THE SOUL SOCIETY.
12:00 P.M., PLUS OR MINUS 15 MINUTES.
WITHIN A 20 METER RADIUS OF YUMIZAWA CHILDREN'S PARK.
A HOLLOW WILL APPEAR.
PRO-BABLY...
IT WILL ATTACK THE CHILD.
!!
!
AAAAAAAH!!

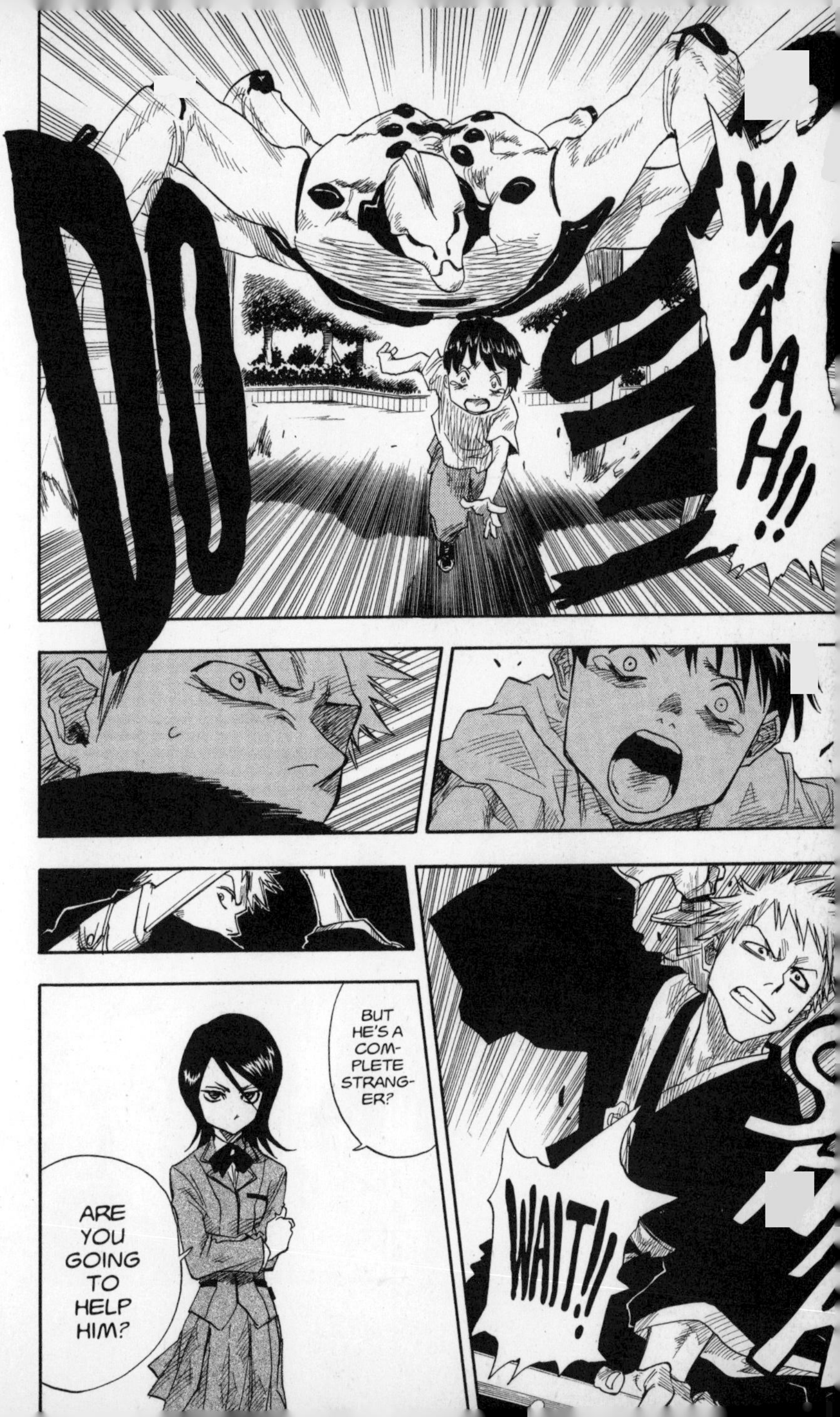
WAAAH!!
DO
WAIT!!
BUT HE'S A COM-PLETE STRANG-ER?
ARE YOU GOING TO HELP HIM?

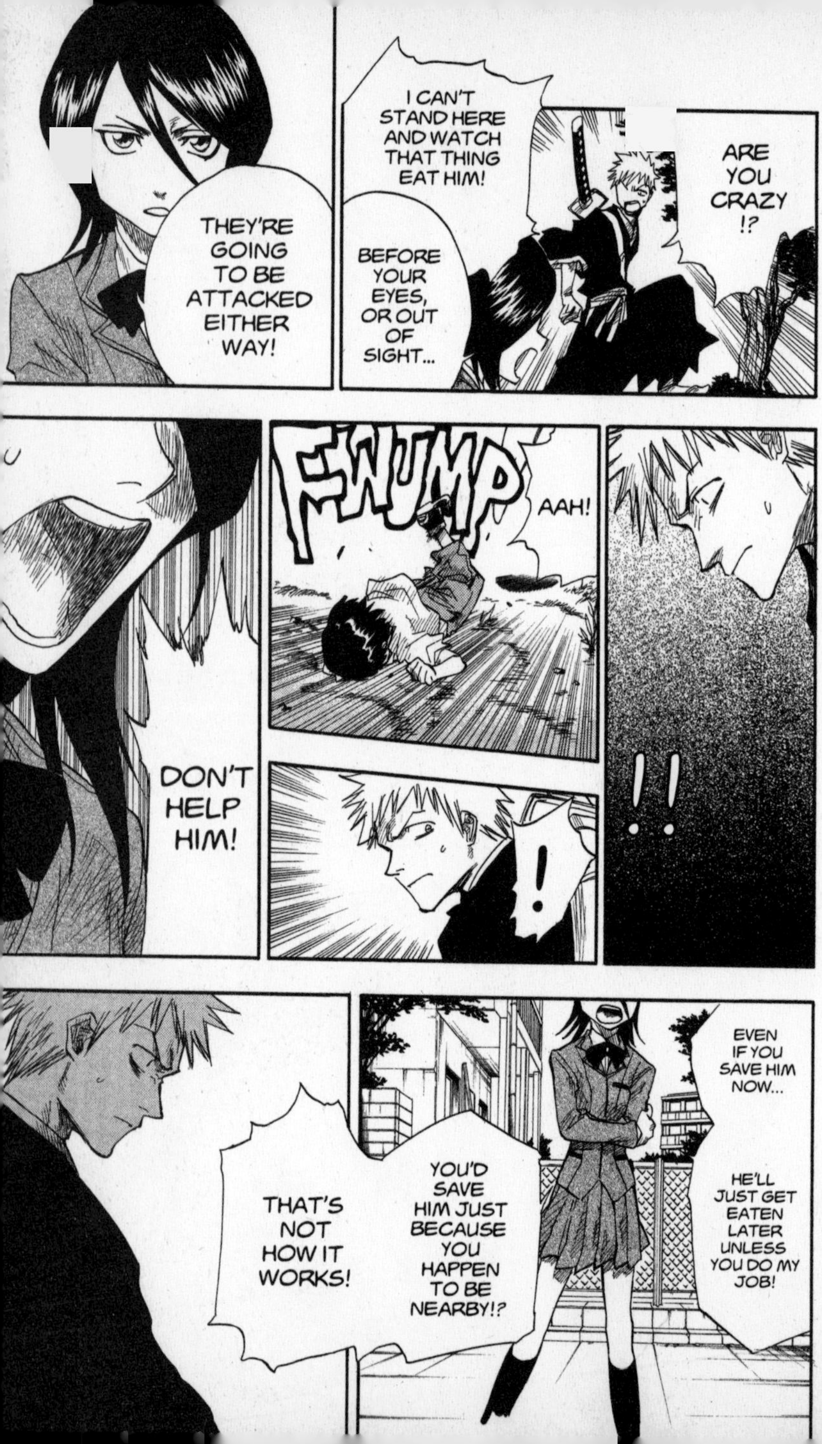
ARE YOU CRAZY !?
I CAN'T STAND HERE AND WATCH THAT THING EAT HIM!
BEFORE YOUR EYES, OR OUT OF SIGHT...
THEY'RE GOING TO BE ATTACKED EITHER WAY!
!!
FWUMP
AAH!
!
DON'T HELP HIM!
EVEN IF YOU SAVE HIM NOW...
HE'LL JUST GET EATEN LATER UNLESS YOU DO MY JOB!
YOU'D SAVE HIM JUST BECAUSE YOU HAPPEN TO BE NEARBY!?
THAT'S NOT HOW IT WORKS!

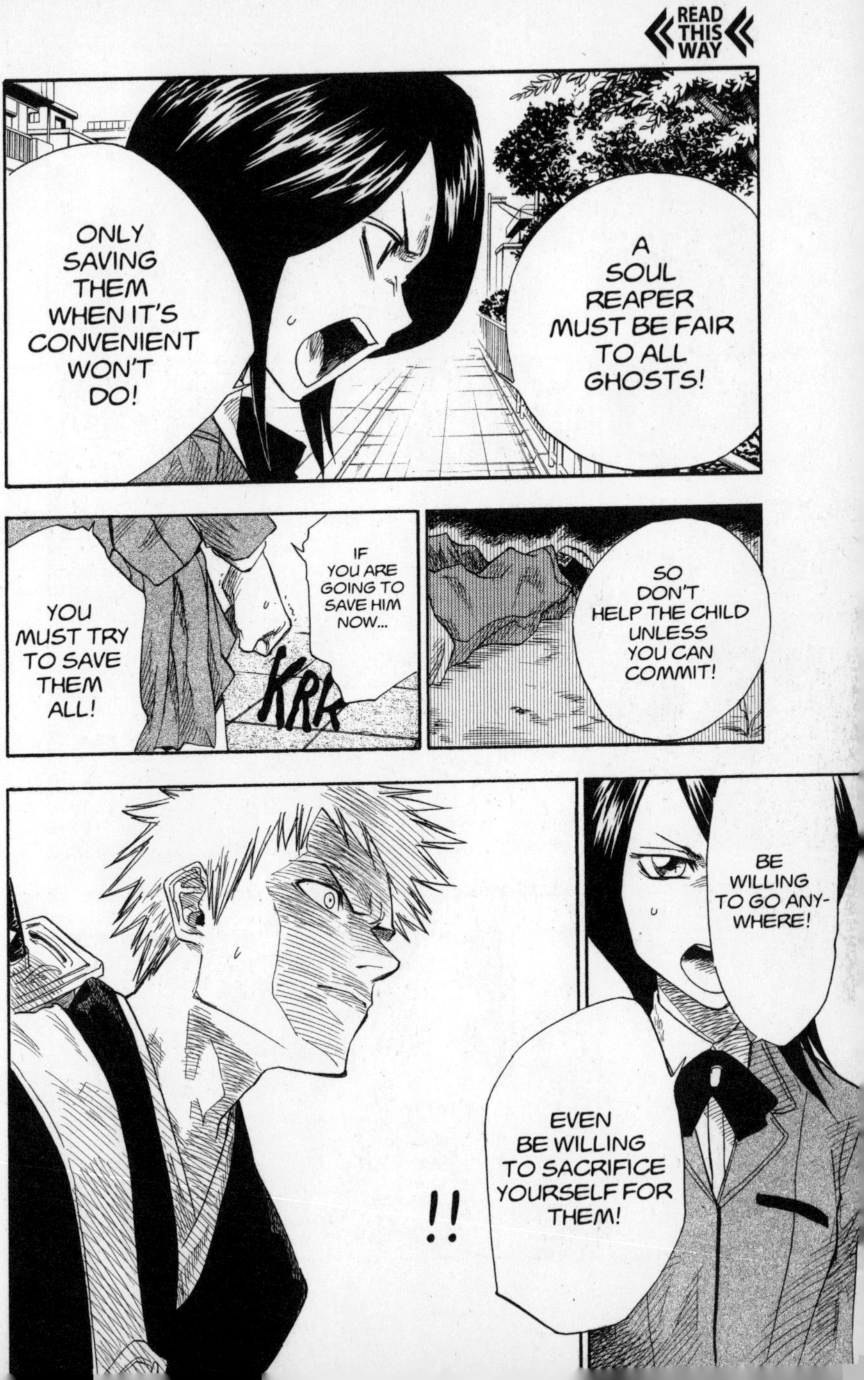
READ THIS WAY
A SOUL REAPER MUST BE FAIR TO ALL GHOSTS!
ONLY SAVING THEM WHEN IT'S CONVENIENT WON'T DO!
SO DON'T HELP THE CHILD UNLESS YOU CAN COMMIT!
IF YOU ARE GOING TO SAVE HIM NOW...
KRK
YOU MUST TRY TO SAVE THEM ALL!
BE WILLING TO GO ANY-WHERE!
EVEN BE WILLING TO SACRIFICE YOURSELF FOR THEM!
!!

READ THIS WAY

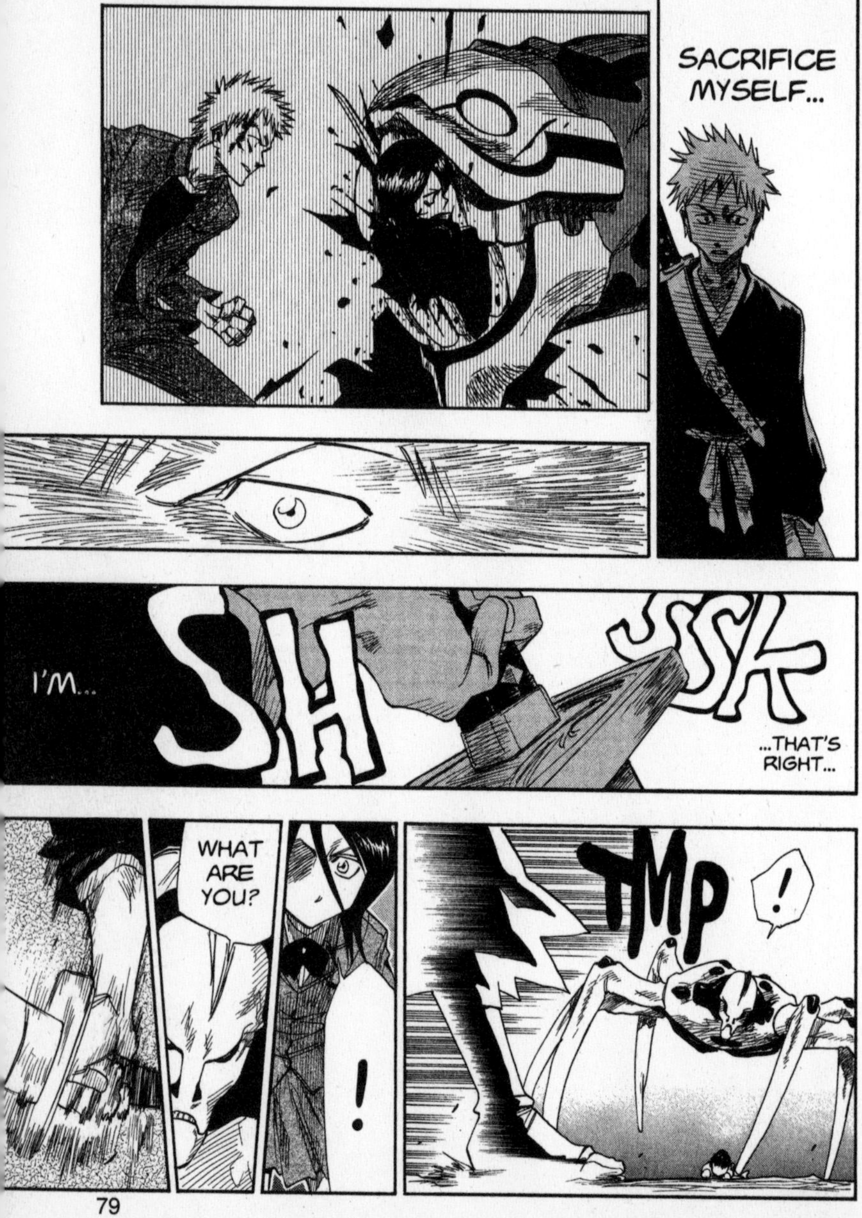
SACRIFICE MYSELF...
SSK
...THAT'S RIGHT...
SH
I'M...
TMP
!
WHAT ARE YOU?
!

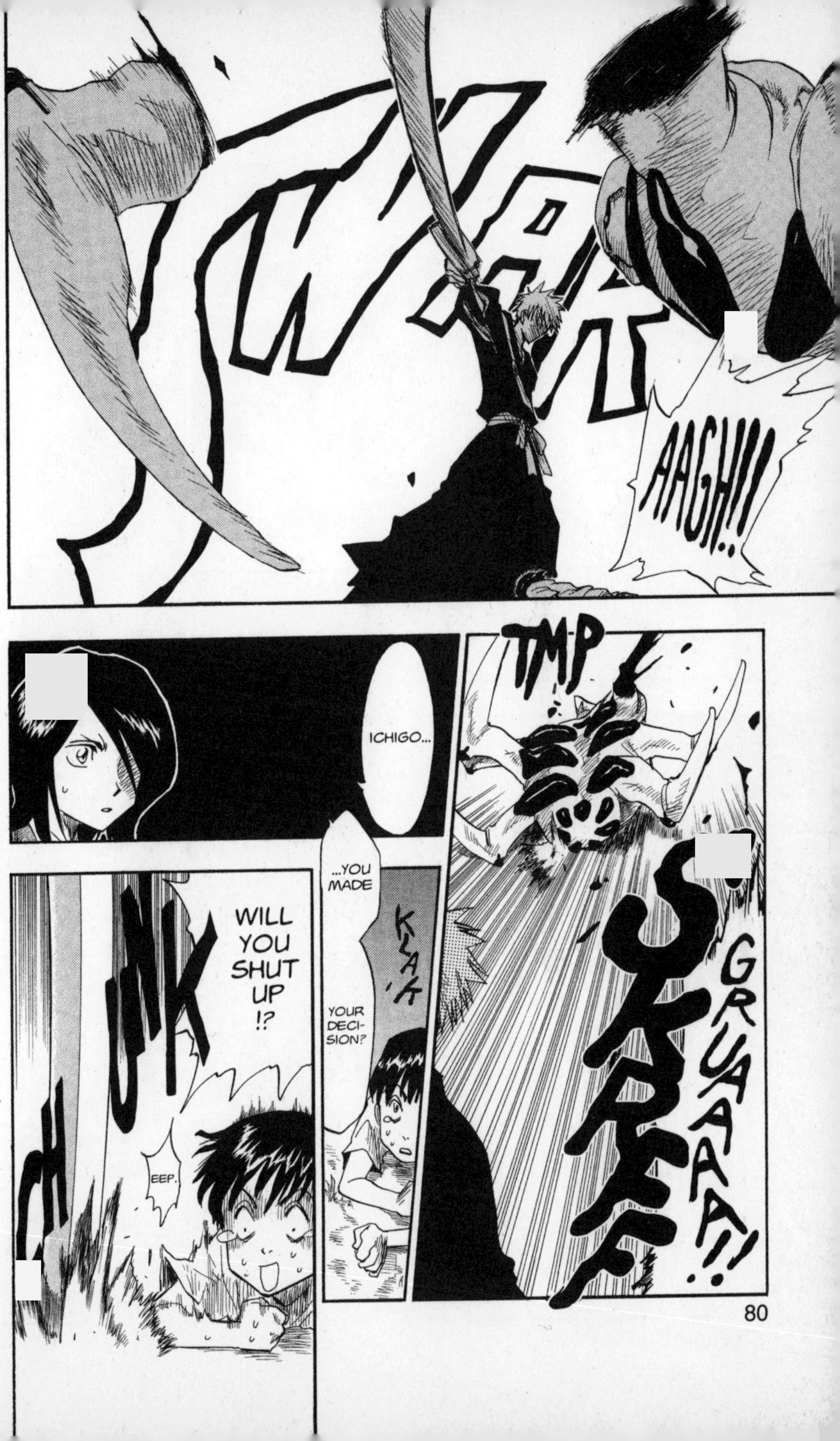
AAGH!!
TMP
GRUAAAA!!
ICHIGO...
...YOU MADE
YOUR DECISION?
KLAK
WILL YOU SHUT UP!?
CHUNK
EEP.

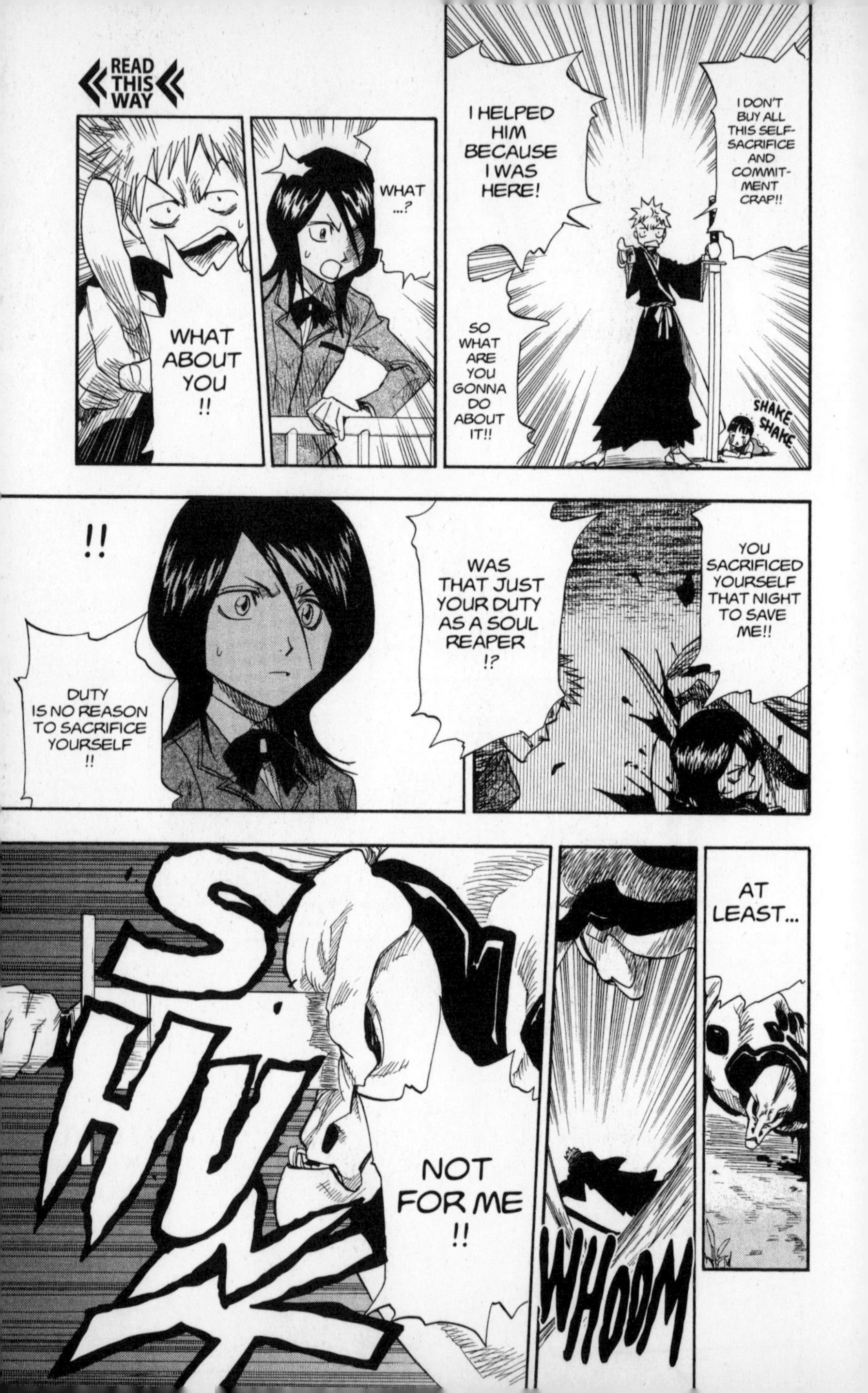
READ THIS WAY
I DON'T BUY ALL THIS SELF-SACRIFICE AND COMMIT-MENT CRAP!!
I HELPED HIM BECAUSE I WAS HERE!
SO WHAT ARE YOU GONNA DO ABOUT IT!!
SHAKE SHAKE
WHAT ...?
WHAT ABOUT YOU !!
YOU SACRIFICED YOURSELF THAT NIGHT TO SAVE ME!!
WAS THAT JUST YOUR DUTY AS A SOUL REAPER !?
!!
DUTY IS NO REASON TO SACRIFICE YOURSELF !!
AT LEAST...
WHOOM
NOT FOR ME !!
SHUK

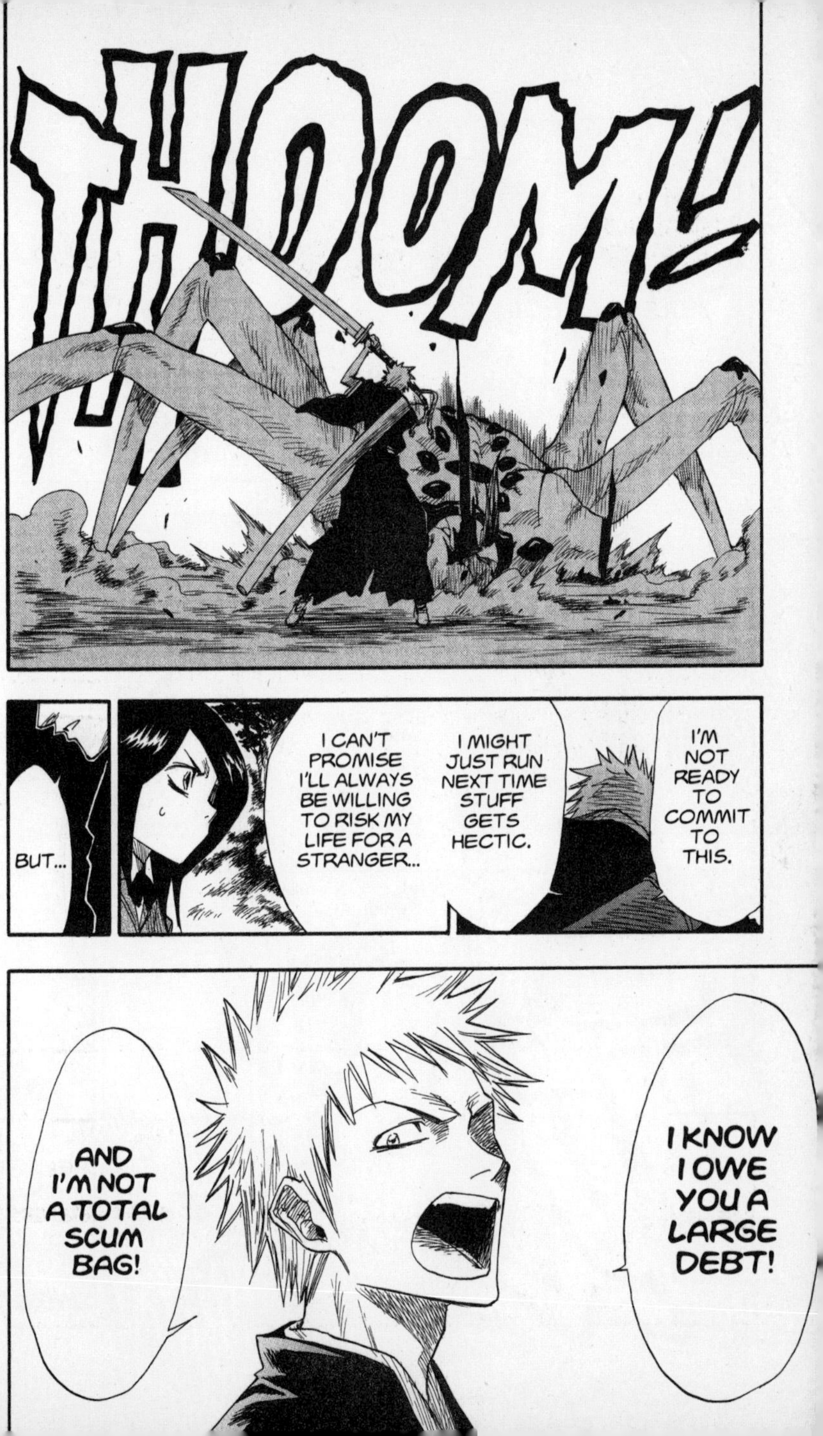
THOOM!
I'M NOT READY TO COMMIT TO THIS.
I MIGHT JUST RUN NEXT TIME STUFF GETS HECTIC.
I CAN'T PROMISE I'LL ALWAYS BE WILLING TO RISK MY LIFE FOR A STRANGER...
BUT...
I KNOW I OWE YOU A LARGE DEBT!
AND I'M NOT A TOTAL SCUM BAG!

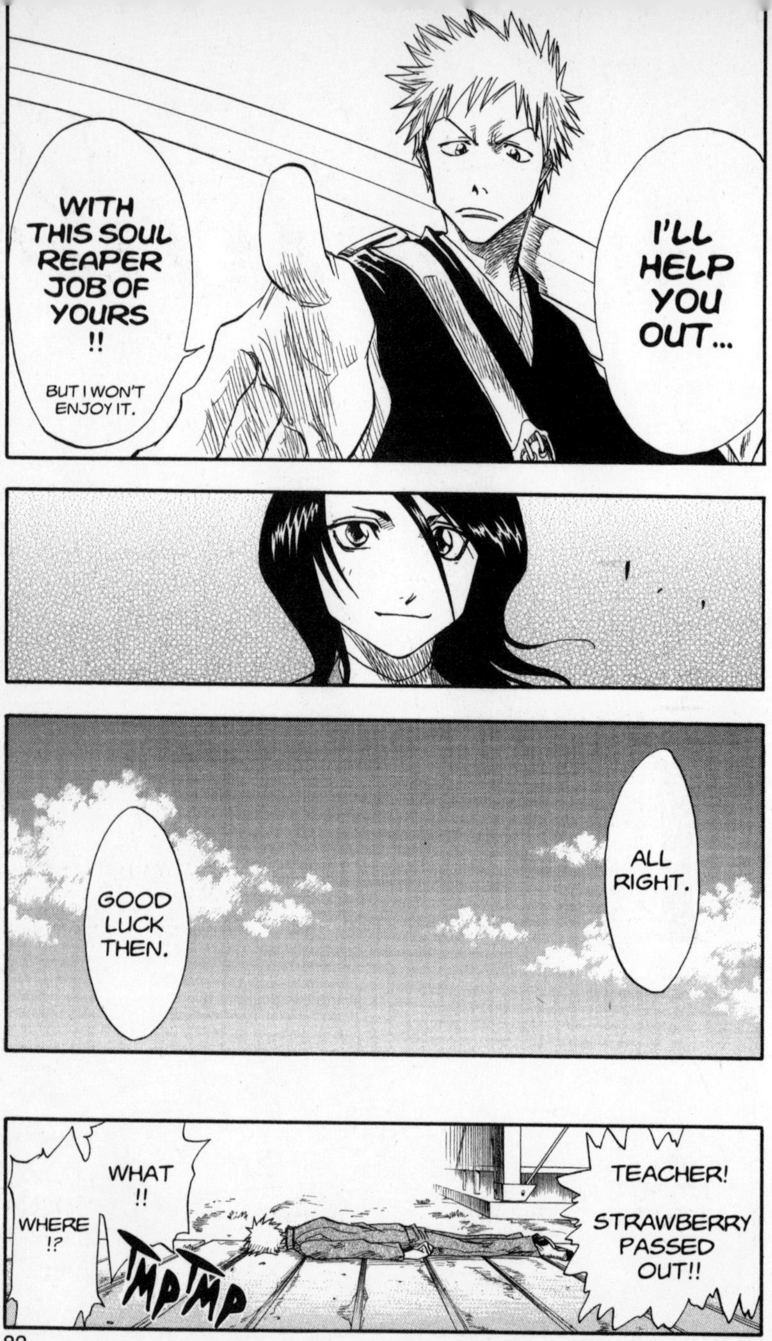
I'LL HELP YOU OUT...
WITH THIS SOUL REAPER JOB OF YOURS!!
BUT I WON'T ENJOY IT.
ALL RIGHT.
GOOD LUCK THEN.
TEACHER!
STRAWBERRY PASSED OUT!!
WHAT!!
WHERE!?
TMP TMP

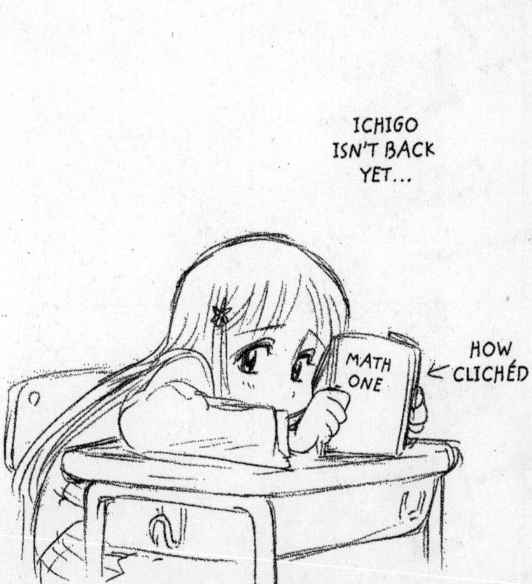
ICHIGO ISN'T BACK YET...
MATH ONE
HOW CLICHÉD

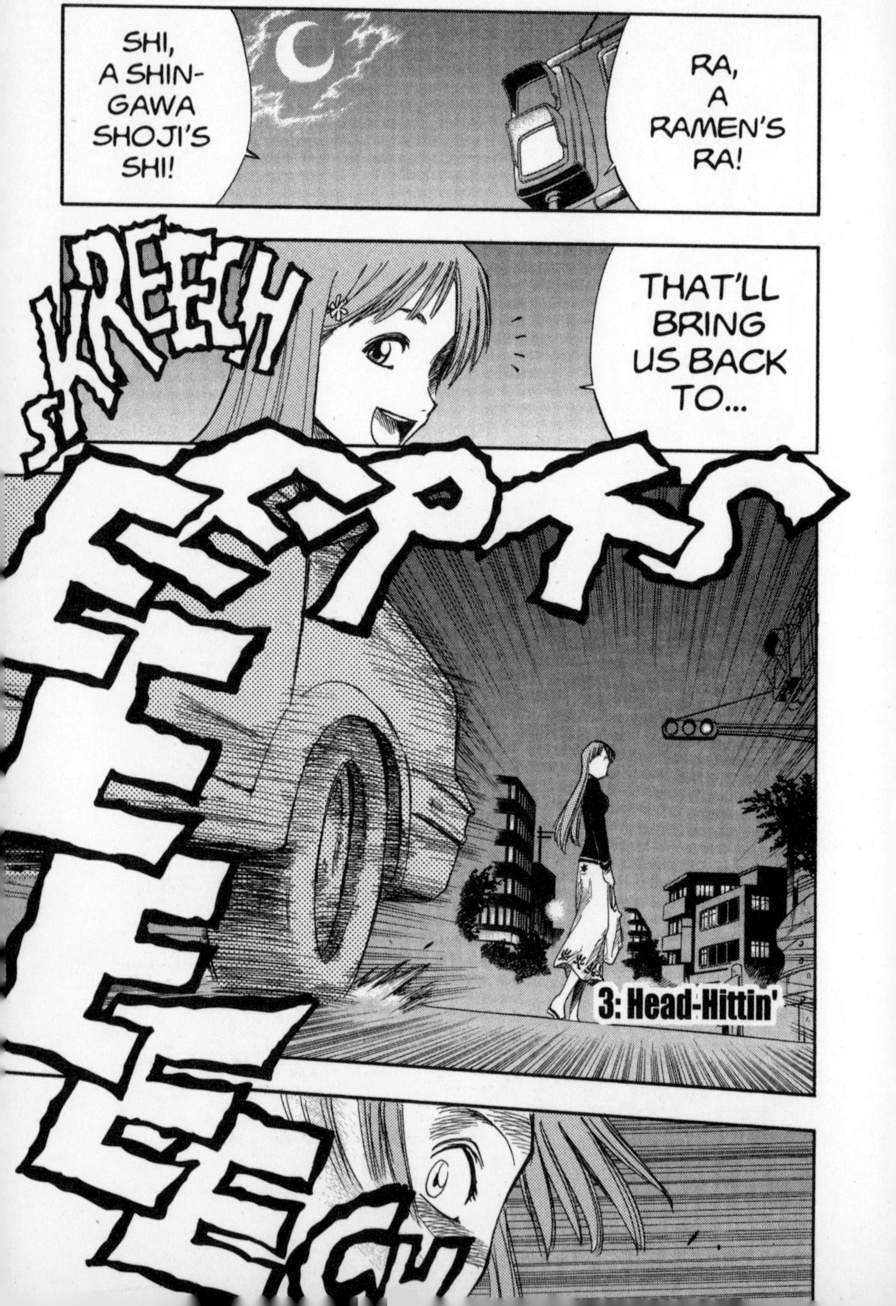
RA, A RAMEN'S RA!
SHI, A SHIN-GAWA SHOJI'S SHI!
THAT'LL BRING US BACK TO...
SKREECH
3: Head-Hittin'

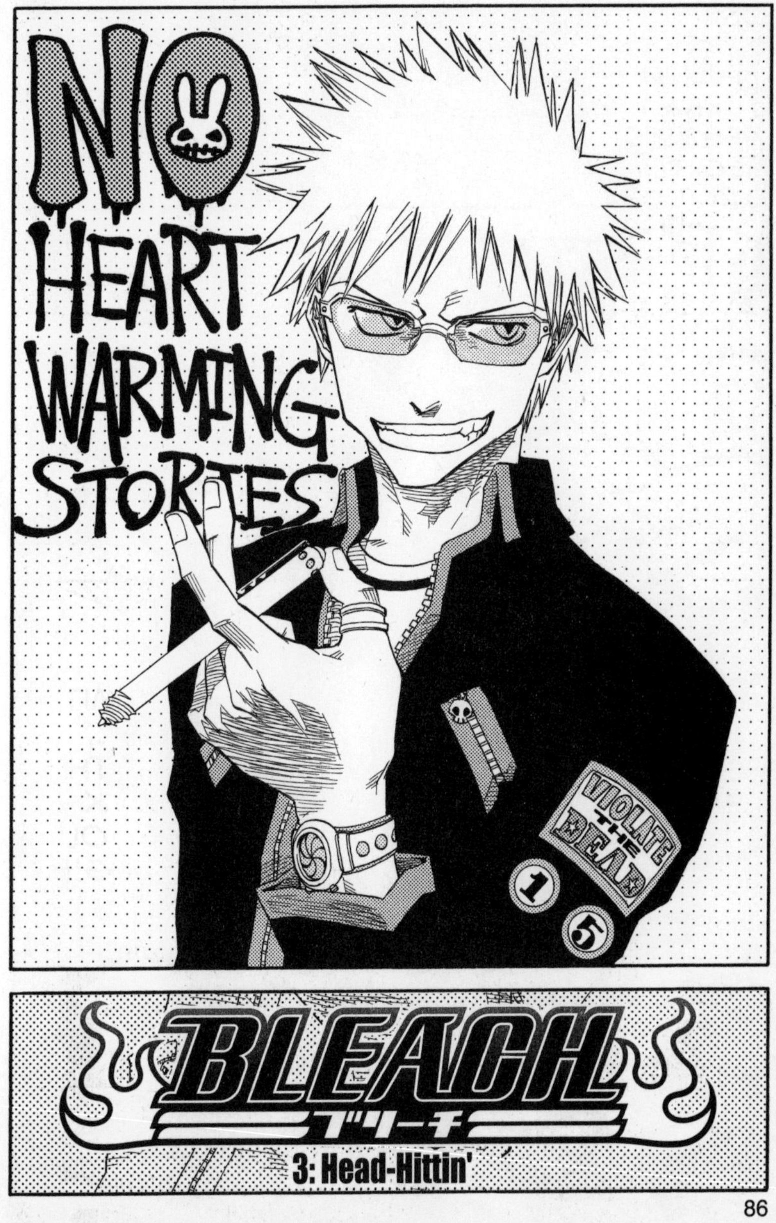
NO HEART WARMING STORIES
VIOLATE THE DEAD
1
5

BLEACH

ブリーチ

3: Head-Hittin'

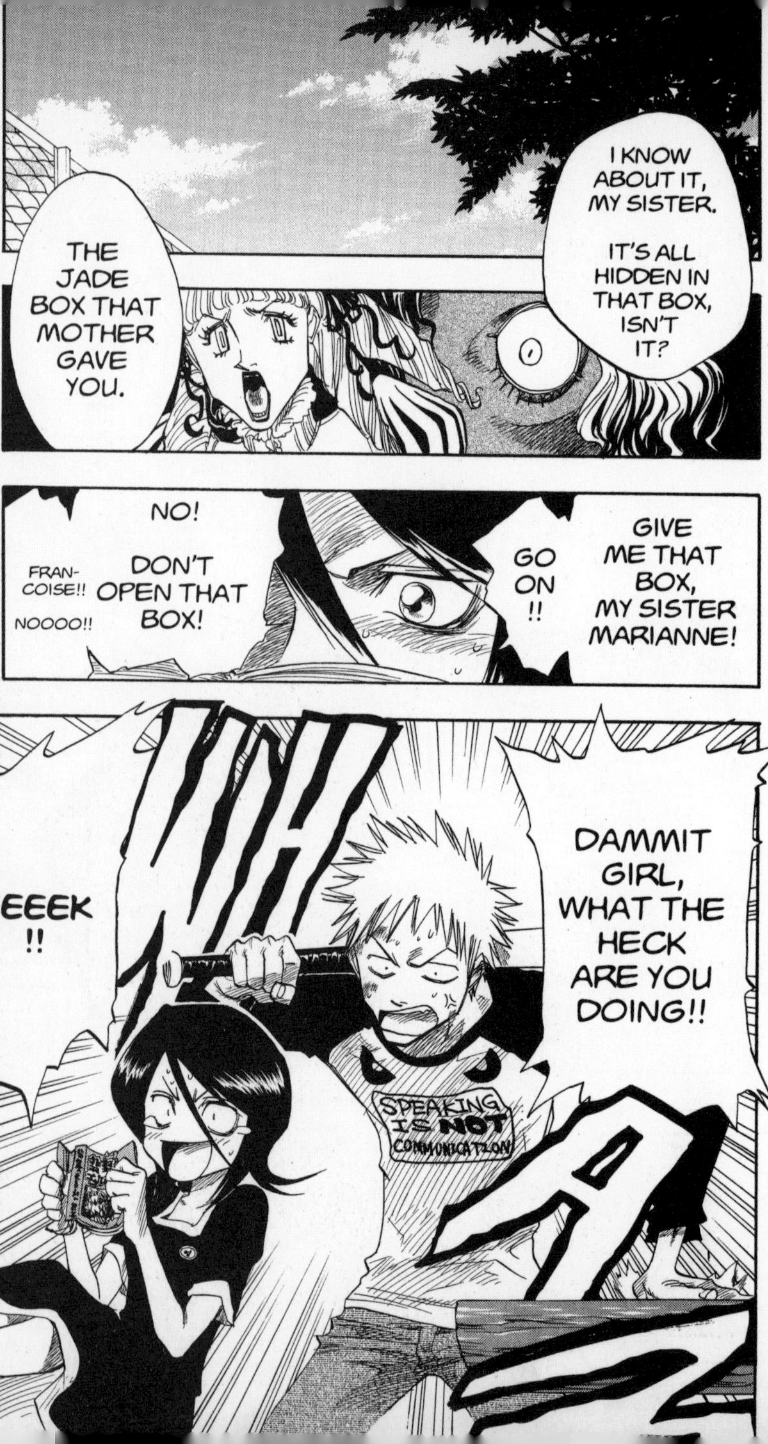
I KNOW ABOUT IT, MY SISTER.
IT'S ALL HIDDEN IN THAT BOX, ISN'T IT?
THE JADE BOX THAT MOTHER GAVE YOU.
GIVE ME THAT BOX, MY SISTER MARIANNE!
GO ON !!
NO!
DON'T OPEN THAT BOX!
FRAN-COISE!!
NOOOO!!
DAMMIT GIRL, WHAT THE HECK ARE YOU DOING!!
SPEAKING IS NOT COMMUNICATION
EEEEK !!

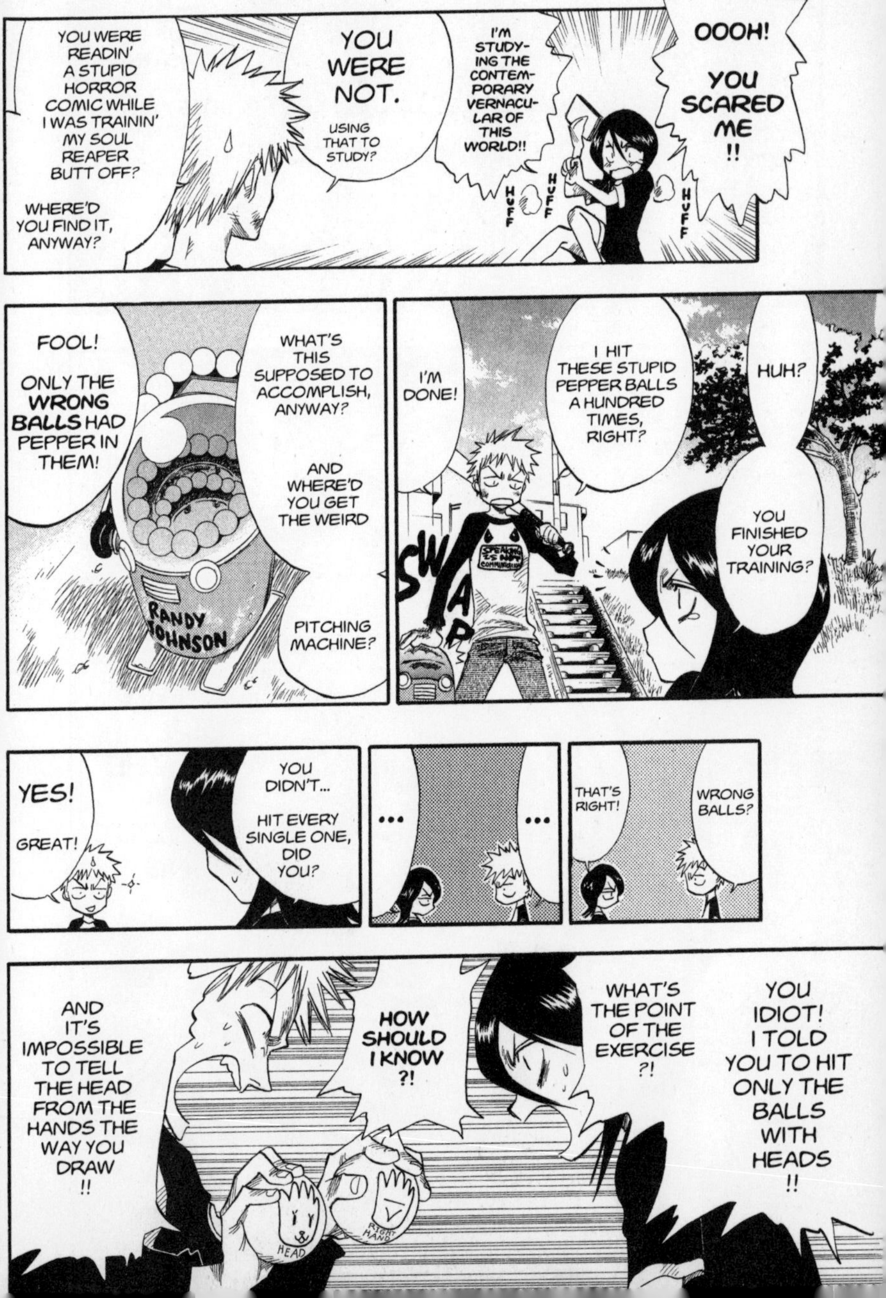
OOOH!
YOU SCARED ME!!
HUFF
HUFF
HUFF
I'M STUDYING THE CONTEMPORARY VERNACULAR OF THIS WORLD!!
YOU WERE NOT.
USING THAT TO STUDY?
YOU WERE READIN' A STUPID HORROR COMIC WHILE I WAS TRAININ' MY SOUL REAPER BUTT OFF?
WHERE'D YOU FIND IT, ANYWAY?
HUH?
YOU FINISHED YOUR TRAINING?
I HIT THESE STUPID PEPPER BALLS A HUNDRED TIMES, RIGHT?
I'M DONE!
SWAP
WHAT'S THIS SUPPOSED TO ACCOMPLISH, ANYWAY?
AND WHERE'D YOU GET THE WEIRD PITCHING MACHINE?
FOOL!
ONLY THE WRONG BALLS HAD PEPPER IN THEM!
RANDY JOHNSON
WRONG BALLS?
THAT'S RIGHT!
...
...
YOU DIDN'T...
HIT EVERY SINGLE ONE, DID YOU?
YES!
GREAT!
YOU IDIOT! I TOLD YOU TO HIT ONLY THE BALLS WITH HEADS!!
WHAT'S THE POINT OF THE EXERCISE?!
HOW SHOULD I KNOW?!
AND IT'S IMPOSSIBLE TO TELL THE HEAD FROM THE HANDS THE WAY YOU DRAW!!
RIGHT HAND
HEAD

READ THIS WAY

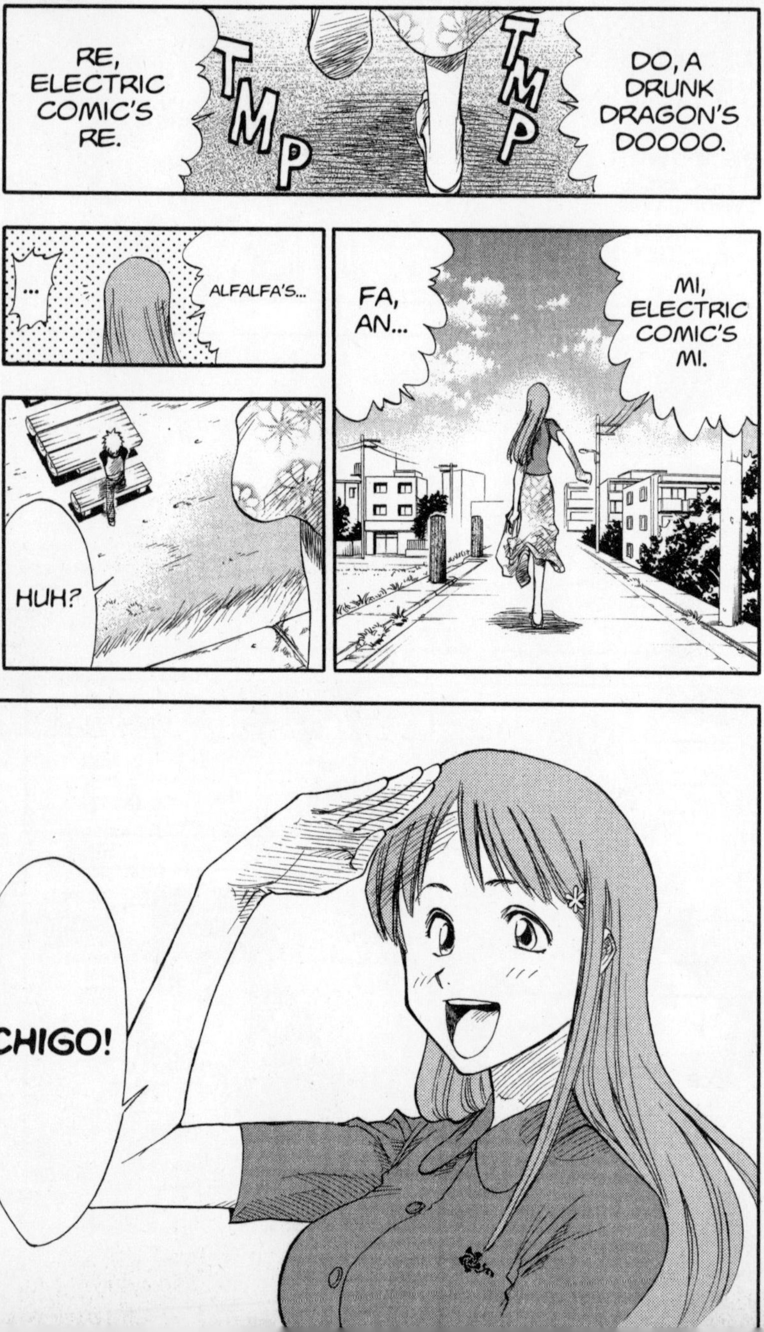
DO, A DRUNK DRAGON'S DOOOOO.
TMP
TMP
RE, ELECTRIC COMIC'S RE.
MI, ELECTRIC COMIC'S MI.
FA, AN...
ALFALFA'S...
...
HUH?
ICHIGO!

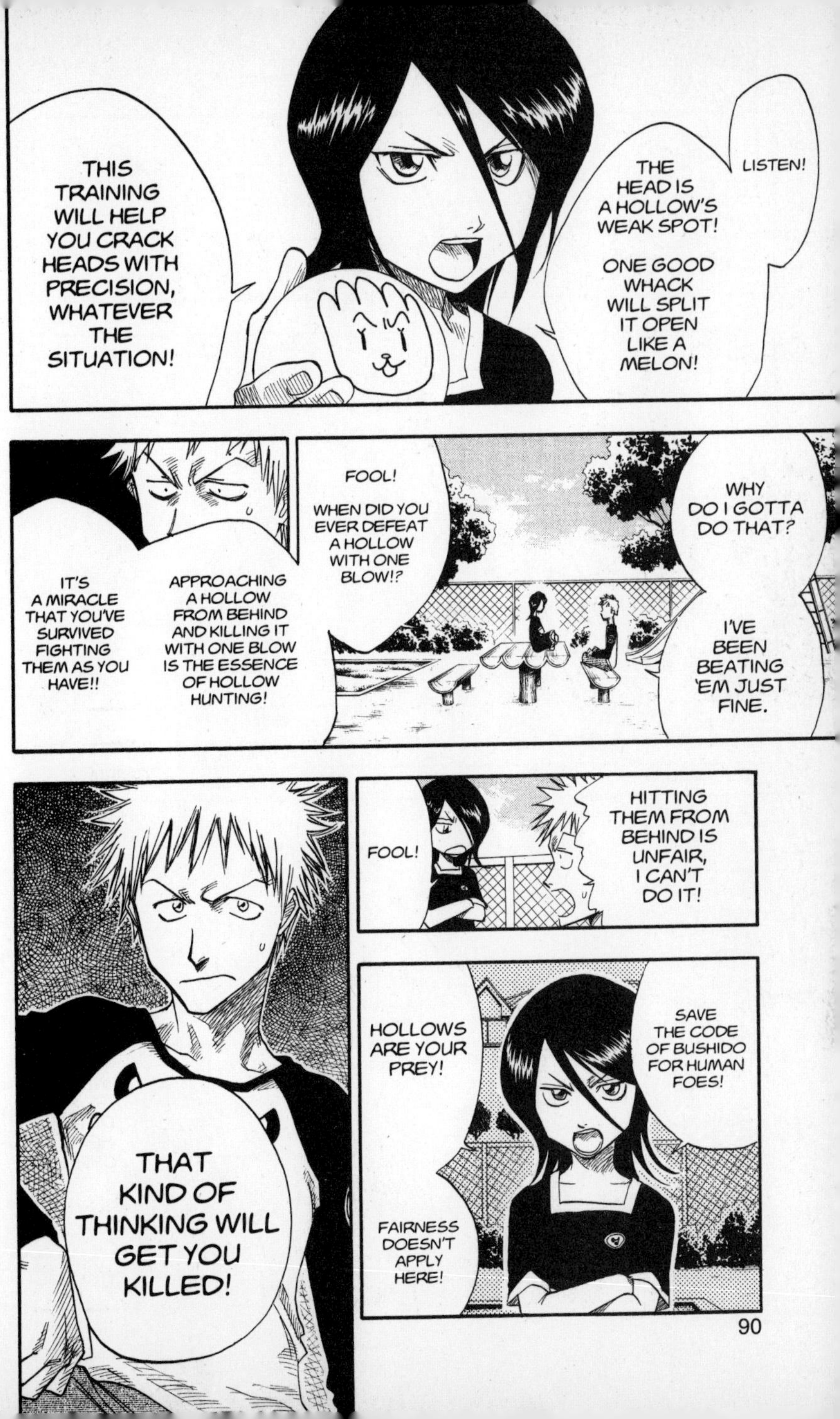
LISTEN!
THE HEAD IS A HOLLOW'S WEAK SPOT!
ONE GOOD WHACK WILL SPLIT IT OPEN LIKE A MELON!
THIS TRAINING WILL HELP YOU CRACK HEADS WITH PRECISION, WHATEVER THE SITUATION!
WHY DO I GOTTA DO THAT?
I'VE BEEN BEATING 'EM JUST FINE.
FOOL!
WHEN DID YOU EVER DEFEAT A HOLLOW WITH ONE BLOW!?
APPROACHING A HOLLOW FROM BEHIND AND KILLING IT WITH ONE BLOW IS THE ESSENCE OF HOLLOW HUNTING!
IT'S A MIRACLE THAT YOU'VE SURVIVED FIGHTING THEM AS YOU HAVE!!
HITTING THEM FROM BEHIND IS UNFAIR, I CAN'T DO IT!
FOOL!
SAVE THE CODE OF BUSHIDO FOR HUMAN FOES!
HOLLOWS ARE YOUR PREY!
FAIRNESS DOESN'T APPLY HERE!
THAT KIND OF THINKING WILL GET YOU KILLED!

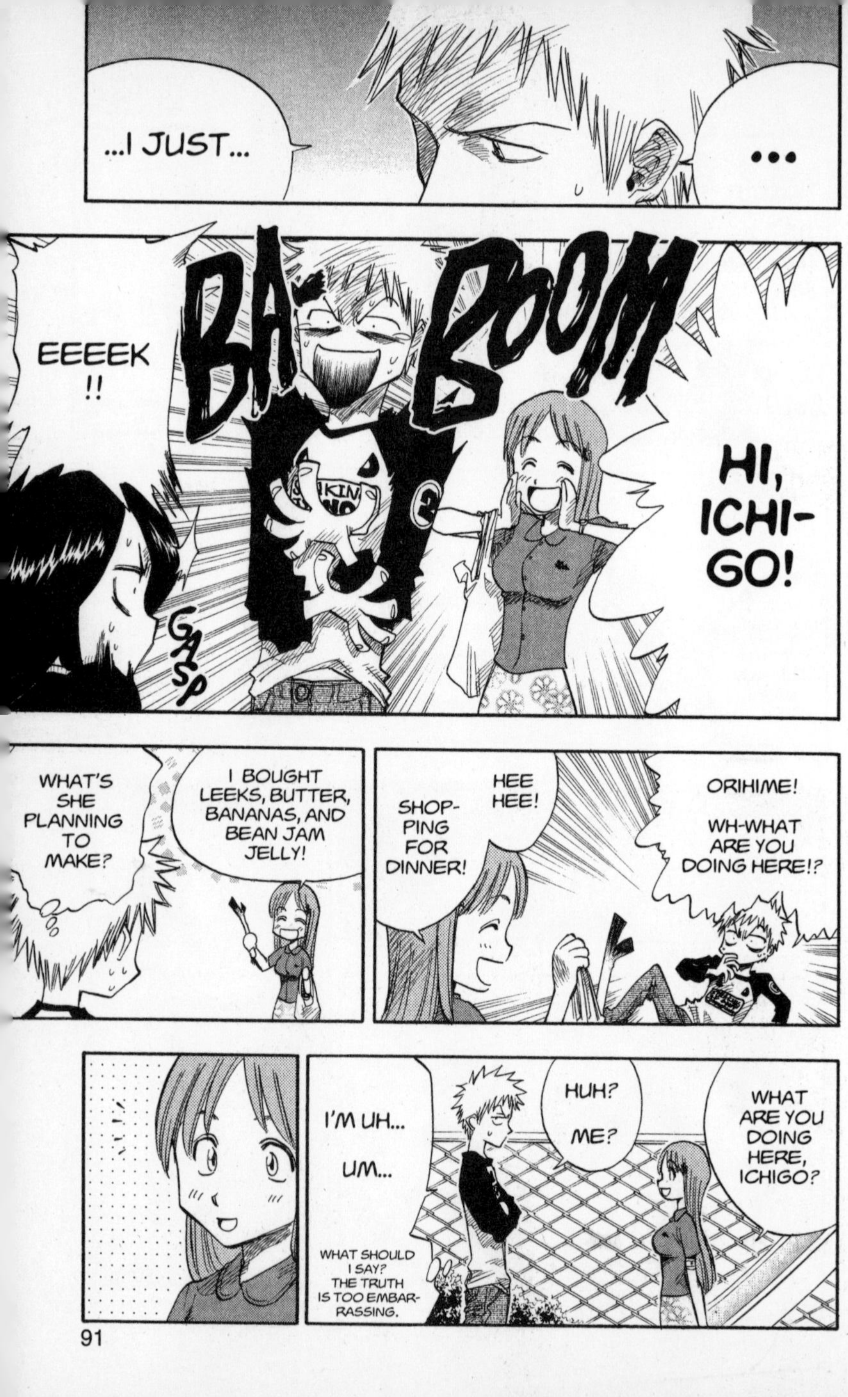
...
...I JUST...
HI, ICHIGO!
BA-BOOM
GASP
EEEEK!!
ORIHIME!
WH-WHAT ARE YOU DOING HERE!?
HEE HEE!
SHOPPING FOR DINNER!
I BOUGHT LEEKS, BUTTER, BANANAS, AND BEAN JAM JELLY!
WHAT'S SHE PLANNING TO MAKE?
WHAT ARE YOU DOING HERE, ICHIGO?
HUH?
ME?
I'M UH...
UM...
WHAT SHOULD I SAY? THE TRUTH IS TOO EMBARRASSING.

READ THIS WAY

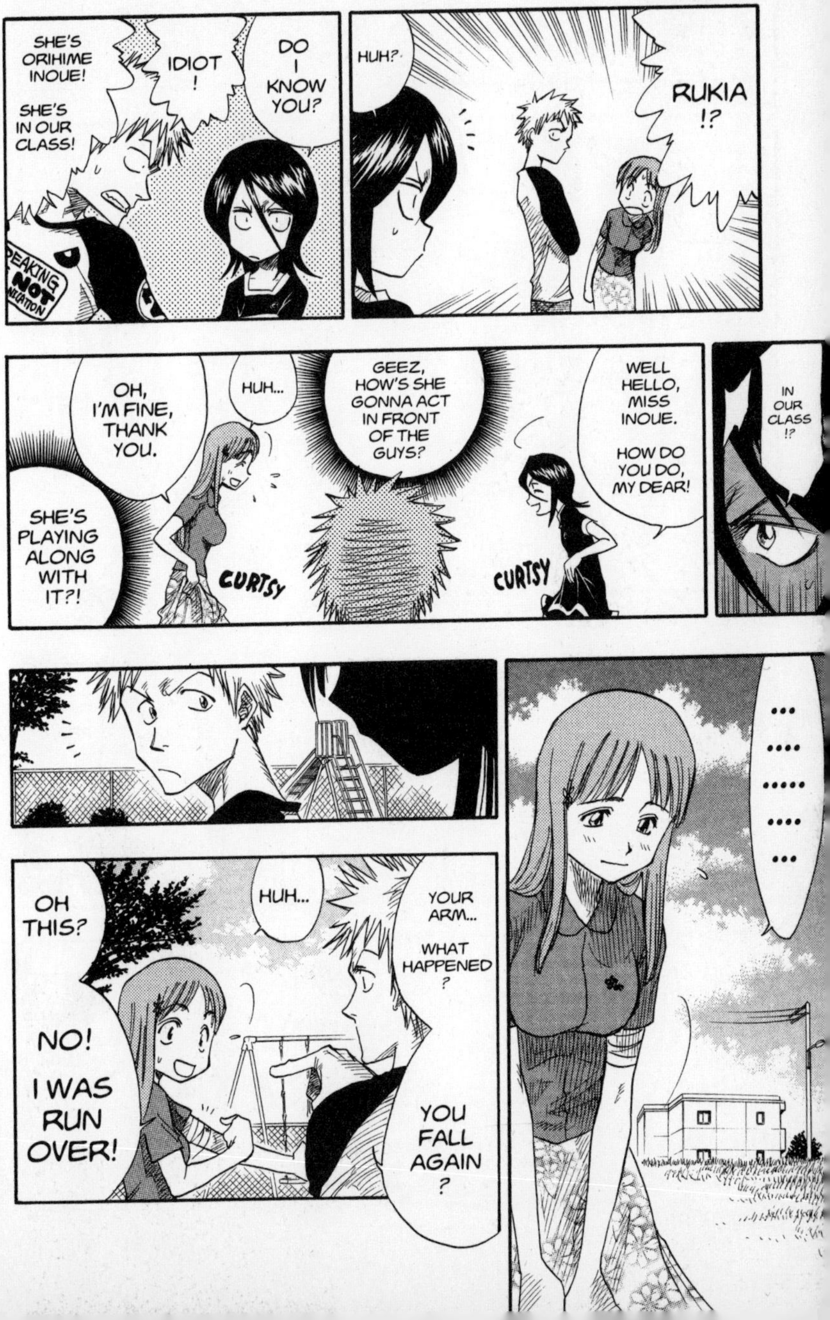

RUKIA !?
HUH?
DO I KNOW YOU?
IDIOT!
SHE'S ORIHIME INOUE!
SHE'S IN OUR CLASS!
IN OUR CLASS !?
WELL HELLO, MISS INOUE.
HOW DO YOU DO, MY DEAR!
CURTSY
GEEZ, HOW'S SHE GONNA ACT IN FRONT OF THE GUYS?
HUH...
OH, I'M FINE, THANK YOU.
SHE'S PLAYING ALONG WITH IT?!
CURTSY
... .
YOUR ARM...
WHAT HAPPENED?
YOU FALL AGAIN?
HUH...
OH THIS?
NO!
I WAS RUN OVER!

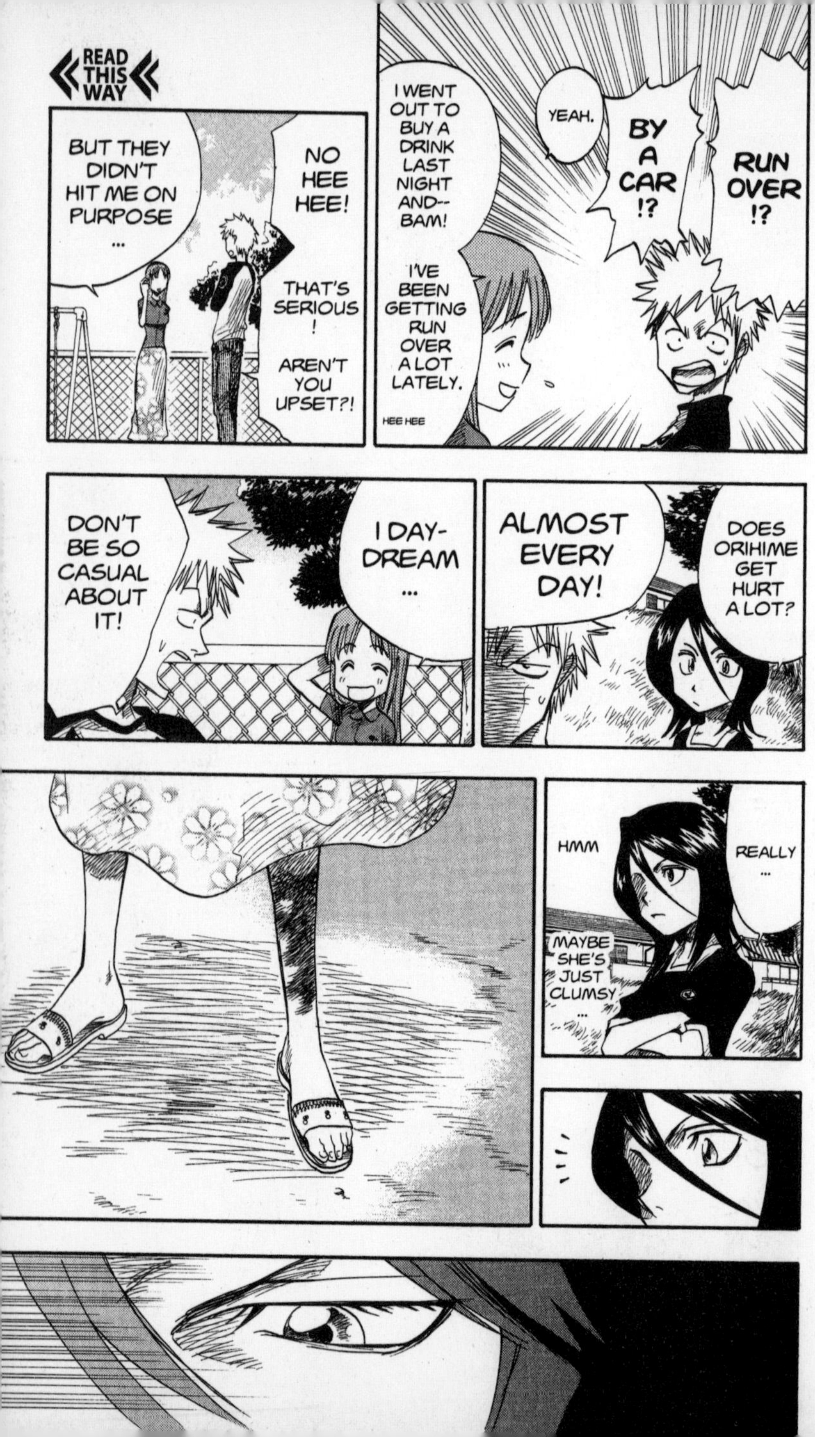
READ THIS WAY
RUN OVER !?
BY A CAR !?
YEAH.
I WENT OUT TO BUY A DRINK LAST NIGHT AND-- BAM!
I'VE BEEN GETTING RUN OVER A LOT LATELY.
HEE HEE
NO HEE HEE!
THAT'S SERIOUS! AREN'T YOU UPSET?!
BUT THEY DIDN'T HIT ME ON PURPOSE ...
DOES ORIHIME GET HURT A LOT?
ALMOST EVERY DAY!
I DAY-DREAM ...
DON'T BE SO CASUAL ABOUT IT!
REALLY ...
HMM
MAYBE SHE'S JUST CLUMSY ...

READ THIS WAY

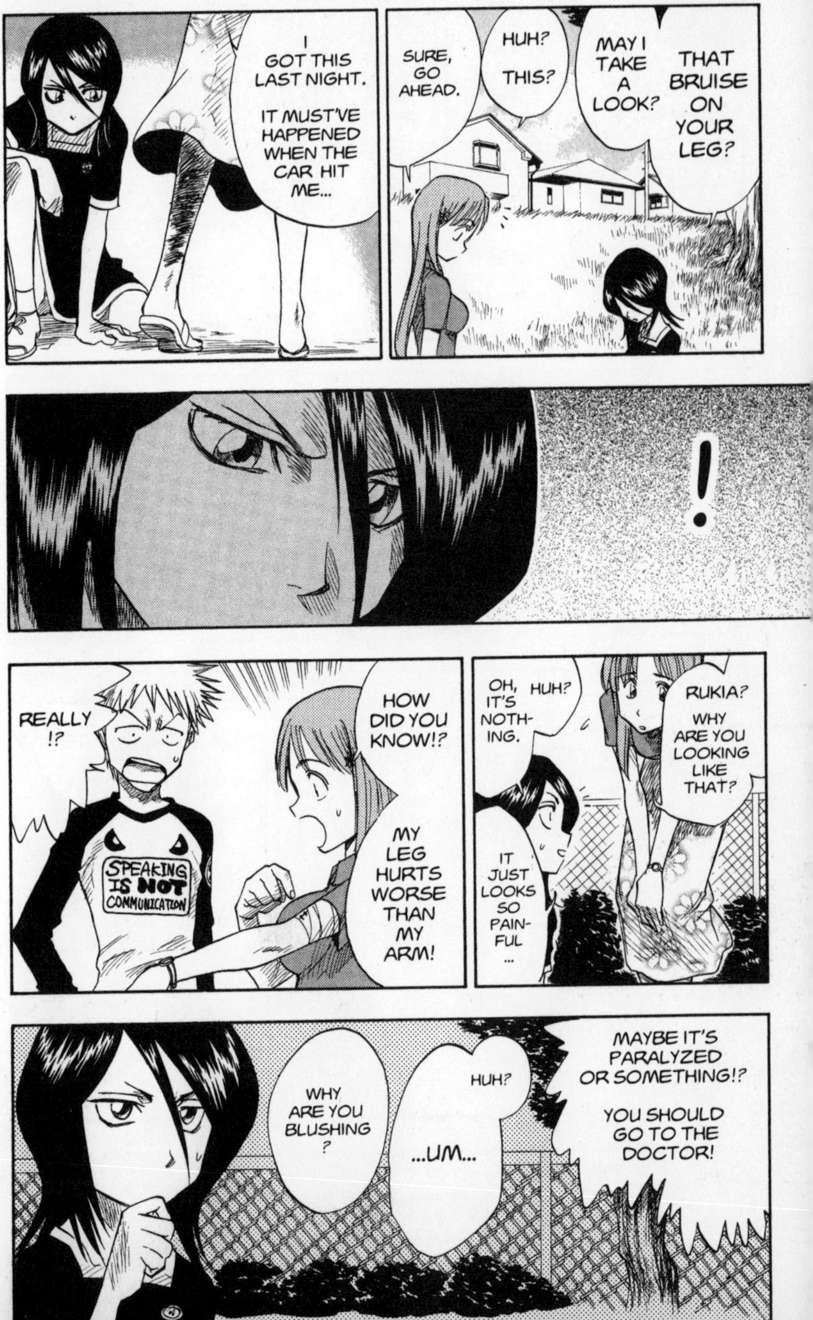
THAT BRUISE ON YOUR LEG?
MAY I TAKE A LOOK?
HUH? THIS?
SURE, GO AHEAD.
I GOT THIS LAST NIGHT.
IT MUST'VE HAPPENED WHEN THE CAR HIT ME...
!
RUKIA? WHY ARE YOU LOOKING LIKE THAT?
HUH?
OH, IT'S NOTHING.
IT JUST LOOKS SO PAINFUL...
HOW DID YOU KNOW!?
MY LEG HURTS WORSE THAN MY ARM!
REALLY!?
SPEAKING IS NOT COMMUNICATION
MAYBE IT'S PARALYZED OR SOMETHING!?
YOU SHOULD GO TO THE DOCTOR!
HUH?
...UM...
WHY ARE YOU BLUSHING?

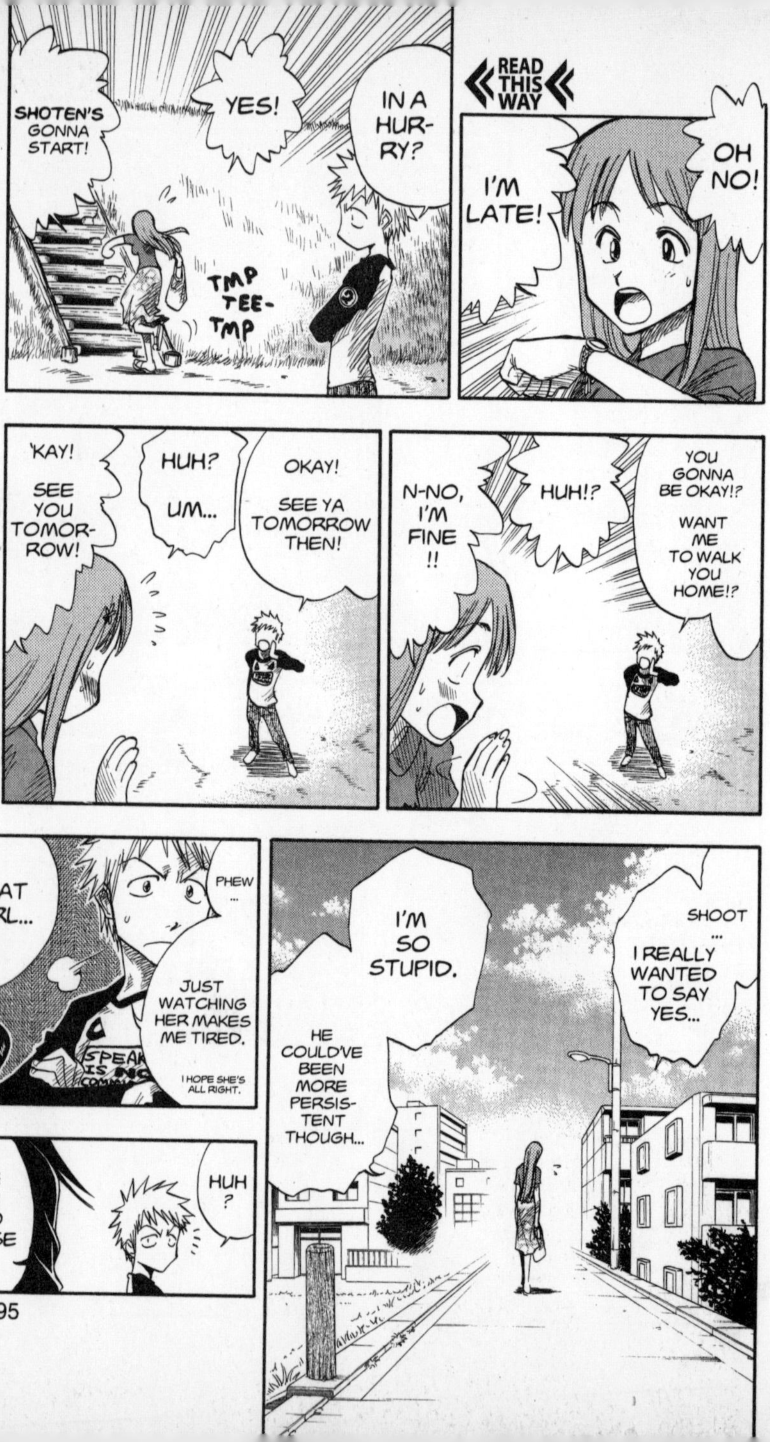
READ THIS WAY
OH NO!
I'M LATE!
IN A HURRY?
YES!
SHOTEN'S GONNA START!
TMP TEE-TMP
YOU GONNA BE OKAY!? WANT ME TO WALK YOU HOME!?
HUH!?
N-NO, I'M FINE!!
OKAY! SEE YA TOMORROW THEN!
HUH? UM...
'KAY! SEE YOU TOMORROW!
SHOOT... I REALLY WANTED TO SAY YES...
I'M SO STUPID.
HE COULD'VE BEEN MORE PERSISTENT THOUGH...
PHEW...
THAT GIRL...
JUST WATCHING HER MAKES ME TIRED.
I HOPE SHE'S ALL RIGHT.
HUH?
ARE YOU TWO CLOSE?

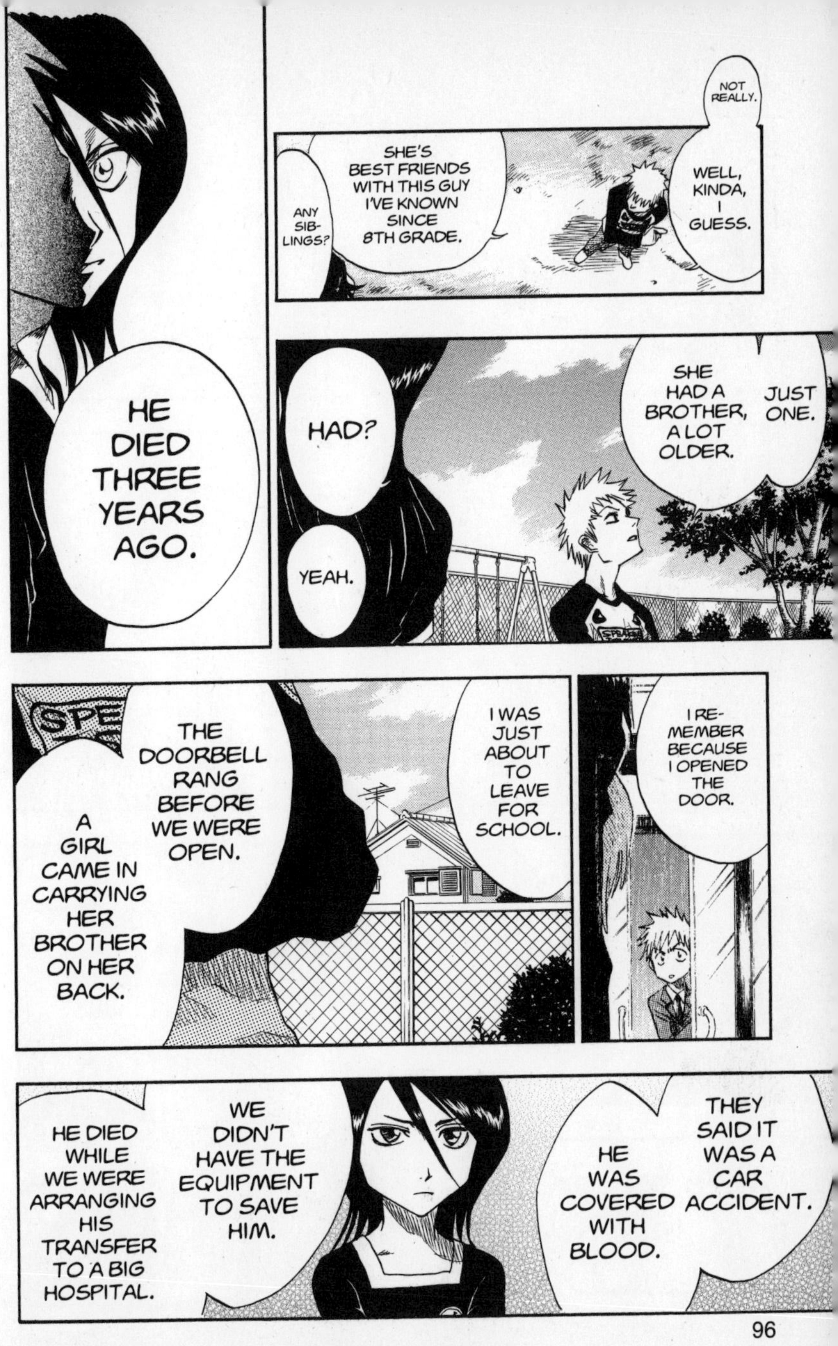
NOT REALLY.
WELL, KINDA, I GUESS.
SHE'S BEST FRIENDS WITH THIS GUY I'VE KNOWN SINCE 8TH GRADE.
ANY SIB-LINGS?
JUST ONE.
SHE HAD A BROTHER, A LOT OLDER.
HAD?
YEAH.
HE DIED THREE YEARS AGO.
I RE-MEMBER BECAUSE I OPENED THE DOOR.
I WAS JUST ABOUT TO LEAVE FOR SCHOOL.
THE DOORBELL RANG BEFORE WE WERE OPEN.
A GIRL CAME IN CARRYING HER BROTHER ON HER BACK.
THEY SAID IT WAS A CAR ACCIDENT.
HE WAS COVERED WITH BLOOD.
WE DIDN'T HAVE THE EQUIPMENT TO SAVE HIM.
HE DIED WHILE WE WERE ARRANGING HIS TRANSFER TO A BIG HOSPITAL.

READ THIS WAY

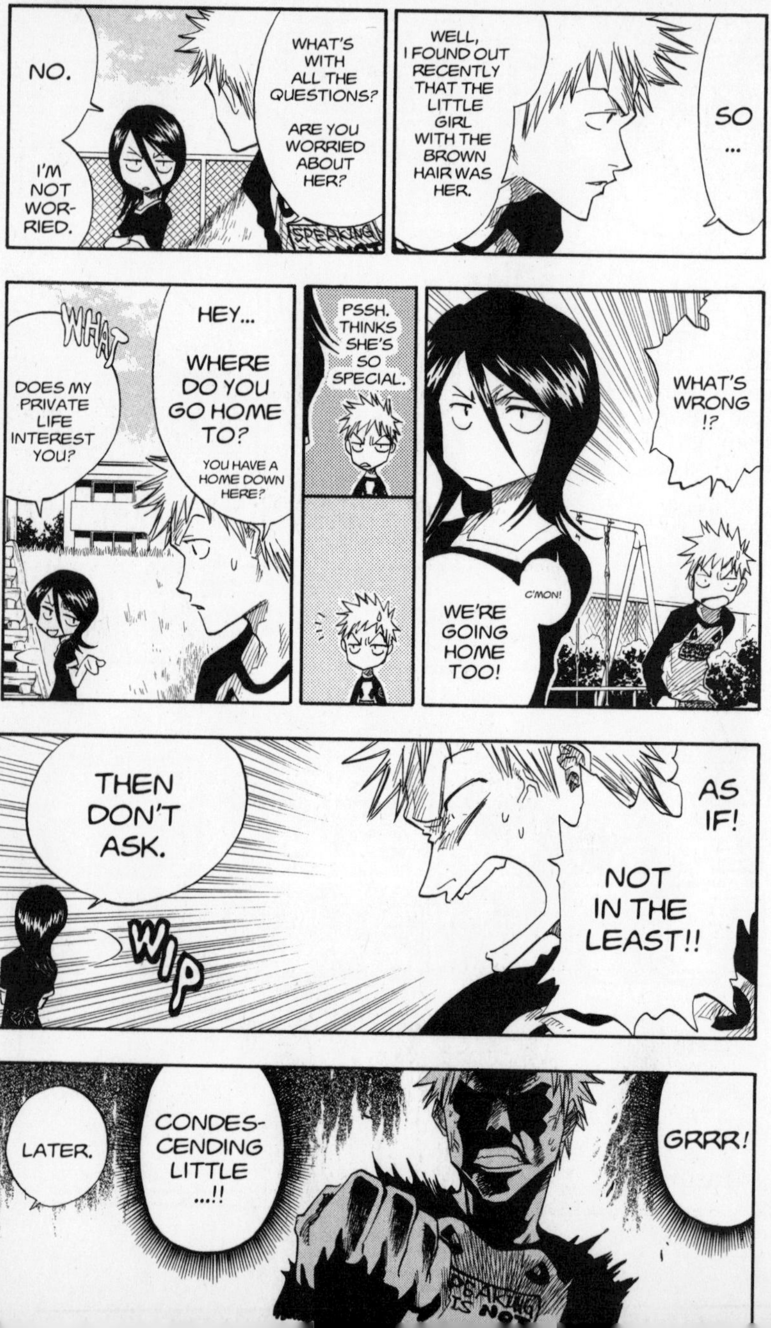
SO ...
WELL, I FOUND OUT RECENTLY THAT THE LITTLE GIRL WITH THE BROWN HAIR WAS HER.
WHAT'S WITH ALL THE QUESTIONS?
ARE YOU WORRIED ABOUT HER?
NO.
I'M NOT WOR-RIED.
WHAT'S WRONG !?
C'MON!
WE'RE GOING HOME TOO!
PSSH. THINKS SHE'S SO SPECIAL.
HEY...
WHERE DO YOU GO HOME TO?
YOU HAVE A HOME DOWN HERE?
WHAT
DOES MY PRIVATE LIFE INTEREST YOU?
AS IF!
NOT IN THE LEAST!!
THEN DON'T ASK.
WIP
GRRR!
CONDES-CENDING LITTLE ...!!
LATER.

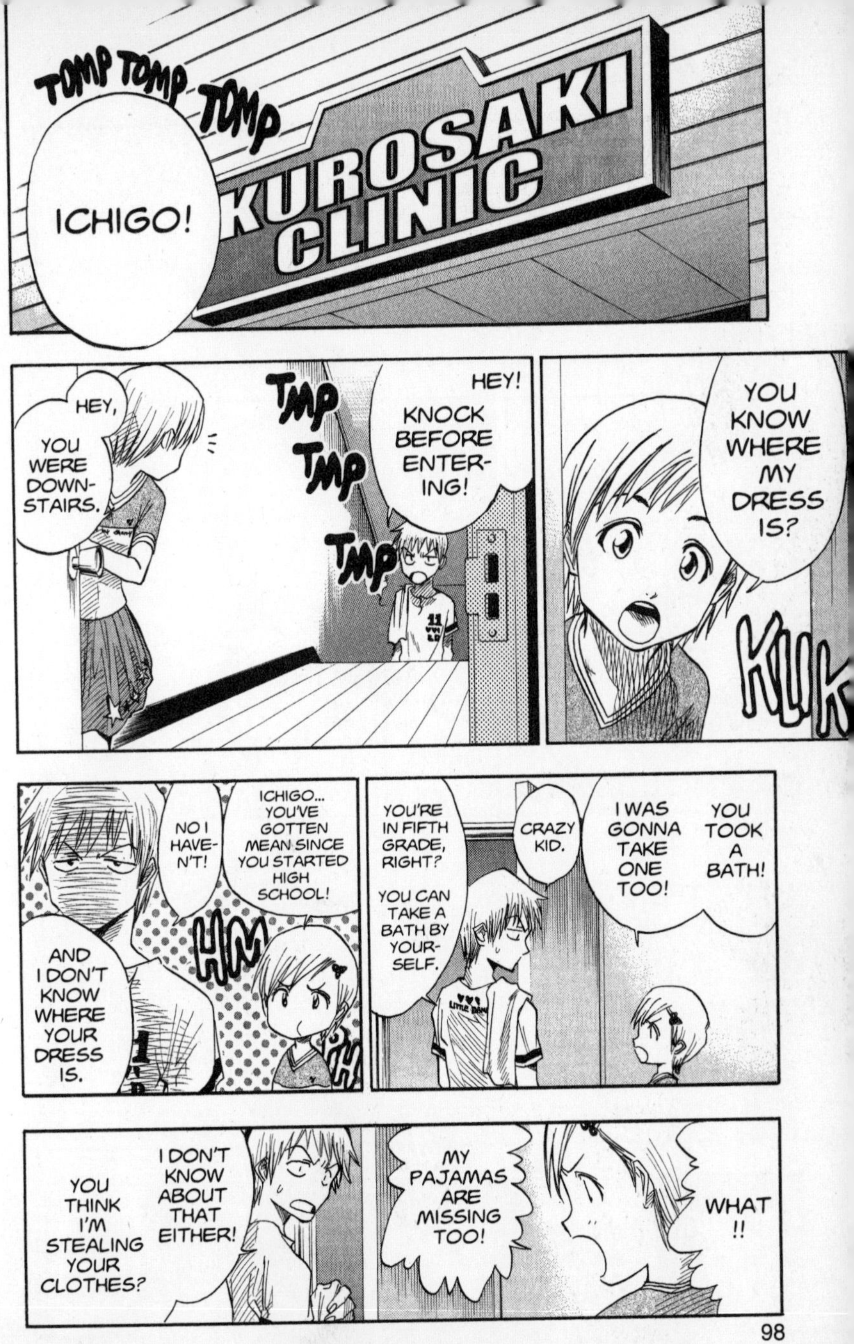
TOMP TOMP TOMP
ICHIGO!
KUROSAKI CLINIC
YOU KNOW WHERE MY DRESS IS?
KLIK
HEY! KNOCK BEFORE ENTERING!
TMP TMP TMP
HEY, YOU WERE DOWNSTAIRS.
YOU TOOK A BATH!
I WAS GONNA TAKE ONE TOO!
CRAZY KID.
YOU'RE IN FIFTH GRADE, RIGHT? YOU CAN TAKE A BATH BY YOURSELF.
ICHIGO... YOU'VE GOTTEN MEAN SINCE YOU STARTED HIGH SCHOOL!
NO I HAVEN'T!
HMPH
AND I DON'T KNOW WHERE YOUR DRESS IS.
WHAT!!
MY PAJAMAS ARE MISSING TOO!
I DON'T KNOW ABOUT THAT EITHER!
YOU THINK I'M STEALING YOUR CLOTHES?

READ THIS WAY

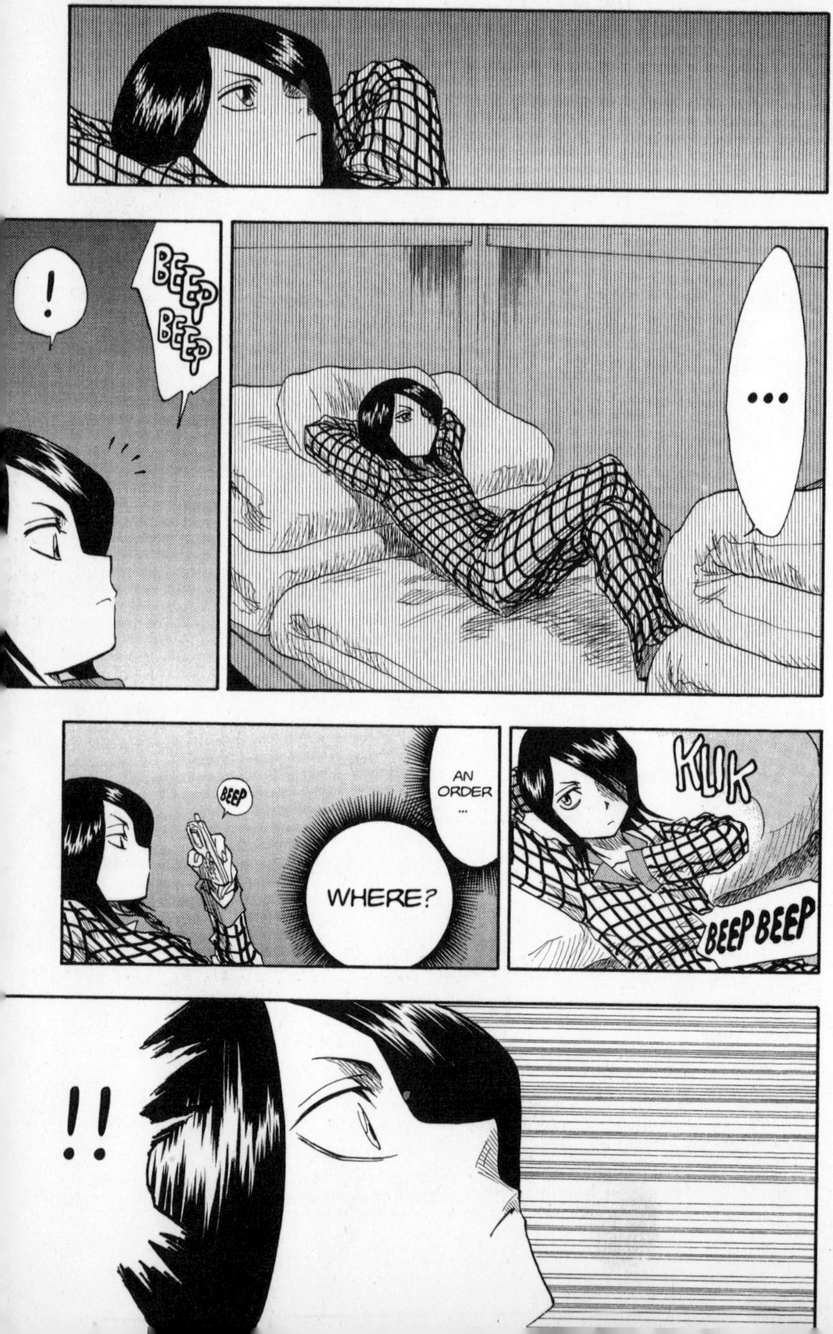
...
BEEP BEEP
!
KLIK
BEEP BEEP
AN ORDER ...
BEEP
WHERE?
!!

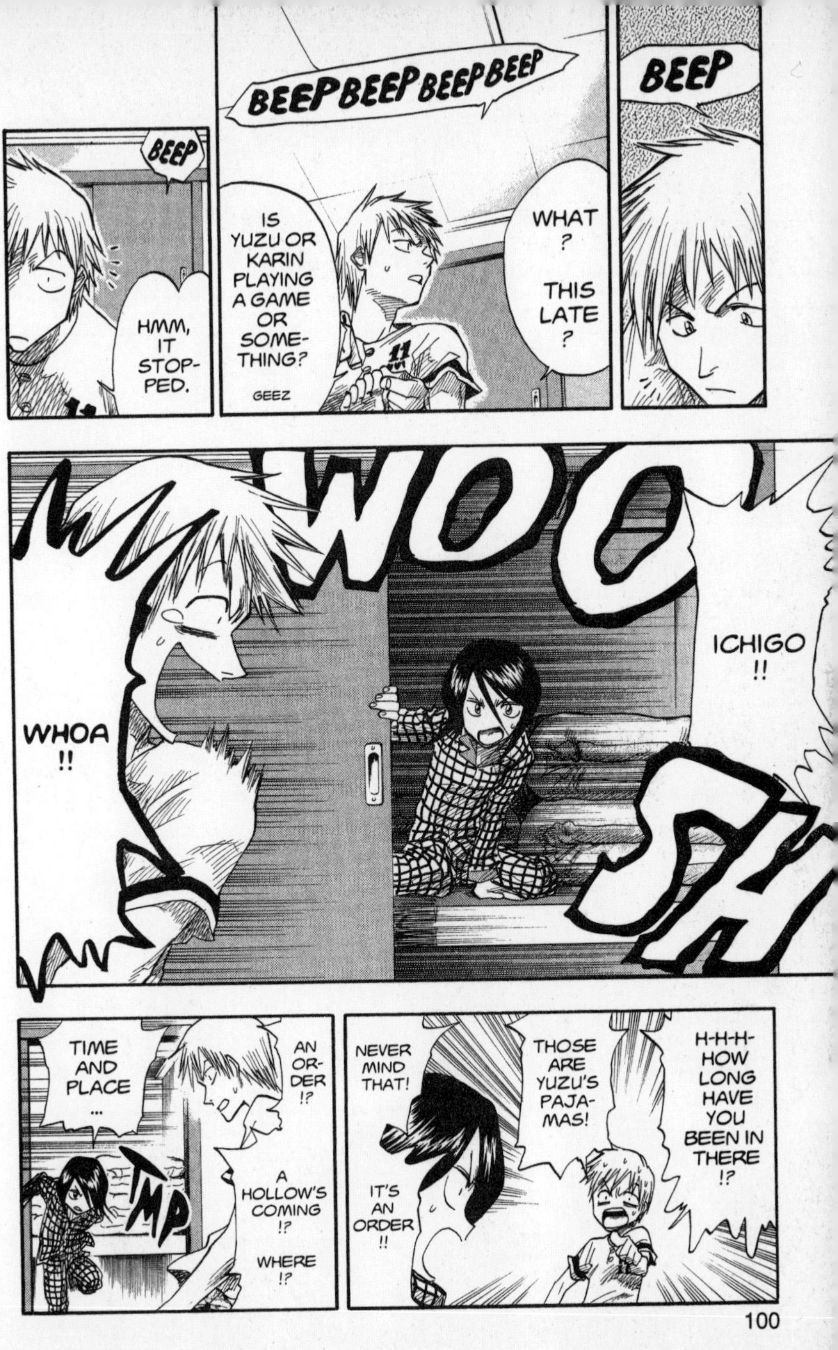
BEEP
BEEP BEEP BEEP BEEP
WHAT? THIS LATE?
IS YUZU OR KARIN PLAYING A GAME OR SOMETHING?
GEEZ
BEEP
HMM, IT STOPPED.
ICHIGO!!
WOO
SH
WHOA!!
H-H-H-HOW LONG HAVE YOU BEEN IN THERE!?
THOSE ARE YUZU'S PAJAMAS!
NEVER MIND THAT!
IT'S AN ORDER!!
AN ORDER!?
TIME AND PLACE...
A HOLLOW'S COMING!?
WHERE!?
TMP

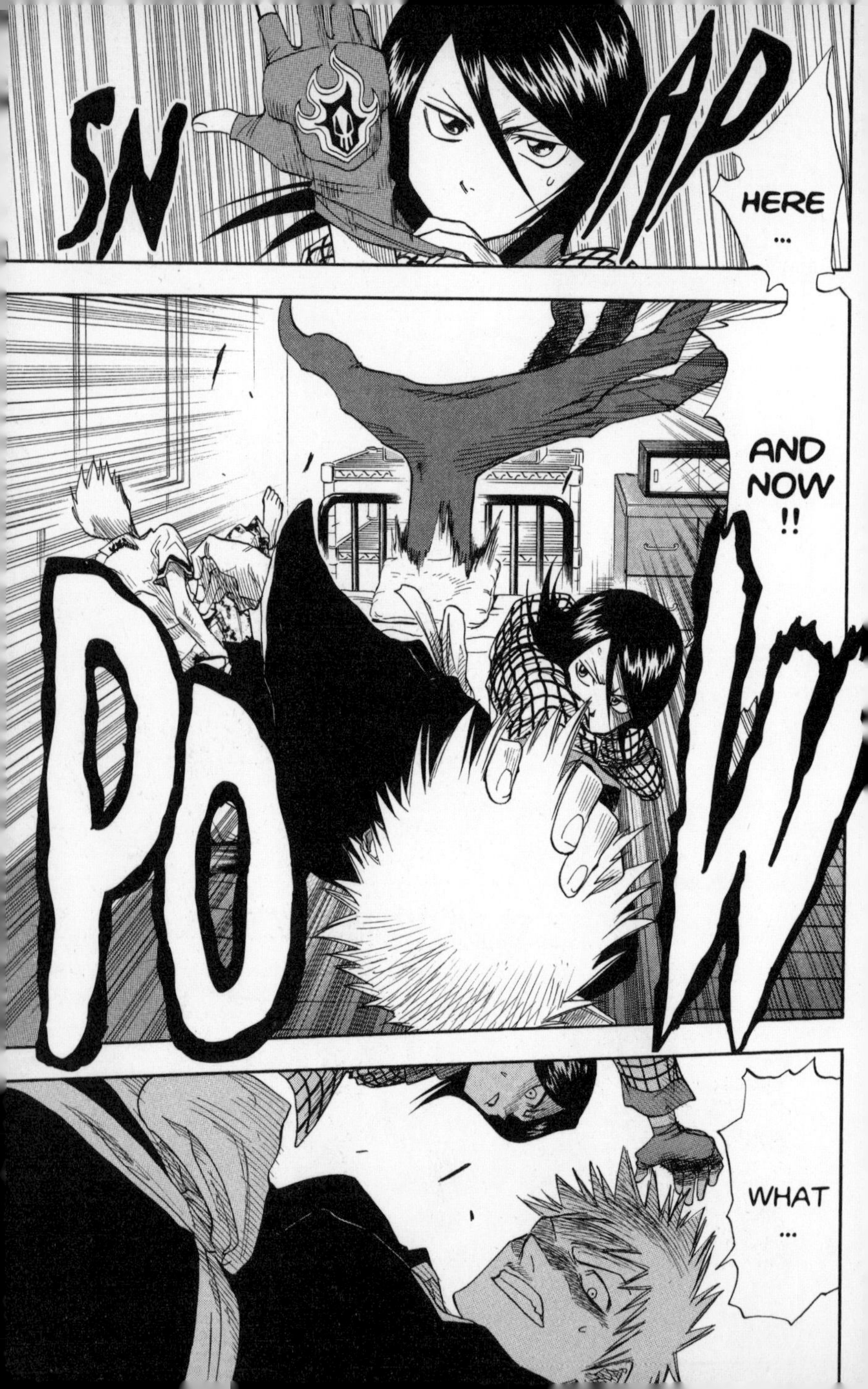
SNAP
HERE ...
AND NOW !!
POW
WHAT ...

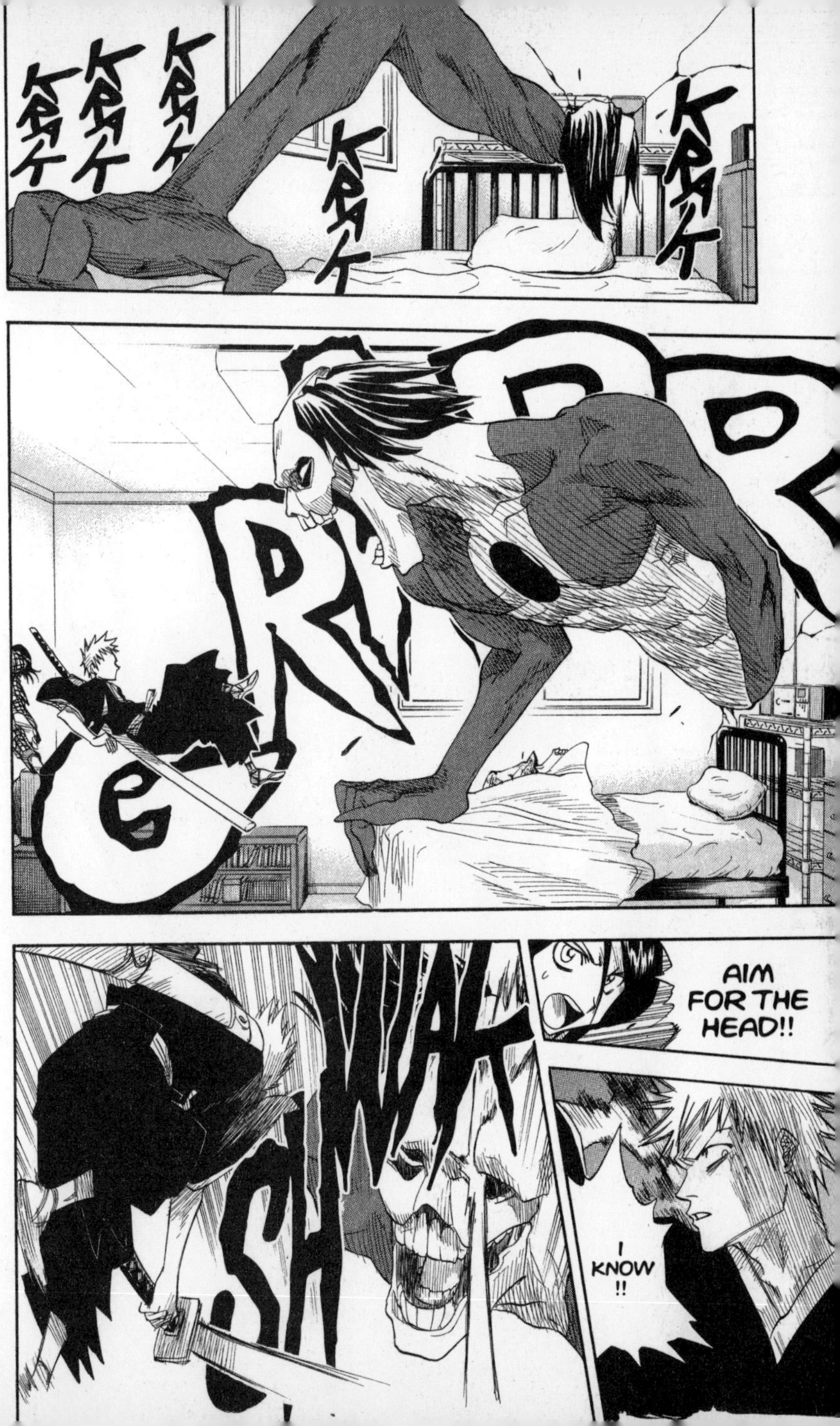
KRAK
KRAK
KRAK
KRAK
KRAK
AIM FOR THE HEAD!!
I KNOW !!

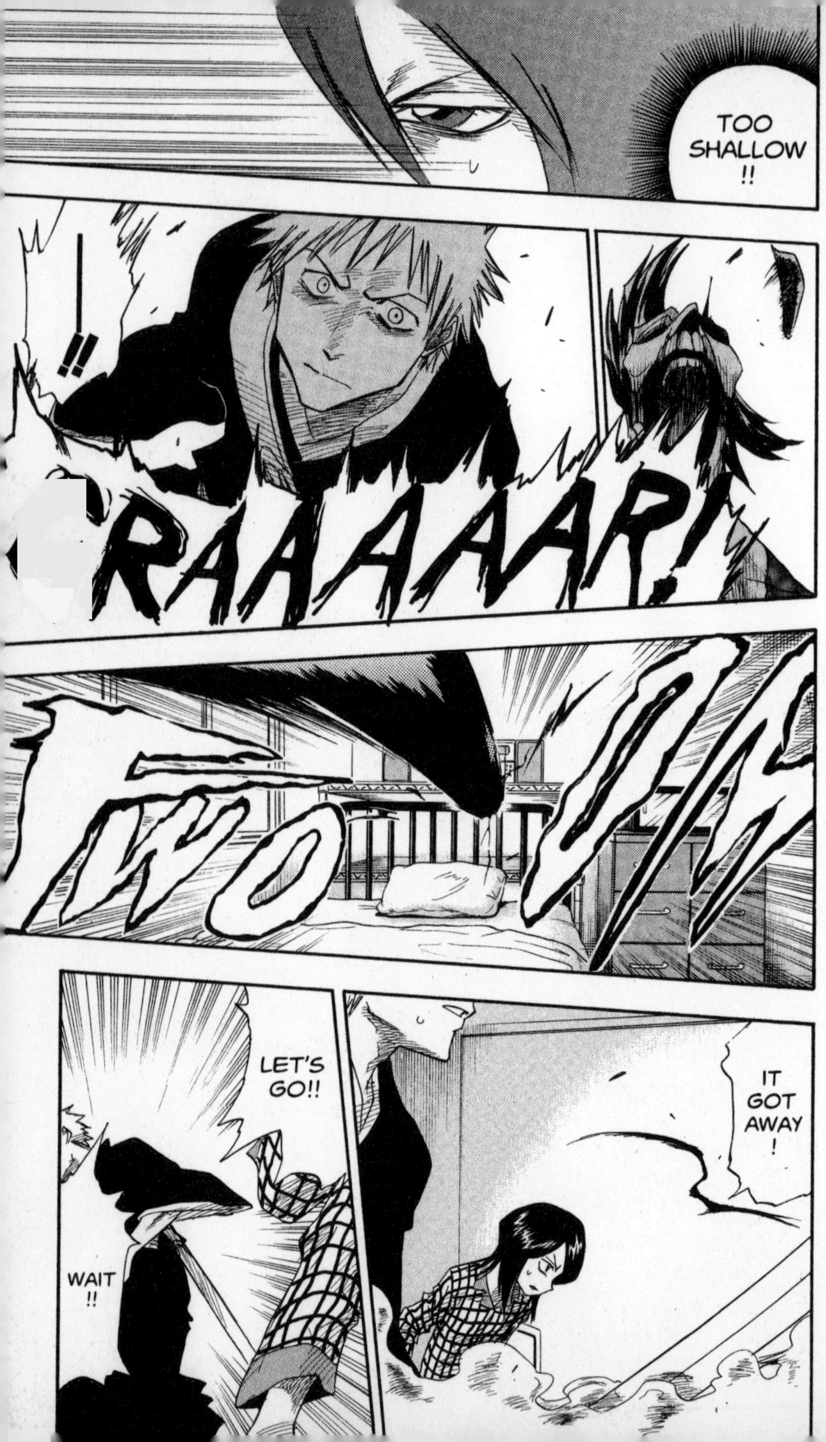
TOO SHALLOW !!
RAAAAAR!
!!
IT GOT AWAY !
LET'S GO!!
WAIT !!

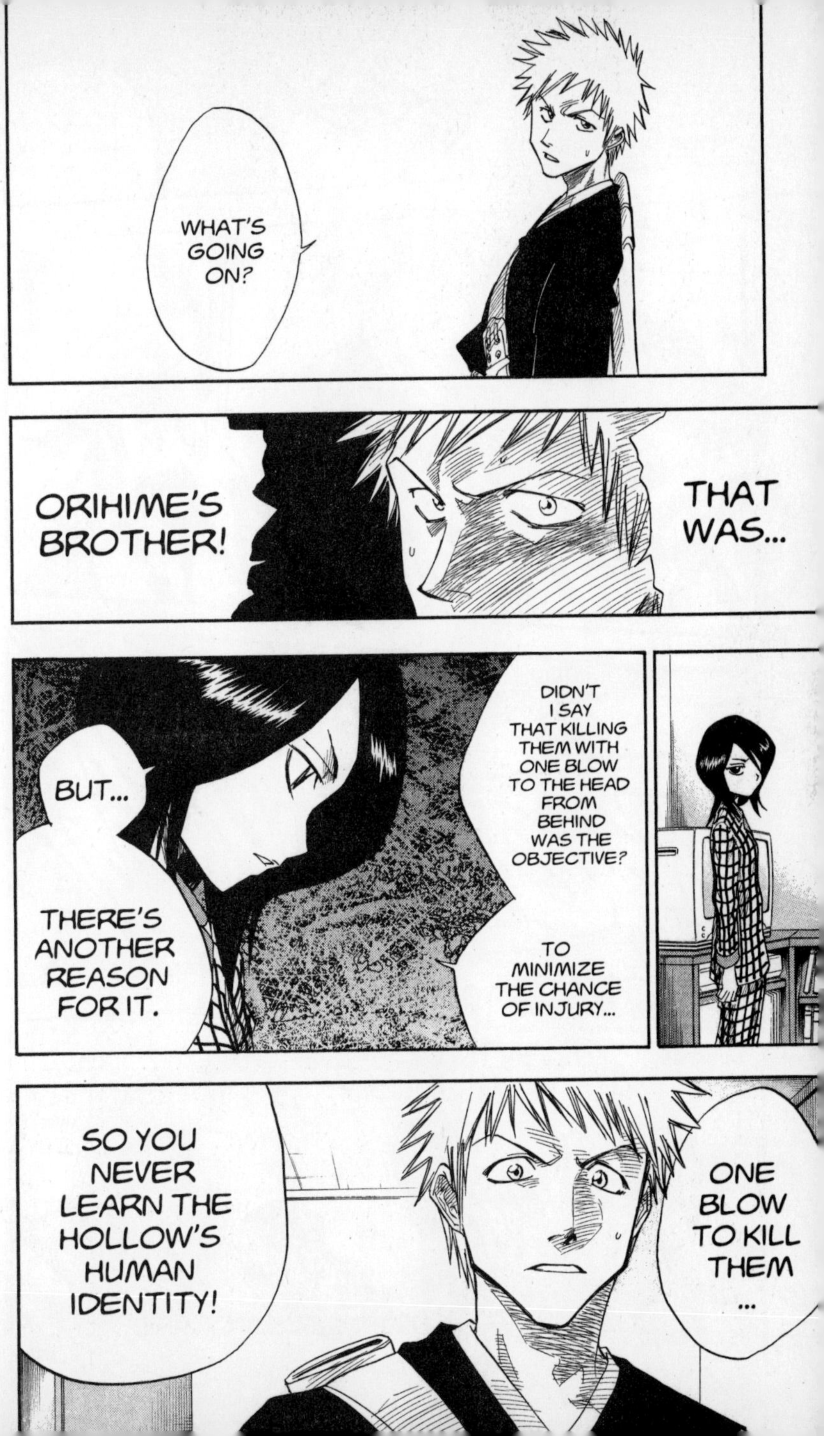
WHAT'S GOING ON?
THAT WAS...
ORIHIME'S BROTHER!
DIDN'T I SAY THAT KILLING THEM WITH ONE BLOW TO THE HEAD FROM BEHIND WAS THE OBJECTIVE?
TO MINIMIZE THE CHANCE OF INJURY...
BUT...
THERE'S ANOTHER REASON FOR IT.
ONE BLOW TO KILL THEM ...
SO YOU NEVER LEARN THE HOLLOW'S HUMAN IDENTITY!

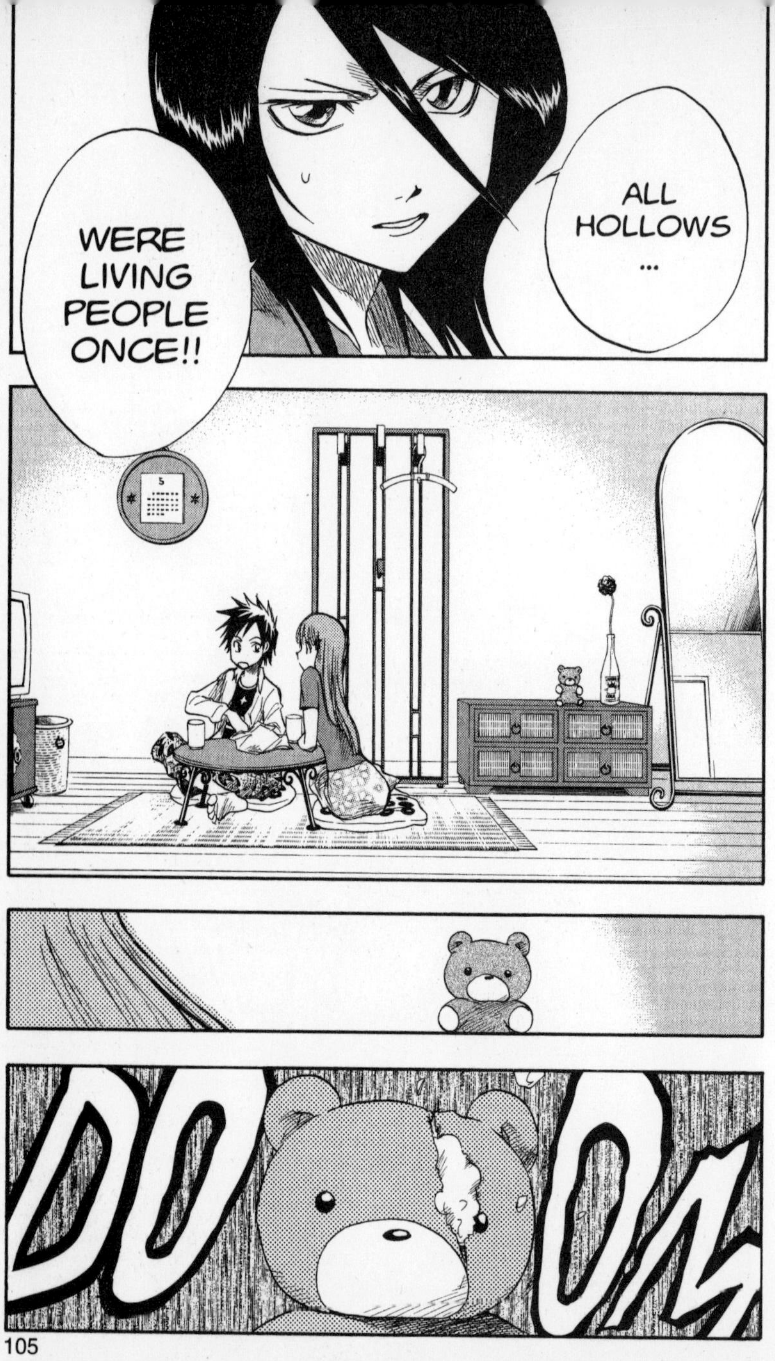
ALL HOLLOWS ...
WERE LIVING PEOPLE ONCE!!
DOOM

SMALL ITEMS SERIES 1

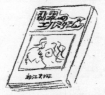

THE COMIC RUKIA IS READING IN EPISODE 3.

"THE JADE HERMITAGE"

WRITTEN BY: MARIE HATSUE

A STORY ABOUT
SOFT-MASOCHIST MARIANNE (OLDER SISTER)
AND HARD-GAY FRANCOISE (YOUNGER SISTER)
DOING ALL SORTS OF THINGS OVER
A JADE BOX GIVEN TO THEM BY THEIR MOTHER
(52-YEAR-OLD-WRESTLER).

SUPER SCARY STUFF

4. WHY DO YOU EAT IT?

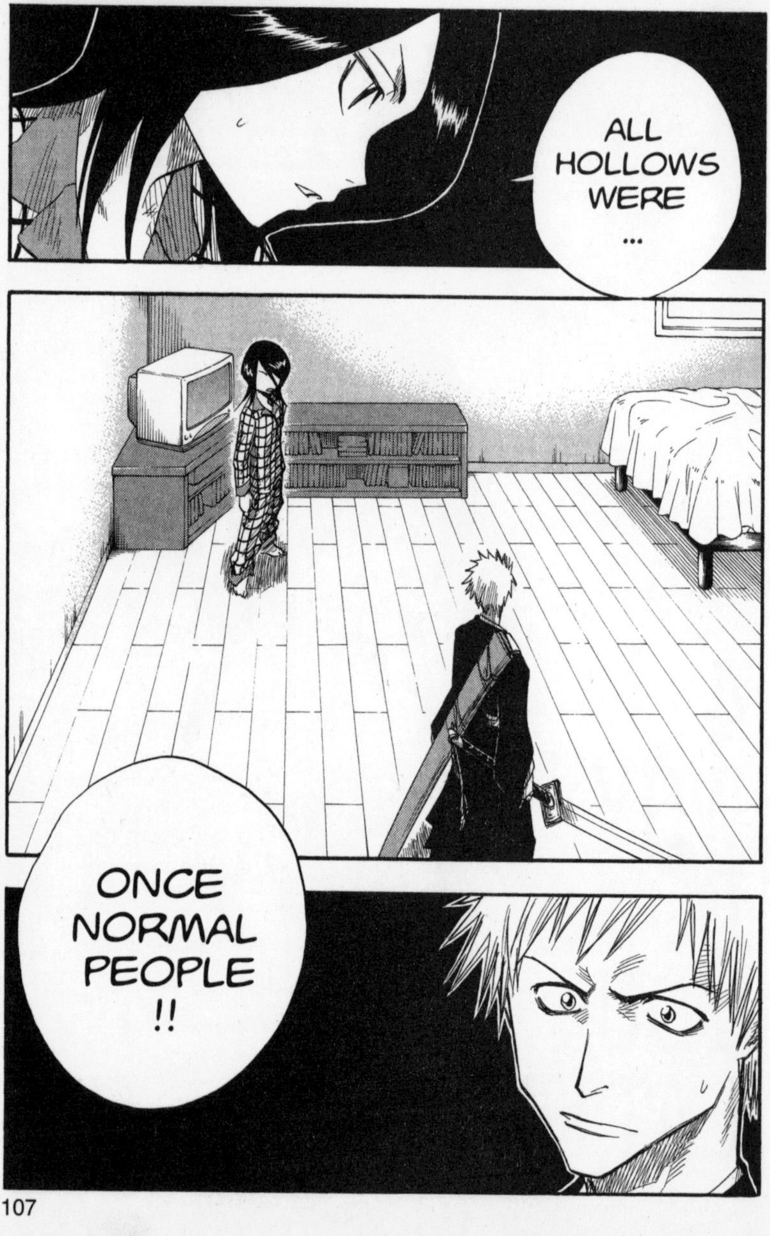
ALL HOLLOWS WERE ...
ONCE NORMAL PEOPLE !!

BLEACH

ブリーチ

4. WHY DO YOU EAT IT?

BIG MARBLE

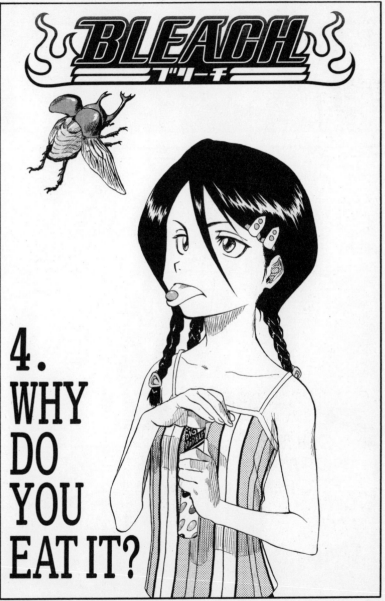

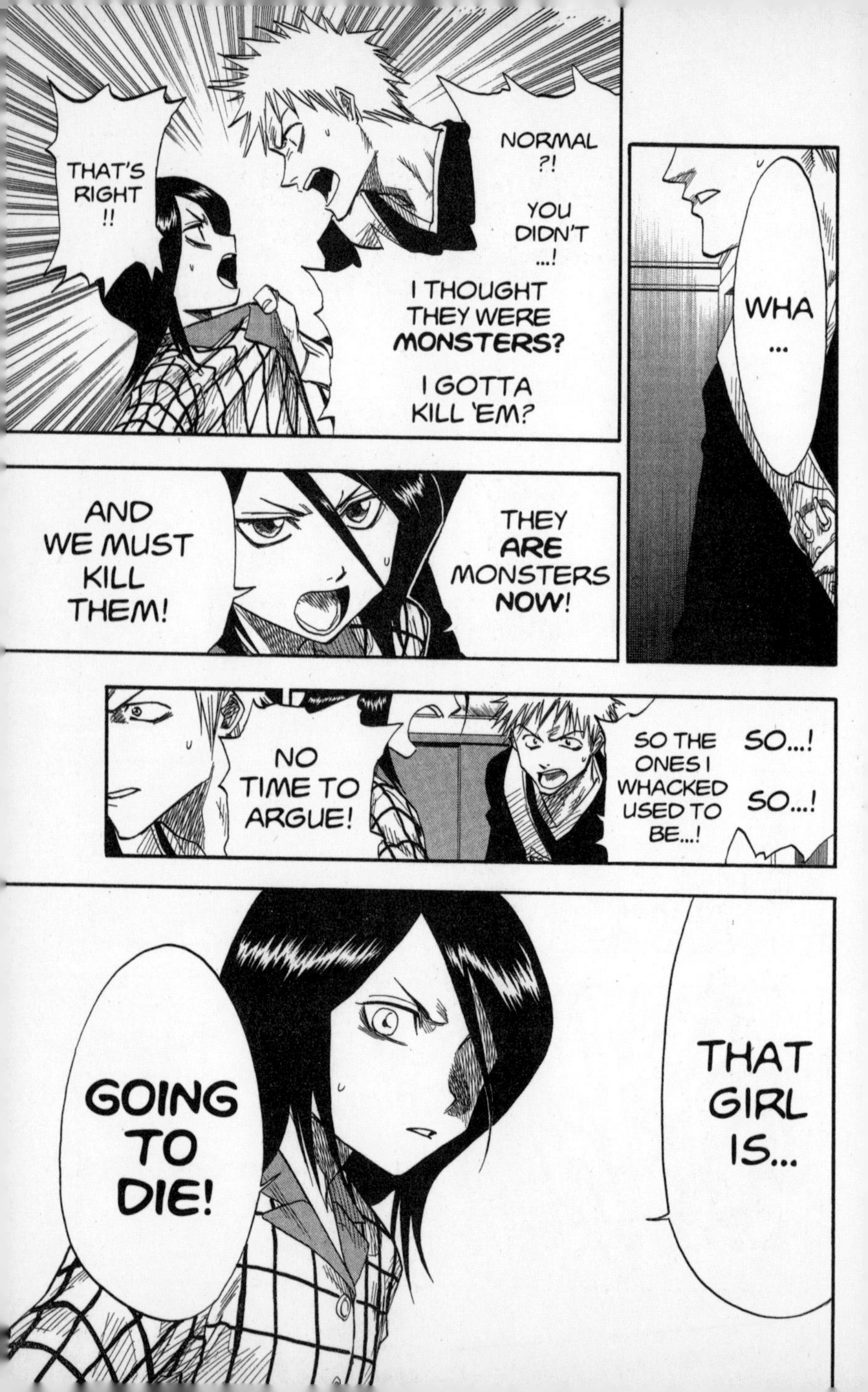
WHA...
NORMAL?!
YOU DIDN'T ...!
I THOUGHT THEY WERE **MONSTERS?**
I GOTTA KILL 'EM?
THAT'S RIGHT!!
THEY **ARE** MONSTERS **NOW!**
AND WE MUST KILL THEM!
SO...!
SO...!
SO THE ONES I WHACKED USED TO BE...!
NO TIME TO ARGUE!
THAT GIRL IS...
GOING TO DIE!

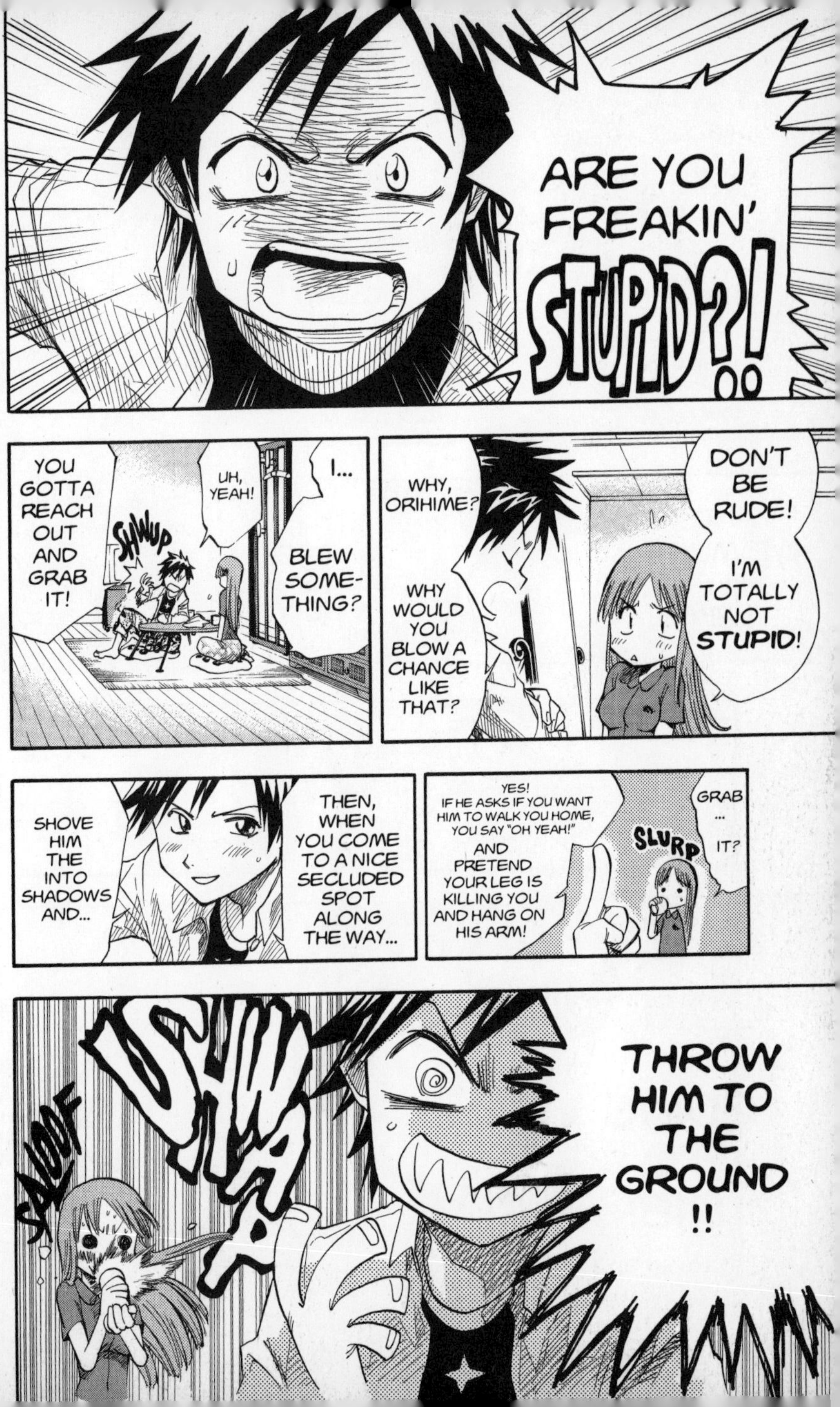
ARE YOU FREAKIN' STUPID?!
DON'T BE RUDE!
I'M TOTALLY NOT STUPID!
WHY, ORIHIME?
WHY WOULD YOU BLOW A CHANCE LIKE THAT?
I...
BLEW SOMETHING?
UH, YEAH!
YOU GOTTA REACH OUT AND GRAB IT!
SHWUP
GRAB ... IT?
SLURP
YES! IF HE ASKS IF YOU WANT HIM TO WALK YOU HOME, YOU SAY "OH YEAH!"
AND PRETEND YOUR LEG IS KILLING YOU AND HANG ON HIS ARM!
THEN, WHEN YOU COME TO A NICE SECLUDED SPOT ALONG THE WAY...
SHOVE HIM THE INTO SHADOWS AND...
THROW HIM TO THE GROUND !!

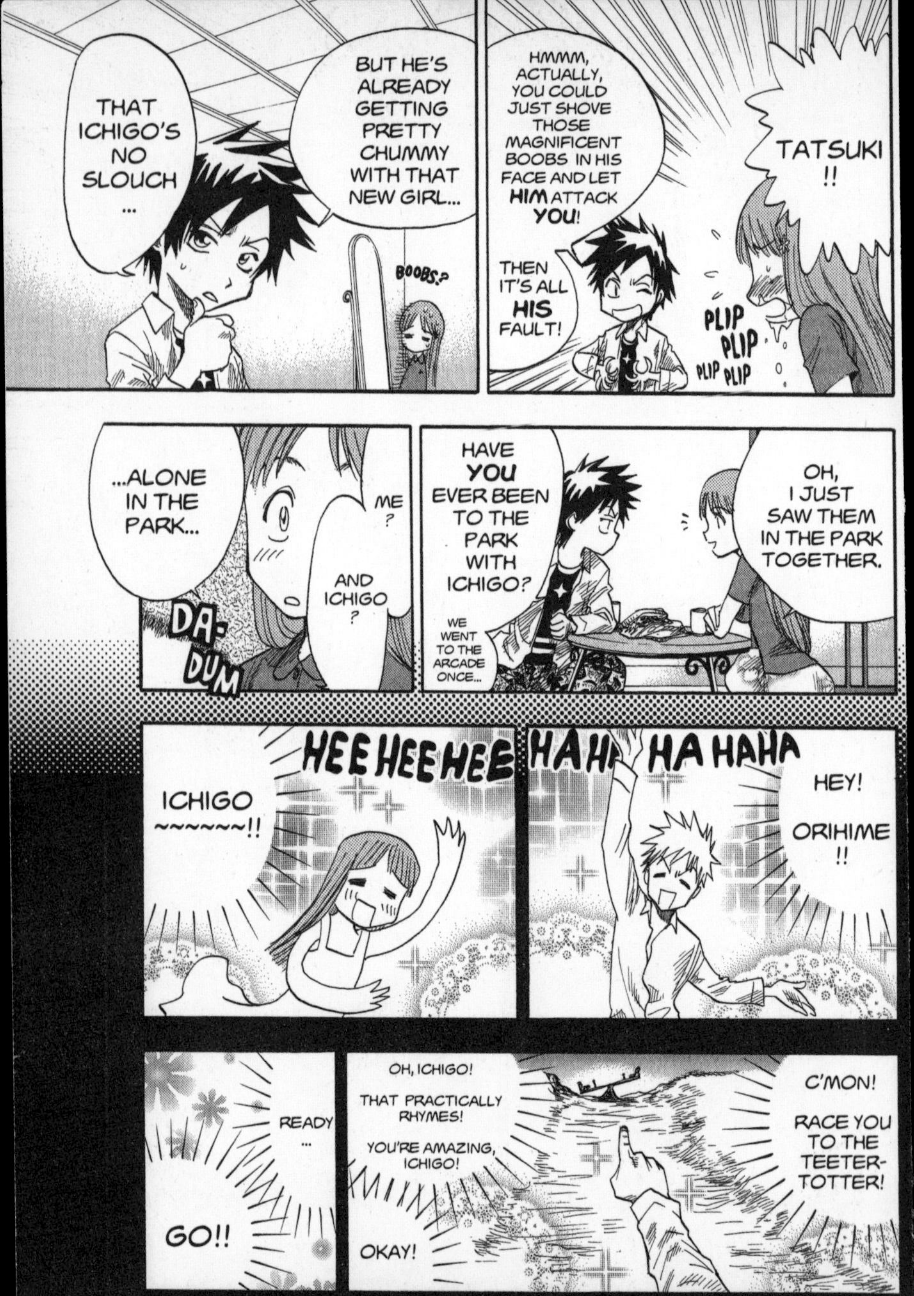
HMMM, ACTUALLY, YOU COULD JUST SHOVE THOSE MAGNIFICENT BOOBS IN HIS FACE AND LET HIM ATTACK YOU!
TATSUKI!!
THEN IT'S ALL HIS FAULT!
PLIP PLIP PLIP PLIP
BUT HE'S ALREADY GETTING PRETTY CHUMMY WITH THAT NEW GIRL...
THAT ICHIGO'S NO SLOUCH...
BOOBS?
OH, I JUST SAW THEM IN THE PARK TOGETHER.
HAVE YOU EVER BEEN TO THE PARK WITH ICHIGO?
WE WENT TO THE ARCADE ONCE...
ME? AND ICHIGO?
...ALONE IN THE PARK...
DA-DUM
HAHA HA HAHA
HEY! ORIHIME!!
HEE HEE HEE
ICHIGO~~~~~~~!!
C'MON! RACE YOU TO THE TEETER-TOTTER!
OH, ICHIGO! THAT PRACTICALLY RHYMES! YOU'RE AMAZING, ICHIGO!
OKAY!
READY...
GO!!

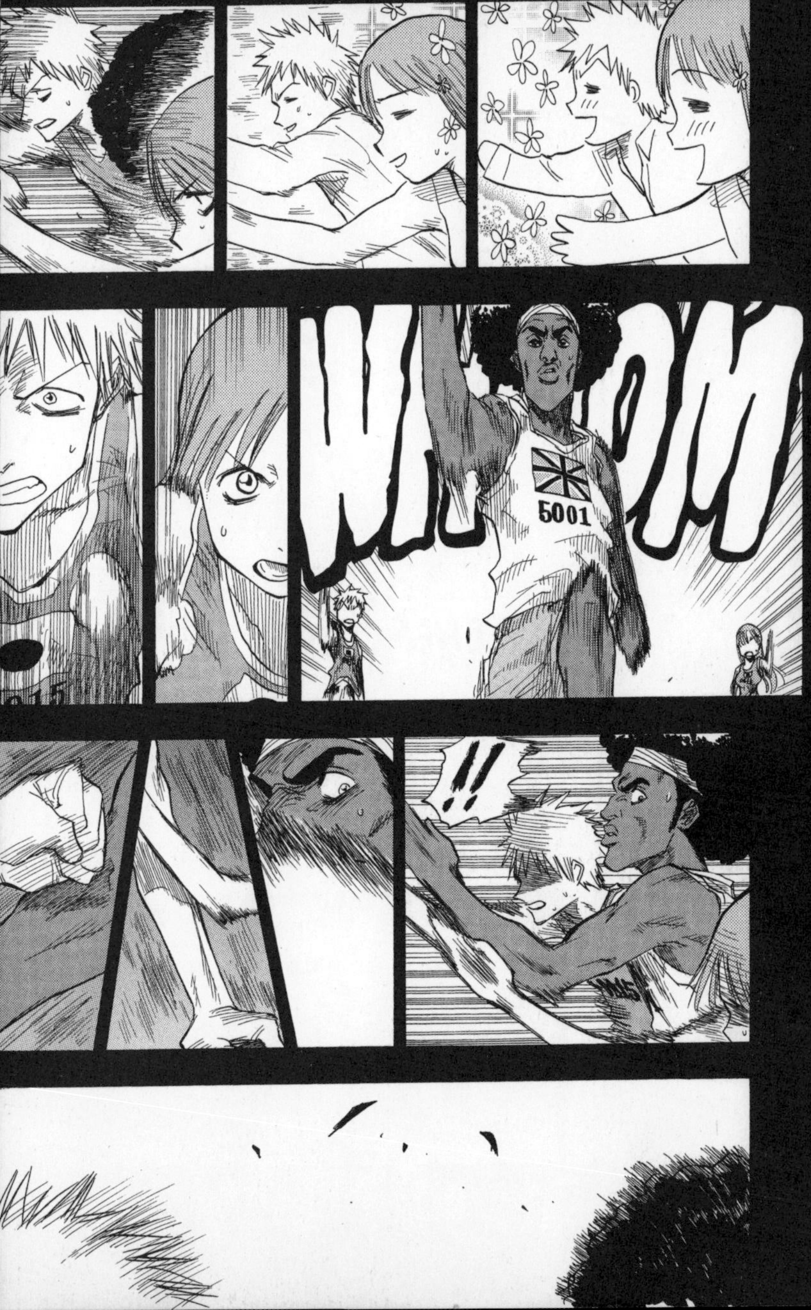
5001
!!

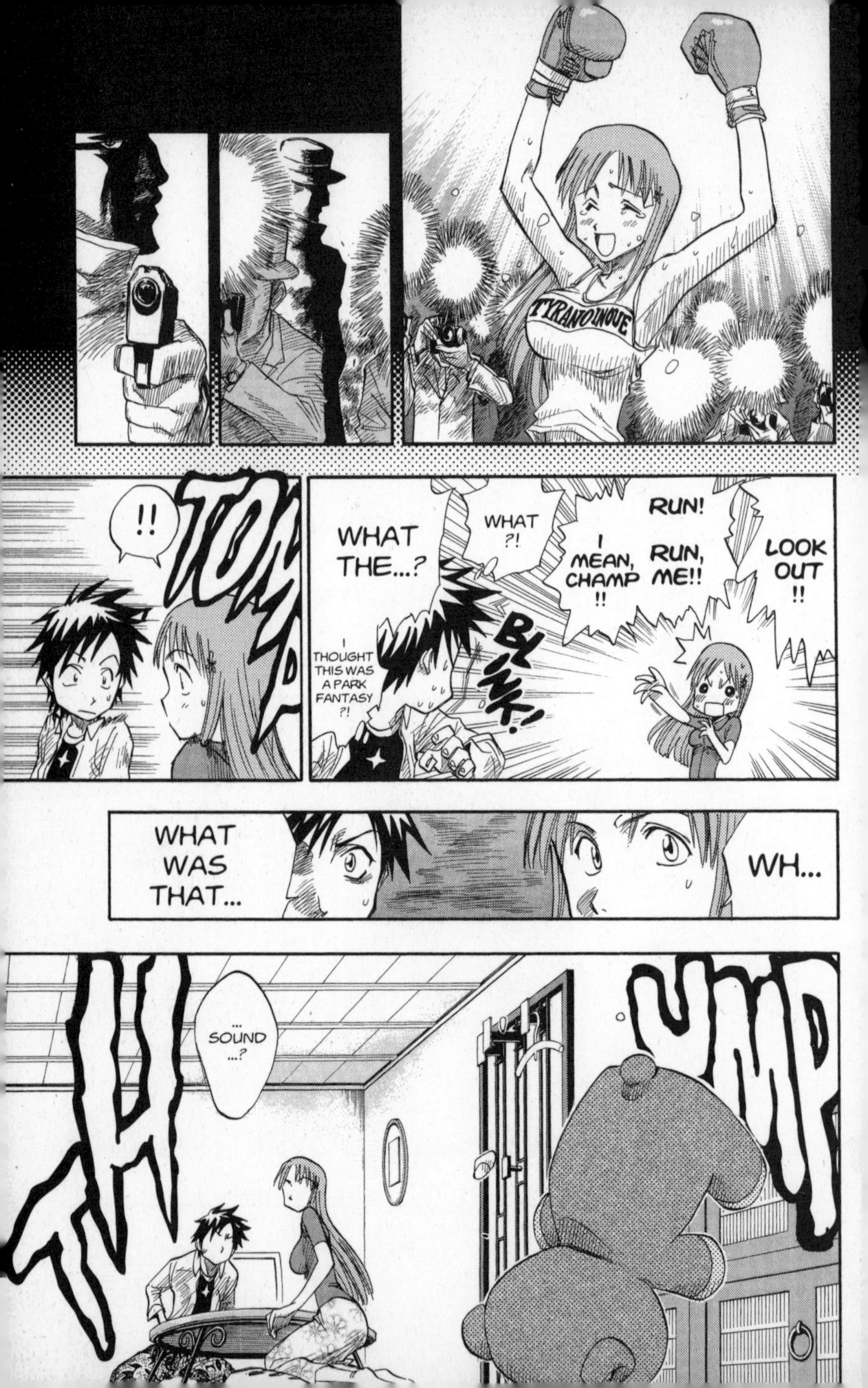
TYRANOINQUE
LOOK OUT !!
RUN!
RUN, ME!!
I MEAN, CHAMP !!
WHAT ?!
WHAT THE...?
BLINK!
I THOUGHT THIS WAS A PARK FANTASY ?!
TOMP
!!
WH...
WHAT WAS THAT...
THUMP
... SOUND ...?

READ THIS WAY

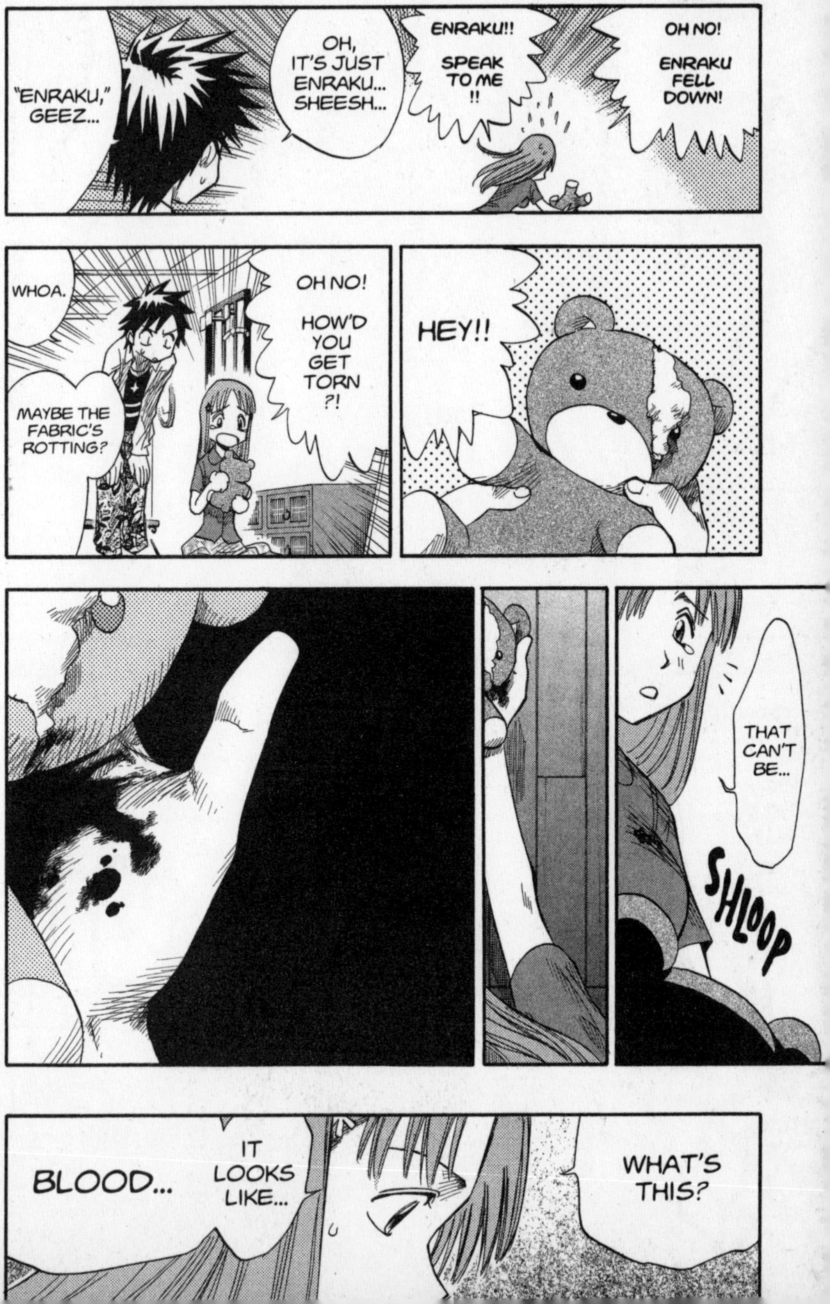
OH NO! ENRAKU FELL DOWN!
ENRAKU!! SPEAK TO ME !!
OH, IT'S JUST ENRAKU... SHEESH...
"ENRAKU," GEEZ...
HEY!!
OH NO! HOW'D YOU GET TORN ?!
WHOA.
MAYBE THE FABRIC'S ROTTING?
THAT CAN'T BE...
SHLOOP
WHAT'S THIS?
IT LOOKS LIKE...
BLOOD...

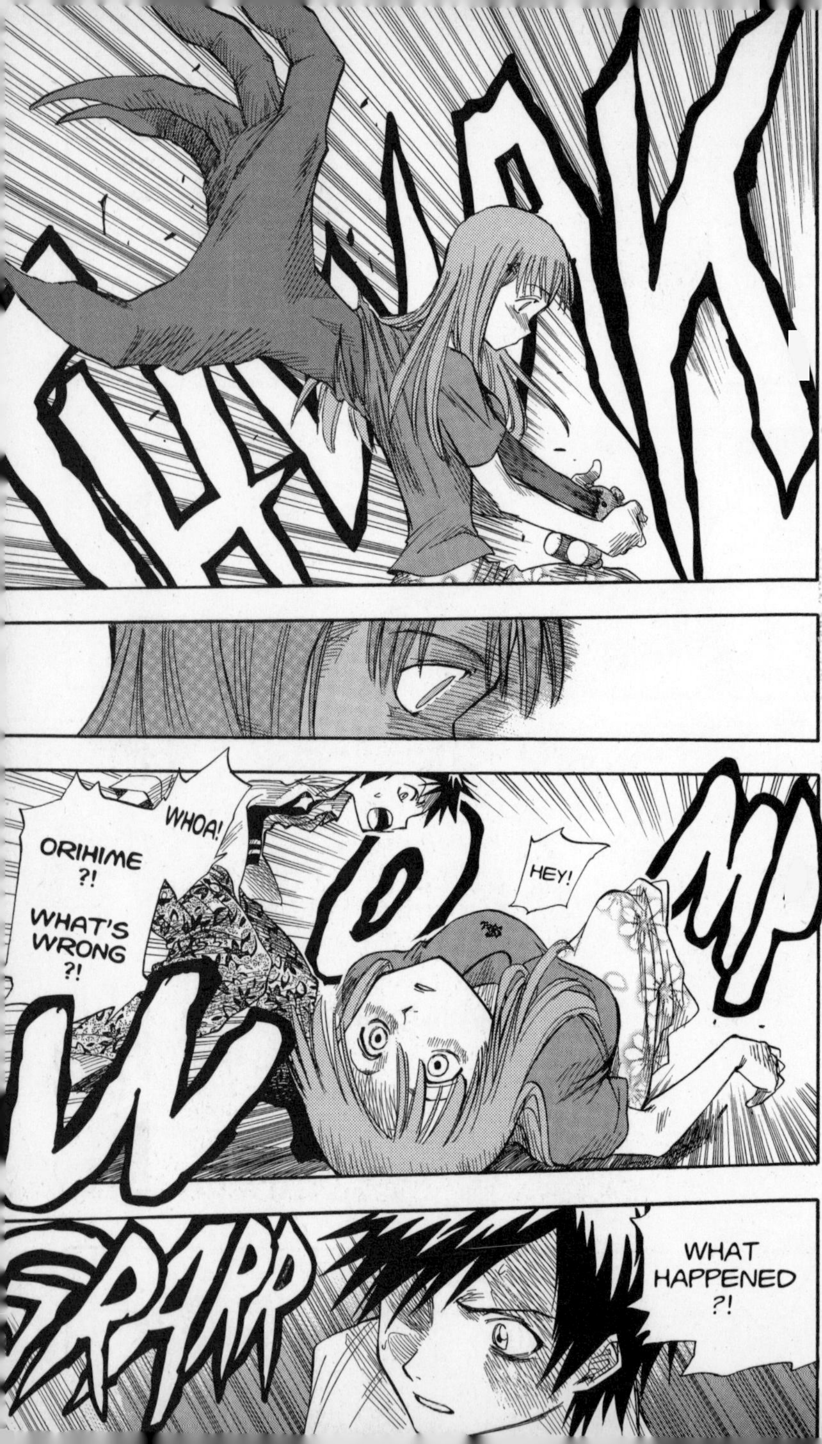
HEY!
WHOA!
ORIHIME ?!
WHAT'S WRONG ?!
WHAT HAPPENED ?!

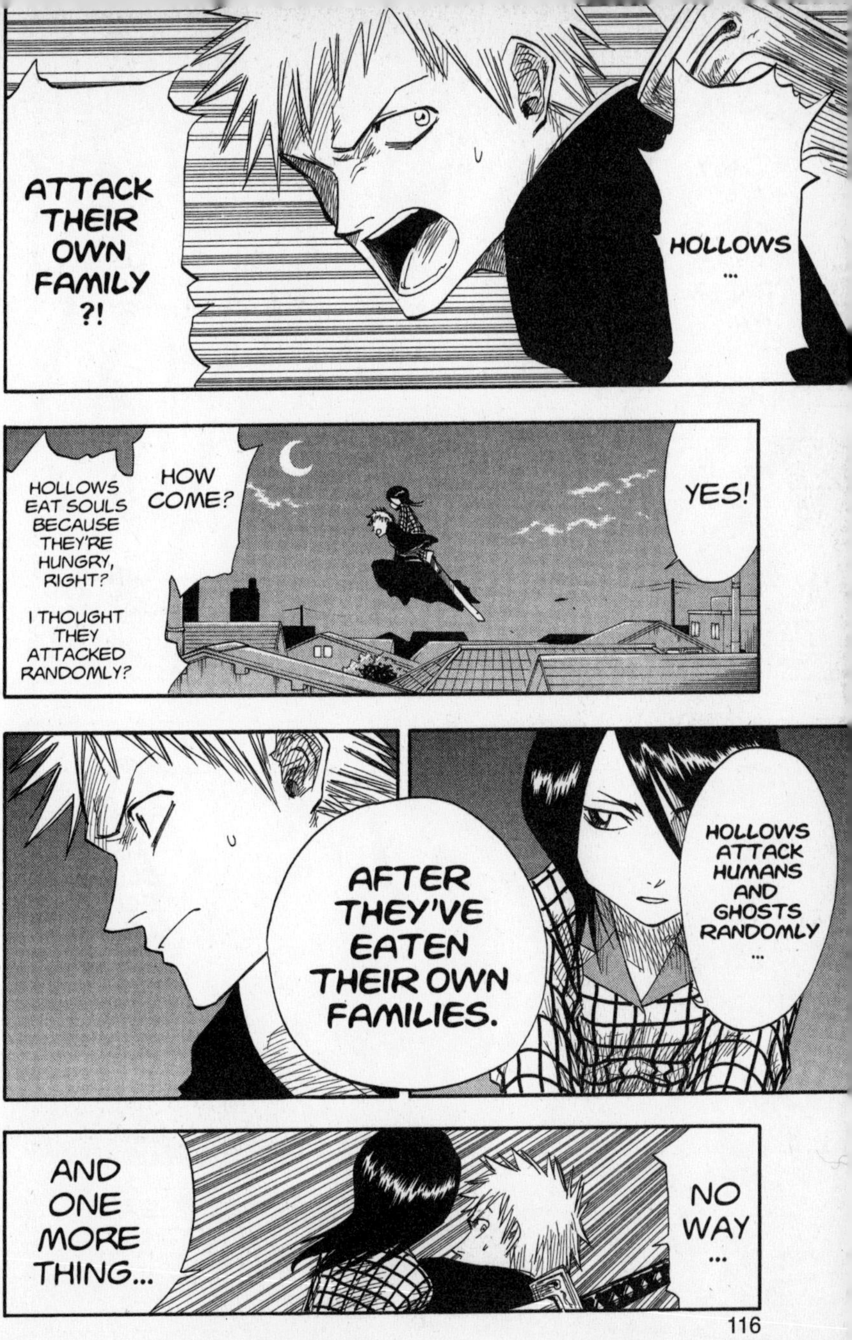
HOLLOWS ...
ATTACK THEIR OWN FAMILY ?!
YES!
HOW COME?
HOLLOWS EAT SOULS BECAUSE THEY'RE HUNGRY, RIGHT?
I THOUGHT THEY ATTACKED RANDOMLY?
HOLLOWS ATTACK HUMANS AND GHOSTS RANDOMLY ...
AFTER THEY'VE EATEN THEIR OWN FAMILIES.
NO WAY ...
AND ONE MORE THING...

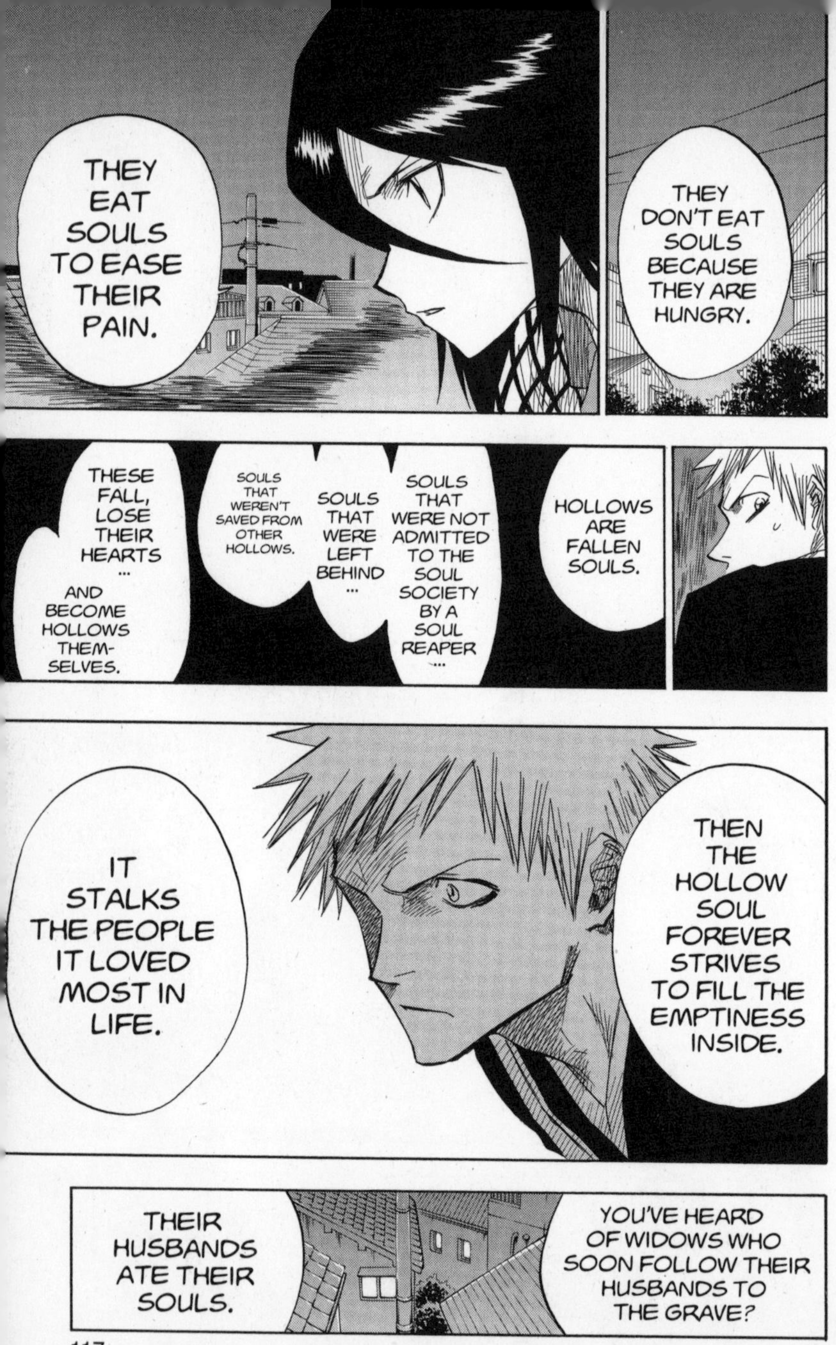
THEY DON'T EAT SOULS BECAUSE THEY ARE HUNGRY.
THEY EAT SOULS TO EASE THEIR PAIN.
HOLLOWS ARE FALLEN SOULS.
SOULS THAT WERE NOT ADMITTED TO THE SOUL SOCIETY BY A SOUL REAPER...
SOULS THAT WERE LEFT BEHIND...
SOULS THAT WEREN'T SAVED FROM OTHER HOLLOWS.
THESE FALL, LOSE THEIR HEARTS... AND BECOME HOLLOWS THEMSELVES.
THEN THE HOLLOW SOUL FOREVER STRIVES TO FILL THE EMPTINESS INSIDE.
IT STALKS THE PEOPLE IT LOVED MOST IN LIFE.
YOU'VE HEARD OF WIDOWS WHO SOON FOLLOW THEIR HUSBANDS TO THE GRAVE?
THEIR HUSBANDS ATE THEIR SOULS.

READ THIS WAY

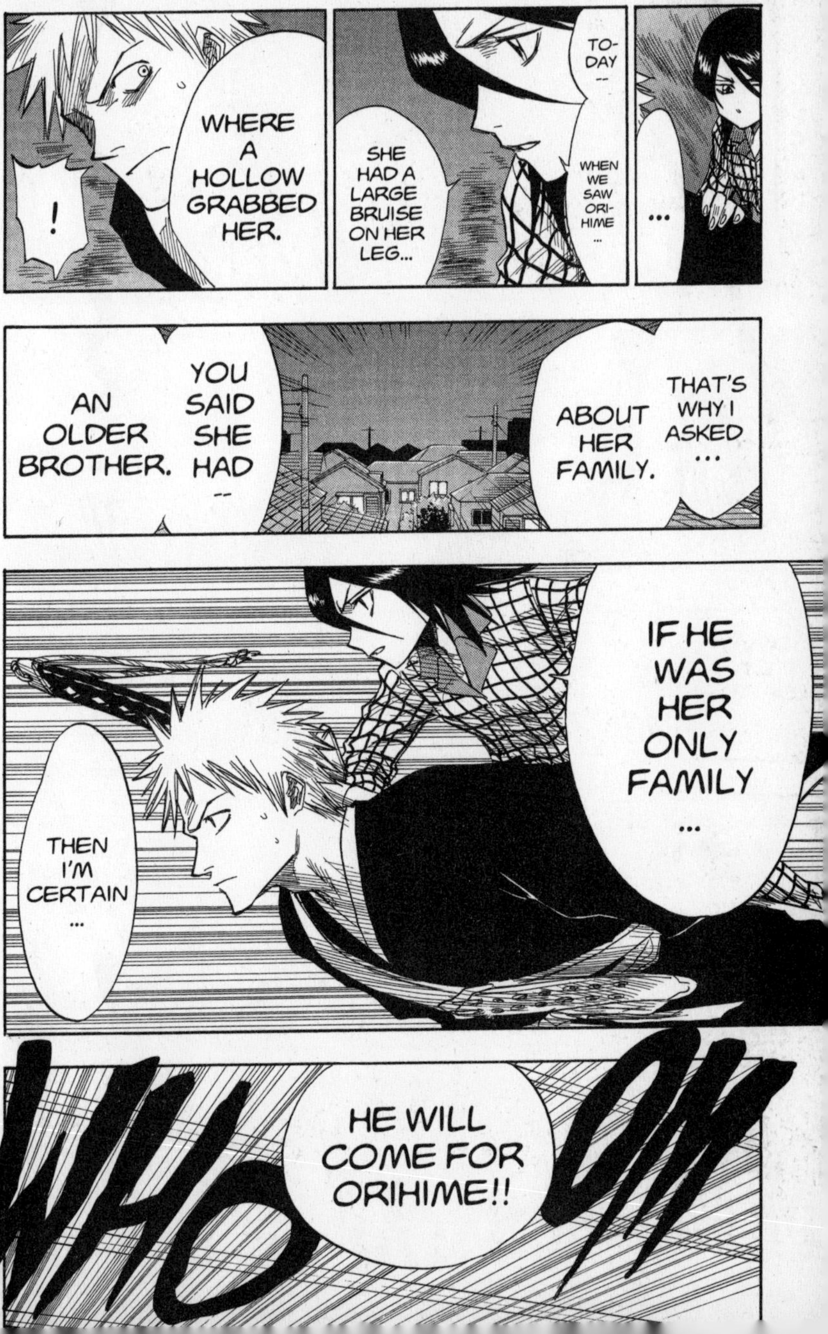
...
TO-DAY --
WHEN WE SAW ORI-HIME ...
SHE HAD A LARGE BRUISE ON HER LEG...
WHERE A HOLLOW GRABBED HER.
!
THAT'S WHY I ASKED ...
ABOUT HER FAMILY.
YOU SAID SHE HAD --
AN OLDER BROTHER.
IF HE WAS HER ONLY FAMILY ...
THEN I'M CERTAIN ...
HE WILL COME FOR ORIHIME!!
WHOOM

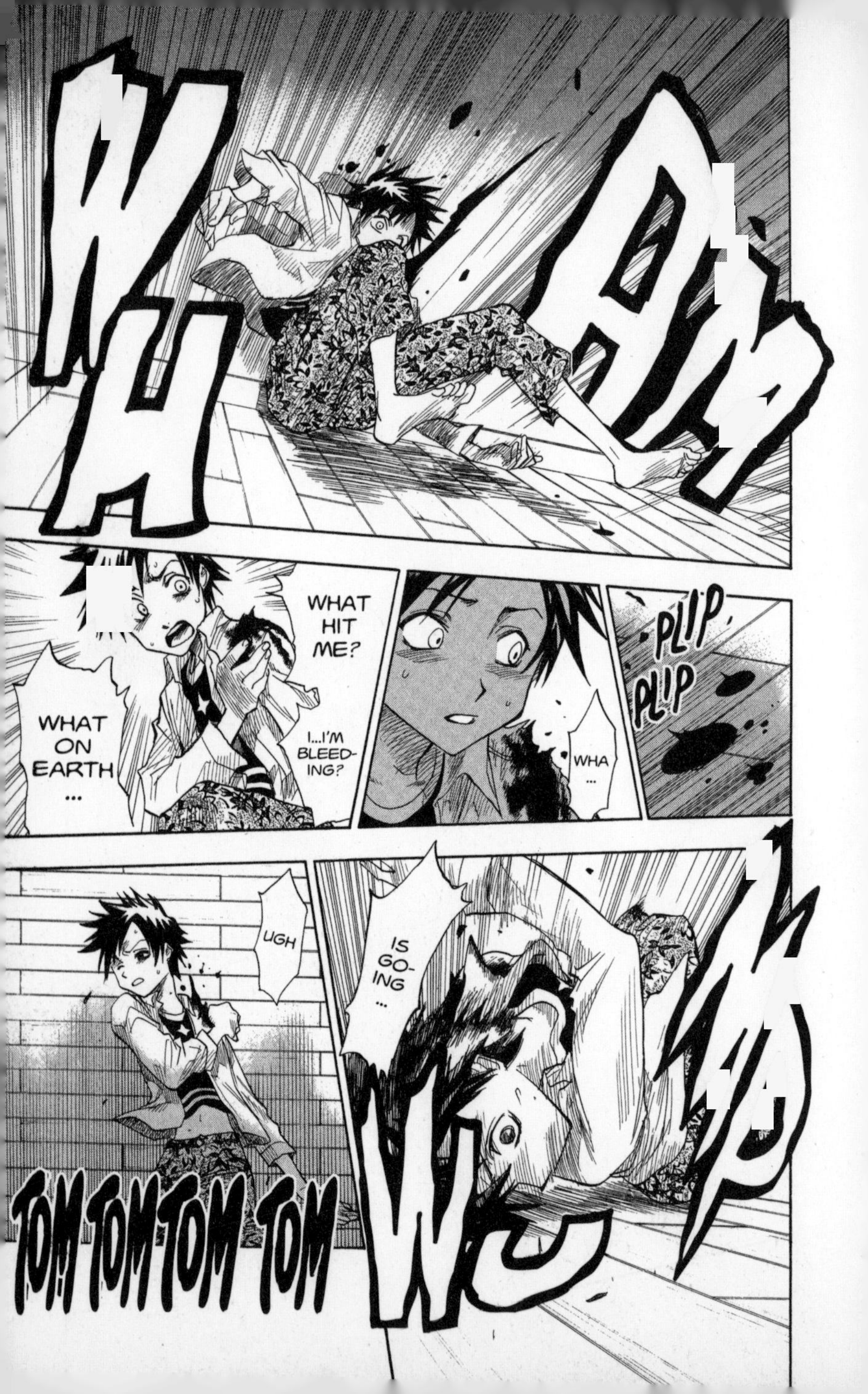
PLIP PLIP
WHA ...
WHAT HIT ME?
I...I'M BLEED-ING?
WHAT ON EARTH ...
IS GO-ING ...
UGH
TOM TOM TOM TOM

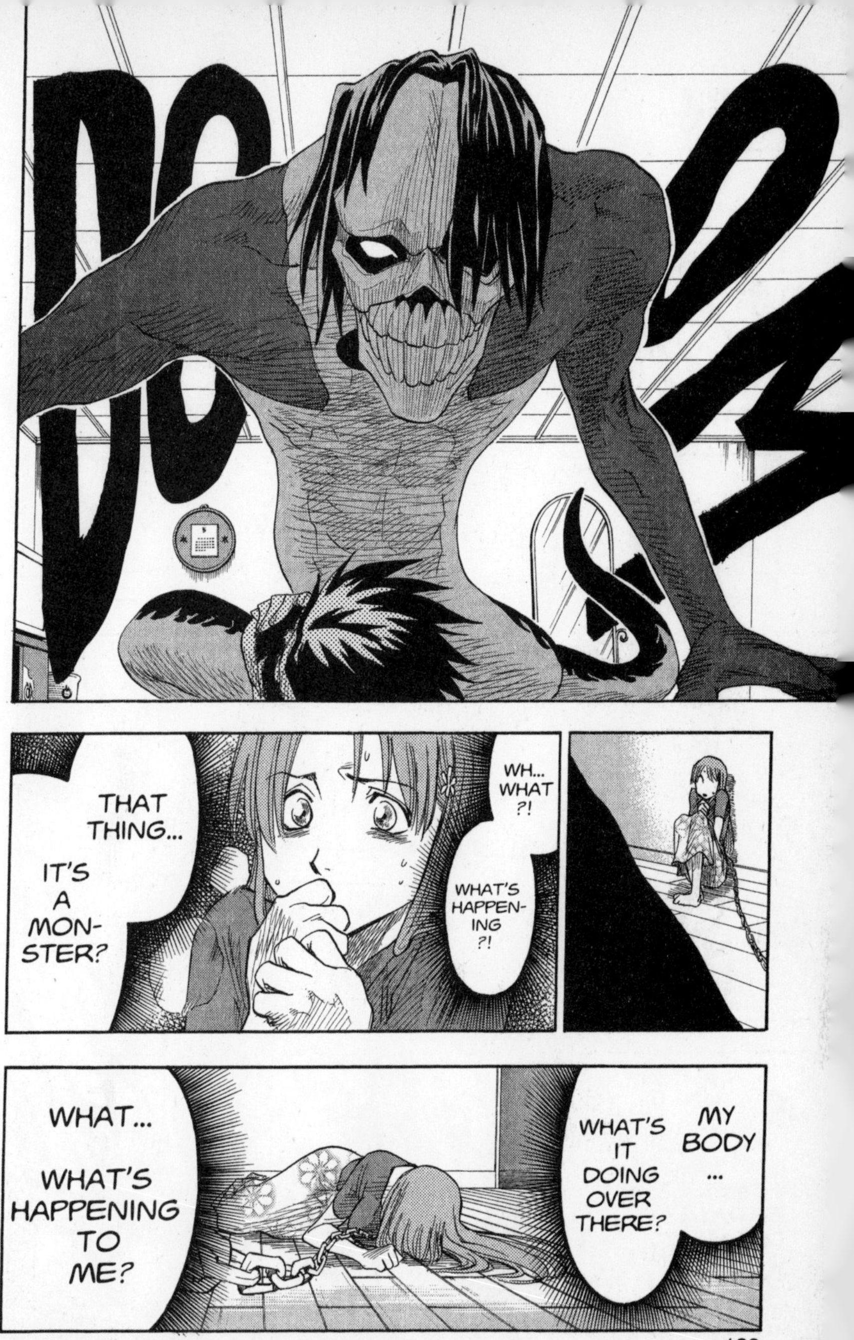
WH... WHAT ?!
WHAT'S HAPPEN- ING ?!
THAT THING...
IT'S A MON- STER?
MY BODY ...
WHAT'S IT DOING OVER THERE?
WHAT...
WHAT'S HAPPENING TO ME?

READ THIS WAY

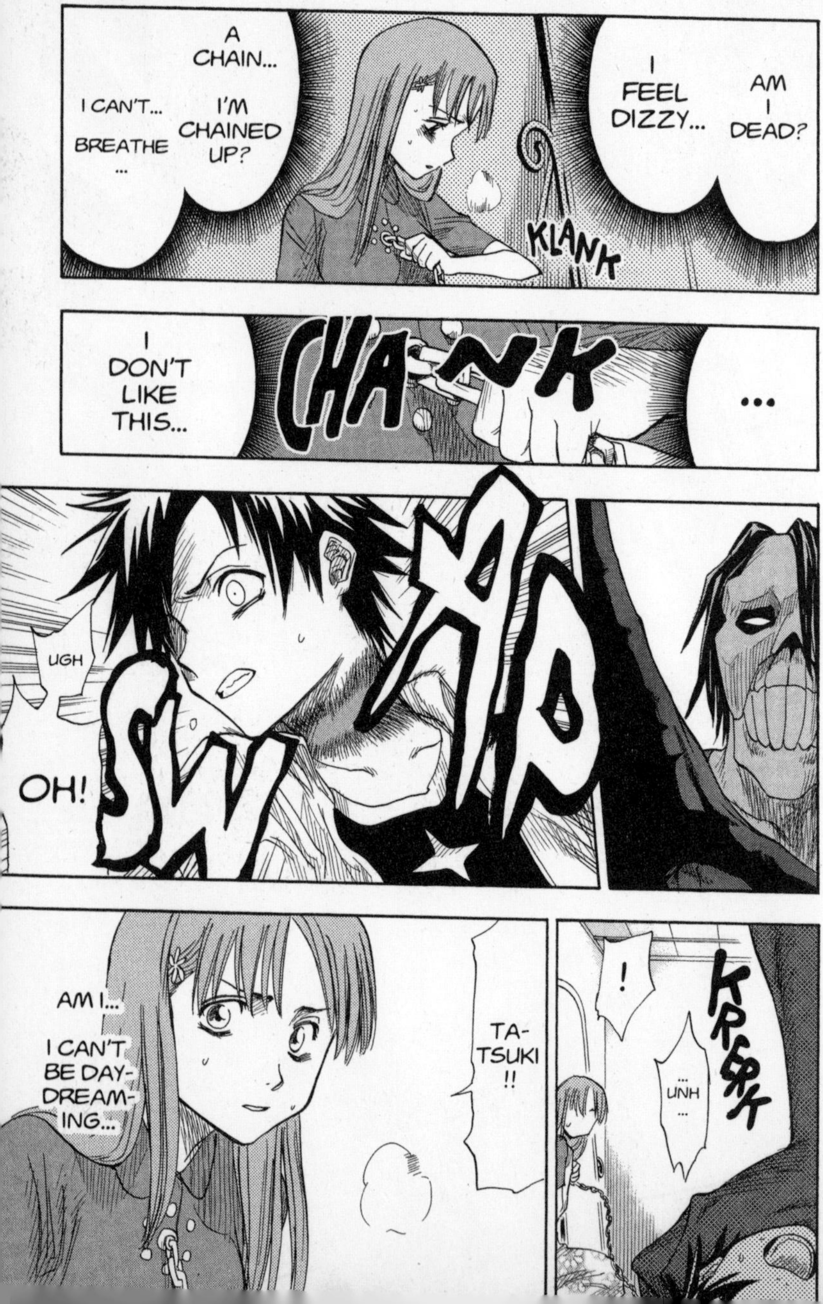
AM I DEAD?
I FEEL DIZZY...
KLANK
A CHAIN... I'M CHAINED UP?
I CAN'T... BREATHE...
...
CHANK
I DON'T LIKE THIS...
SWAP
UGH
OH!
KRRRK
!
...UNH...
TA-TSUKI!!
AM I...
I CAN'T BE DAY-DREAMING...

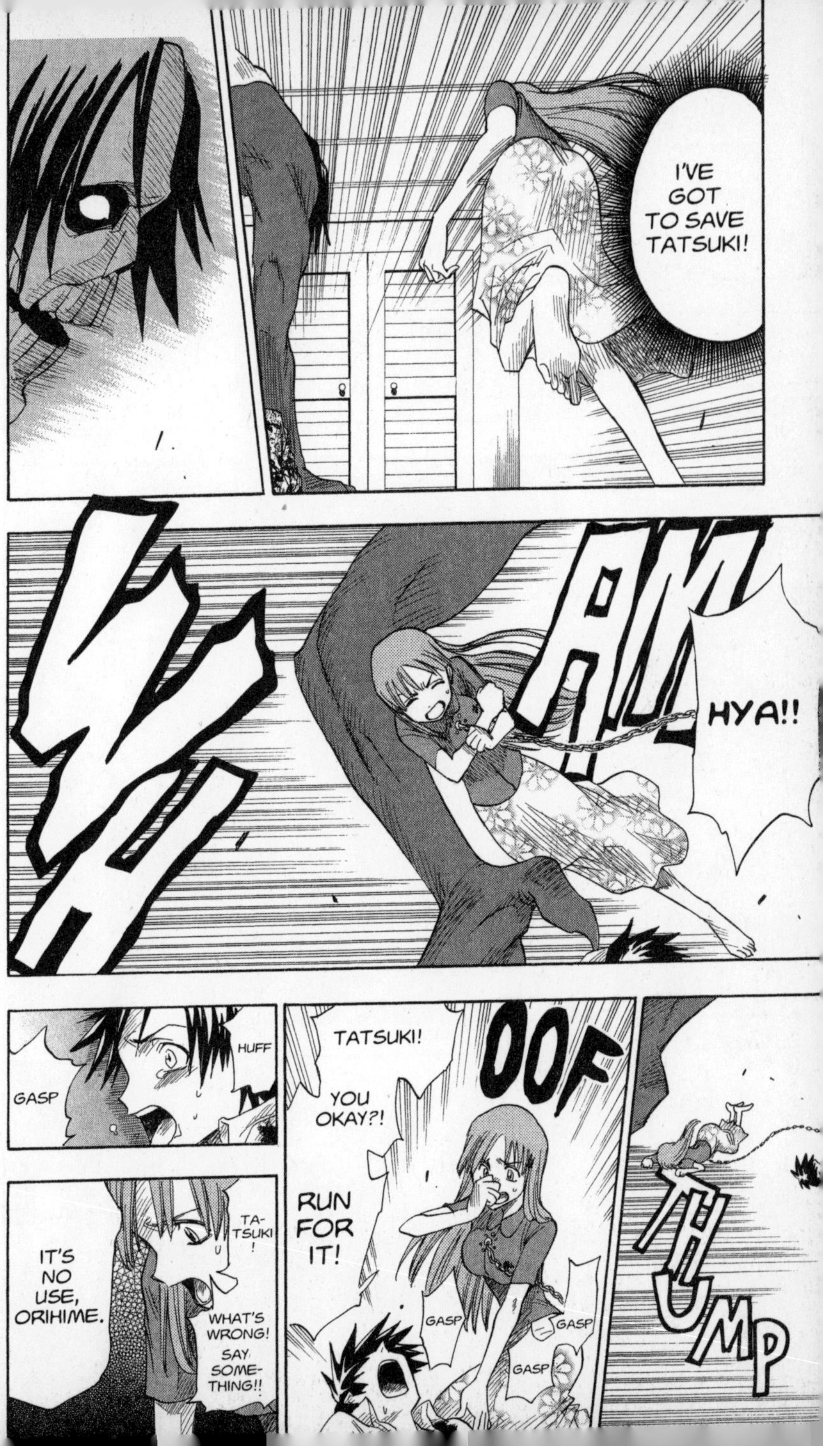
I'VE GOT TO SAVE TATSUKI!
HYA!!
THUMP
OOF
TATSUKI!
YOU OKAY?!
RUN FOR IT!
GASP
GASP
GASP
HUFF
GASP
TA-TSUKI!
WHAT'S WRONG! SAY SOME-THING!!
IT'S NO USE, ORIHIME.

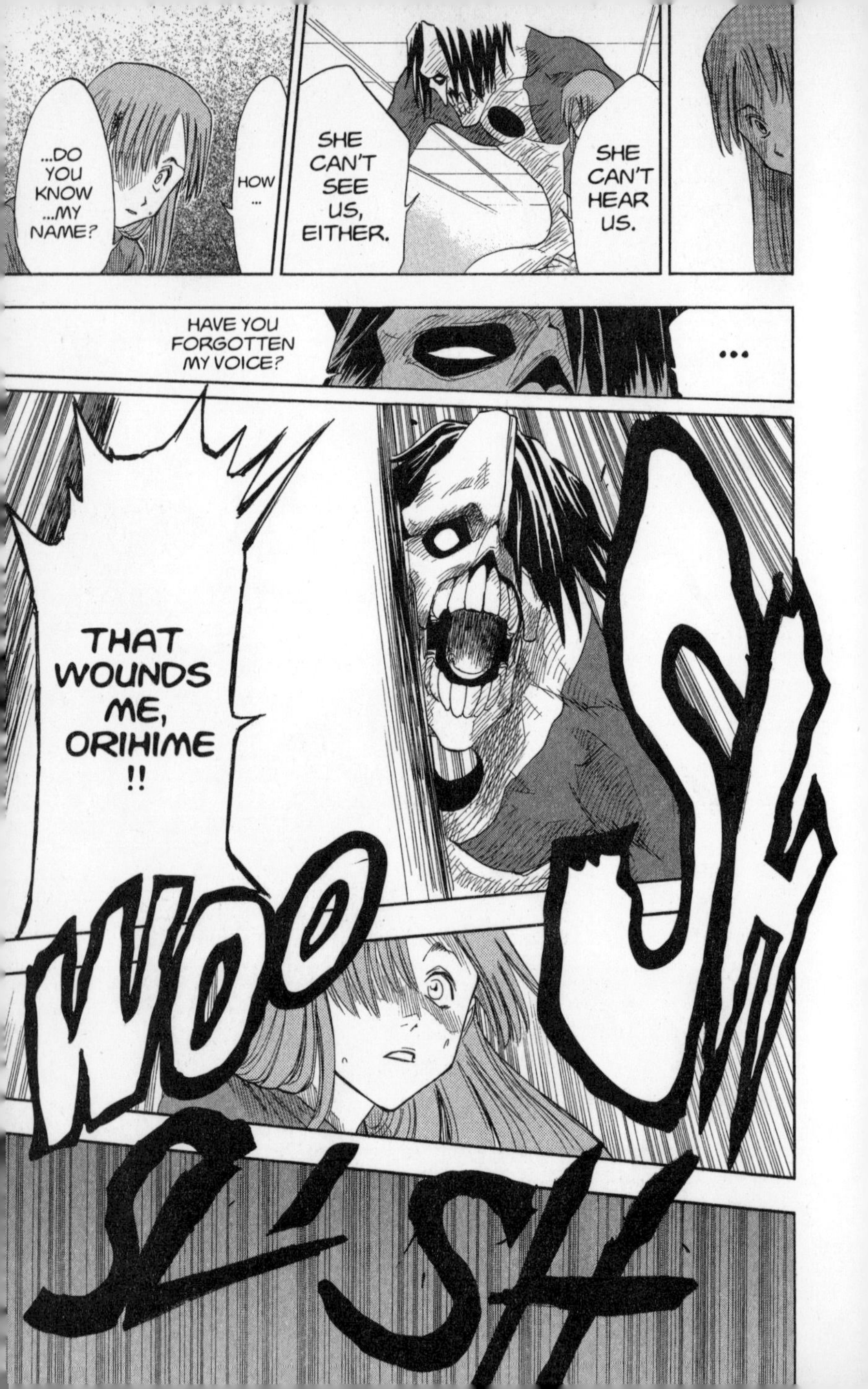
SHE CAN'T HEAR US.
SHE CAN'T SEE US, EITHER.
HOW ...
...DO YOU KNOW ...MY NAME?
...
HAVE YOU FORGOTTEN MY VOICE?
THAT WOUNDS ME, ORIHIME!!
WOOSH

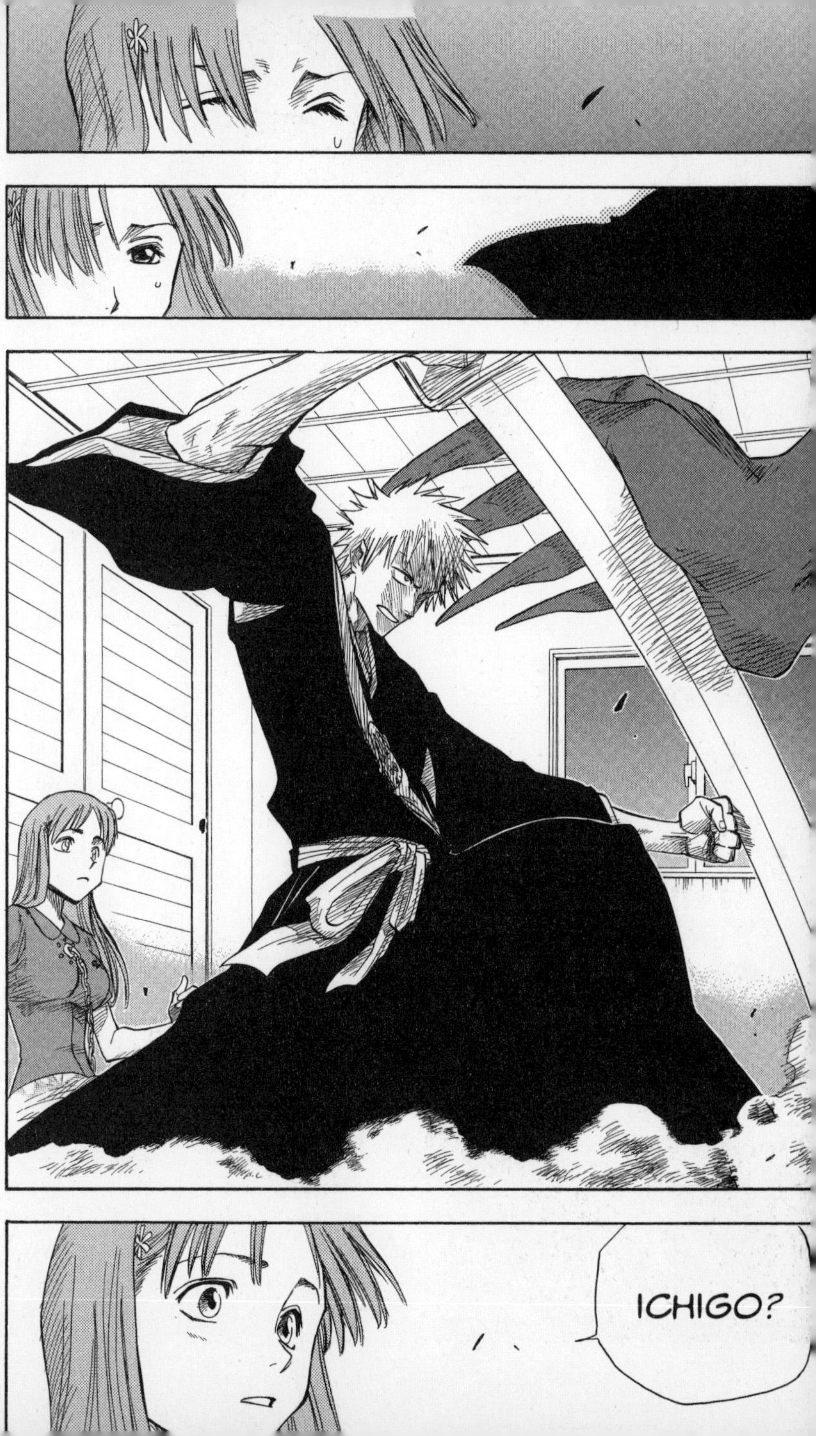
ICHIGO?

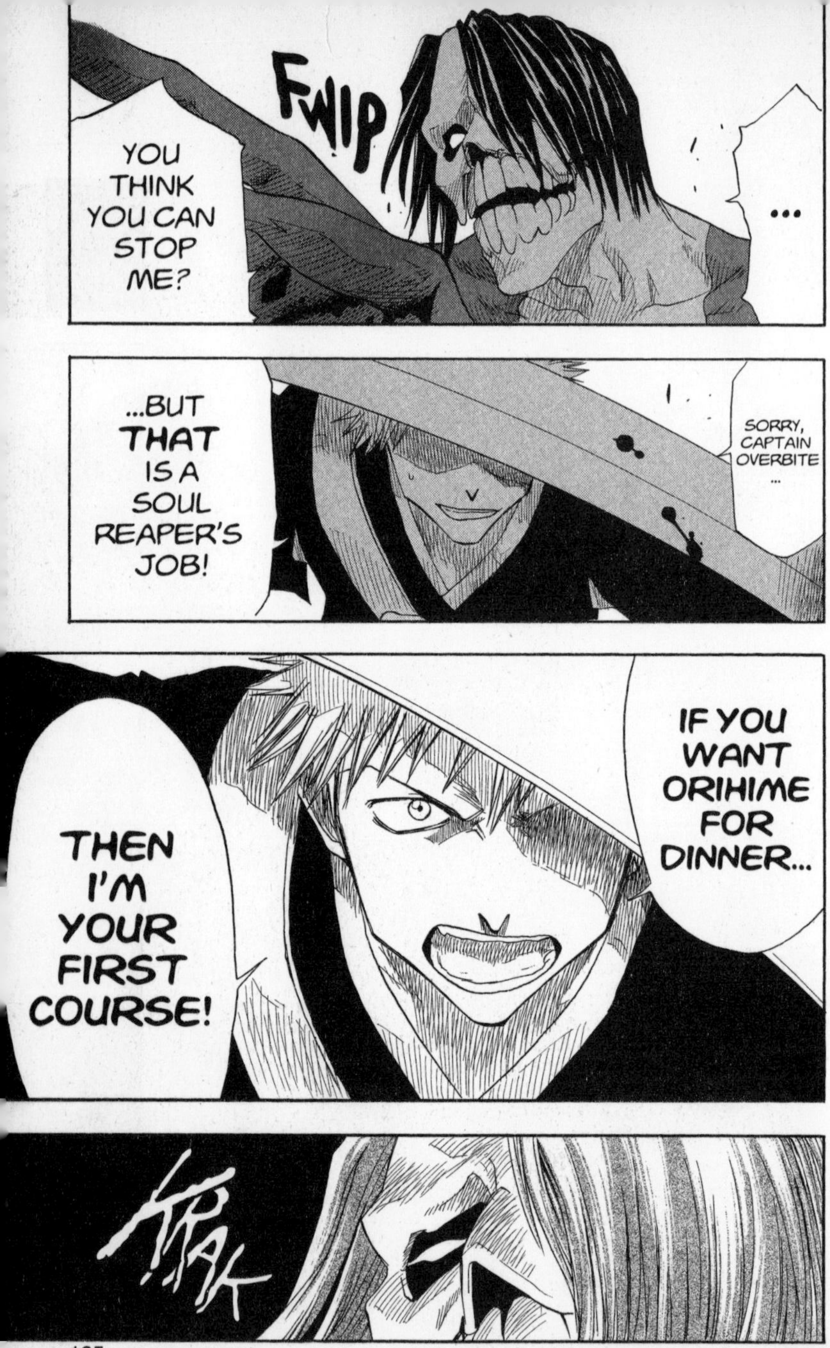
...
FWIP
YOU THINK YOU CAN STOP ME?
SORRY, CAPTAIN OVERBITE ...
...BUT **THAT** IS A SOUL REAPER'S JOB!
IF YOU WANT ORIHIME FOR DINNER...
THEN I'M YOUR FIRST COURSE!
KRAK

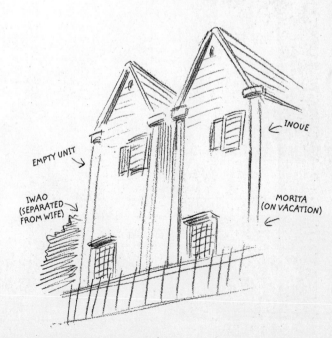

ORIHIME'S HOUSE IS AN APARTMENT.
THIS IS THE STREET SIDE.
APT. 202 IS THE INOUE RESIDENCE

INOUE

EMPTY UNIT

IWAO
(SEPARATED
FROM WIFE)

MORITA
(ON VACATION)

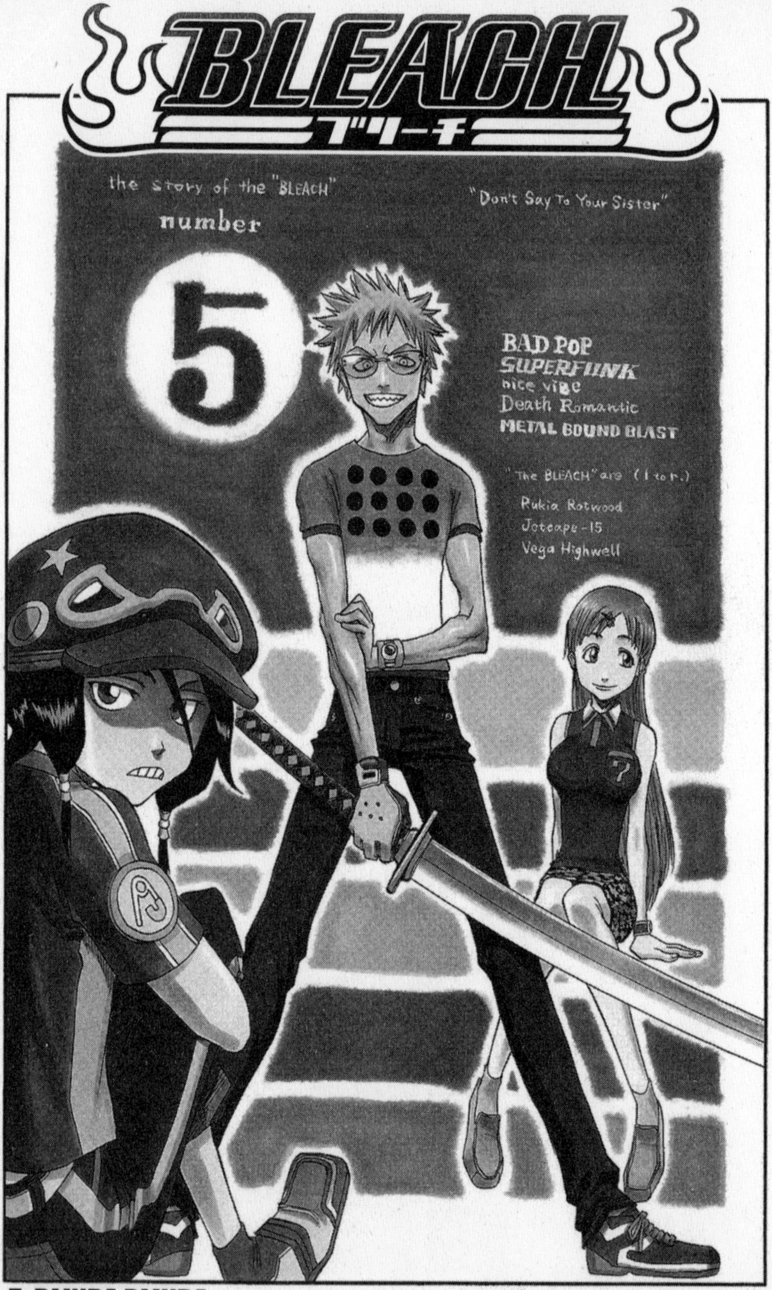
BLEACH
ブリーチ
the story of the "BLEACH"
number
5
"Don't Say To Your Sister"
BAD POP
SUPERFUNK
nice vibe
Death Romantic
METAL BOUND BLAST
"The BLEACH" are (l to r.)
Rukia Rotwood
Jotcape-15
Vega Highwell

5. BLINDA BLINDA

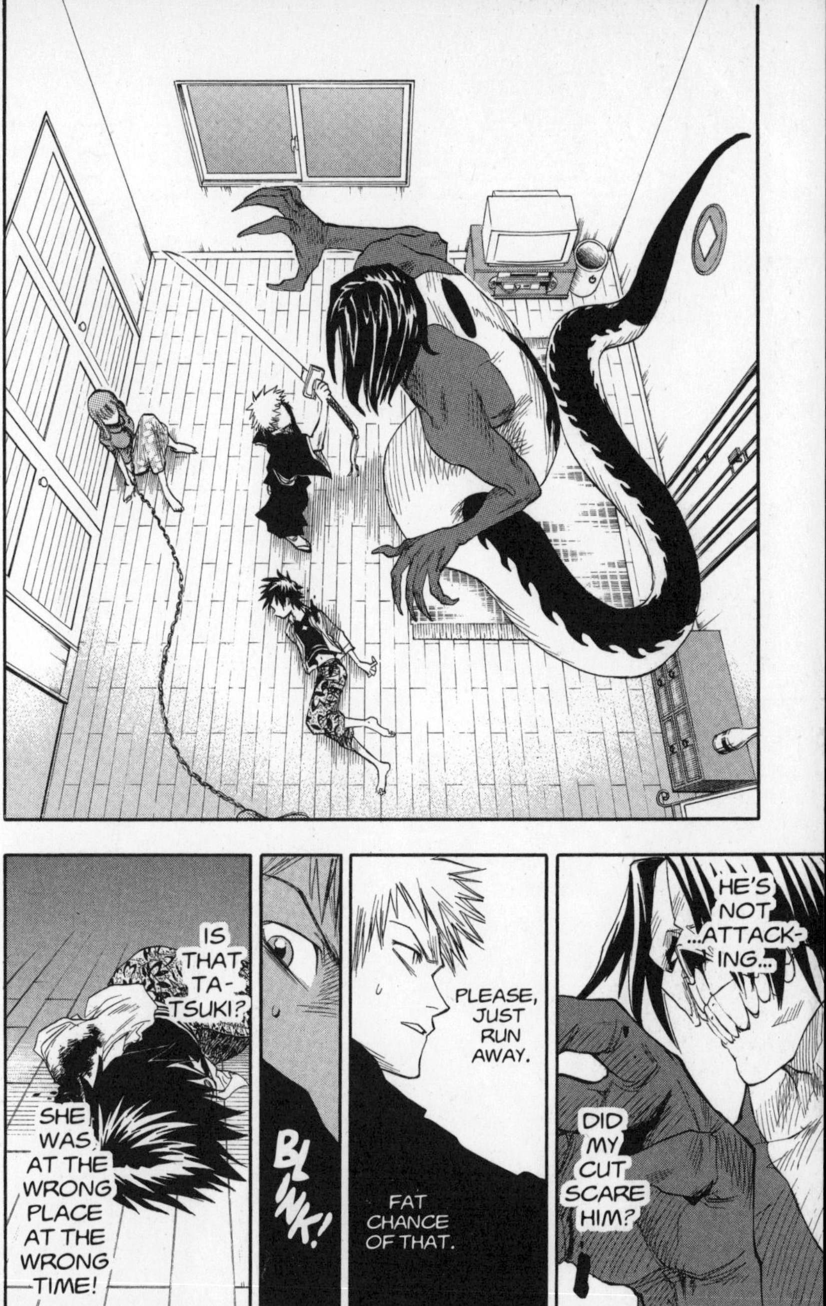
HE'S NOT ...ATTACKING...
DID MY CUT SCARE HIM?
PLEASE, JUST RUN AWAY.
FAT CHANCE OF THAT.
BLINK!
IS THAT TATSUKI?
SHE WAS AT THE WRONG PLACE AT THE WRONG TIME!

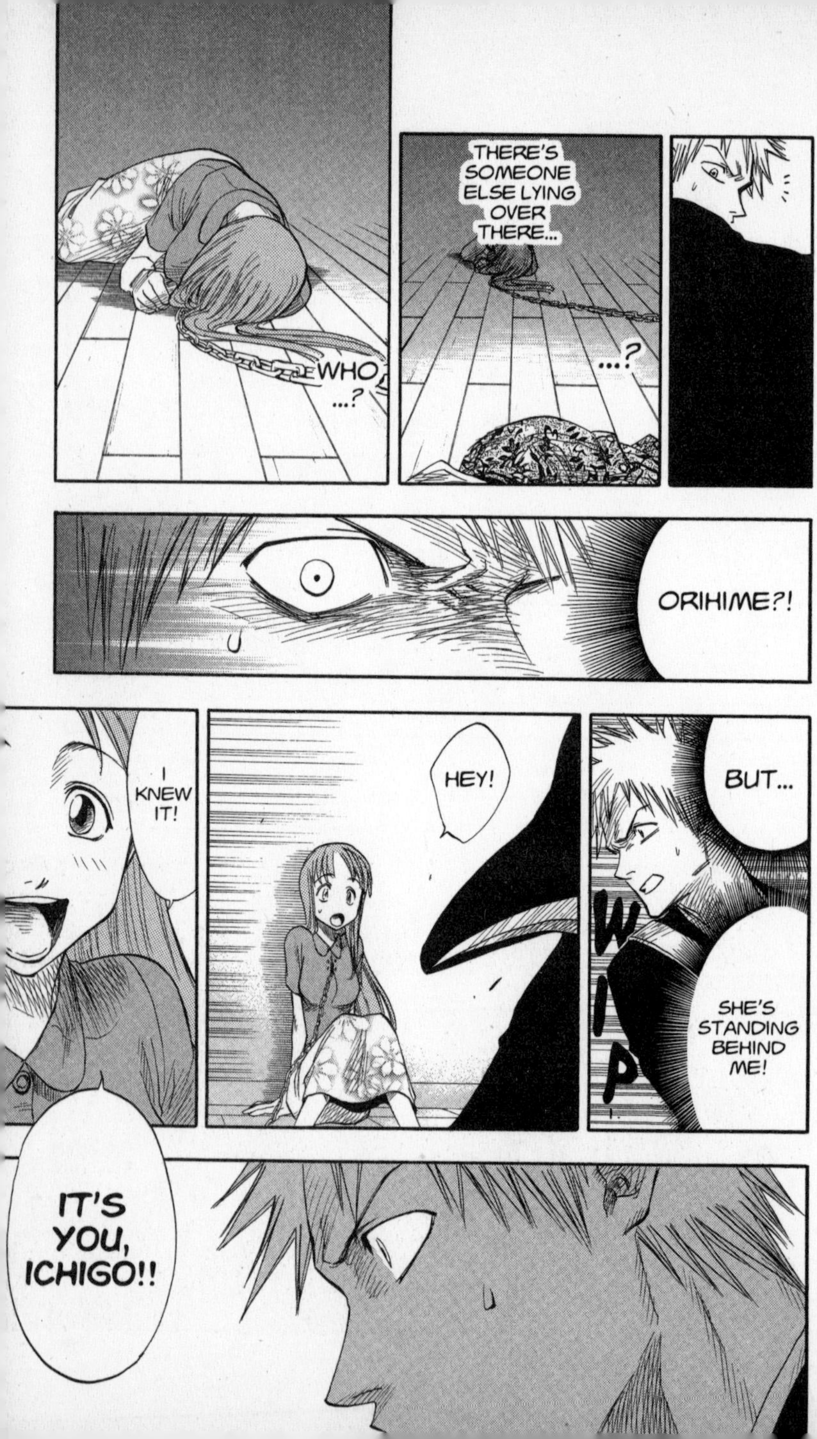
THERE'S SOMEONE ELSE LYING OVER THERE...
...?
WHO ...?
ORIHIME?!
BUT...
WIP
SHE'S STANDING BEHIND ME!
HEY!
I KNEW IT!
IT'S YOU, ICHIGO!!

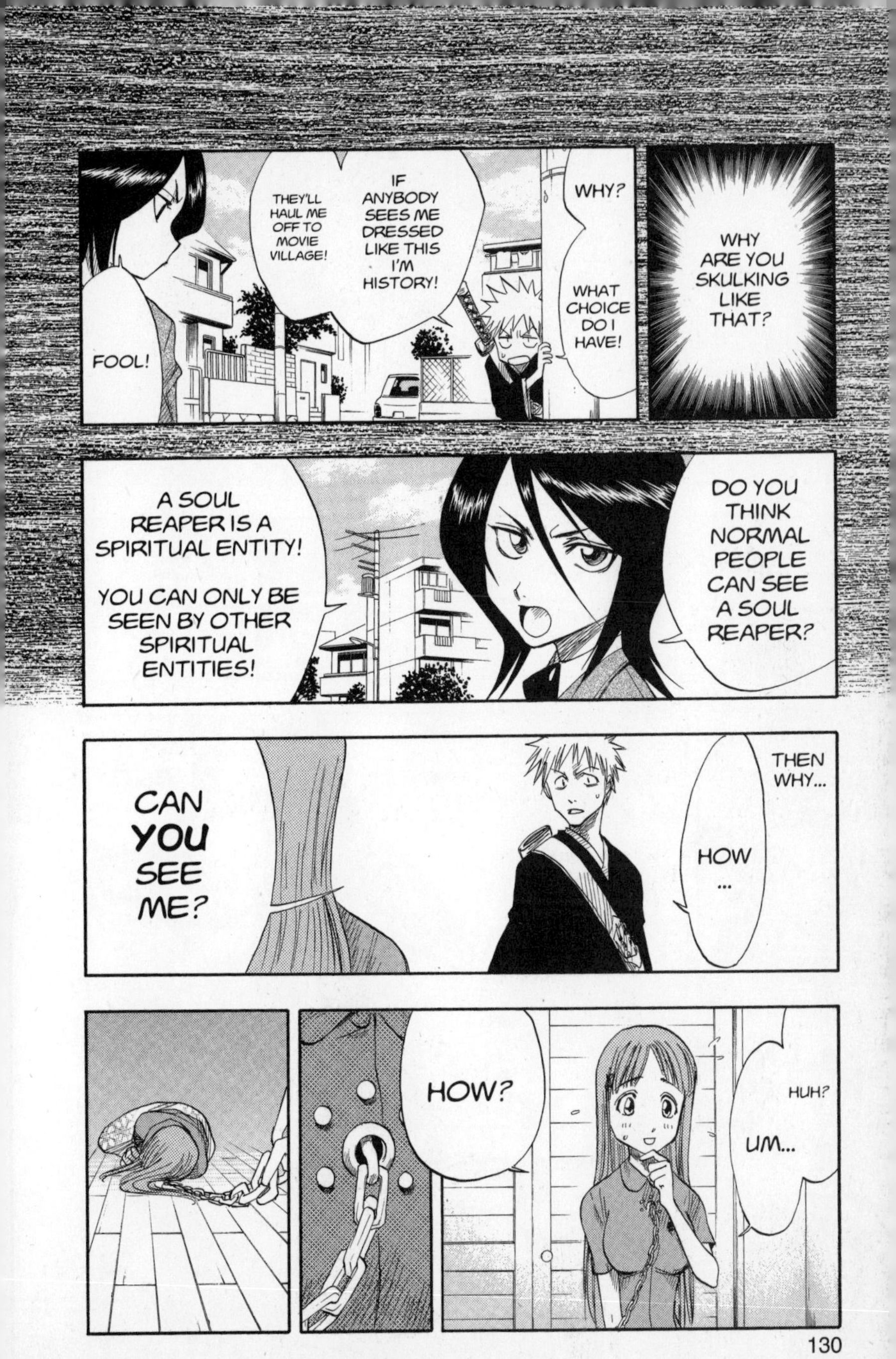
WHY ARE YOU SKULKING LIKE THAT?
WHY?
WHAT CHOICE DO I HAVE!
IF ANYBODY SEES ME DRESSED LIKE THIS I'M HISTORY!
THEY'LL HAUL ME OFF TO MOVIE VILLAGE!
FOOL!
DO YOU THINK NORMAL PEOPLE CAN SEE A SOUL REAPER?
A SOUL REAPER IS A SPIRITUAL ENTITY!
YOU CAN ONLY BE SEEN BY OTHER SPIRITUAL ENTITIES!
THEN WHY...
HOW ...
CAN **YOU** SEE ME?
HUH?
UM...
HOW?

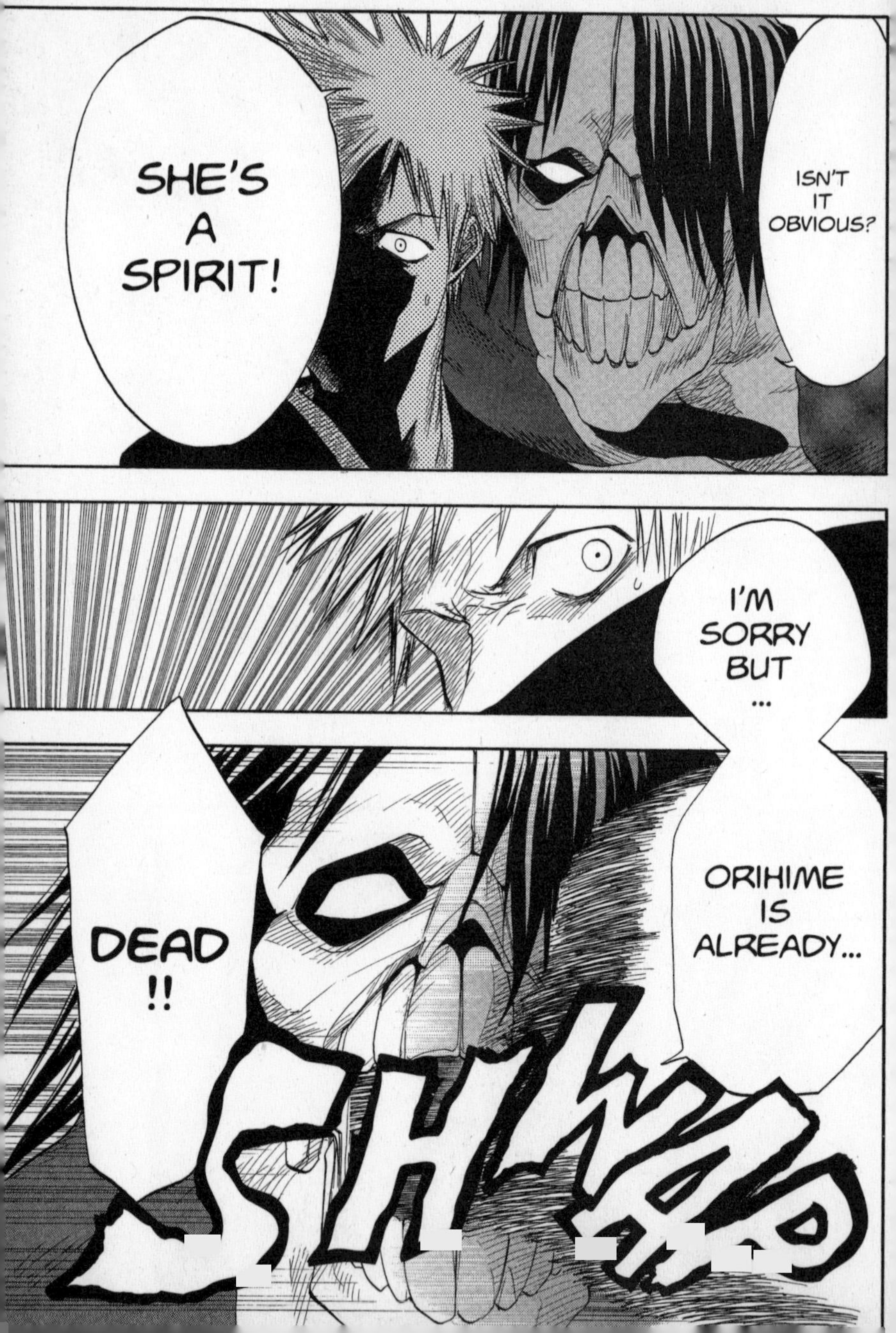
ISN'T IT OBVIOUS?
SHE'S A SPIRIT!
I'M SORRY BUT ...
ORIHIME IS ALREADY...
DEAD !!

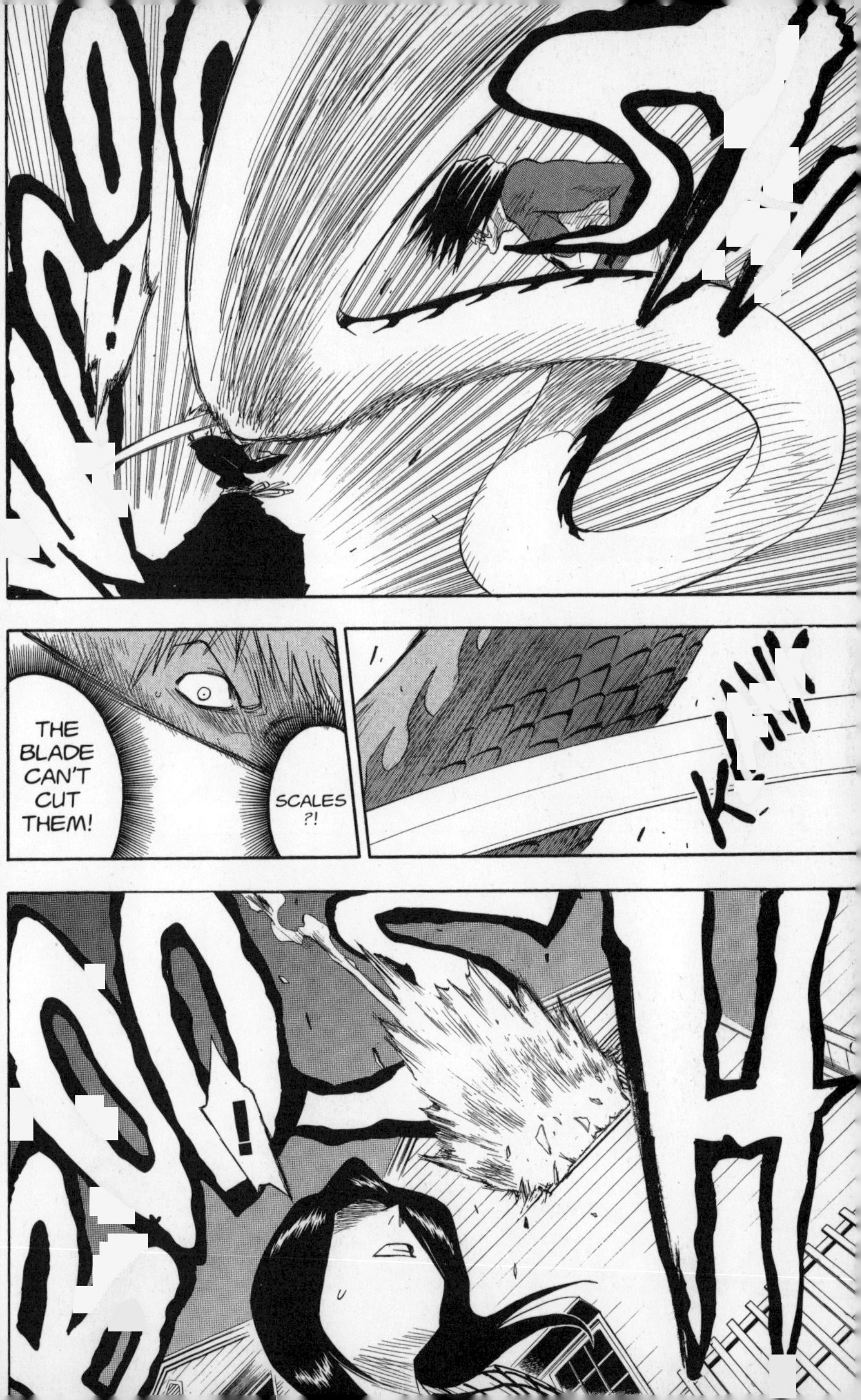
SCALES ?!
THE BLADE CAN'T CUT THEM!

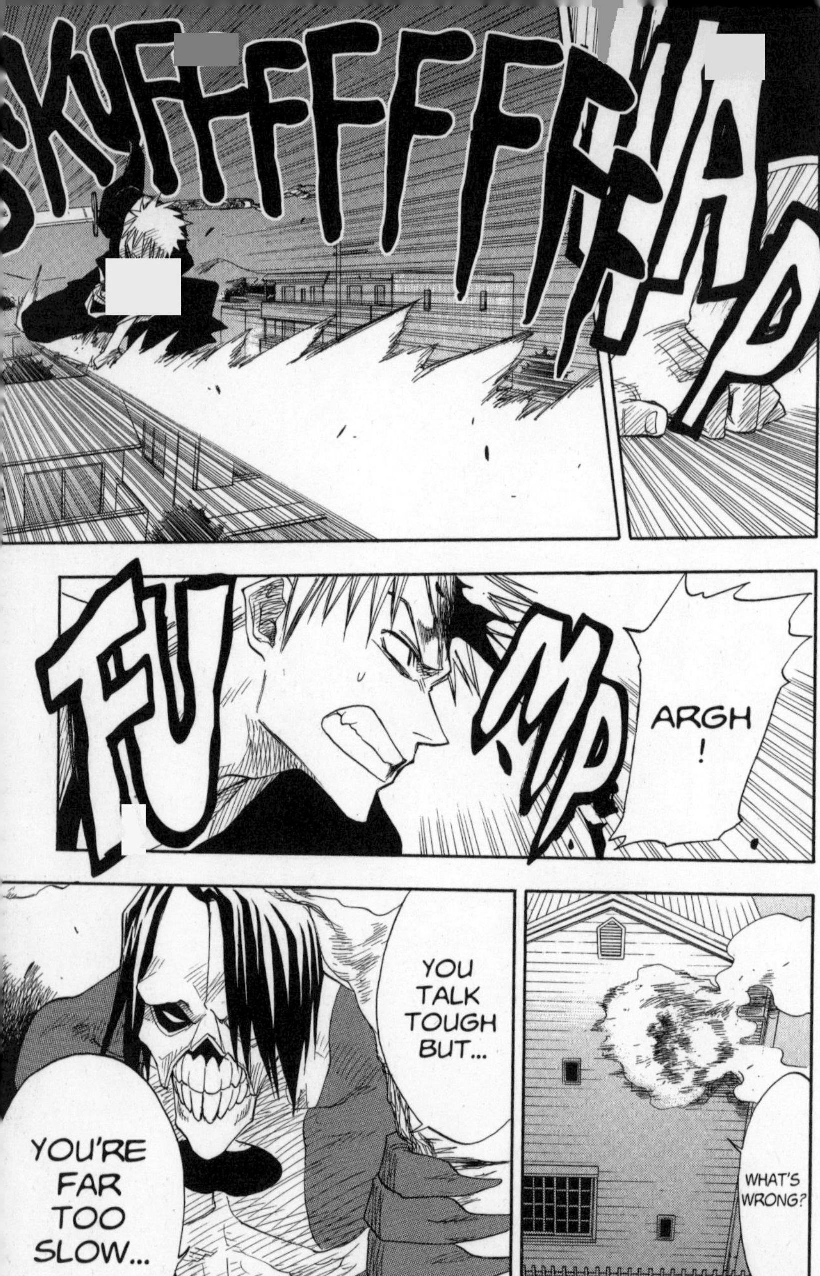
FUMP
ARGH!
WHAT'S WRONG?
YOU TALK TOUGH BUT...
YOU'RE FAR TOO SLOW...

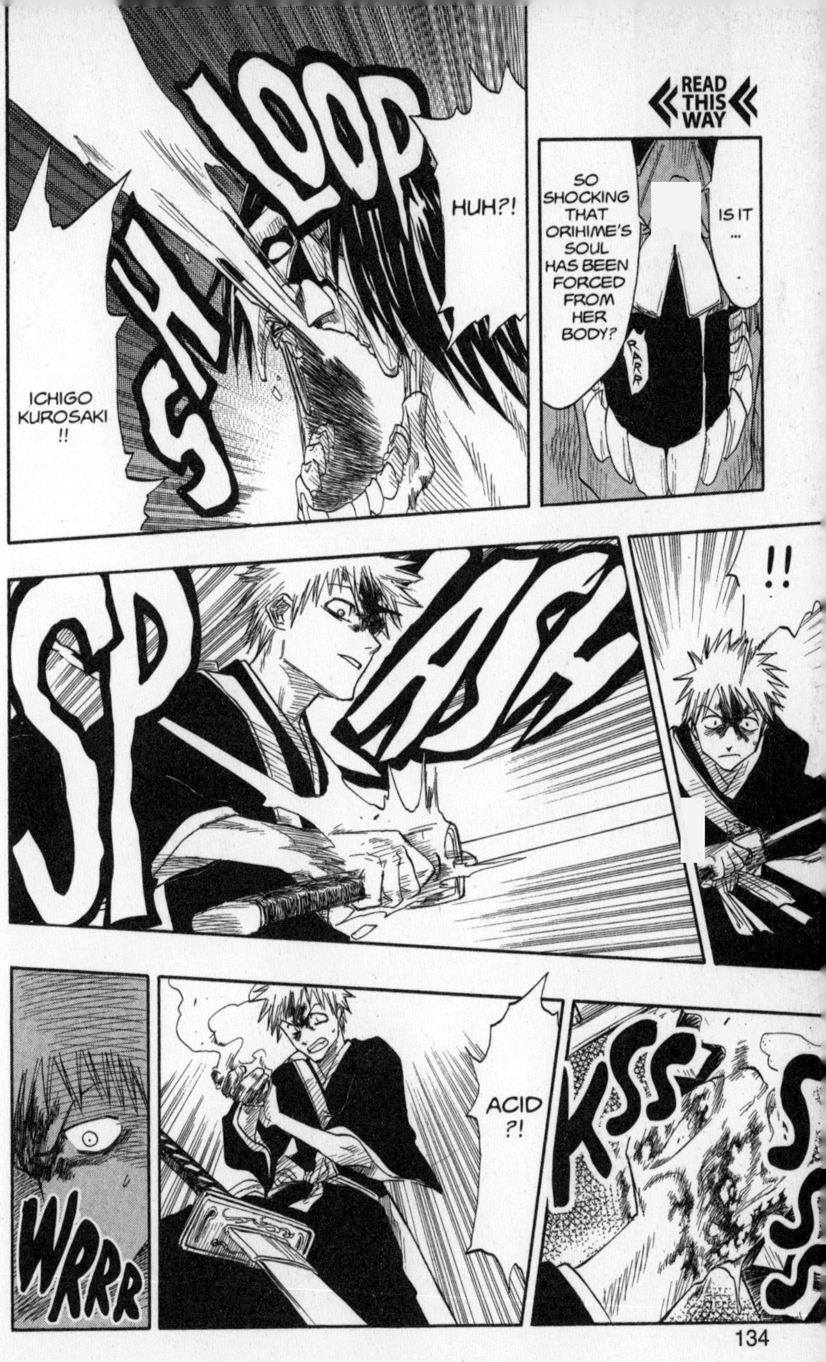
READ THIS WAY
IS IT ...
SO SHOCKING THAT ORIHIME'S SOUL HAS BEEN FORCED FROM HER BODY?
RARR
HUH?!
SHLOOP
ICHIGO KUROSAKI !!
!!
SPLASH
KSSSS
ACID ?!
WRRR

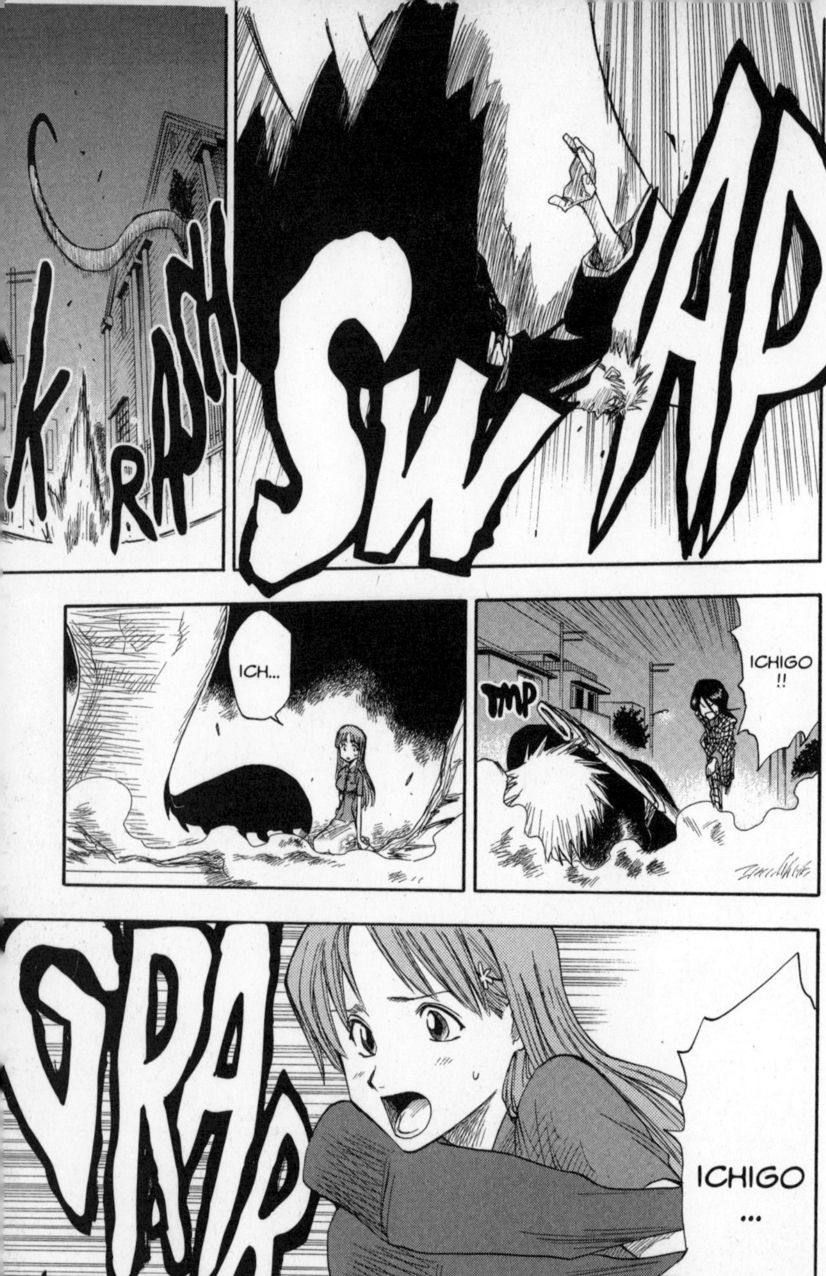
SWAP
KRASH
ICHIGO !!
TMP
ICH...
ICHIGO ...
GRAB

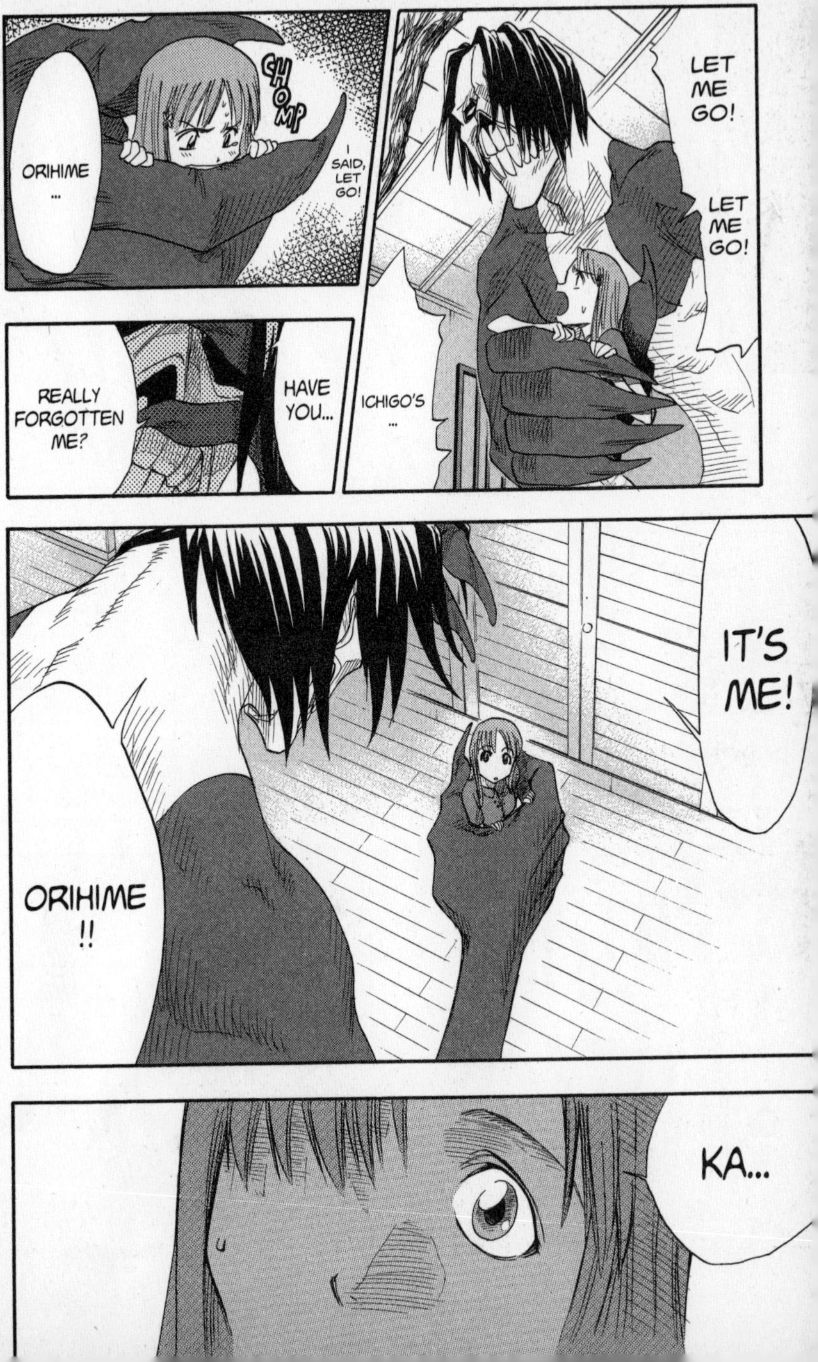
LET ME GO!
LET ME GO!
ICHIGO'S ...
I SAID, LET GO!
CHOMP
ORIHIME ...
HAVE YOU...
REALLY FORGOTTEN ME?
IT'S ME!
ORIHIME !!
KA...

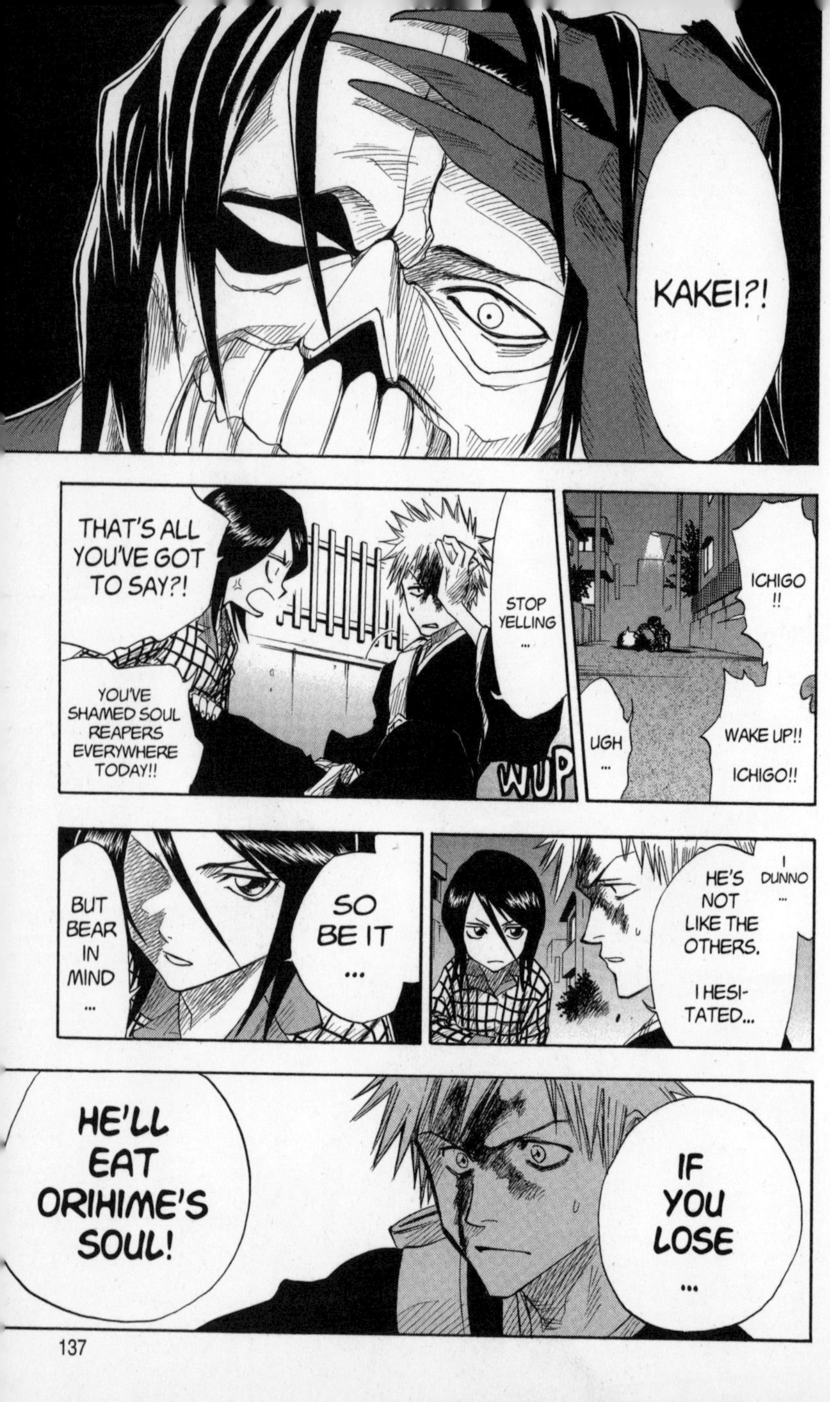
KAKEI?!
ICHIGO!!
WAKE UP!!
ICHIGO!!
UGH ...
STOP YELLING ...
WUP
THAT'S ALL YOU'VE GOT TO SAY?!
YOU'VE SHAMED SOUL REAPERS EVERYWHERE TODAY!!
I DUNNO ...
HE'S NOT LIKE THE OTHERS.
I HESITATED...
SO BE IT ...
BUT BEAR IN MIND ...
IF YOU LOSE ...
HE'LL EAT ORIHIME'S SOUL!

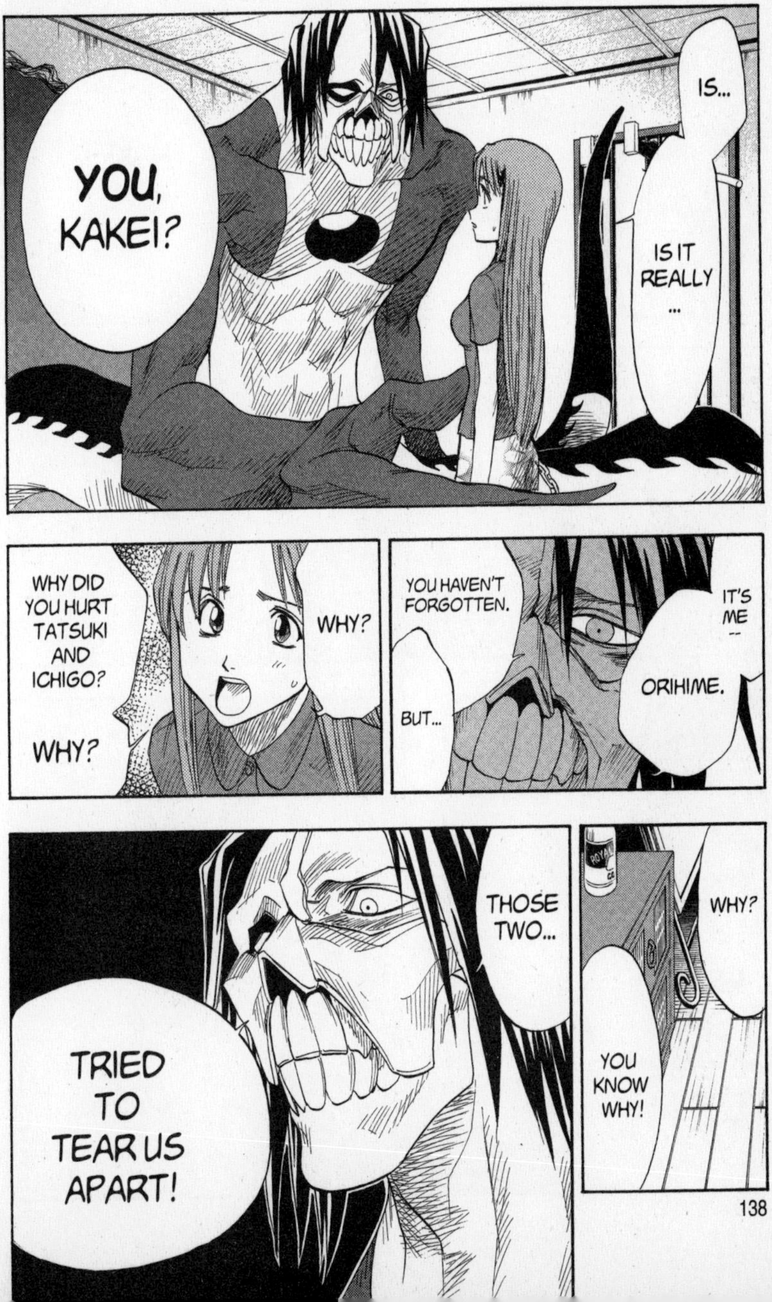
IS... IS IT REALLY ...
YOU, KAKEI?
IT'S ME -- ORIHIME.
YOU HAVEN'T FORGOTTEN.
BUT...
WHY?
WHY DID YOU HURT TATSUKI AND ICHIGO?
WHY?
WHY?
YOU KNOW WHY!
THOSE TWO...
TRIED TO TEAR US APART!

READ THIS WAY

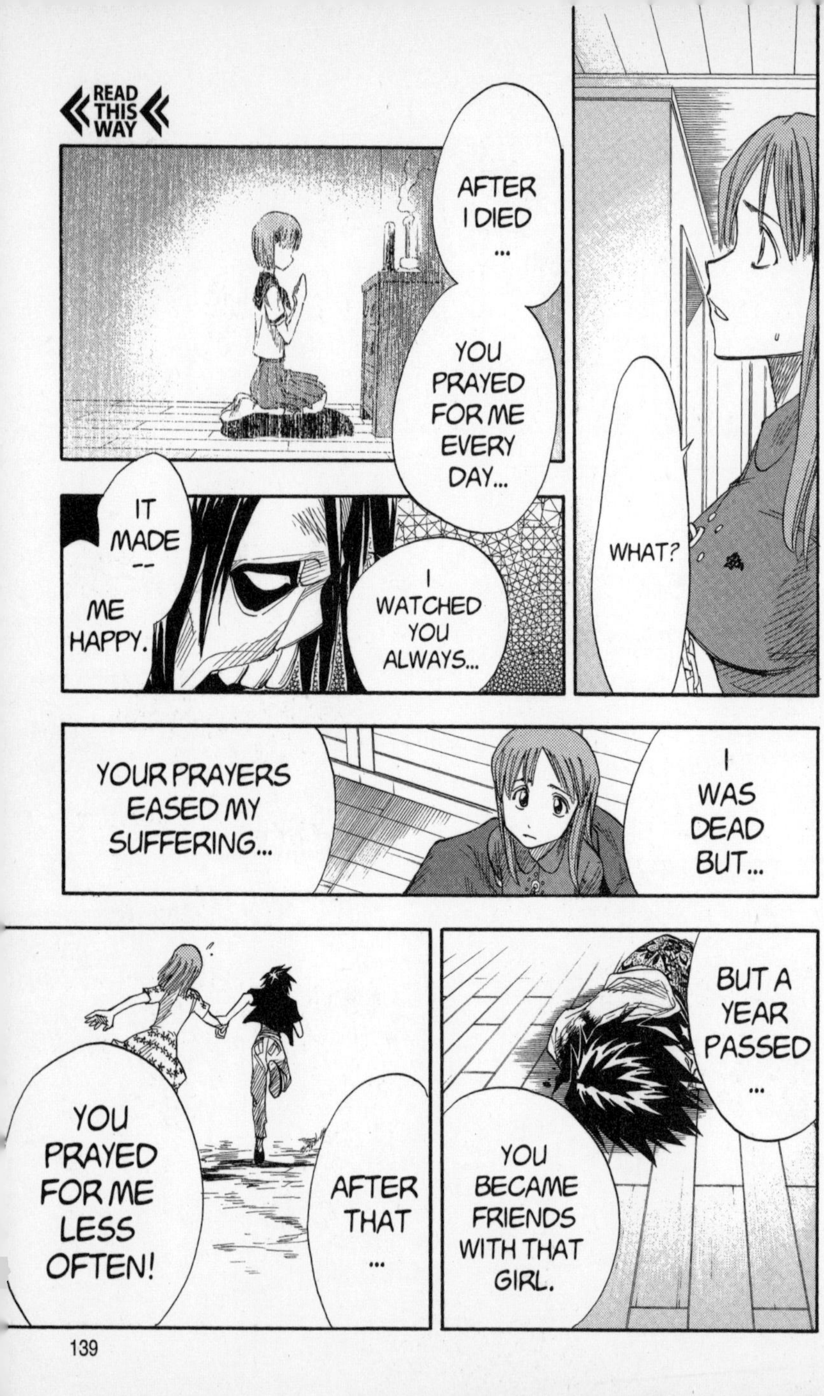
AFTER I DIED ...
YOU PRAYED FOR ME EVERY DAY...
WHAT?
I WATCHED YOU ALWAYS...
IT MADE -- ME HAPPY.
I WAS DEAD BUT...
YOUR PRAYERS EASED MY SUFFERING...
BUT A YEAR PASSED ...
YOU BECAME FRIENDS WITH THAT GIRL.
AFTER THAT ...
YOU PRAYED FOR ME LESS OFTEN!

READ THIS WAY

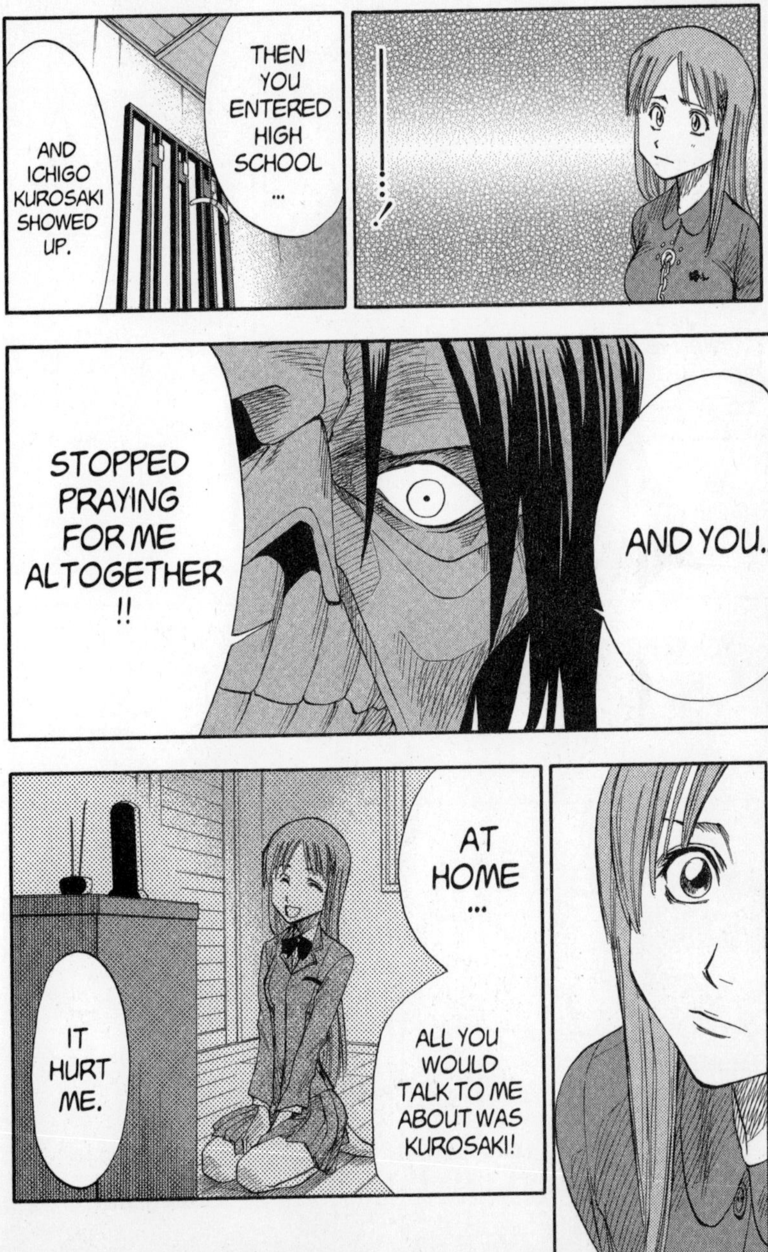
……!
THEN YOU ENTERED HIGH SCHOOL ...
AND ICHIGO KUROSAKI SHOWED UP.
AND YOU...
STOPPED PRAYING FOR ME ALTOGETHER !!
AT HOME ...
ALL YOU WOULD TALK TO ME ABOUT WAS KUROSAKI!
IT HURT ME.

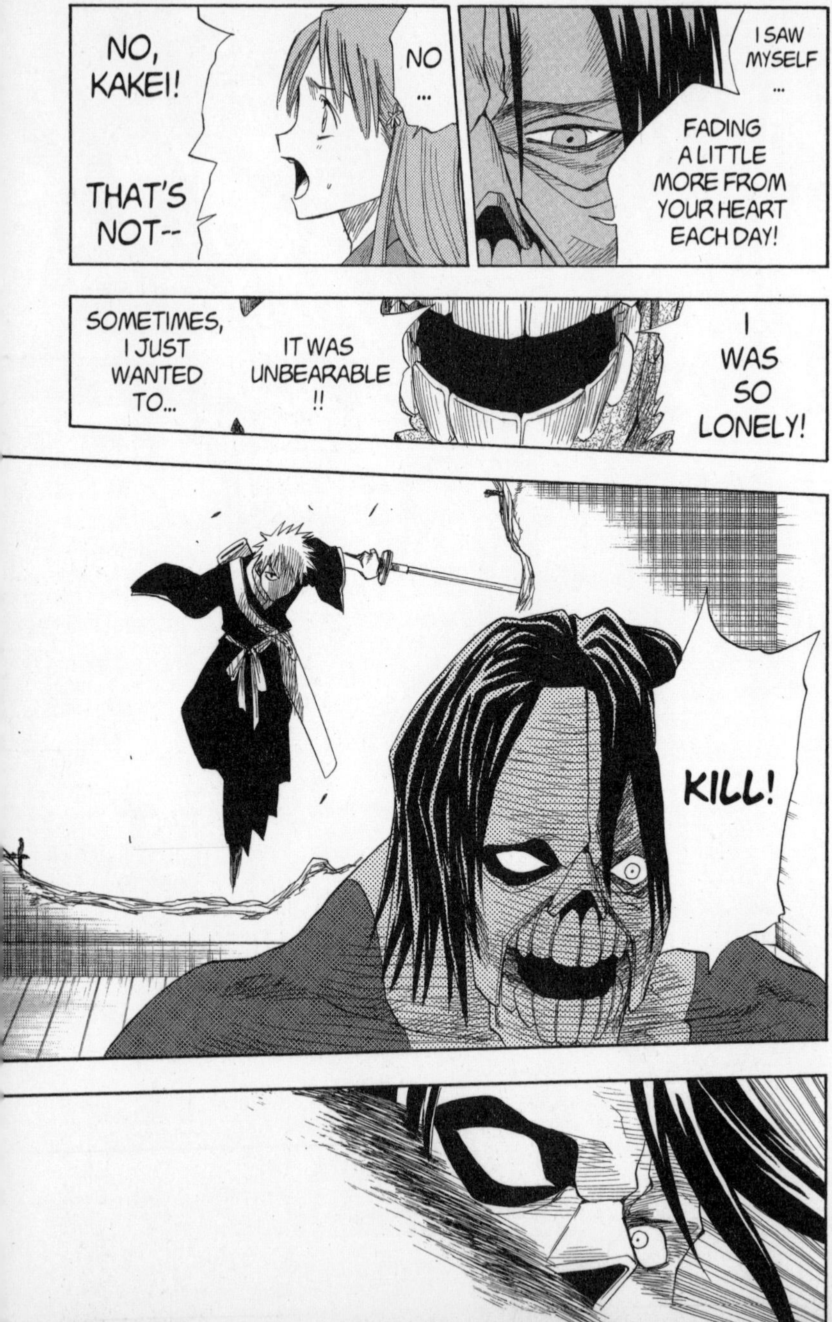
I SAW MYSELF ... FADING A LITTLE MORE FROM YOUR HEART EACH DAY!
NO ...
NO, KAKEI!
THAT'S NOT--
I WAS SO LONELY!
IT WAS UNBEARABLE !!
SOMETIMES, I JUST WANTED TO...
KILL!

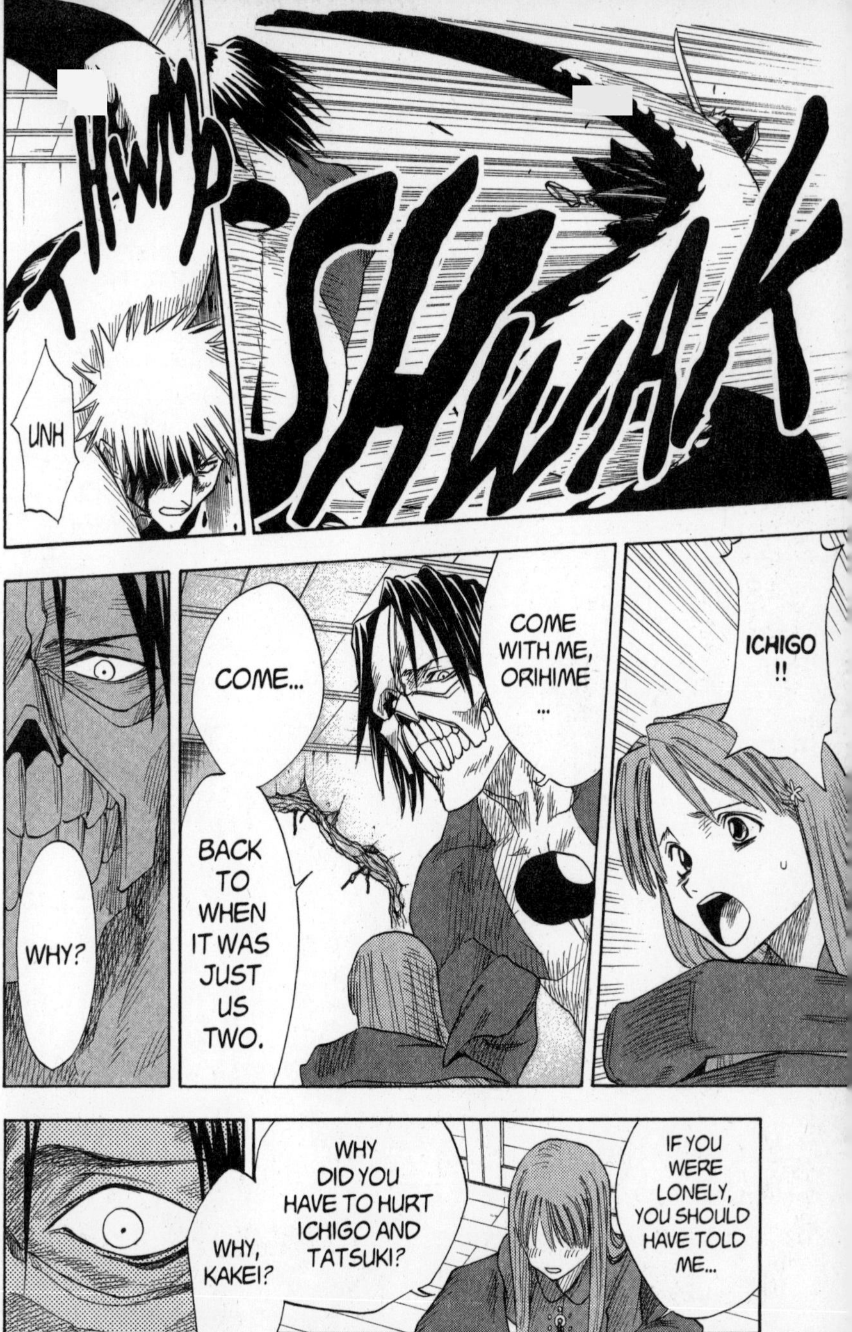
THWUMP
SHWAK
UNH
ICHIGO !!
COME WITH ME, ORIHIME ...
COME...
BACK TO WHEN IT WAS JUST US TWO.
WHY?
IF YOU WERE LONELY, YOU SHOULD HAVE TOLD ME...
WHY DID YOU HAVE TO HURT ICHIGO AND TATSUKI?
WHY, KAKEI?

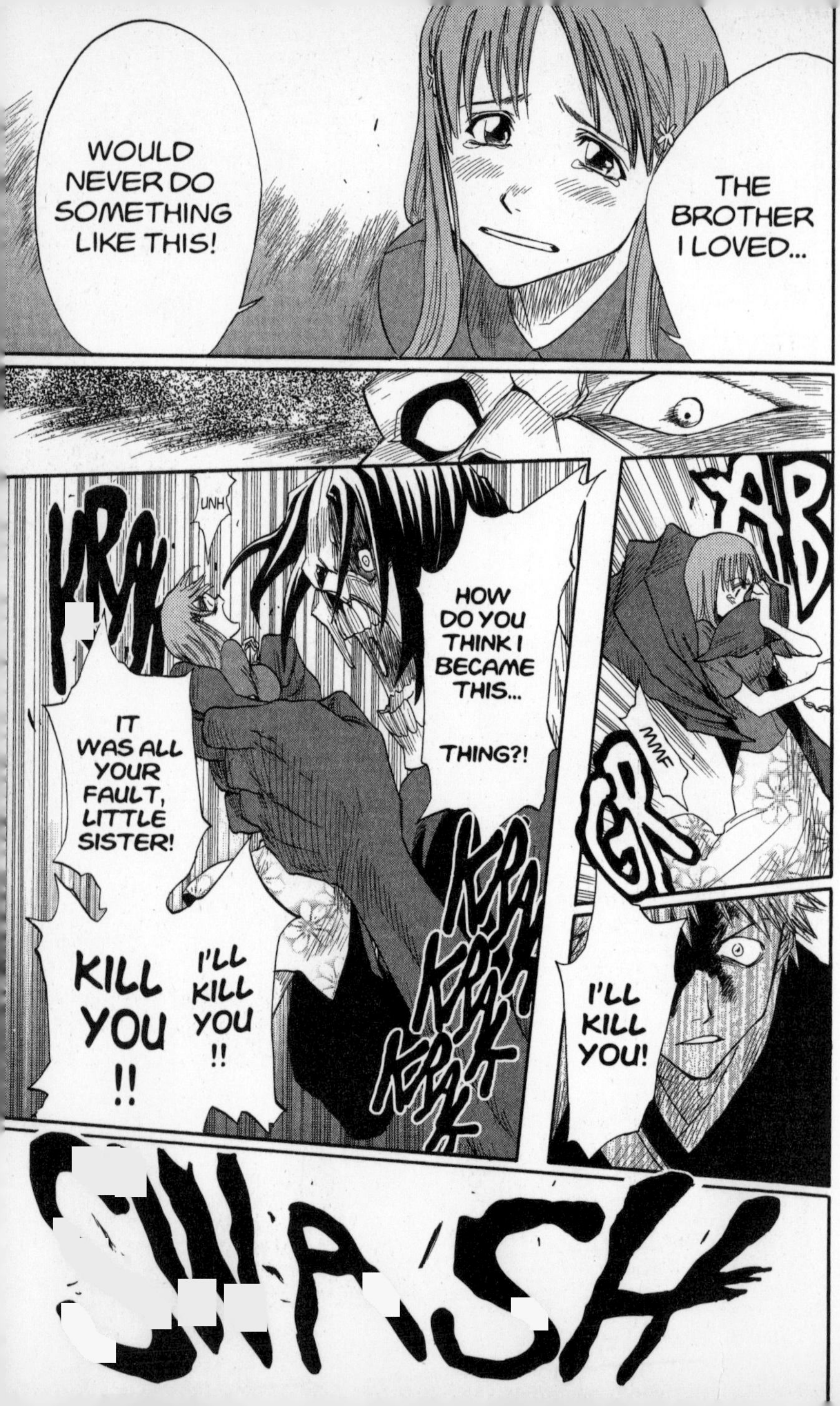
THE BROTHER I LOVED...
WOULD NEVER DO SOMETHING LIKE THIS!
MMF
I'LL KILL YOU!
UNH
HOW DO YOU THINK I BECAME THIS...
THING?!
IT WAS ALL YOUR FAULT, LITTLE SISTER!
I'LL KILL YOU !!
KILL YOU !!

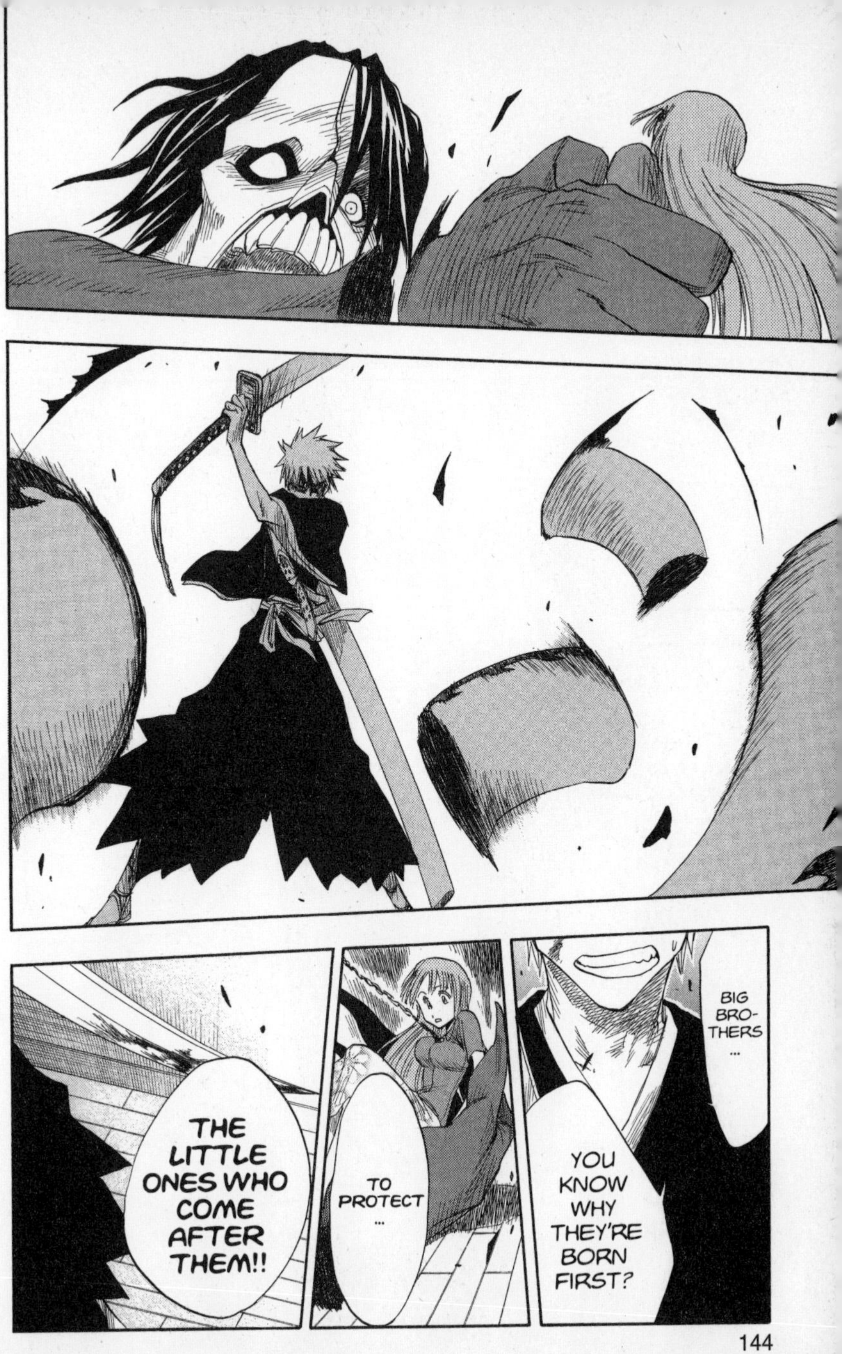
BIG BRO-THERS...
YOU KNOW WHY THEY'RE BORN FIRST?
TO PROTECT...
THE LITTLE ONES WHO COME AFTER THEM!!

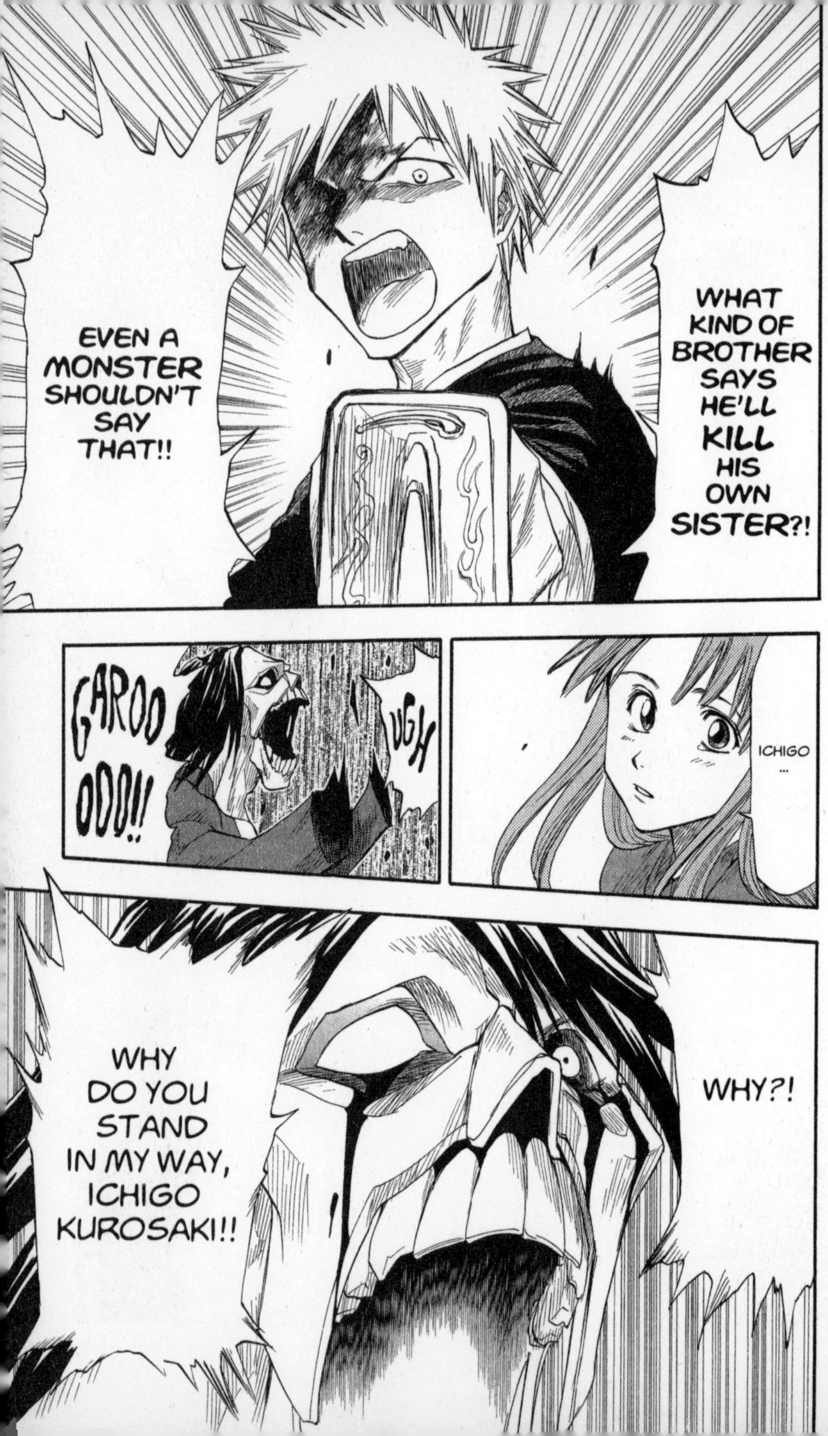
WHAT KIND OF BROTHER SAYS HE'LL KILL HIS OWN SISTER?!
EVEN A MONSTER SHOULDN'T SAY THAT!!
ICHIGO ...
UGH
GAROOOOO!!
WHY?!
WHY DO YOU STAND IN MY WAY, ICHIGO KUROSAKI!!

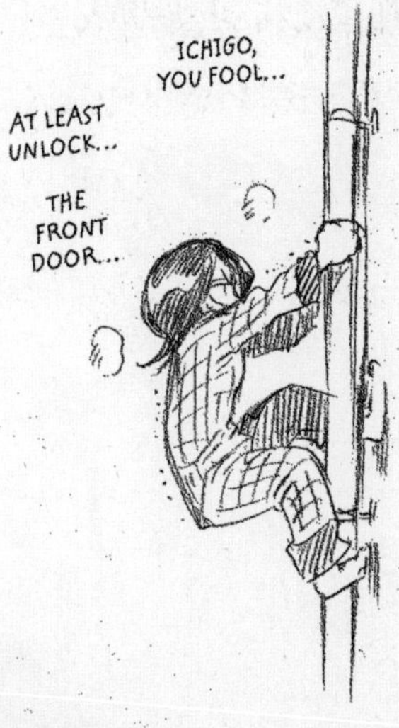
ICHIGO, YOU FOOL...
AT LEAST UNLOCK...
THE FRONT DOOR...

6. Microcrack.

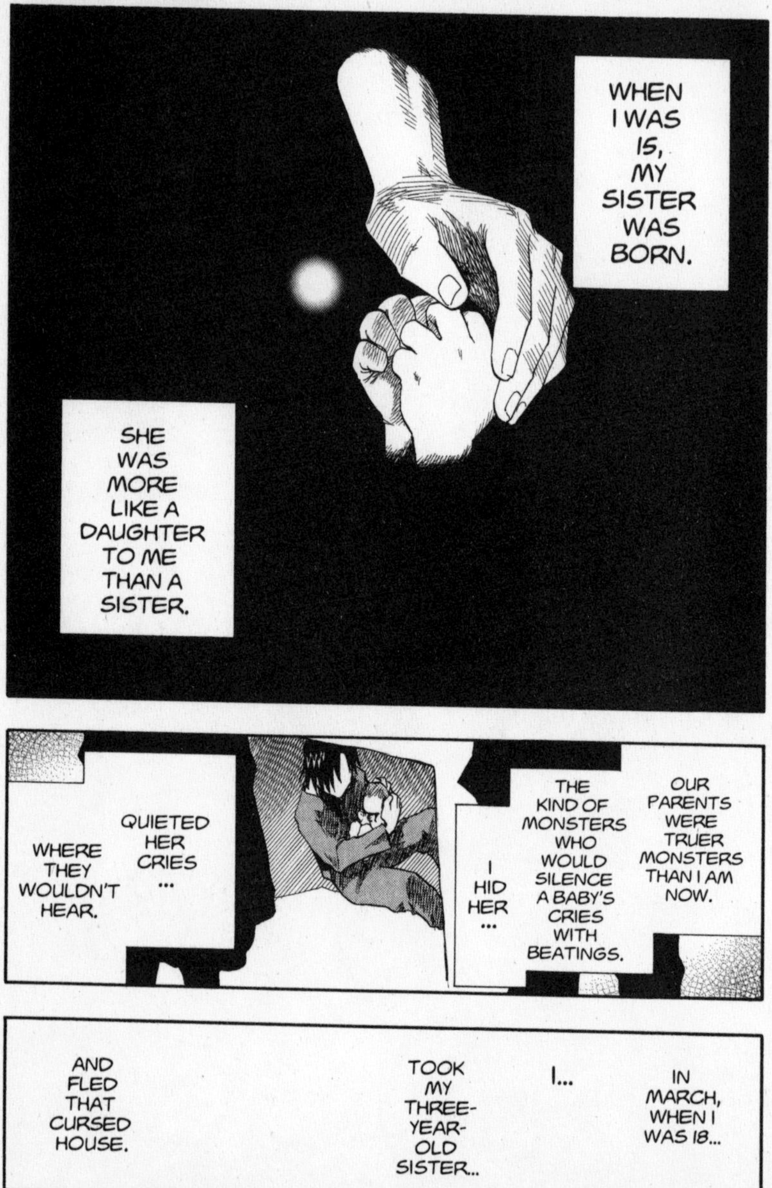
WHEN I WAS 15, MY SISTER WAS BORN.
SHE WAS MORE LIKE A DAUGHTER TO ME THAN A SISTER.
OUR PARENTS WERE TRUER MONSTERS THAN I AM NOW.
THE KIND OF MONSTERS WHO WOULD SILENCE A BABY'S CRIES WITH BEATINGS.
I HID HER...
QUIETED HER CRIES...
WHERE THEY WOULDN'T HEAR.
IN MARCH, WHEN I WAS 18...
I...
TOOK MY THREE-YEAR-OLD SISTER...
AND FLED THAT CURSED HOUSE.

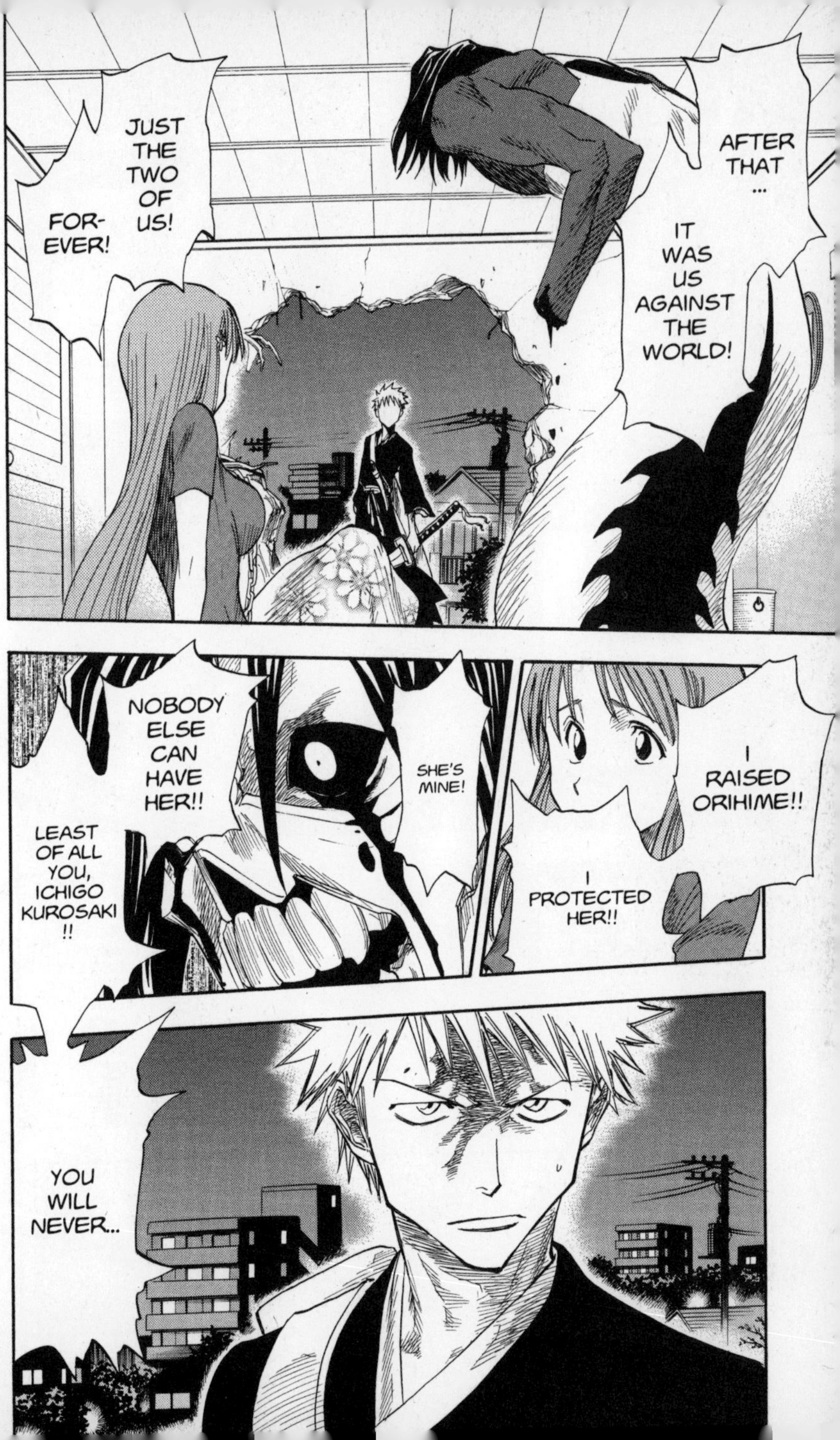
AFTER THAT ...
IT WAS US AGAINST THE WORLD!
JUST THE TWO OF US!
FOR-EVER!
I RAISED ORIHIME!!
I PROTECTED HER!!
NOBODY ELSE CAN HAVE HER!!
SHE'S MINE!
LEAST OF ALL YOU, ICHIGO KUROSAKI!!
YOU WILL NEVER...

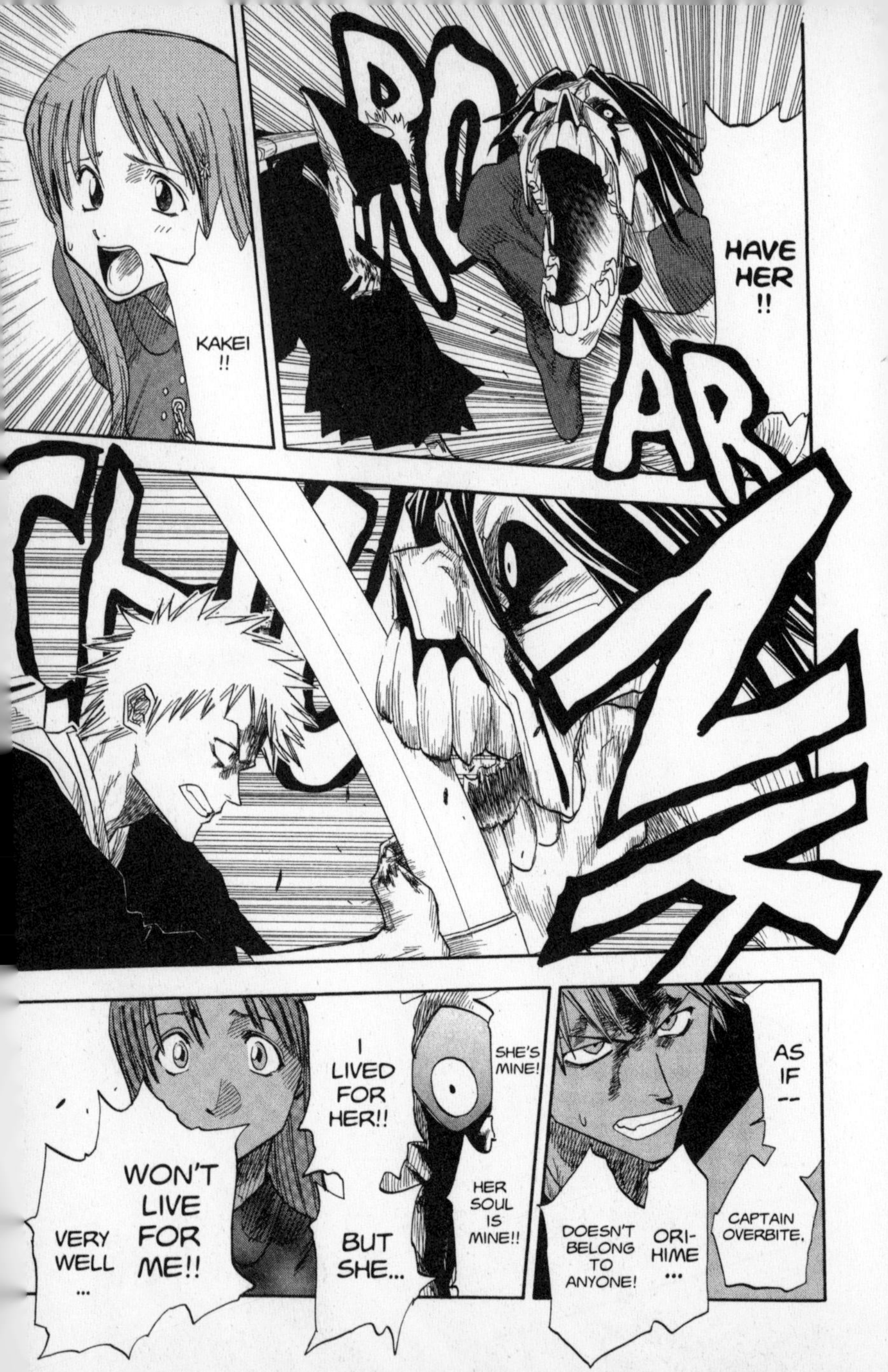
HAVE HER !!
KAKEI !!
AS IF --
CAPTAIN OVERBITE.
ORI-HIME ...
DOESN'T BELONG TO ANYONE!
SHE'S MINE!
I LIVED FOR HER!!
HER SOUL IS MINE!!
BUT SHE...
WON'T LIVE FOR ME!!
VERY WELL ...

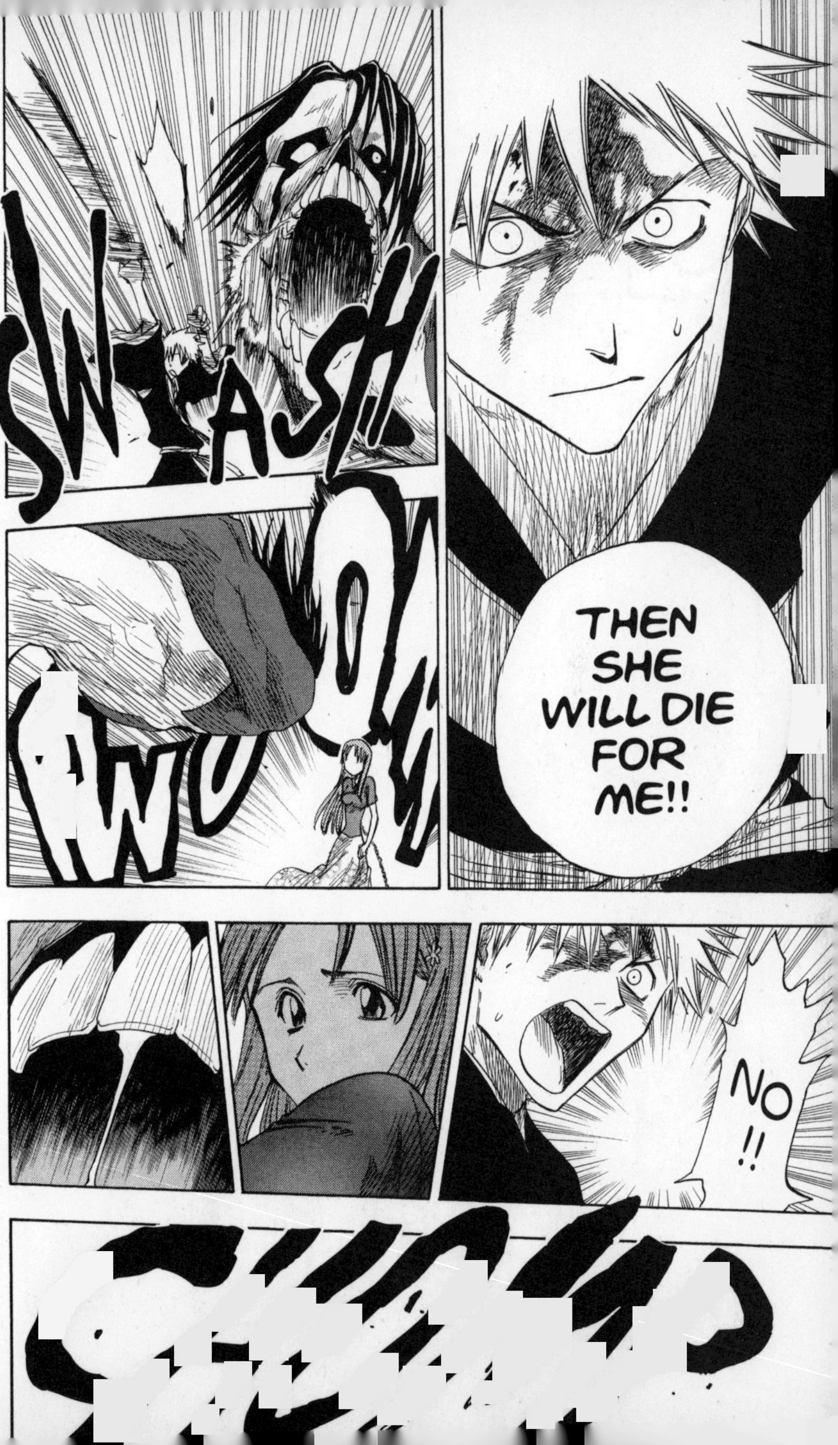
THEN SHE WILL DIE FOR ME!!
SWASH
NO!!

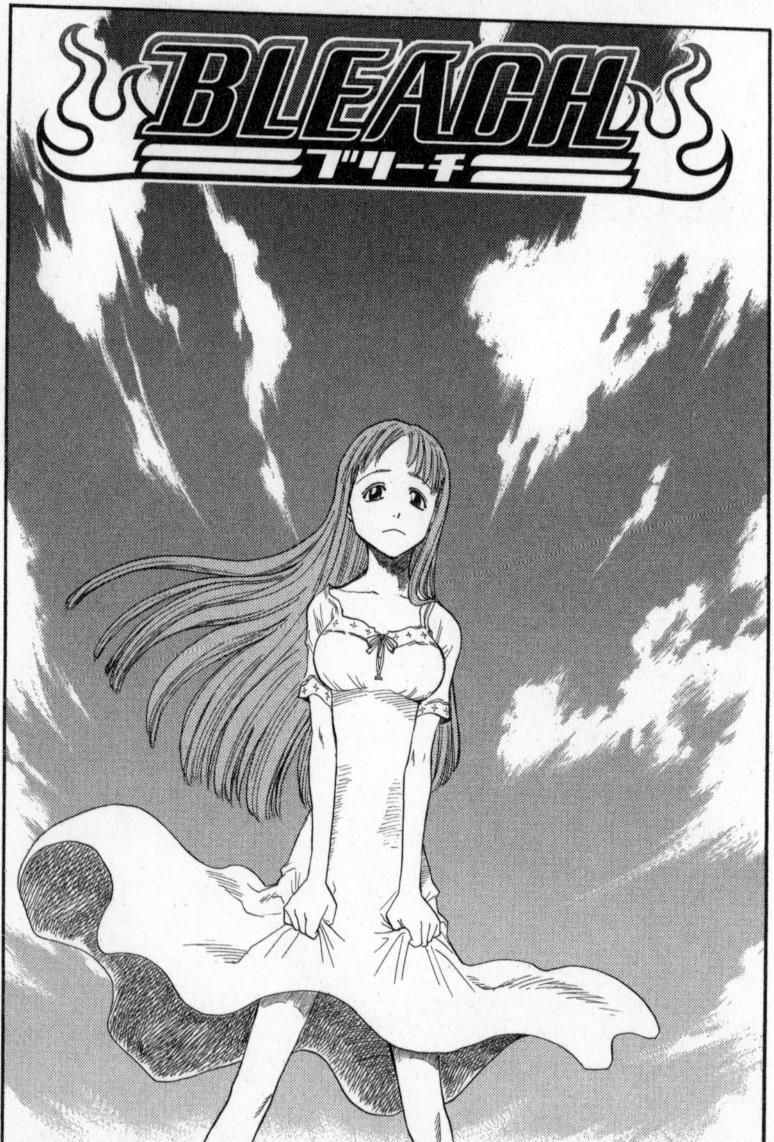
BLEACH
ブリーチ
6. Microcrack.

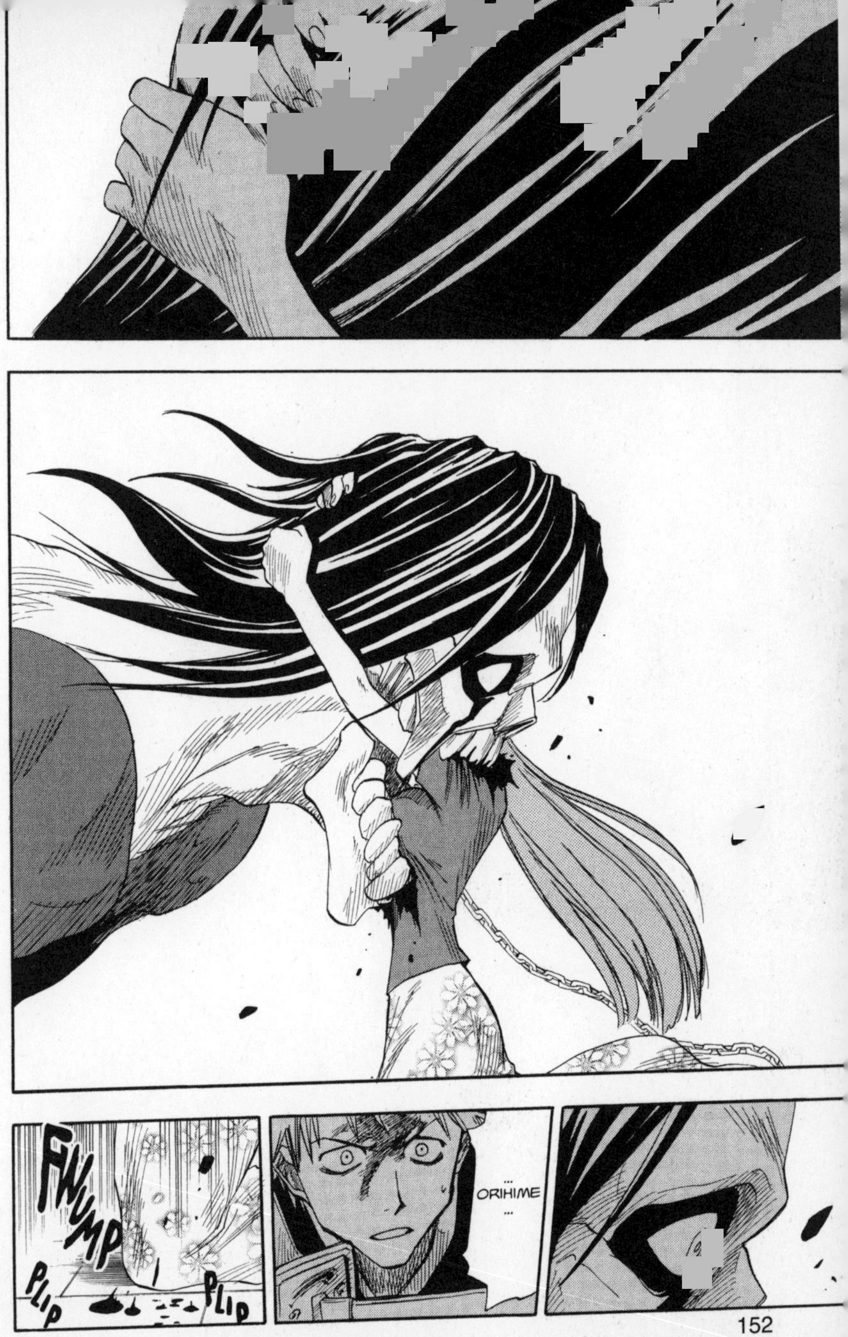
... ORIHIME ...
FWUMP
PLIP
PLIP

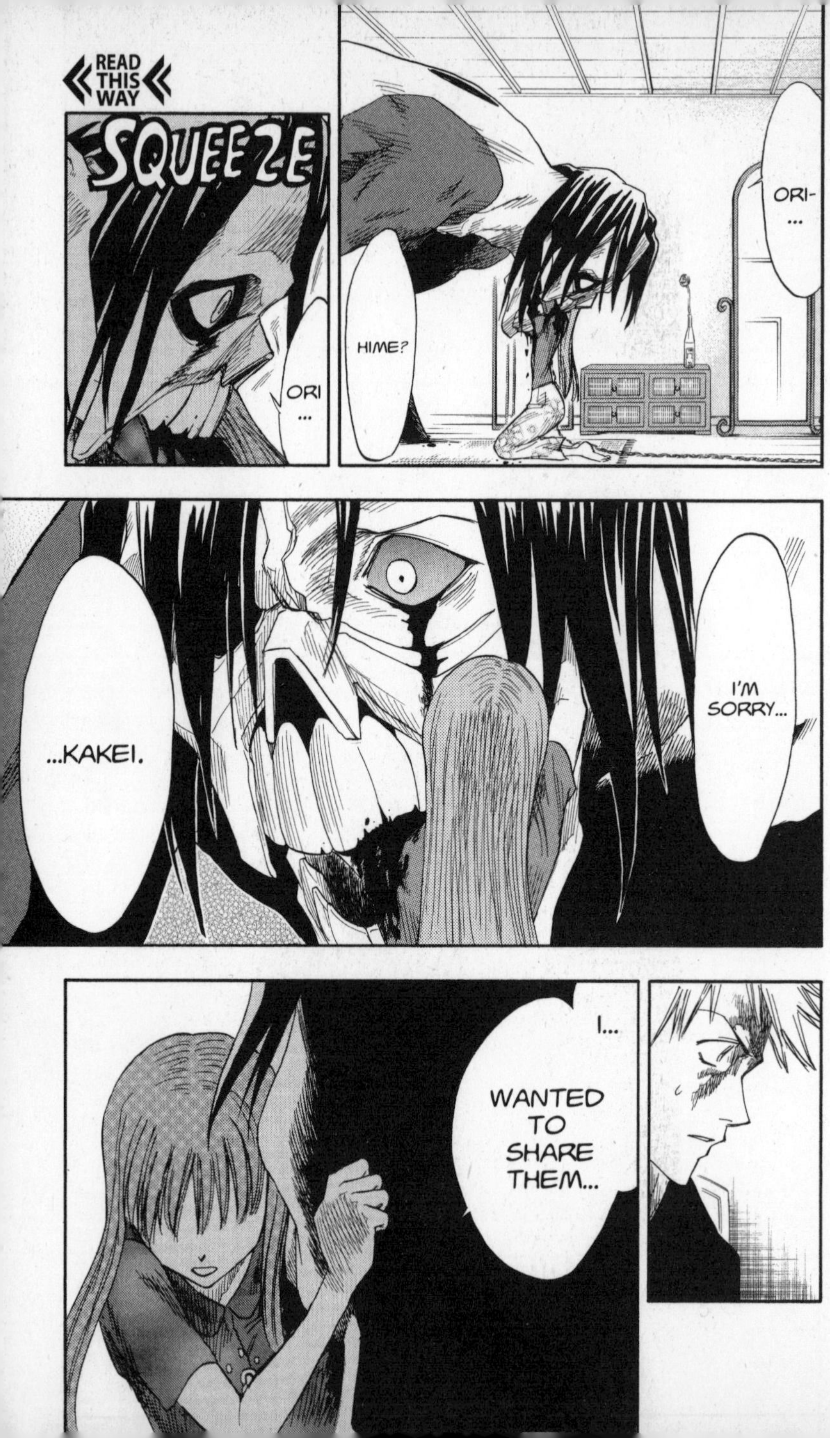
READ THIS WAY
ORI-...
HIME?
SQUEEZE
ORI...
I'M SORRY...
...KAKEI.
I...
WANTED TO SHARE THEM...

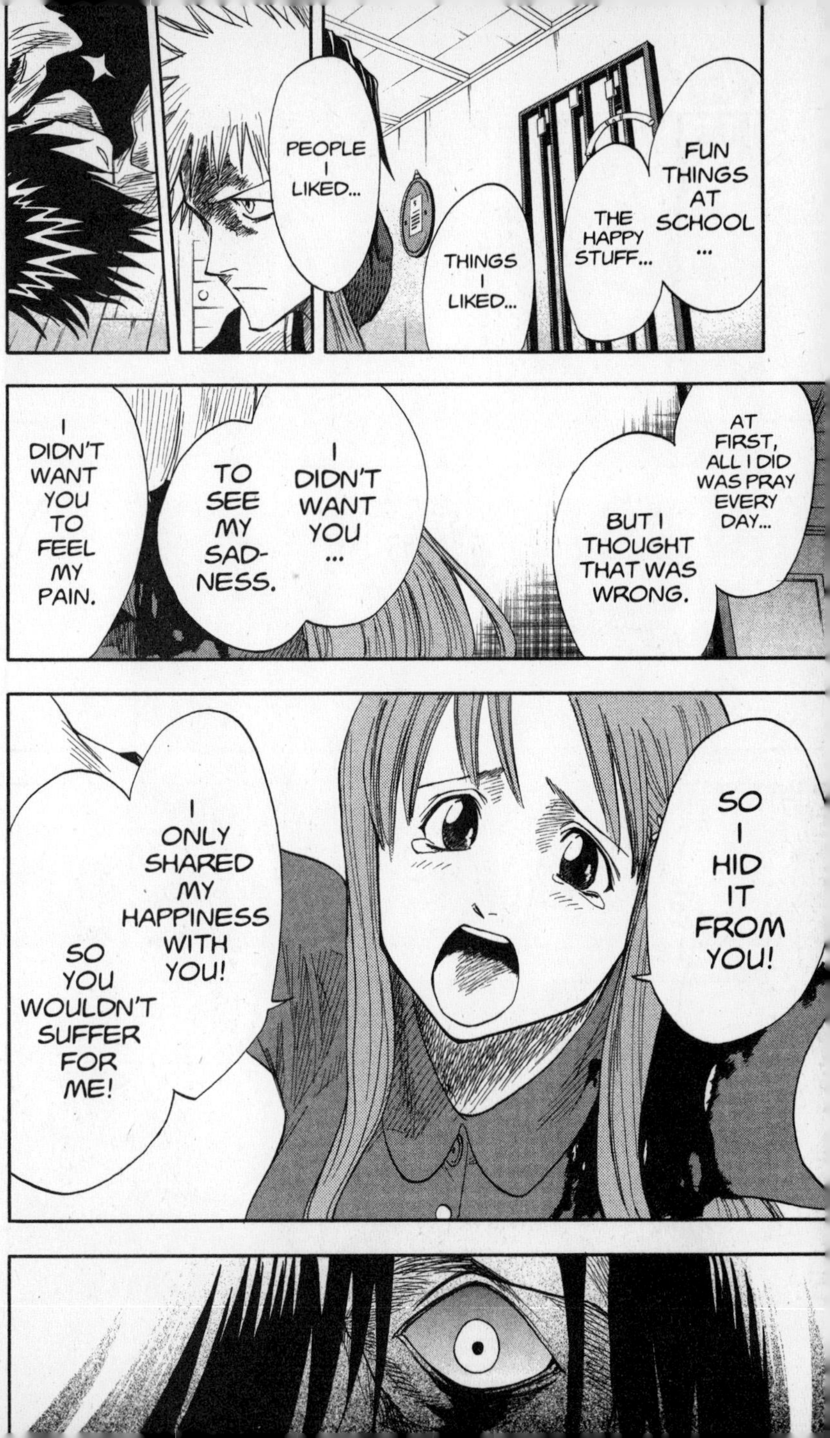
FUN THINGS AT SCHOOL...
THE HAPPY STUFF...
THINGS I LIKED...
PEOPLE I LIKED...
AT FIRST, ALL I DID WAS PRAY EVERY DAY...
BUT I THOUGHT THAT WAS WRONG.
I DIDN'T WANT YOU...
TO SEE MY SADNESS.
I DIDN'T WANT YOU TO FEEL MY PAIN.
SO I HID IT FROM YOU!
I ONLY SHARED MY HAPPINESS WITH YOU!
SO YOU WOULDN'T SUFFER FOR ME!

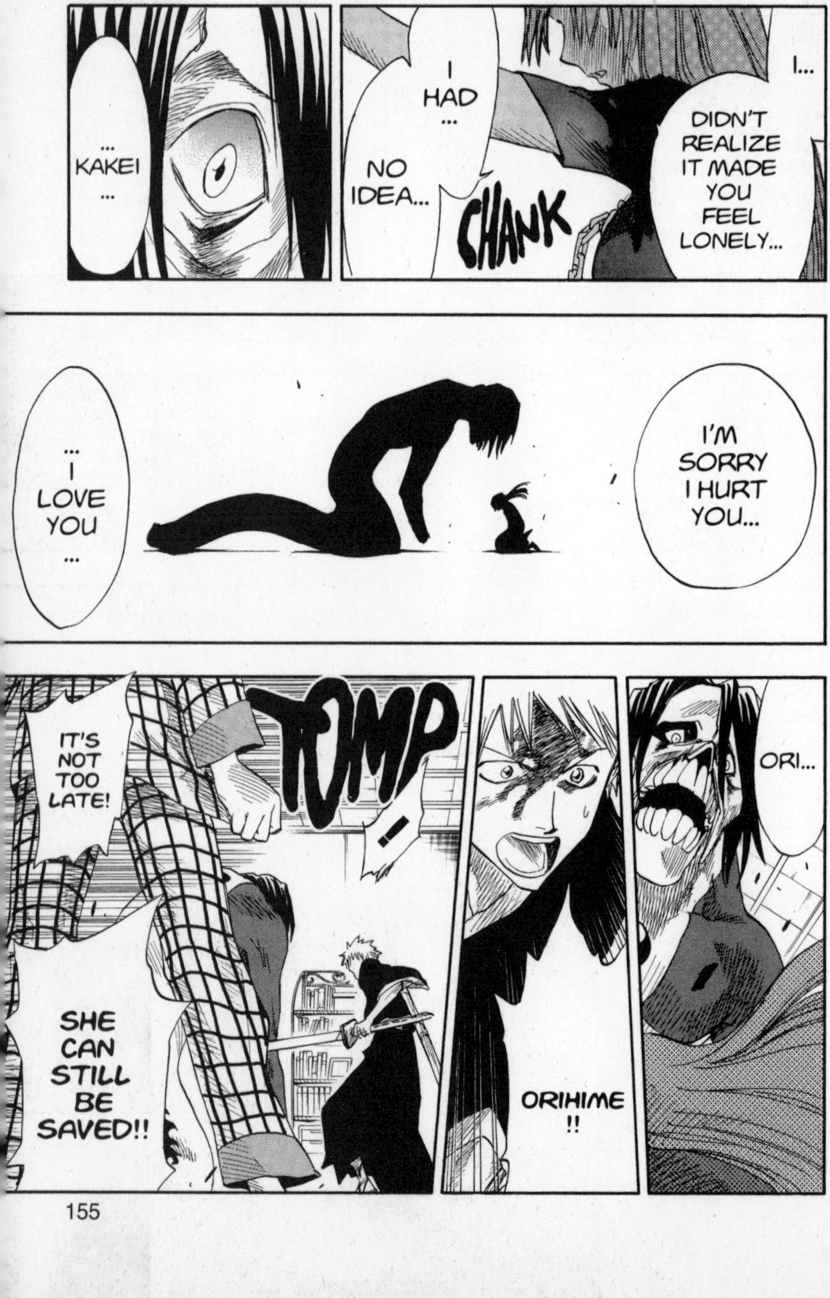
I...
DIDN'T REALIZE IT MADE YOU FEEL LONELY...
I HAD ... NO IDEA...
CHANK
... KAKEI ...
I'M SORRY I HURT YOU...
... I LOVE YOU ...
ORI...
ORIHIME !!
TOMP
IT'S NOT TOO LATE!
SHE CAN STILL BE SAVED!!

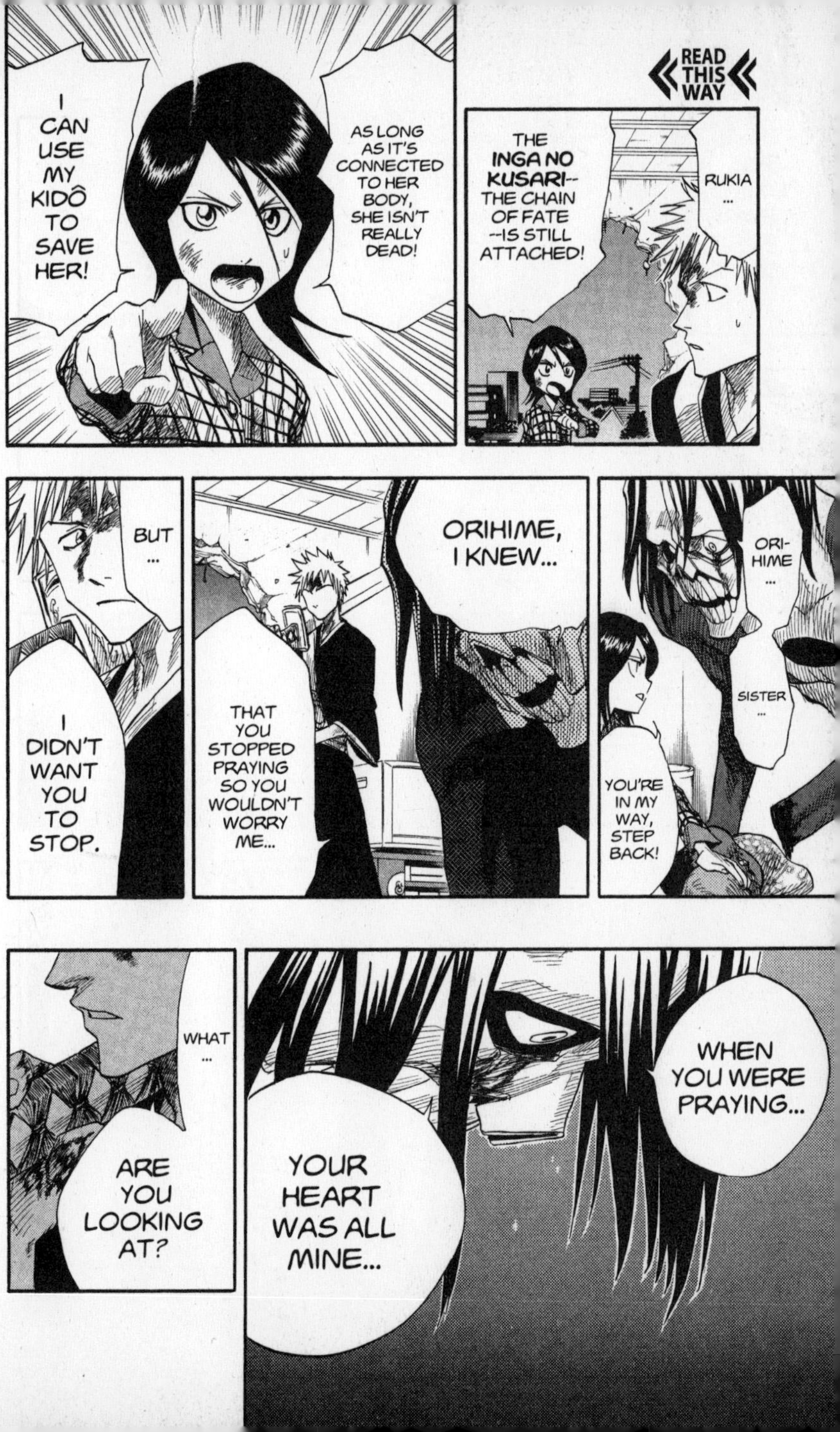
READ THIS WAY
RUKIA ...
THE INGA NO KUSARI-- THE CHAIN OF FATE --IS STILL ATTACHED!
AS LONG AS IT'S CONNECTED TO HER BODY, SHE ISN'T REALLY DEAD!
I CAN USE MY KIDÔ TO SAVE HER!
ORI- HIME ...
SISTER ...
YOU'RE IN MY WAY, STEP BACK!
ORIHIME, I KNEW...
THAT YOU STOPPED PRAYING SO YOU WOULDN'T WORRY ME...
BUT ...
I DIDN'T WANT YOU TO STOP.
WHEN YOU WERE PRAYING...
YOUR HEART WAS ALL MINE...
WHAT ...
ARE YOU LOOKING AT?

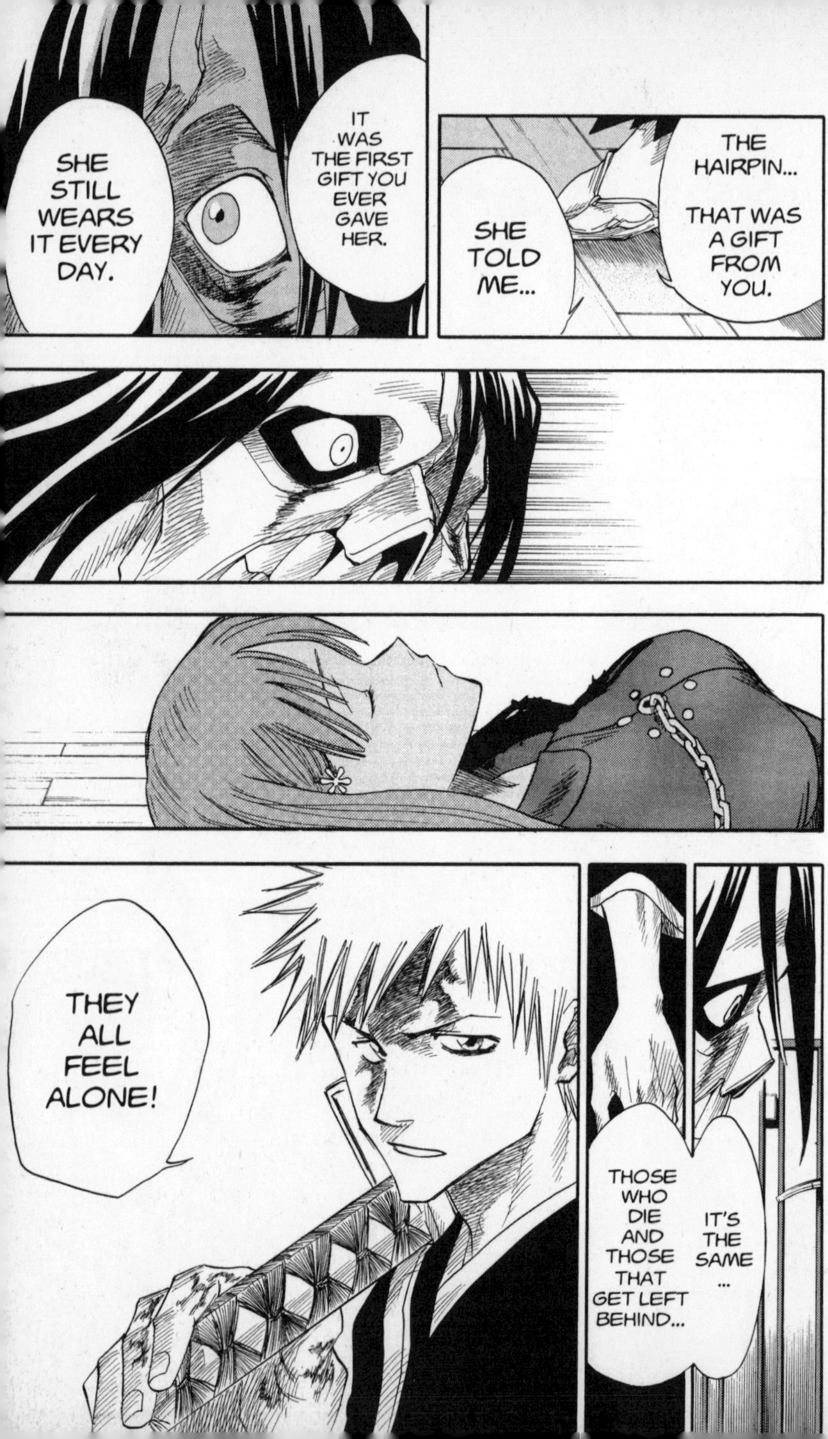
THE HAIRPIN... THAT WAS A GIFT FROM YOU.
SHE TOLD ME...
IT WAS THE FIRST GIFT YOU EVER GAVE HER.
SHE STILL WEARS IT EVERY DAY.
IT'S THE SAME ...
THOSE WHO DIE AND THOSE THAT GET LEFT BEHIND...
THEY ALL FEEL ALONE!

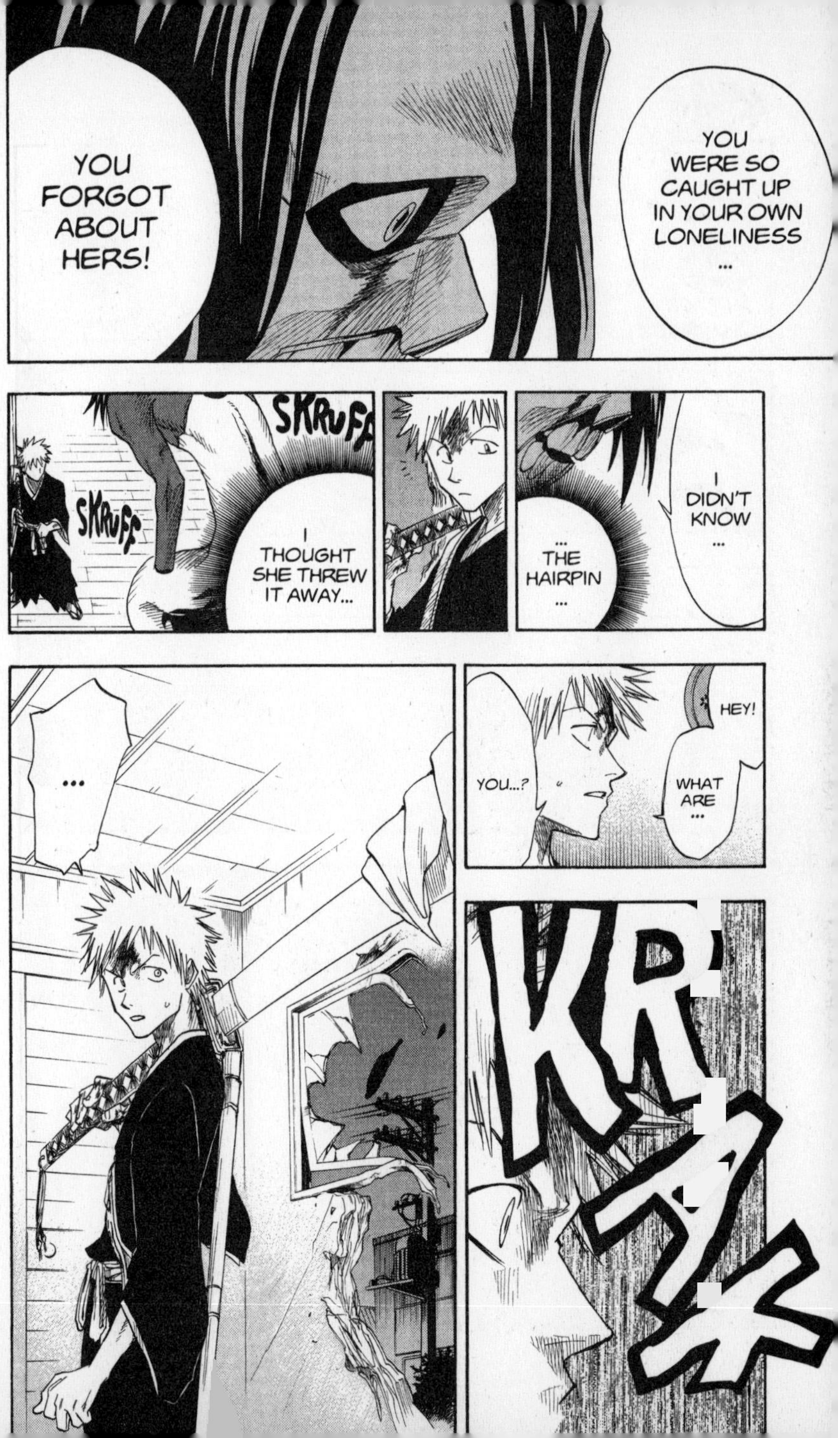
YOU WERE SO CAUGHT UP IN YOUR OWN LONELINESS ...
YOU FORGOT ABOUT HERS!
I DIDN'T KNOW ...
... THE HAIRPIN ...
SKRUFF
I THOUGHT SHE THREW IT AWAY...
SKRUFF
HEY! WHAT ARE ...
YOU...?
KRAK
...

READ THIS WAY

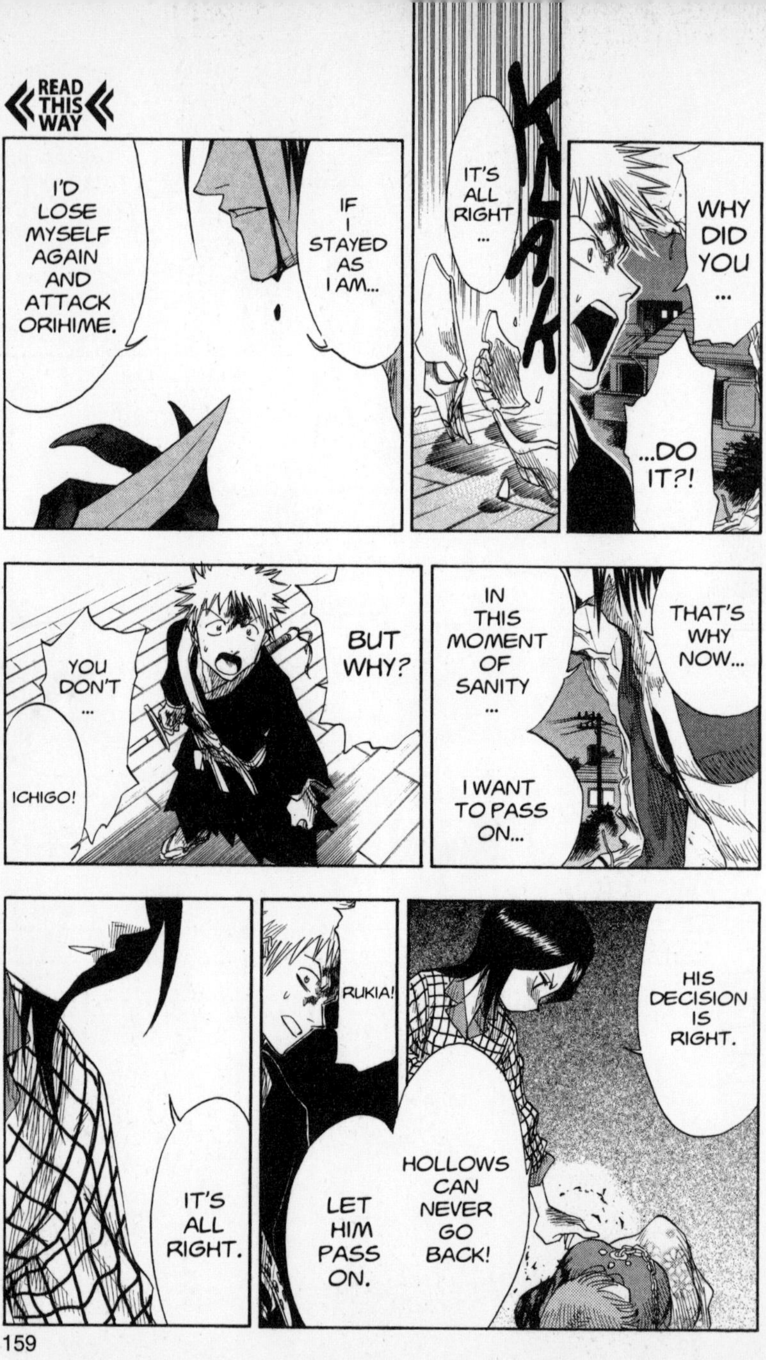
WHY DID YOU ...
...DO IT?!
IT'S ALL RIGHT ...
KLAK
IF I STAYED AS I AM...
I'D LOSE MYSELF AGAIN AND ATTACK ORIHIME.
THAT'S WHY NOW...
IN THIS MOMENT OF SANITY ...
I WANT TO PASS ON...
BUT WHY?
YOU DON'T ...
ICHIGO!
HIS DECISION IS RIGHT.
HOLLOWS CAN NEVER GO BACK!
LET HIM PASS ON.
RUKIA!
IT'S ALL RIGHT.

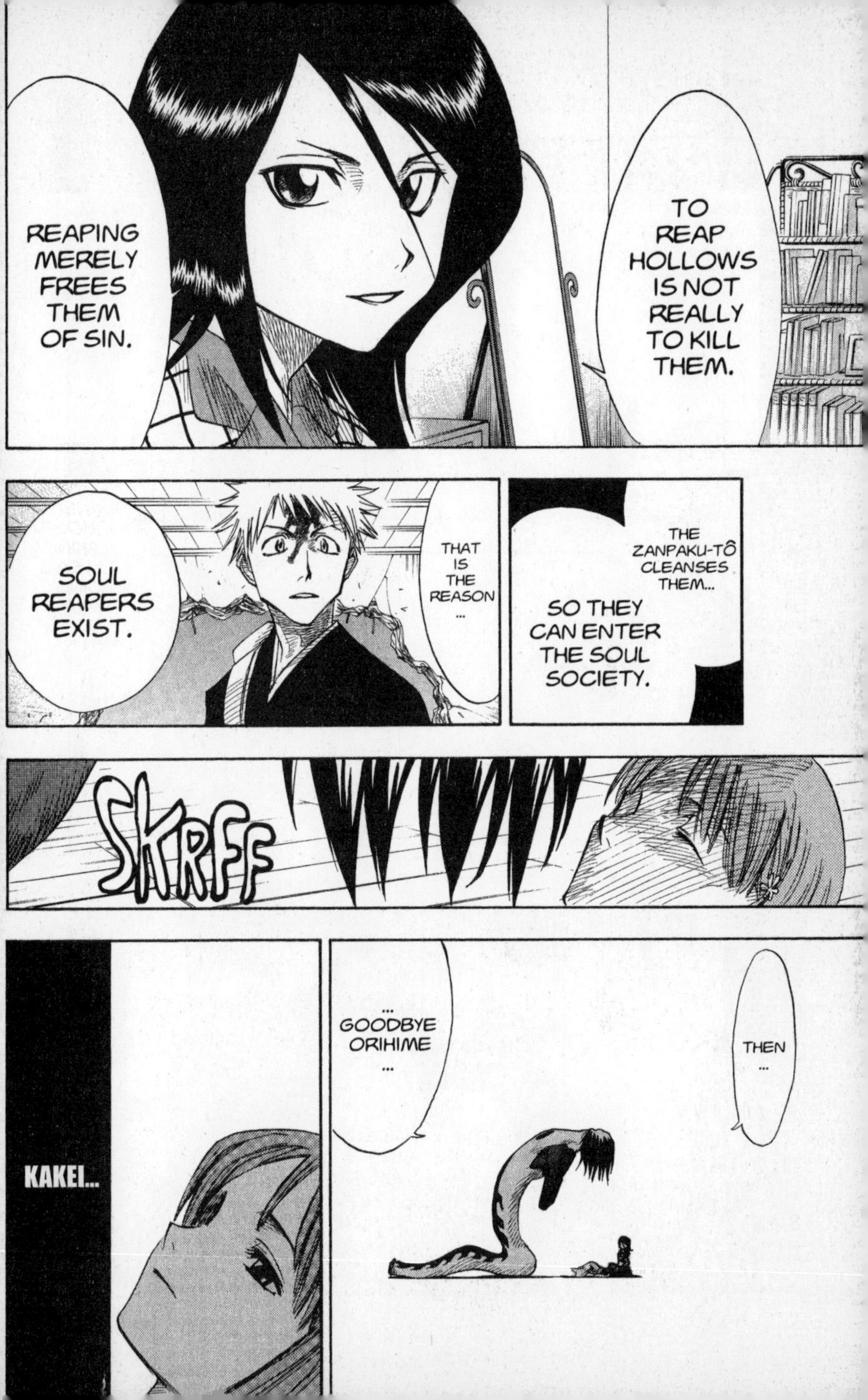
TO REAP HOLLOWS IS NOT REALLY TO KILL THEM.
REAPING MERELY FREES THEM OF SIN.
THE ZANPAKU-TÔ CLEANSES THEM...
SO THEY CAN ENTER THE SOUL SOCIETY.
THAT IS THE REASON ...
SOUL REAPERS EXIST.
SKRFF
THEN ...
... GOODBYE ORIHIME ...
KAKEI...

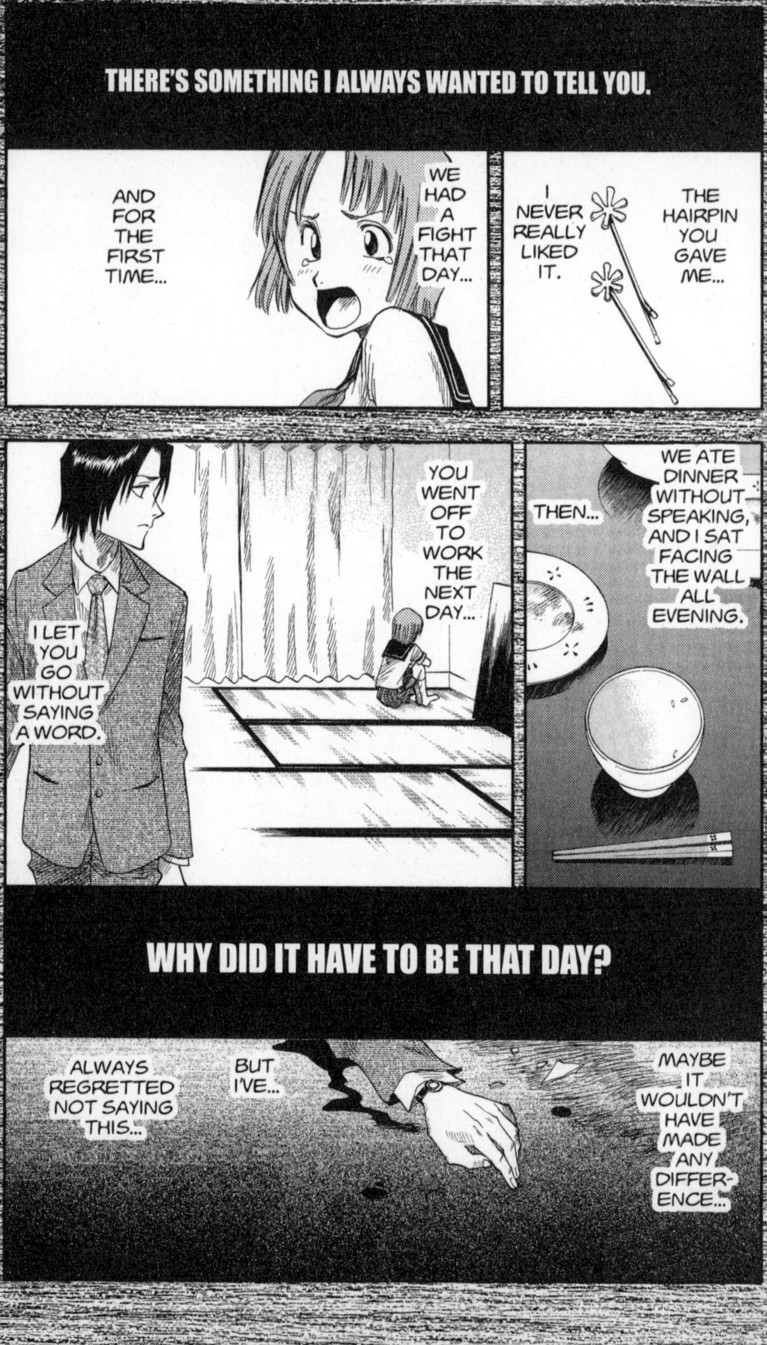
THERE'S SOMETHING I ALWAYS WANTED TO TELL YOU.
THE HAIRPIN YOU GAVE ME...
I NEVER REALLY LIKED IT.
WE HAD A FIGHT THAT DAY...
AND FOR THE FIRST TIME...
WE ATE DINNER WITHOUT SPEAKING, AND I SAT FACING THE WALL ALL EVENING.
THEN...
YOU WENT OFF TO WORK THE NEXT DAY...
I LET YOU GO WITHOUT SAYING A WORD.
WHY DID IT HAVE TO BE THAT DAY?
MAYBE IT WOULDN'T HAVE MADE ANY DIFFERENCE...
BUT I'VE...
ALWAYS REGRETTED NOT SAYING THIS...

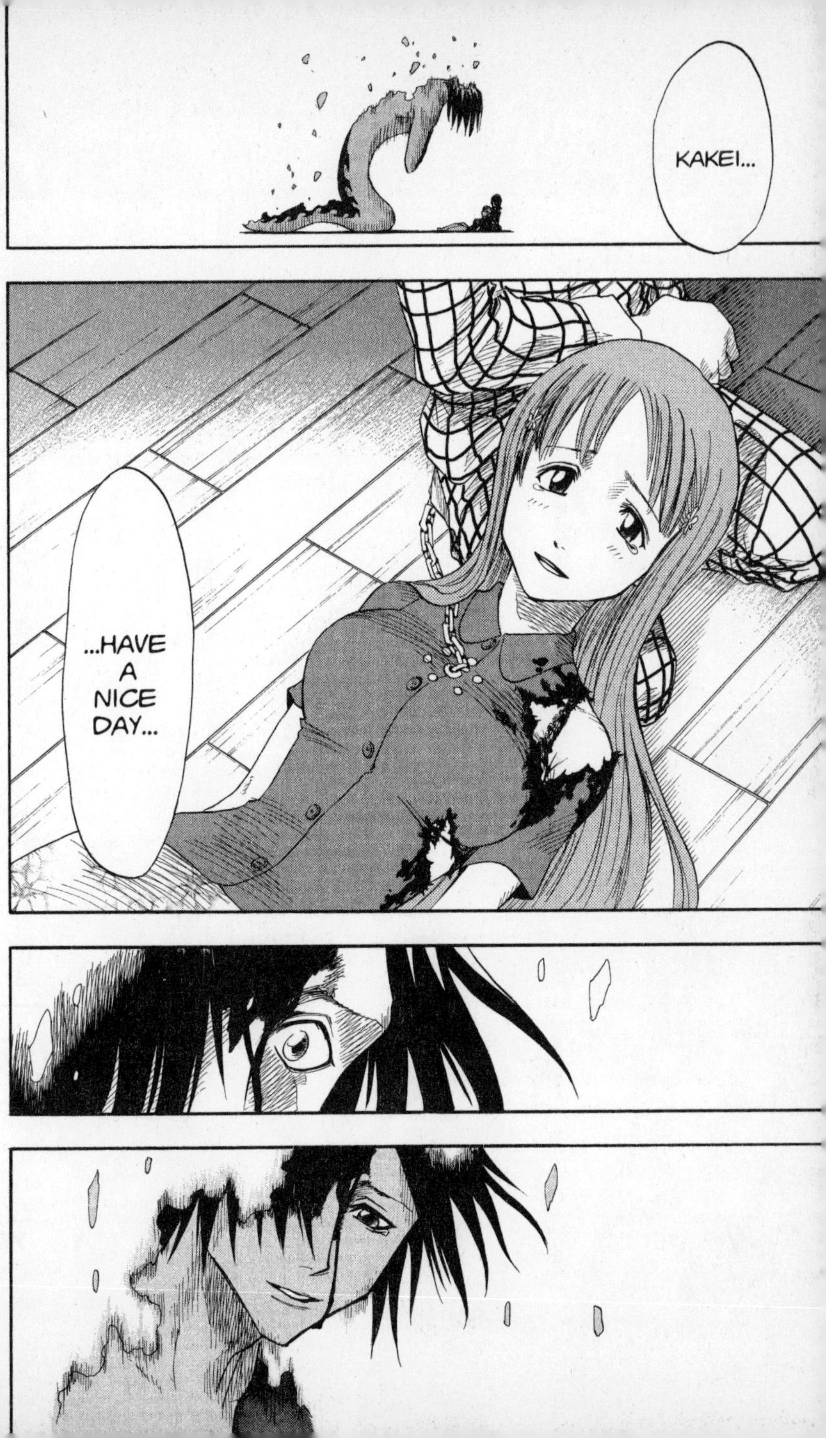
KAKEI...
...HAVE A NICE DAY...

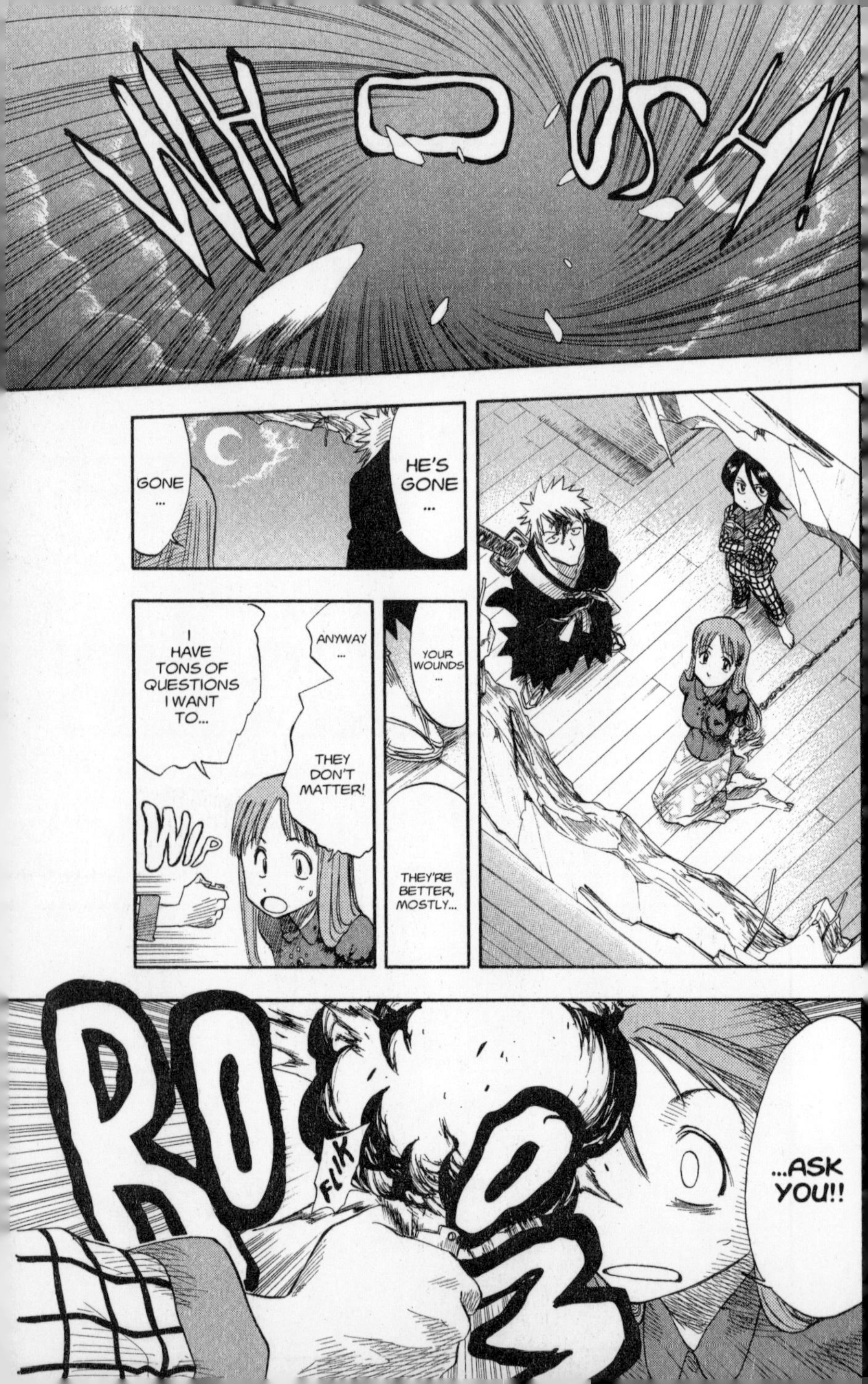
WHOOSH!
HE'S GONE ...
GONE ...
YOUR WOUNDS ...
THEY'RE BETTER, MOSTLY...
ANYWAY ...
THEY DON'T MATTER!
I HAVE TONS OF QUESTIONS I WANT TO...
WIP
...ASK YOU!!
ROOM
FLIK

READ THIS WAY

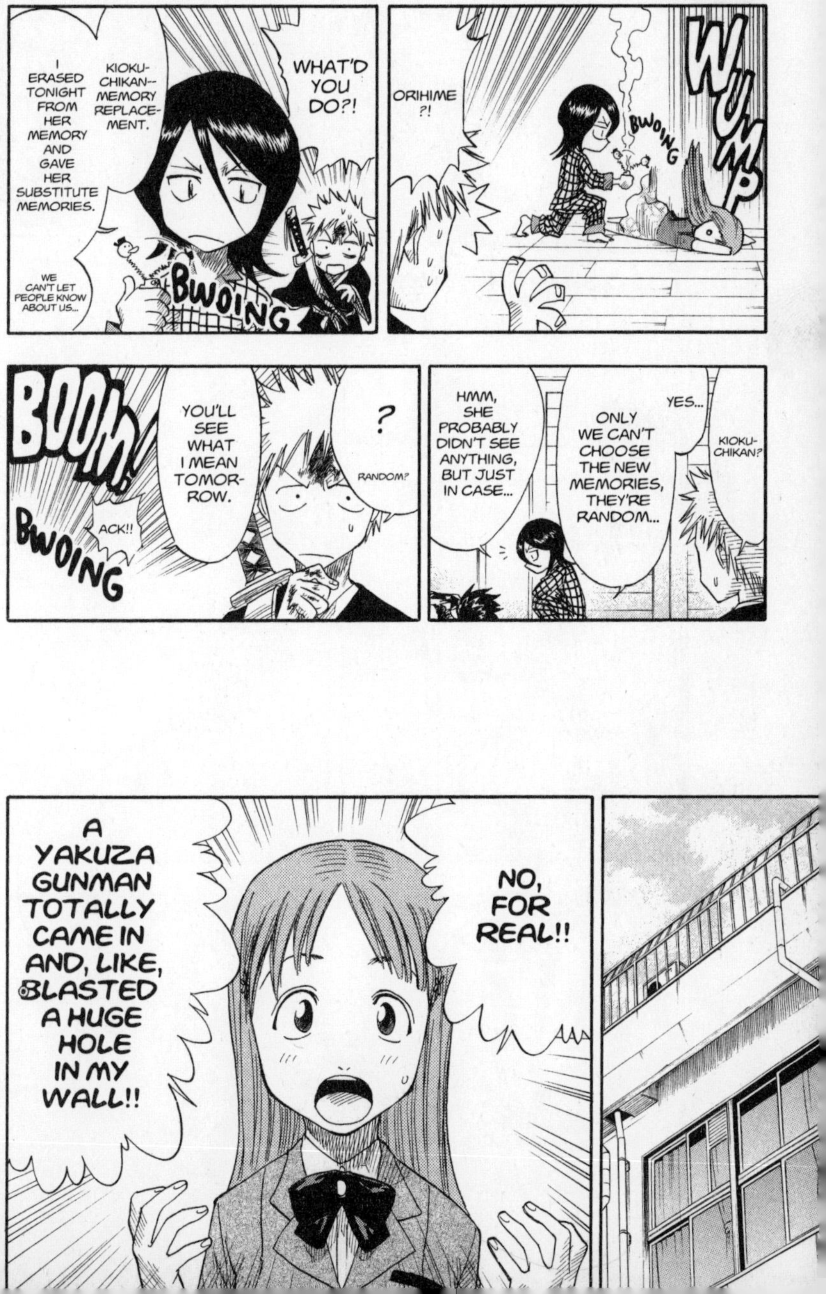

WUMP
BWOING
ORIHIME ?!
WHAT'D YOU DO?!
KIOKU-CHIKAN-- MEMORY REPLACEMENT.
I ERASED TONIGHT FROM HER MEMORY AND GAVE HER SUBSTITUTE MEMORIES.
WE CAN'T LET PEOPLE KNOW ABOUT US...
BWOING
KIOKU-CHIKAN?
YES...
ONLY WE CAN'T CHOOSE THE NEW MEMORIES, THEY'RE RANDOM...
HMM, SHE PROBABLY DIDN'T SEE ANYTHING, BUT JUST IN CASE...
?
RANDOM?
YOU'LL SEE WHAT I MEAN TOMORROW.
BOOM!
ACK!!
BWOING
NO, FOR REAL!!
A YAKUZA GUNMAN TOTALLY CAME IN AND, LIKE, BLASTED A HUGE HOLE IN MY WALL!!

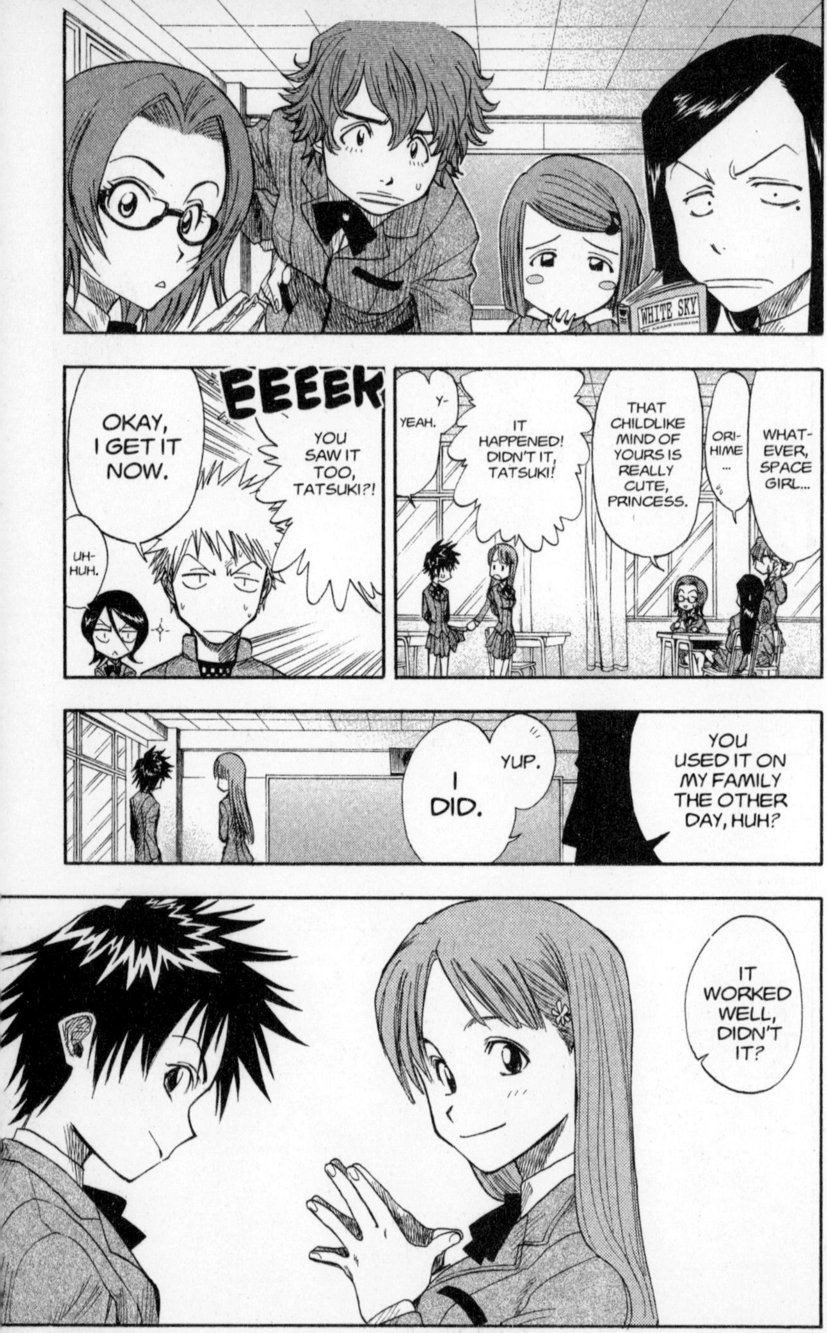
WHITE SKY
WHAT-EVER, SPACE GIRL...
ORI-HIME ...
THAT CHILDLIKE MIND OF YOURS IS REALLY CUTE, PRINCESS.
IT HAPPENED! DIDN'T IT, TATSUKI!
Y-YEAH.
EEEEK
YOU SAW IT TOO, TATSUKI?!
OKAY, I GET IT NOW.
UH-HUH.
YOU USED IT ON MY FAMILY THE OTHER DAY, HUH?
YUP.
I DID.
IT WORKED WELL, DIDN'T IT?

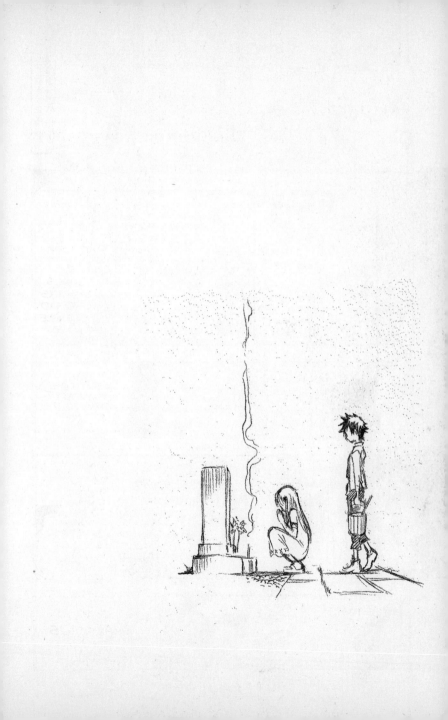

7: THE PINK CHEEKED PARAKEET

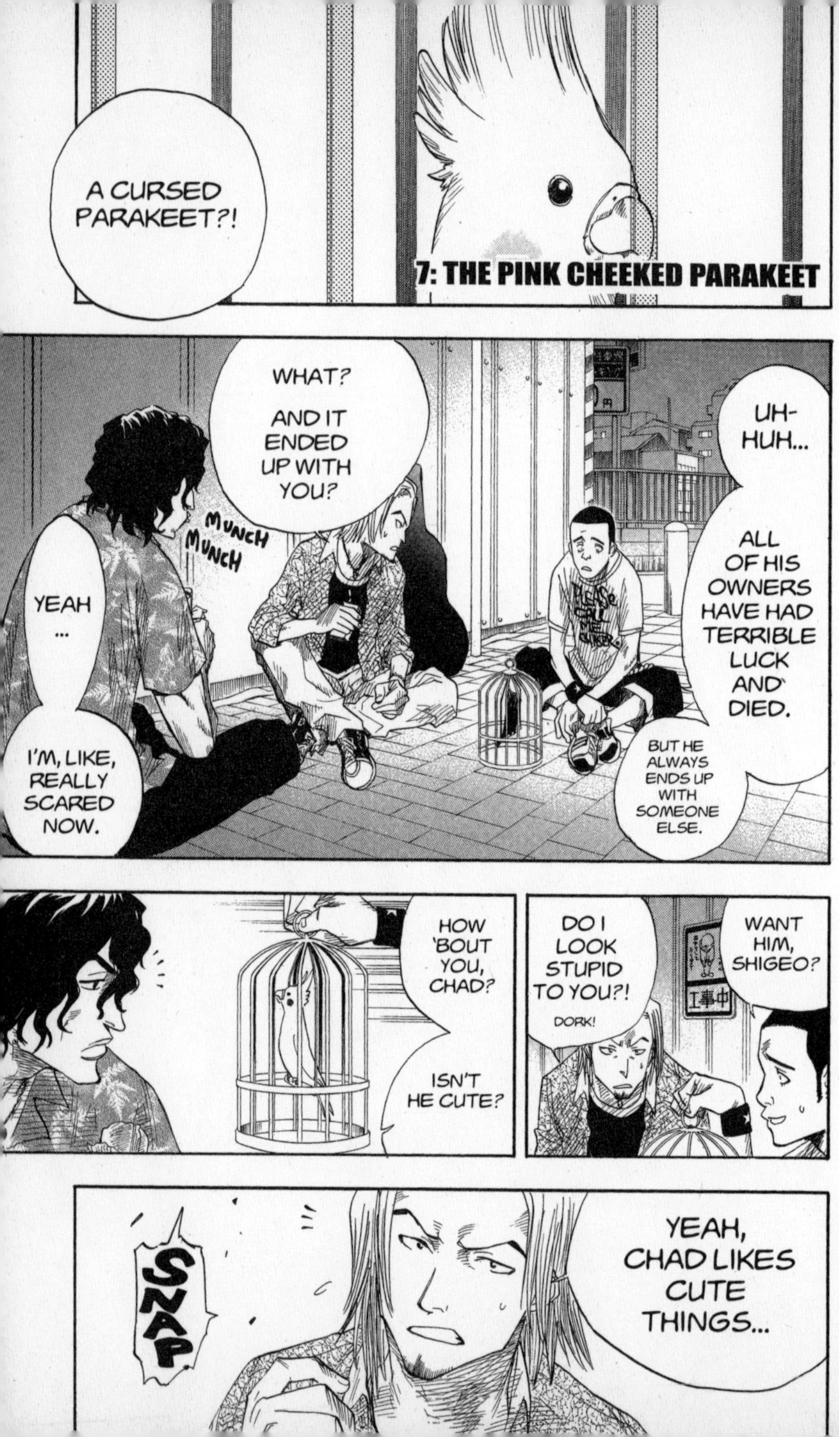
A CURSED PARAKEET?!
UH-HUH...
ALL OF HIS OWNERS HAVE HAD TERRIBLE LUCK AND DIED.
BUT HE ALWAYS ENDS UP WITH SOMEONE ELSE.
WHAT?
AND IT ENDED UP WITH YOU?
MUNCH MUNCH
YEAH ...
I'M, LIKE, REALLY SCARED NOW.
WANT HIM, SHIGEO?
工事中
DO I LOOK STUPID TO YOU?!
DORK!
HOW 'BOUT YOU, CHAD?
ISN'T HE CUTE?
YEAH, CHAD LIKES CUTE THINGS...
SNAP

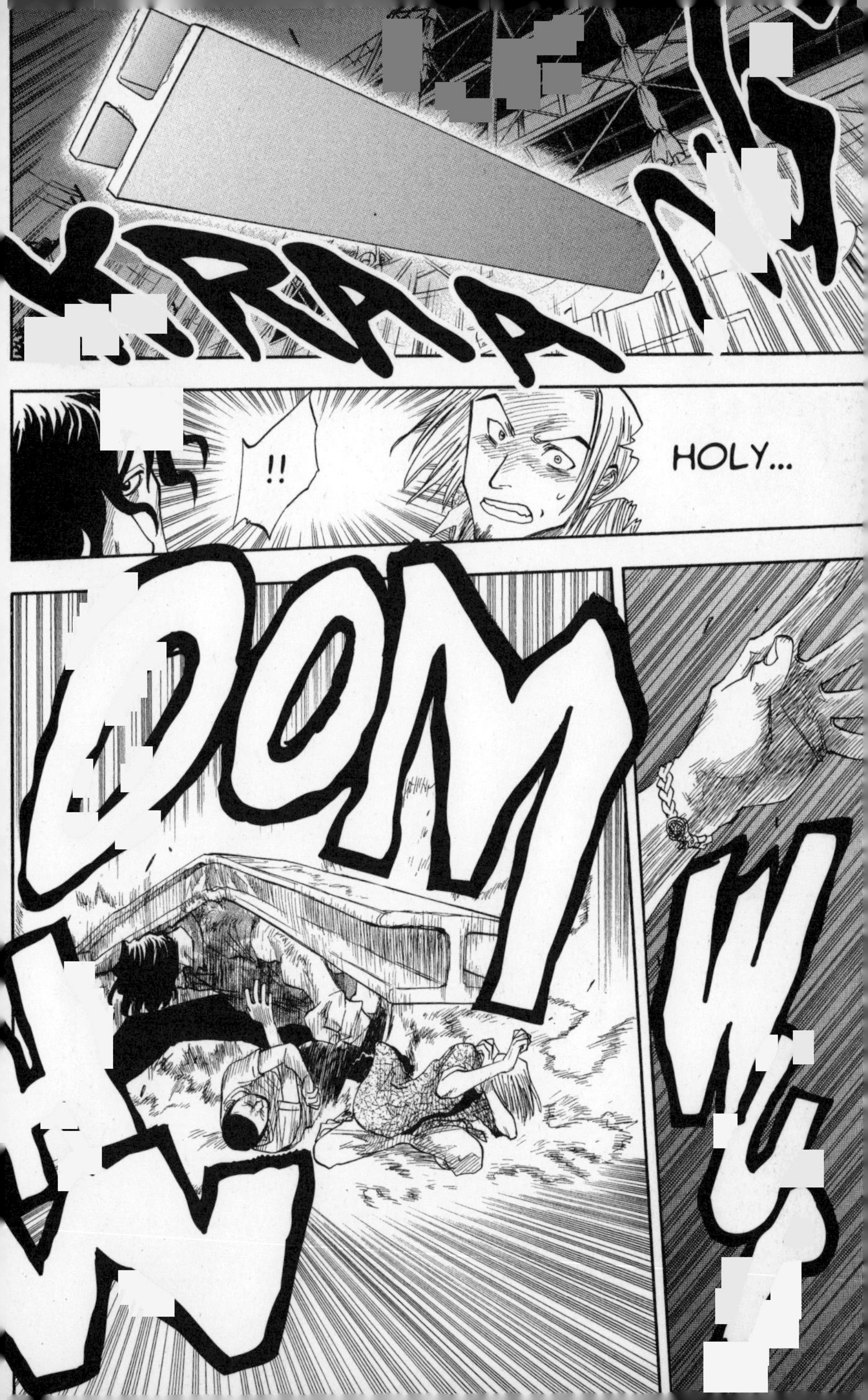
HOLY...
!!

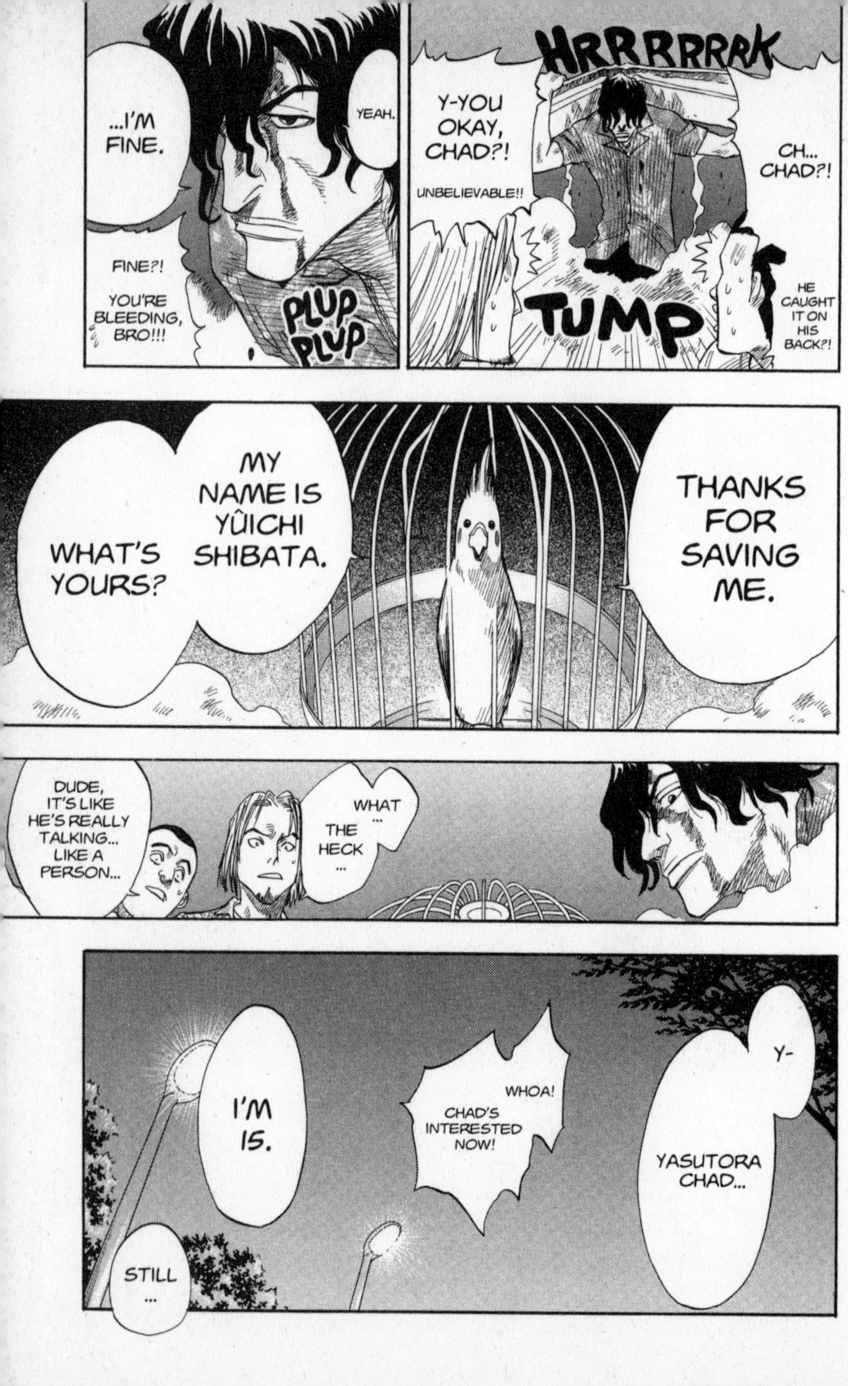
HRRRRRRK
CH... CHAD?!
Y-YOU OKAY, CHAD?!
UNBELIEVABLE!!
HE CAUGHT IT ON HIS BACK?!
TUMP
YEAH.
...I'M FINE.
FINE?!
YOU'RE BLEEDING, BRO!!!
PLUP PLUP
THANKS FOR SAVING ME.
MY NAME IS YÛICHI SHIBATA.
WHAT'S YOURS?
WHAT... THE HECK...
DUDE, IT'S LIKE HE'S REALLY TALKING... LIKE A PERSON...
Y-
YASUTORA CHAD...
WHOA! CHAD'S INTERESTED NOW!
I'M IS.
STILL...

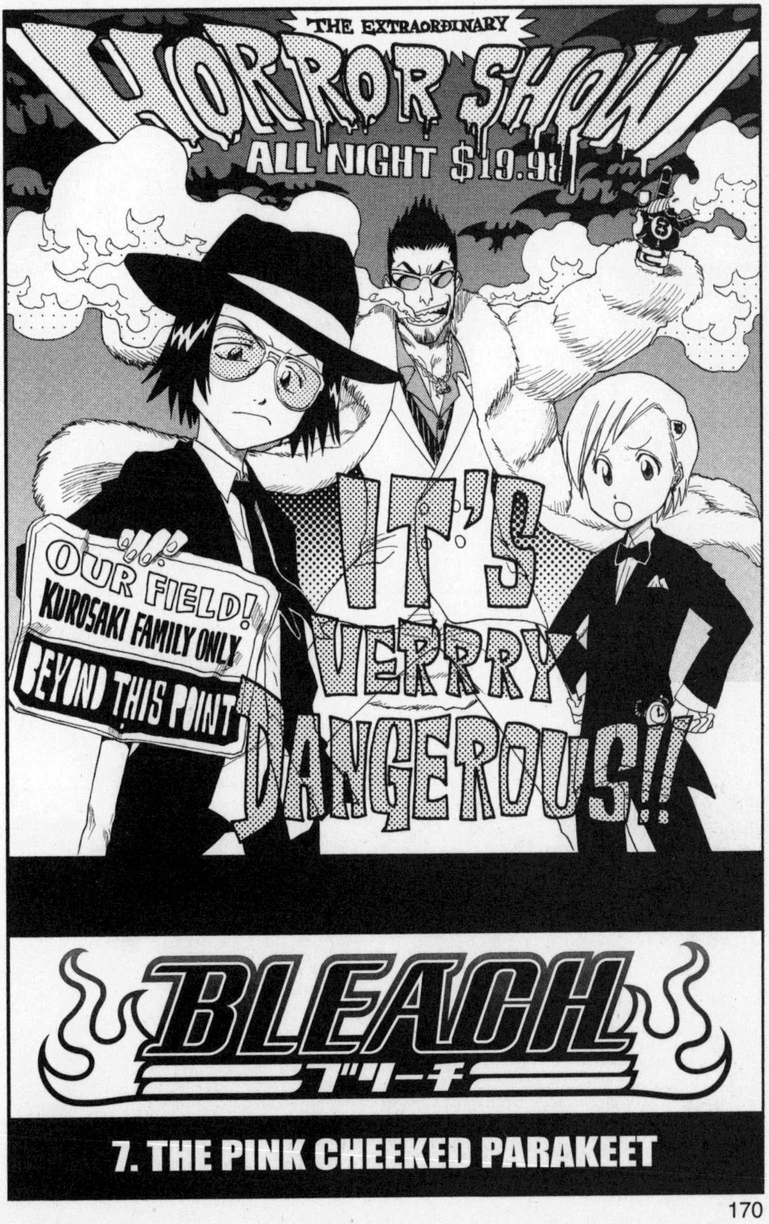
THE EXTRAORDINARY
HORROR SHOW
ALL NIGHT $19.9
OUR FIELD! KUROSAKI FAMILY ONLY BEYOND THIS POINT
IT'S VERRRY DANGEROUS!!

BLEACH
ブリーチ

7. THE PINK CHEEKED PARAKEET

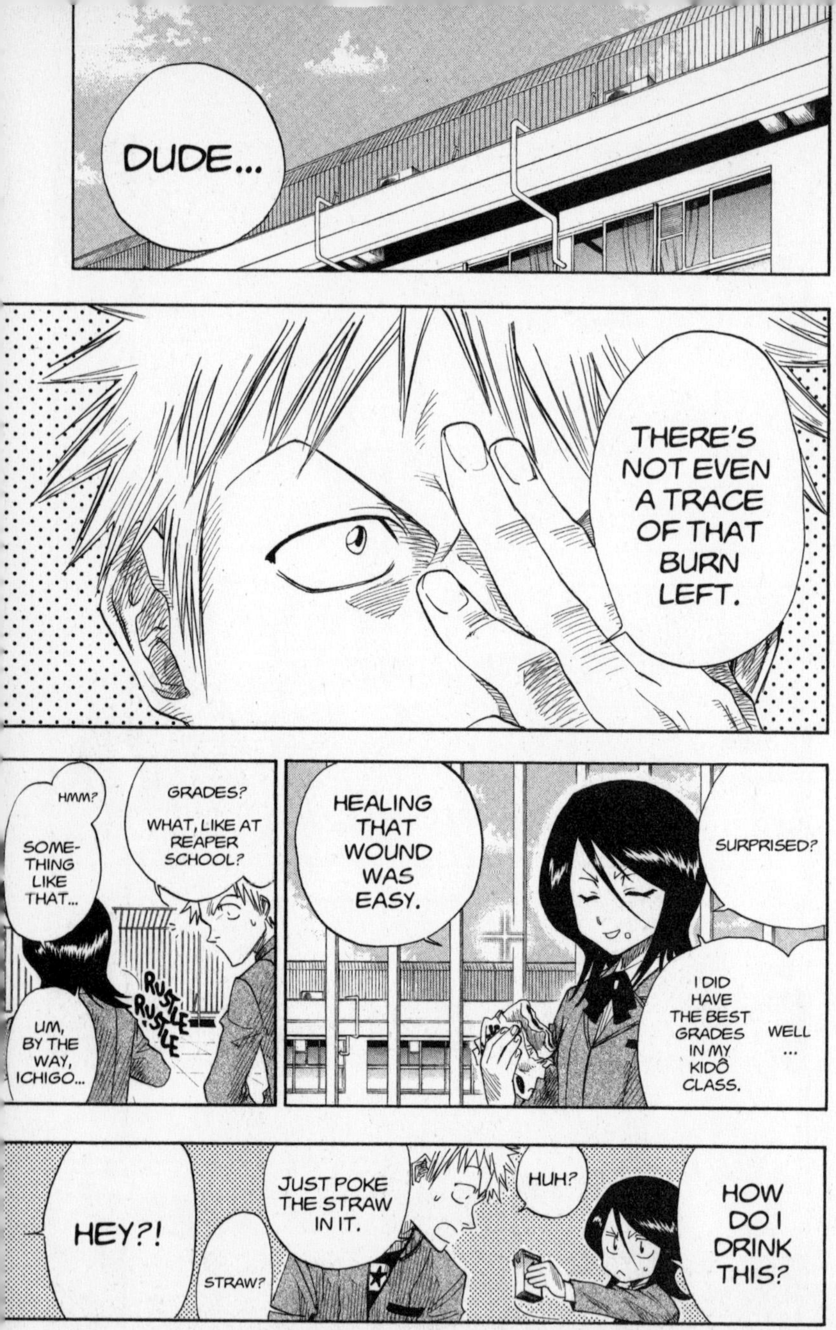
DUDE...
THERE'S NOT EVEN A TRACE OF THAT BURN LEFT.
SURPRISED?
WELL...
I DID HAVE THE BEST GRADES IN MY KIDÔ CLASS.
HEALING THAT WOUND WAS EASY.
GRADES?
WHAT, LIKE AT REAPER SCHOOL?
HMM?
SOME-THING LIKE THAT...
RUSTLE RUSTLE
UM, BY THE WAY, ICHIGO...
HOW DO I DRINK THIS?
HUH?
JUST POKE THE STRAW IN IT.
STRAW?
HEY?!

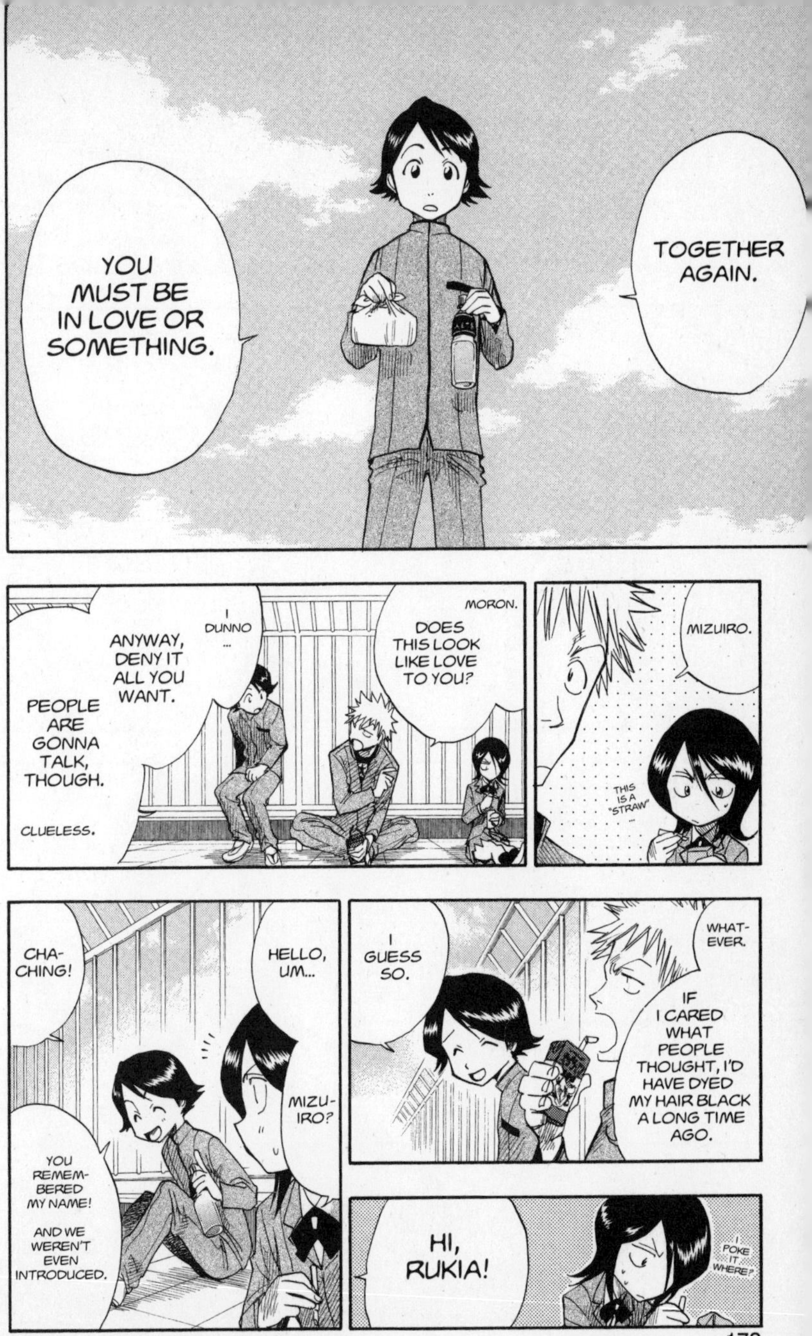
TOGETHER AGAIN.
YOU MUST BE IN LOVE OR SOMETHING.
MIZUIRO.
THIS IS A "STRAW"...
MORON.
DOES THIS LOOK LIKE LOVE TO YOU?
I DUNNO...
ANYWAY, DENY IT ALL YOU WANT.
PEOPLE ARE GONNA TALK, THOUGH.
CLUELESS.
WHAT-EVER.
IF I CARED WHAT PEOPLE THOUGHT, I'D HAVE DYED MY HAIR BLACK A LONG TIME AGO.
I GUESS SO.
I POKE IT WHERE?
HI, RUKIA!
HELLO, UM...
CHA-CHING!
MIZU-IRO?
YOU REMEM-BERED MY NAME!
AND WE WEREN'T EVEN INTRODUCED.

READ THIS WAY

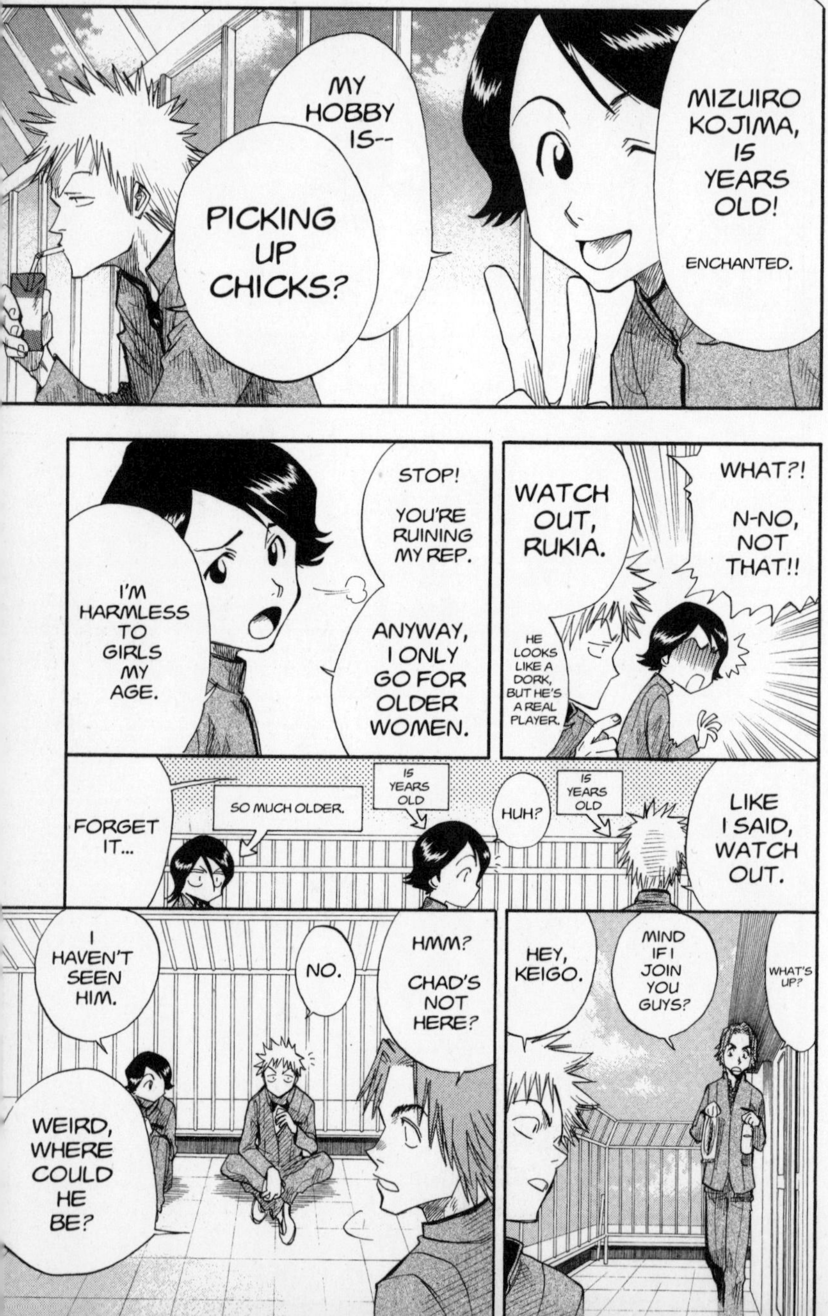

MIZUIRO KOJIMA, 15 YEARS OLD!
ENCHANTED.
MY HOBBY IS--
PICKING UP CHICKS?
WHAT?!
N-NO, NOT THAT!!
WATCH OUT, RUKIA.
HE LOOKS LIKE A DORK, BUT HE'S A REAL PLAYER.
STOP!
YOU'RE RUINING MY REP.
ANYWAY, I ONLY GO FOR OLDER WOMEN.
I'M HARMLESS TO GIRLS MY AGE.
LIKE I SAID, WATCH OUT.
15 YEARS OLD
HUH?
15 YEARS OLD
SO MUCH OLDER.
FORGET IT...
WHAT'S UP?
MIND IF I JOIN YOU GUYS?
HEY, KEIGO.
HMM?
CHAD'S NOT HERE?
NO.
I HAVEN'T SEEN HIM.
WEIRD, WHERE COULD HE BE?

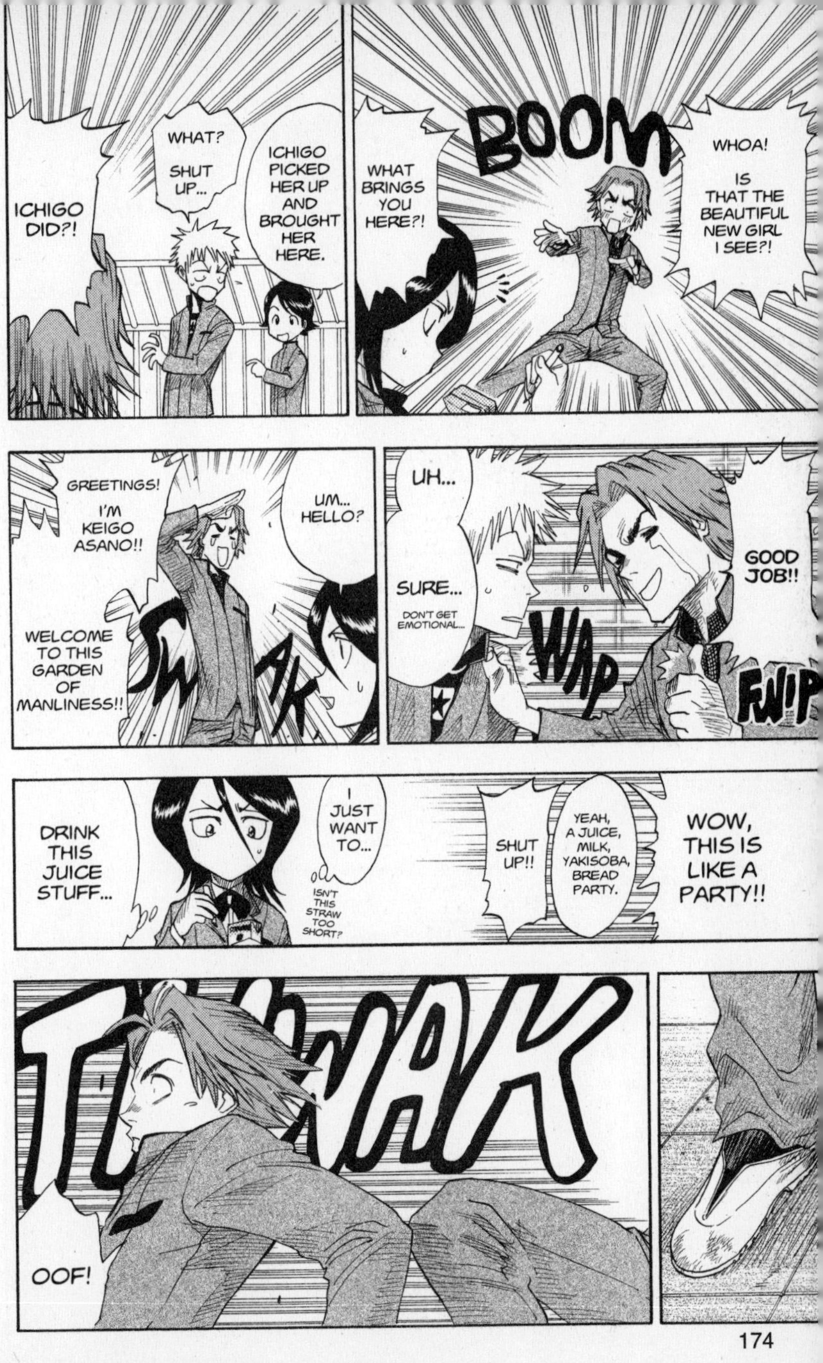
WHOA!
IS THAT THE BEAUTIFUL NEW GIRL I SEE?!
BOOM
WHAT BRINGS YOU HERE?!
ICHIGO PICKED HER UP AND BROUGHT HER HERE.
WHAT?
SHUT UP...
ICHIGO DID?!
GOOD JOB!!
FWIP
WAP
UH...
SURE...
DON'T GET EMOTIONAL...
UM... HELLO?
GREETINGS!
I'M KEIGO ASANO!!
WELCOME TO THIS GARDEN OF MANLINESS!!
WOW, THIS IS LIKE A PARTY!!
YEAH, A JUICE, MILK, YAKISOBA, BREAD PARTY.
SHUT UP!!
I JUST WANT TO...
ISN'T THIS STRAW TOO SHORT?
DRINK THIS JUICE STUFF...
OOF!

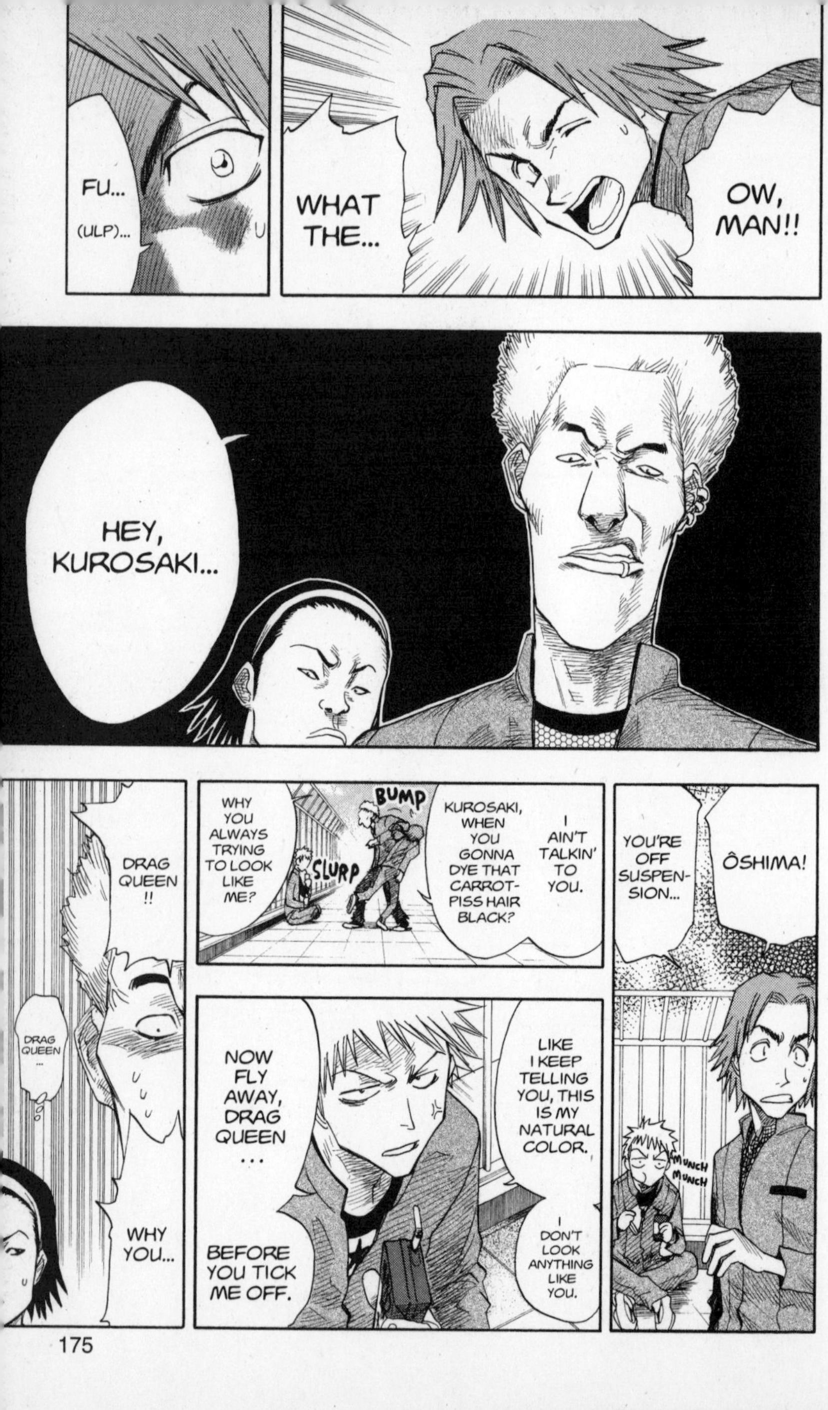
OW, MAN!!
WHAT THE...
FU...
(ULP)...
HEY, KUROSAKI...
ÔSHIMA!
YOU'RE OFF SUSPENSION...
MUNCH MUNCH
I AIN'T TALKIN' TO YOU.
KUROSAKI, WHEN YOU GONNA DYE THAT CARROT-PISS HAIR BLACK?
BUMP
SLURP
WHY YOU ALWAYS TRYING TO LOOK LIKE ME?
LIKE I KEEP TELLING YOU, THIS IS MY NATURAL COLOR.
I DON'T LOOK ANYTHING LIKE YOU.
NOW FLY AWAY, DRAG QUEEN . . .
BEFORE YOU TICK ME OFF.
DRAG QUEEN !!
DRAG QUEEN ...
WHY YOU...

READ THIS WAY

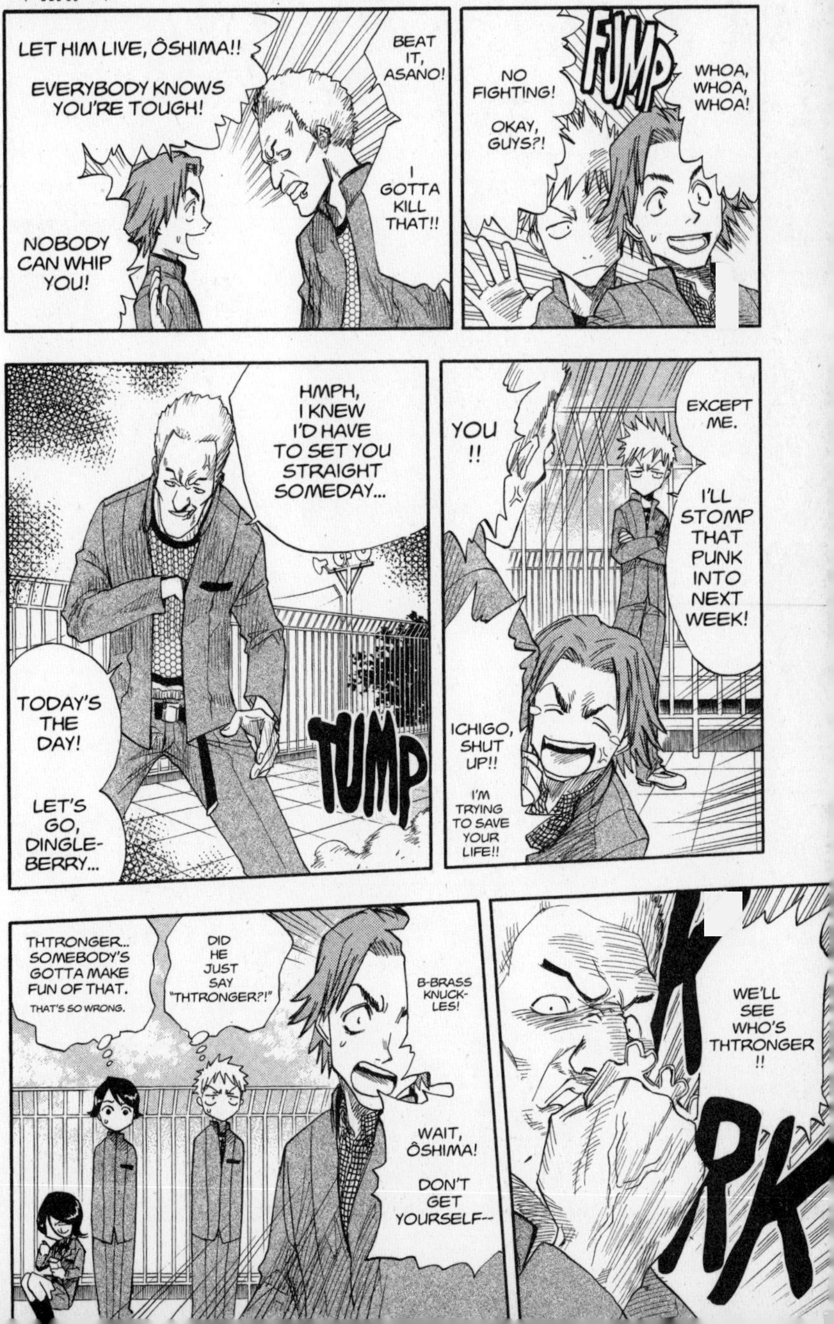
FUMP
WHOA, WHOA, WHOA!
NO FIGHTING!
OKAY, GUYS?!
BEAT IT, ASANO!
I GOTTA KILL THAT!!
LET HIM LIVE, ÔSHIMA!!
EVERYBODY KNOWS YOU'RE TOUGH!
NOBODY CAN WHIP YOU!
EXCEPT ME.
I'LL STOMP THAT PUNK INTO NEXT WEEK!
YOU!!
ICHIGO, SHUT UP!!
I'M TRYING TO SAVE YOUR LIFE!!
HMPH, I KNEW I'D HAVE TO SET YOU STRAIGHT SOMEDAY...
TUMP
TODAY'S THE DAY!
LET'S GO, DINGLE-BERRY...
WE'LL SEE WHO'S THTRONGER!!
B-BRASS KNUCK-LES!
DID HE JUST SAY "THTRONGER?!"
THTRONGER... SOMEBODY'S GOTTA MAKE FUN OF THAT.
THAT'S SO WRONG.
WAIT, ÔSHIMA!
DON'T GET YOURSELF--

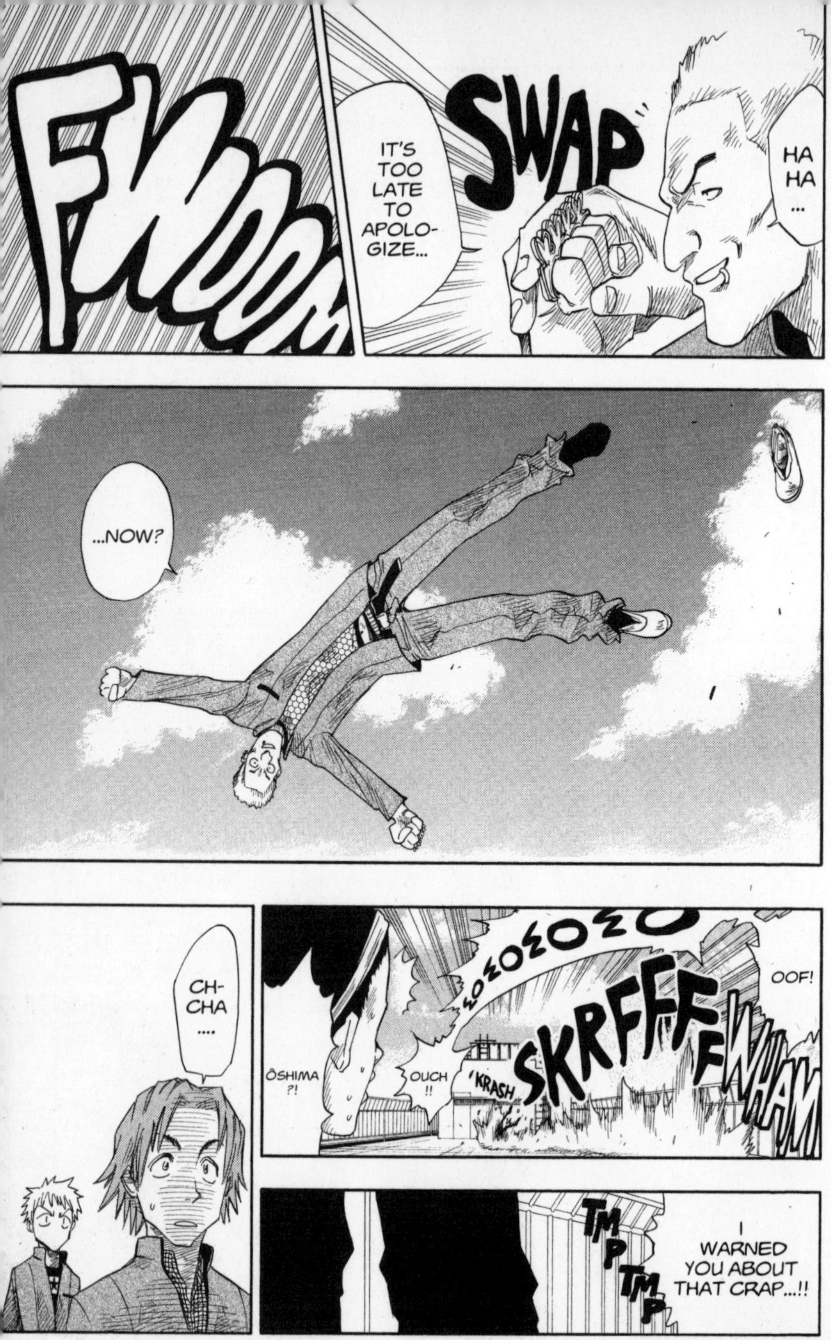
HA HA ...
SWAP
IT'S TOO LATE TO APOLO-GIZE...
FWOOO
...NOW?
OOF!
WHAM
SKRFFFF
'KRASH
OUCH !!
ÔSHIMA ?!
I WARNED YOU ABOUT THAT CRAP...!!
TMP TMP
CH-CHA ....

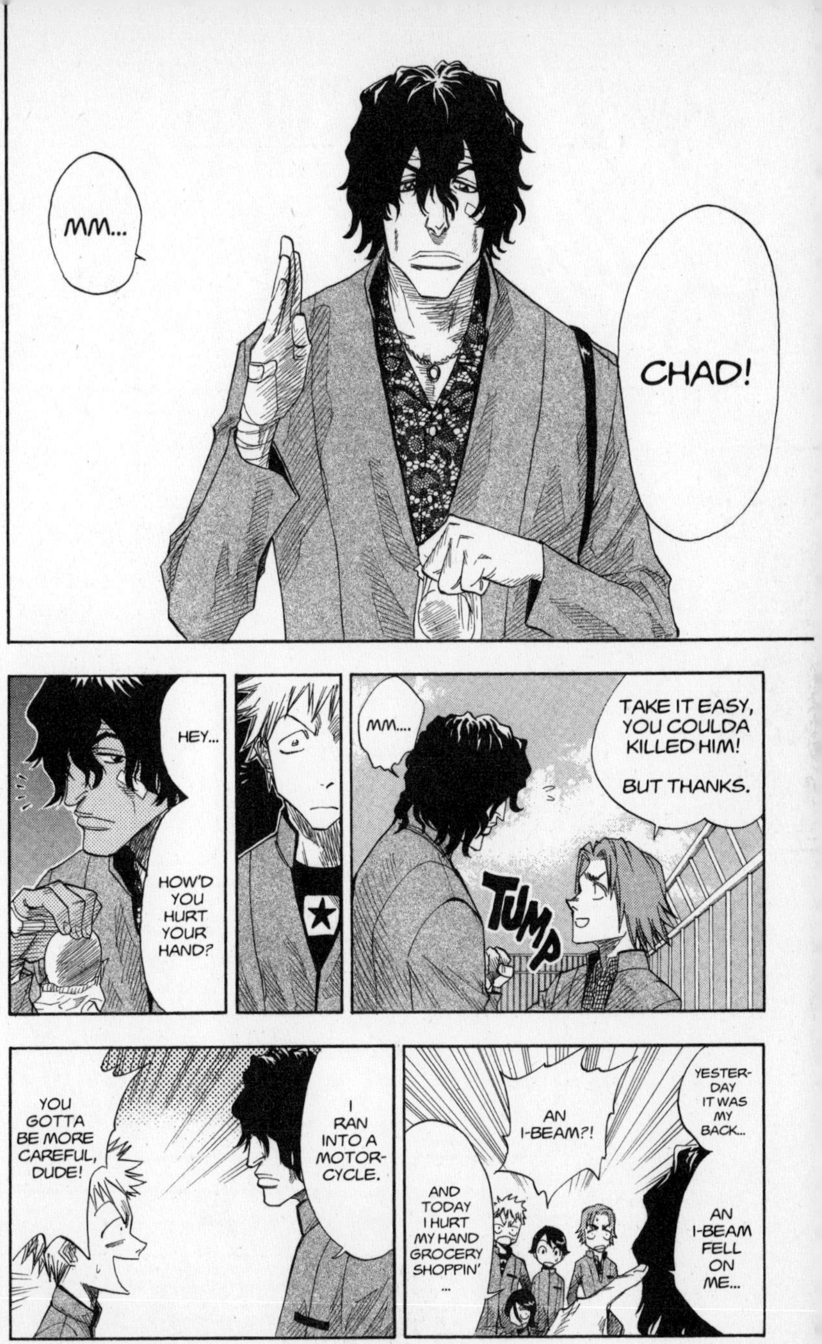
CHAD!
MM...
TAKE IT EASY, YOU COULDA KILLED HIM!
BUT THANKS.
TUMP
MM....
HEY...
HOW'D YOU HURT YOUR HAND?
YESTER-DAY IT WAS MY BACK...
AN I-BEAM FELL ON ME...
AN I-BEAM?!
AND TODAY I HURT MY HAND GROCERY SHOPPIN' ...
I RAN INTO A MOTOR-CYCLE.
YOU GOTTA BE MORE CAREFUL, DUDE!

READ THIS WAY

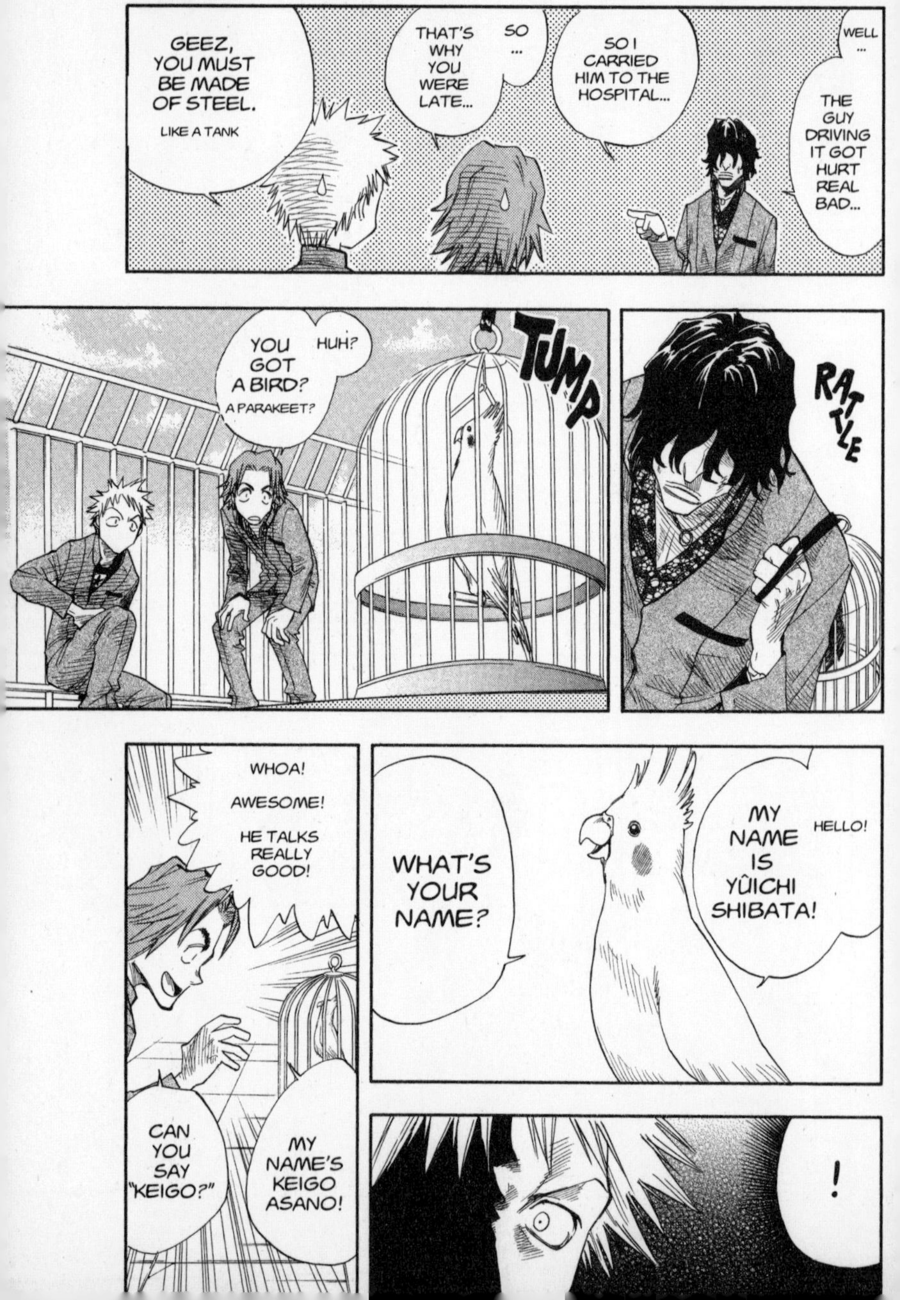
WELL ...
THE GUY DRIVING IT GOT HURT REAL BAD...
SO I CARRIED HIM TO THE HOSPITAL...
SO ...
THAT'S WHY YOU WERE LATE...
GEEZ, YOU MUST BE MADE OF STEEL.
LIKE A TANK
RATTLE
TUMP
HUH?
YOU GOT A BIRD?
A PARAKEET?
HELLO!
MY NAME IS YÛICHI SHIBATA!
WHAT'S YOUR NAME?
!
WHOA!
AWESOME!
HE TALKS REALLY GOOD!
MY NAME'S KEIGO ASANO!
CAN YOU SAY "KEIGO?"

READ THIS WAY

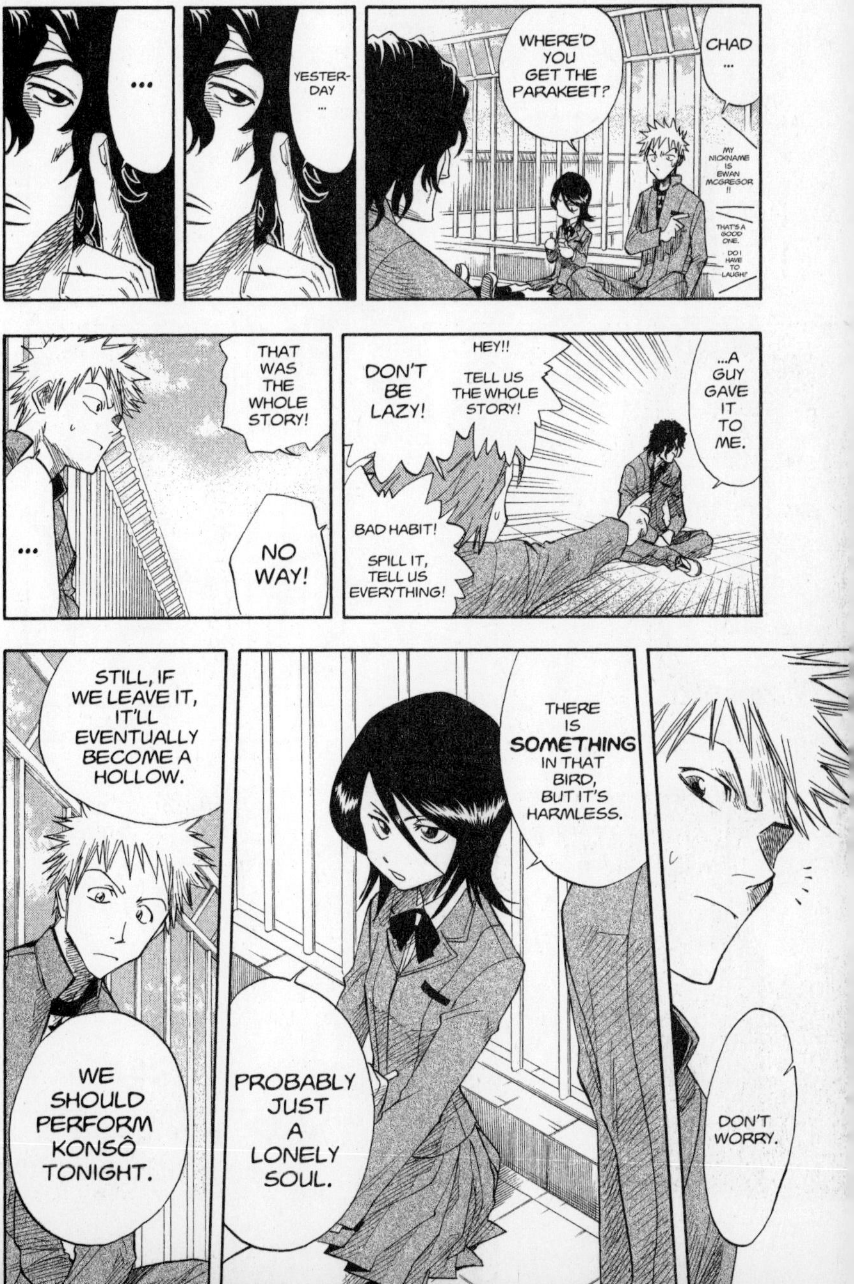

CHAD ...
WHERE'D YOU GET THE PARAKEET?
MY NICKNAME IS EWAN MCGREGOR!!
THAT'S A GOOD ONE.
DO I HAVE TO LAUGH?
YESTER-DAY ...
...
...A GUY GAVE IT TO ME.
HEY!!
TELL US THE WHOLE STORY!
DON'T BE LAZY!
BAD HABIT!
SPILL IT, TELL US EVERYTHING!
THAT WAS THE WHOLE STORY!
NO WAY!
...
DON'T WORRY.
THERE IS **SOMETHING** IN THAT BIRD, BUT IT'S HARMLESS.
PROBABLY JUST A LONELY SOUL.
STILL, IF WE LEAVE IT, IT'LL EVENTUALLY BECOME A HOLLOW.
WE SHOULD PERFORM KONSÔ TONIGHT.

READ THIS WAY

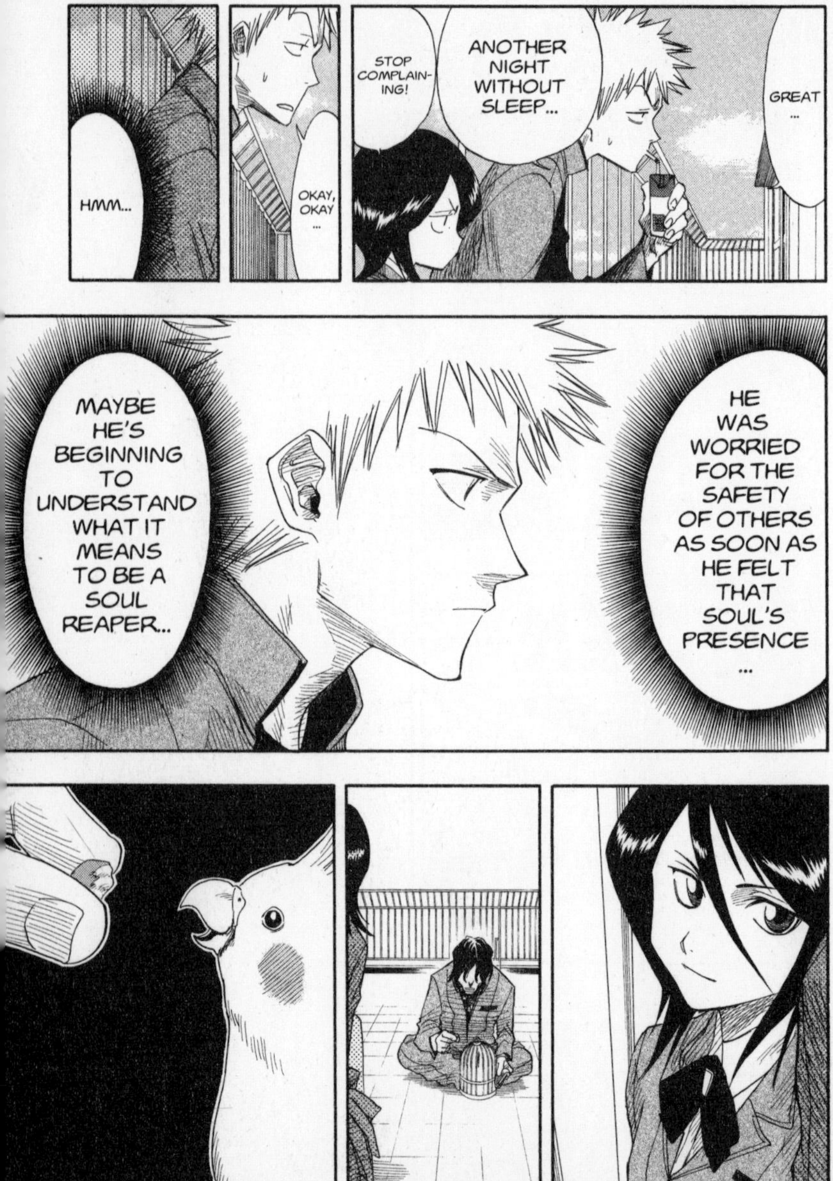
GREAT ...
ANOTHER NIGHT WITHOUT SLEEP...
STOP COMPLAINING!
OKAY, OKAY ...
HMM...
HE WAS WORRIED FOR THE SAFETY OF OTHERS AS SOON AS HE FELT THAT SOUL'S PRESENCE ...
MAYBE HE'S BEGINNING TO UNDERSTAND WHAT IT MEANS TO BE A SOUL REAPER...

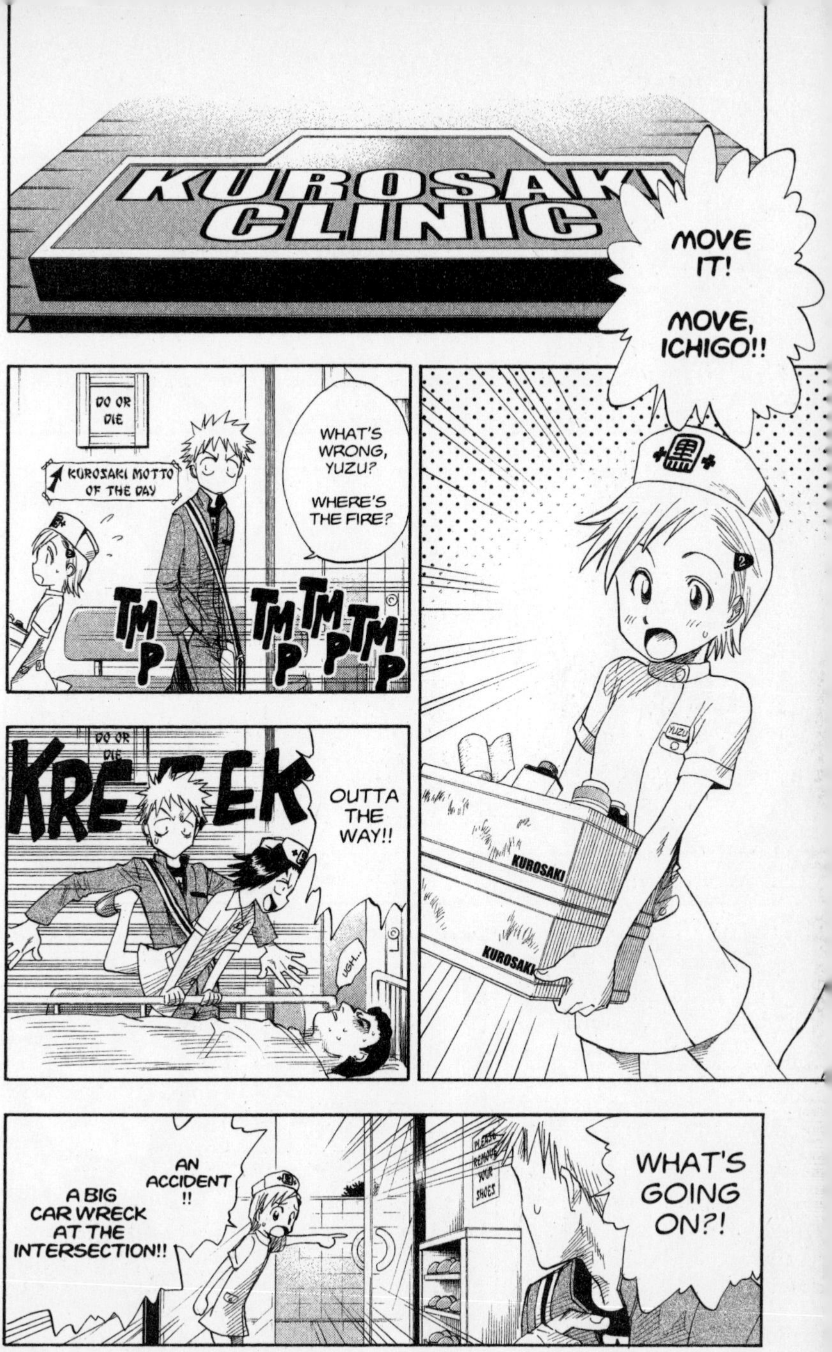
KUROSAKI CLINIC
MOVE IT!
MOVE, ICHIGO!!
YUZU
KUROSAKI
KUROSAKI
DO OR DIE
KUROSAKI MOTTO OF THE DAY
WHAT'S WRONG, YUZU?
WHERE'S THE FIRE?
TMP TMP TMP TMP
DO OR DIE
KREEEK
OUTTA THE WAY!!
UGH...
WHAT'S GOING ON?!
PLEASE REMOVE YOUR SHOES
AN ACCIDENT!!
A BIG CAR WRECK AT THE INTERSECTION!!

READ THIS WAY

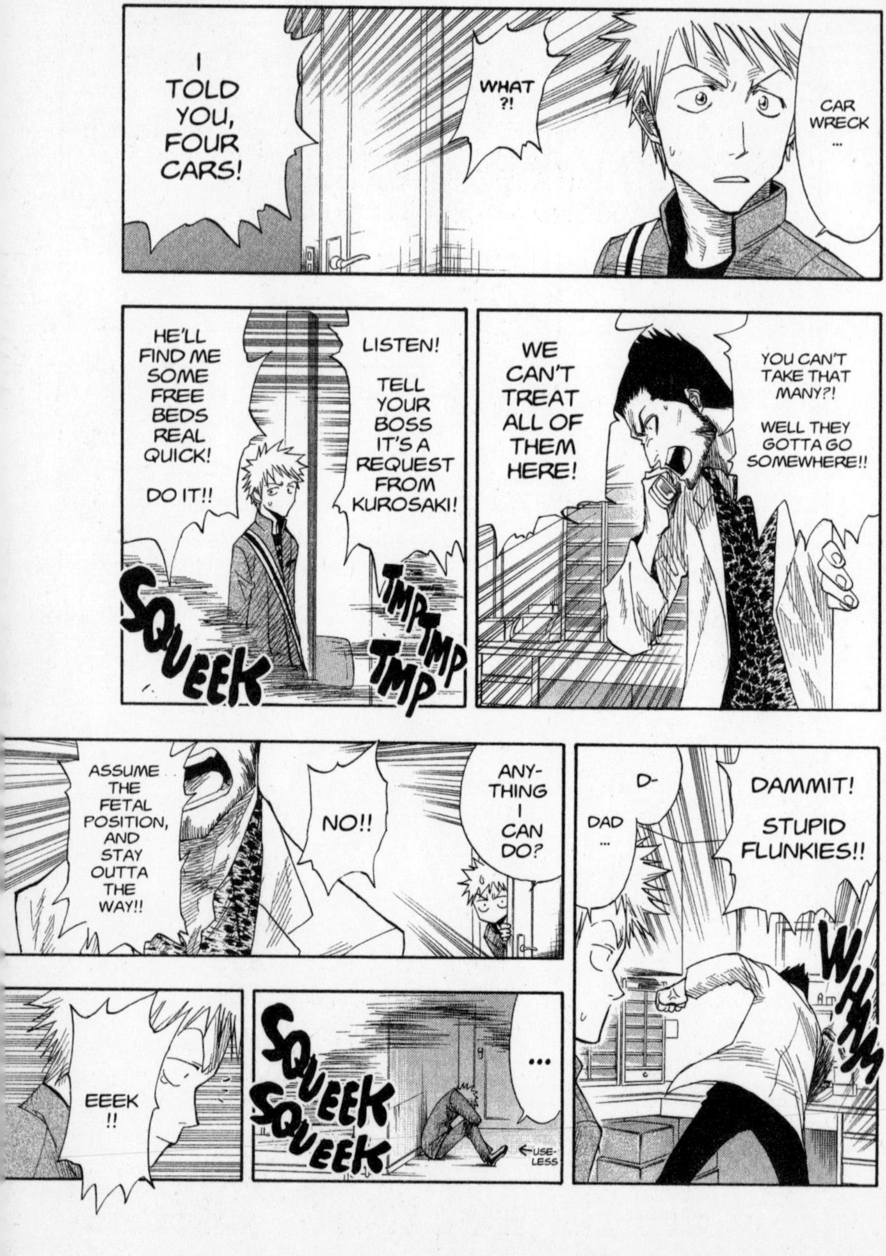
CAR WRECK ...
WHAT ?!
I TOLD YOU, FOUR CARS!
YOU CAN'T TAKE THAT MANY?!
WELL THEY GOTTA GO SOMEWHERE!!
WE CAN'T TREAT ALL OF THEM HERE!
LISTEN!
TELL YOUR BOSS IT'S A REQUEST FROM KUROSAKI!
HE'LL FIND ME SOME FREE BEDS REAL QUICK!
DO IT!!
TMP TMP TMP
SQUEEK
DAMMIT!
STUPID FLUNKIES!!
D-
DAD ...
WHAM
ANYTHING I CAN DO?
NO!!
ASSUME THE FETAL POSITION, AND STAY OUTTA THE WAY!!
...
SQUEEK SQUEEK
← USELESS
EEEK !!

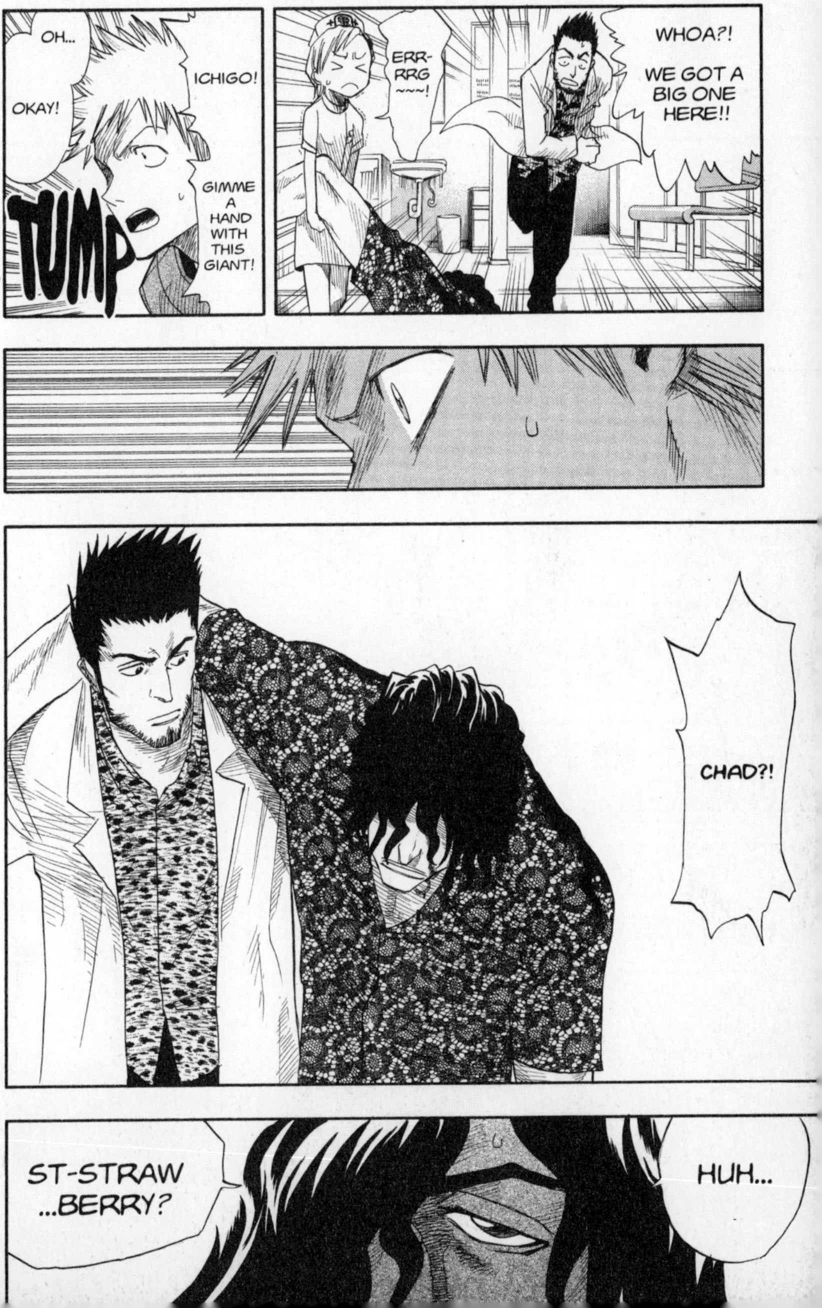
WHOA?! WE GOT A BIG ONE HERE!!
ERR-RRG ~~~!
ICHIGO!
GIMME A HAND WITH THIS GIANT!
OH...
OKAY!
TUMP
CHAD?!
HUH...
ST-STRAW ...BERRY?

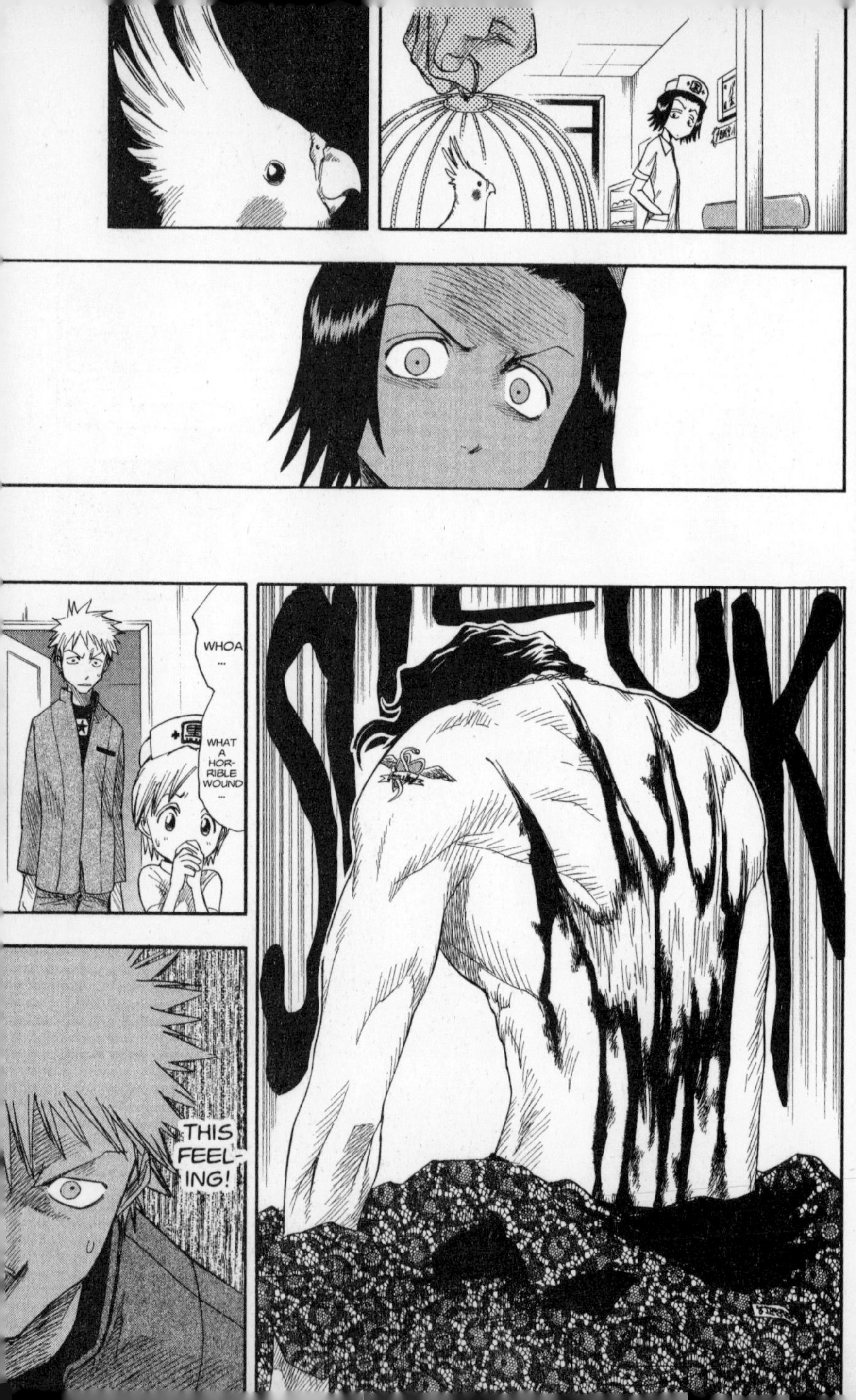
WHOA ...
WHAT A HOR-RIBLE WOUND ...
THIS FEEL-ING!

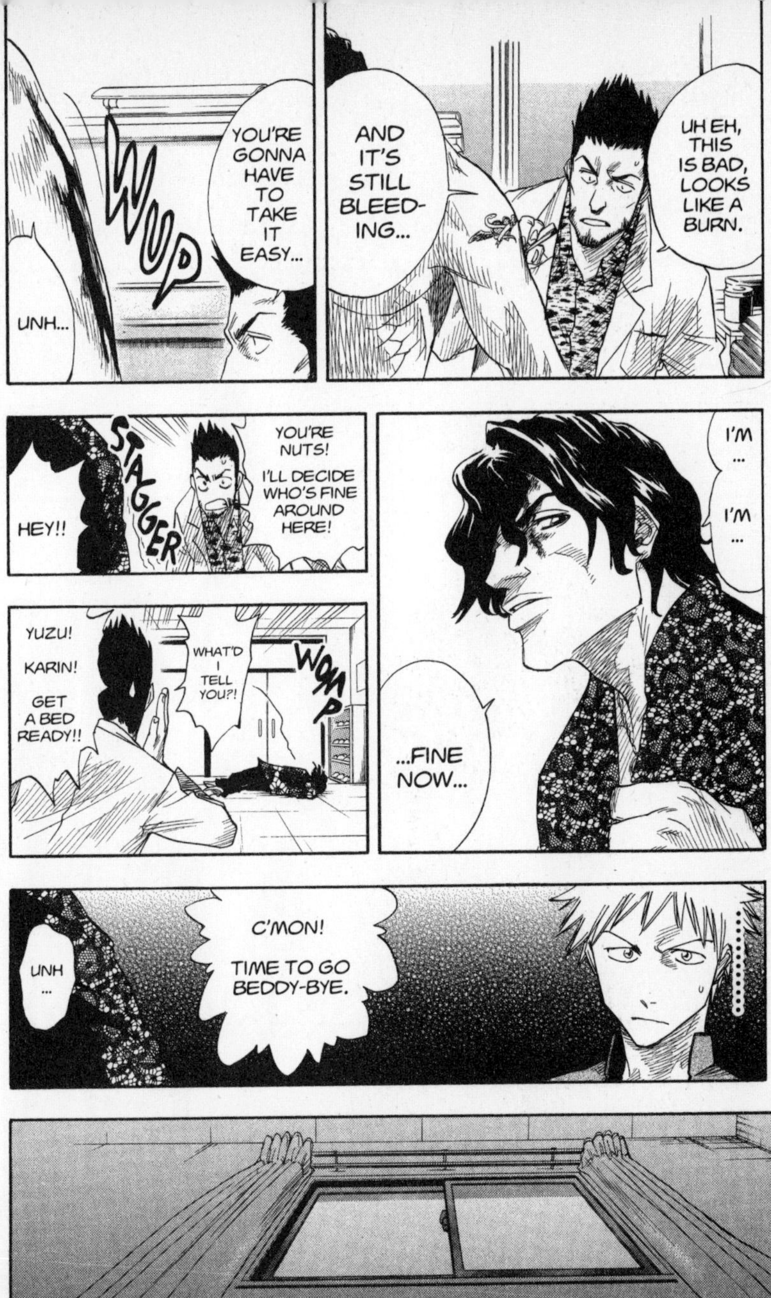
UH EH, THIS IS BAD, LOOKS LIKE A BURN.
AND IT'S STILL BLEEDING...
YOU'RE GONNA HAVE TO TAKE IT EASY...
WUP
UNH...
I'M ... I'M ...
...FINE NOW...
STAGGER
YOU'RE NUTS! I'LL DECIDE WHO'S FINE AROUND HERE!
HEY!!
WOMP
WHAT'D I TELL YOU?!
YUZU! KARIN! GET A BED READY!!
C'MON! TIME TO GO BEDDY-BYE.
UNH ...

READ THIS WAY

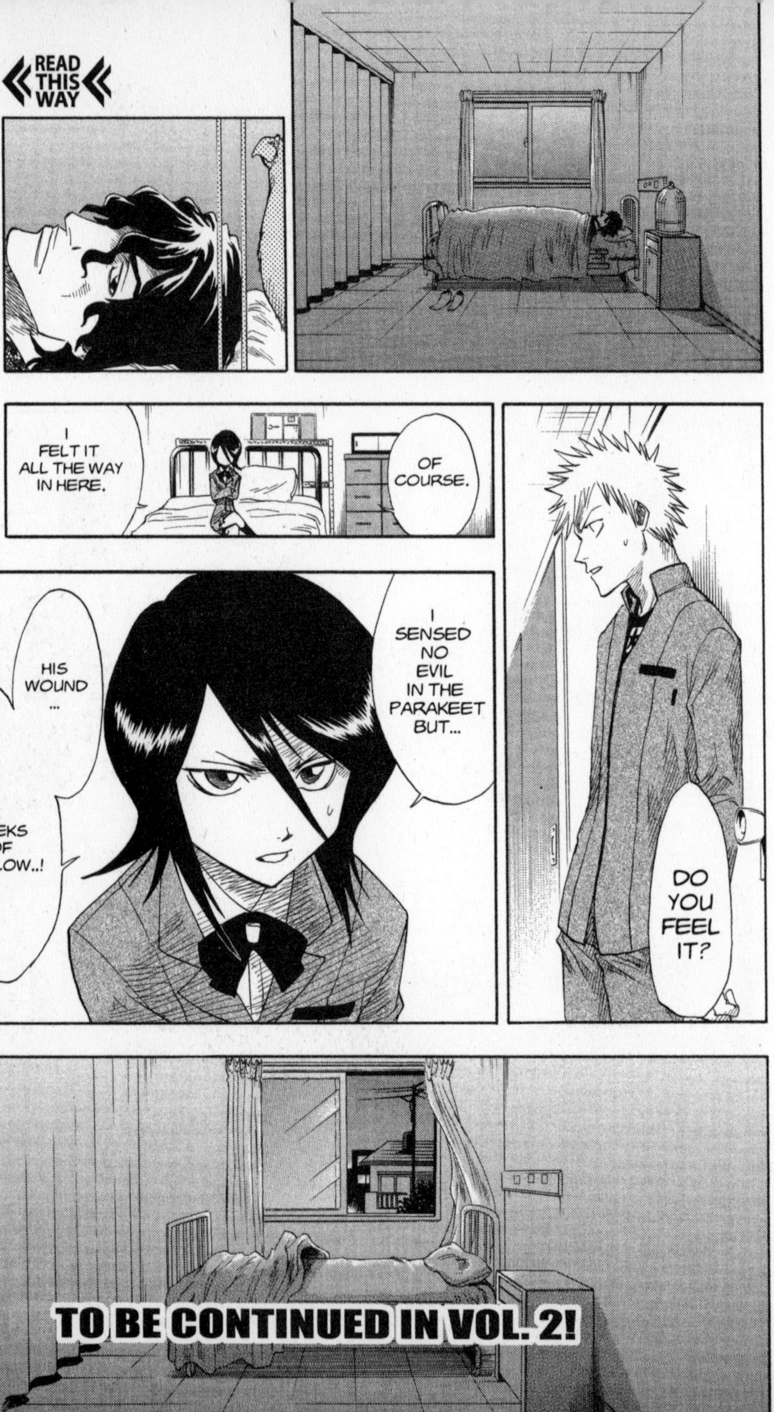
DO YOU FEEL IT?
OF COURSE.
I FELT IT ALL THE WAY IN HERE.
I SENSED NO EVIL IN THE PARAKEET BUT...
HIS WOUND ...
REEKS OF HOLLOW..!
TO BE CONTINUED IN VOL. 2!

OVERALL ATTENDANCE SCORE 13	ICHIGO KUROSAKI	クロサキ・イチゴ
MALE STUDENT ATTENDANCE SCORE 6		

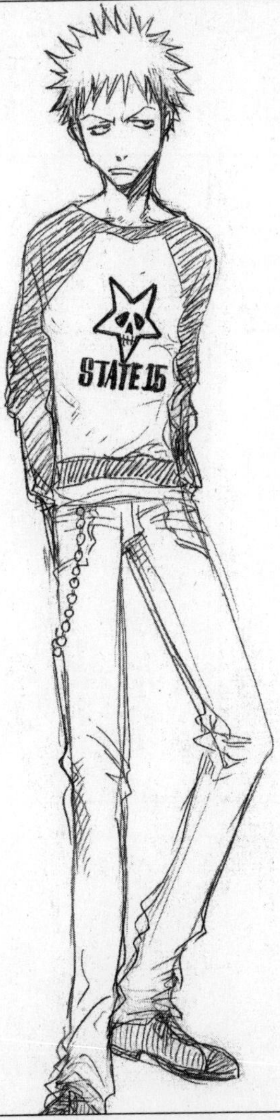
STATE 15

174 CM
61 KG
BLOOD TYPE AO
D.O.B. JULY 15TH

- LIKES SLIM FIT SHIRTS AND PANTS
- LIKES CHOCOLATE AND KARASHI MENTAIKO
- FAVORITE CELEBRITIES ARE MIKE NESS AND AL PACINO
- PERSON HE RESPECTS MOST IS WILLIAM SHAKESPEARE
- HOW TO PRONOUNCE NAME, ICHIGO EMPHASIS ON THE "I." ACCENTED LIKE "ECHIGO."

THEME SONG

BAD RELIGION

"NEWS FROM THE FRONT"

RECORDED IN
"STRANGER THAN FICTION"

OVERALL ATTENDANCE SCORE 11	RUKIA KUCHIKI	クチキ・ルキア
FEMALE STUDENT ATTENDANCE SCORE 6		

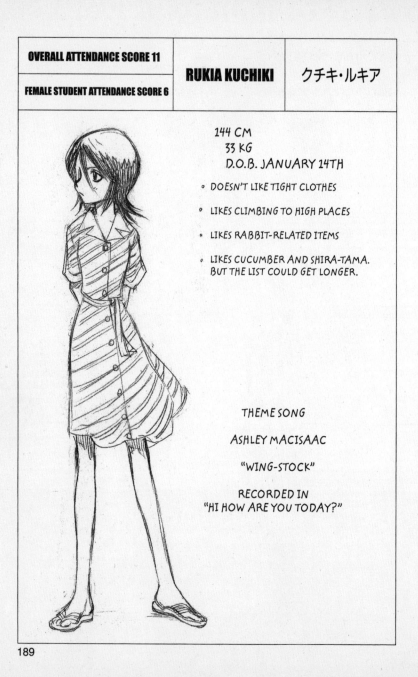

144 CM
33 KG
D.O.B. JANUARY 14TH

- DOESN'T LIKE TIGHT CLOTHES

- LIKES CLIMBING TO HIGH PLACES

- LIKES RABBIT-RELATED ITEMS

- LIKES CUCUMBER AND SHIRA-TAMA. BUT THE LIST COULD GET LONGER.

THEME SONG

ASHLEY MACISAAC

"WING-STOCK"

RECORDED IN
"HI HOW ARE YOU TODAY?"

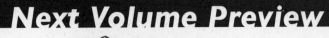

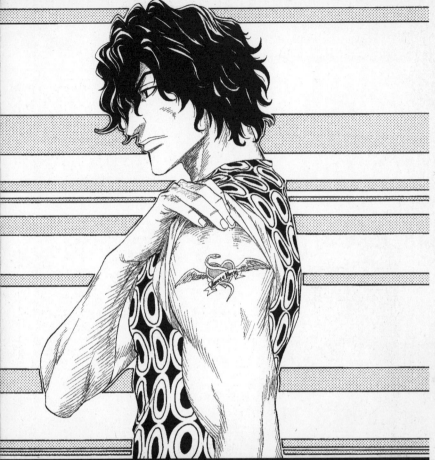

Chad escapes from the Kurosaki Clinic with a parakeet in tow, but it's no ordinary talking bird. A powerful Hollow is after the human soul that resides inside the well-spoken parakeet, and Ichigo and company have another fight on their hands. Much to everyone's surprise, Chad is able to hold his own against the powerful Hollow even though he can't see it! Later, Rukia does some impulse buying at a specialty shop that deals in unauthorized Soul Reaper items, but she ends up getting much more than she bargained for. All this and more, on sale in July 2004!

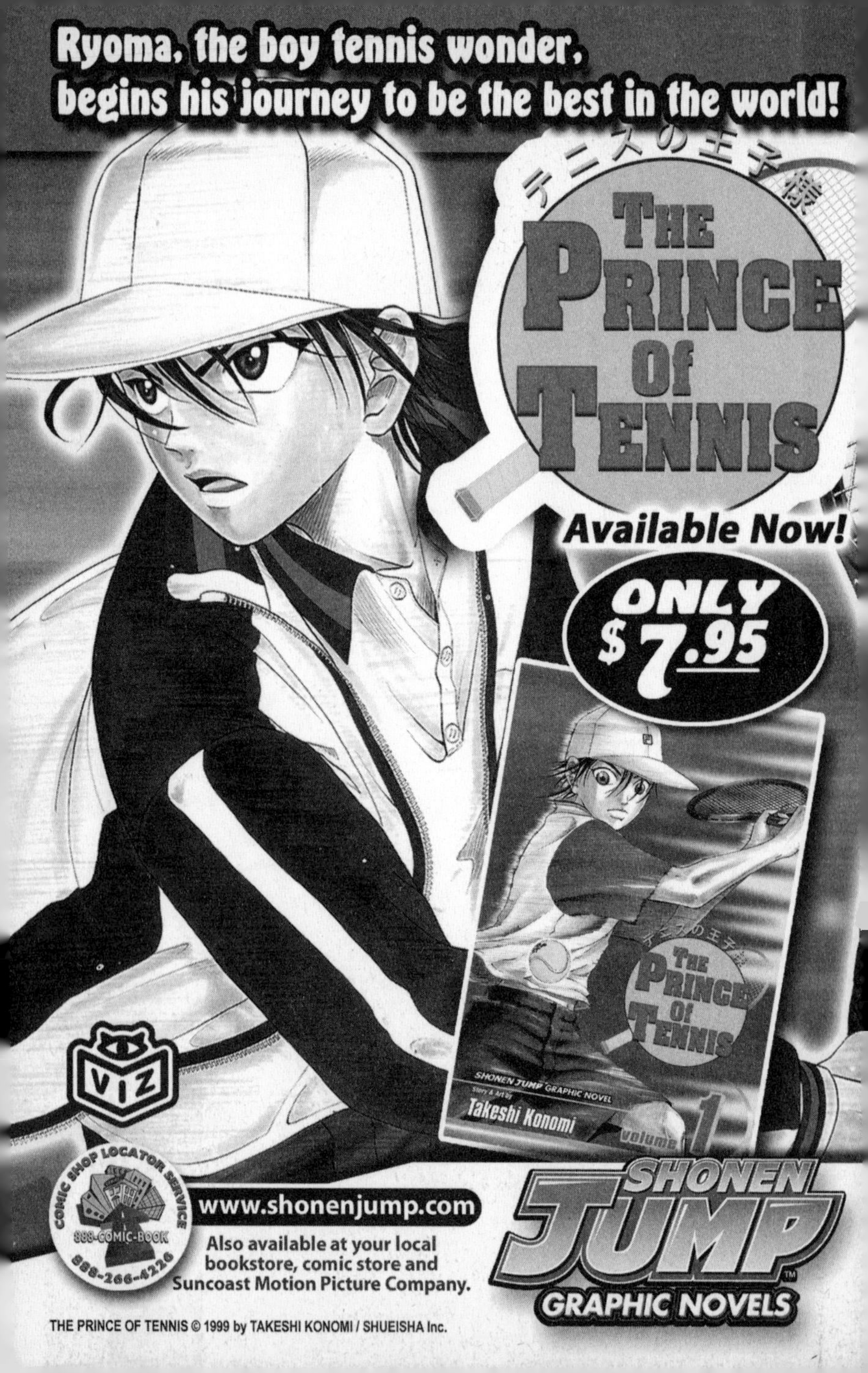
Ryoma, the boy tennis wonder, begins his journey to be the best in the world!
テニスの王子様
THE PRINCE OF TENNIS
Available Now!
ONLY $7.95
テニスの王子様
THE PRINCE OF TENNIS
SHONEN JUMP GRAPHIC NOVEL
Story & Art by
Takeshi Konomi
volume 1
VIZ
COMIC SHOP LOCATOR SERVICE
888-COMIC-BOOK
888-266-4226
www.shonenjump.com
Also available at your local bookstore, comic store and Suncoast Motion Picture Company.
SHONEN JUMP
GRAPHIC NOVELS
THE PRINCE OF TENNIS © 1999 by TAKESHI KONOMI / SHUEISHA Inc.

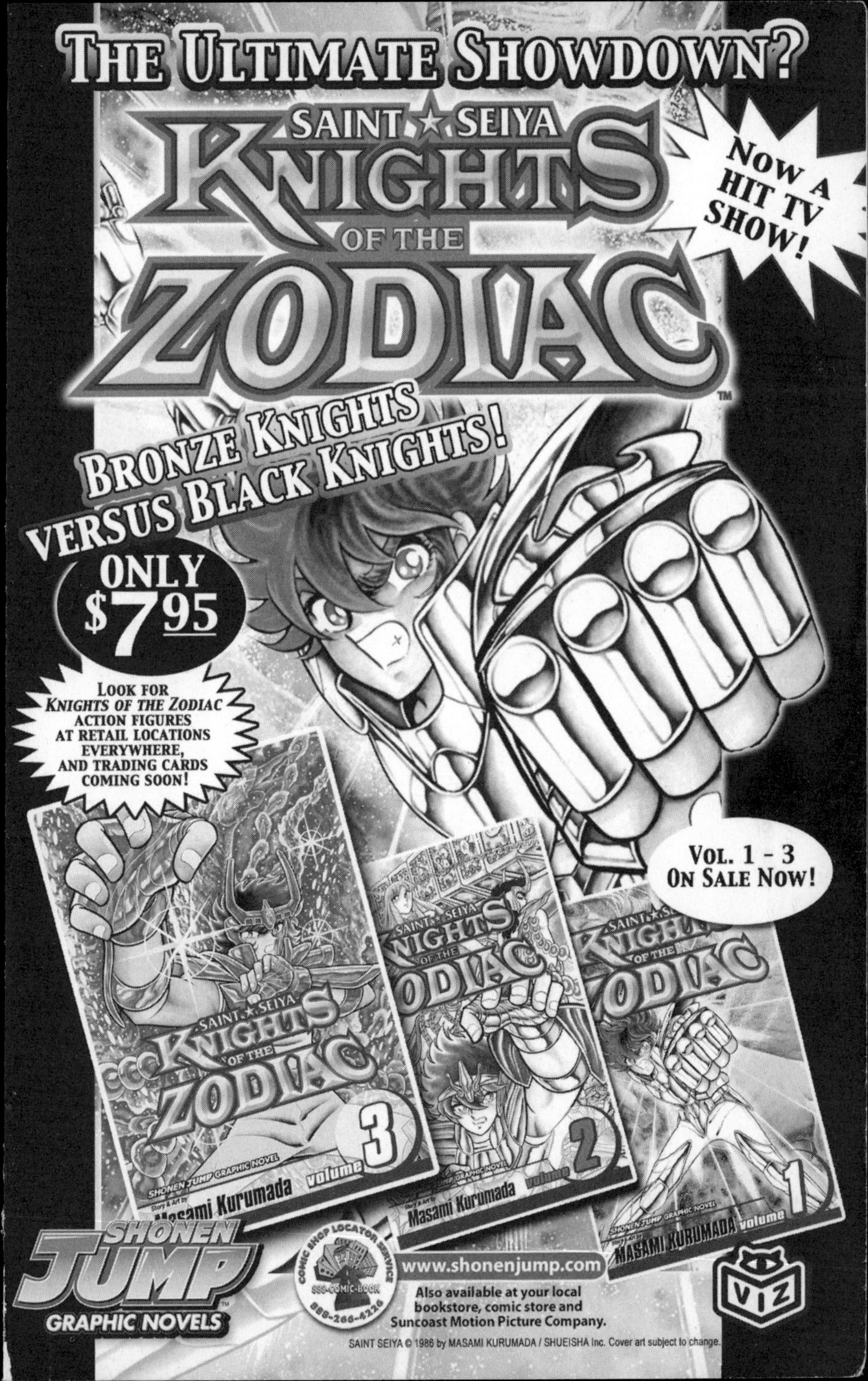
THE ULTIMATE SHOWDOWN?
SAINT ★ SEIYA
KNIGHTS OF THE ZODIAC™
NOW A HIT TV SHOW!
BRONZE KNIGHTS VERSUS BLACK KNIGHTS!
ONLY $7.95
LOOK FOR KNIGHTS OF THE ZODIAC ACTION FIGURES AT RETAIL LOCATIONS EVERYWHERE, AND TRADING CARDS COMING SOON!
VOL. 1 - 3 ON SALE NOW!
SAINT ★ SEIYA KNIGHTS OF THE ZODIAC
SHONEN JUMP GRAPHIC NOVEL
Story & Art by Masami Kurumada
volume 3
volume 2
volume 1
SHONEN JUMP GRAPHIC NOVELS
COMIC SHOP LOCATOR SERVICE
888-COMIC-BOOK
888-266-4226
www.shonenjump.com
Also available at your local bookstore, comic store and Suncoast Motion Picture Company.
VIZ
SAINT SEIYA © 1986 by MASAMI KURUMADA / SHUEISHA Inc. Cover art subject to change.

SHONEN JUMP
THE WORLD'S MOST POPULAR MANGA

COMPLETE OUR SURVEY AND LET US KNOW WHAT YOU THINK!

☐ Please check here if you DO NOT wish to receive information or future offers from VIZ

Name: _____

Address: _____

City:_____ State:_____ Zip:_____

E-mail: _____

☐ Male   ☐ Female   Date of Birth (mm/dd/yyyy): ___/___/_____   (Under 13? Parental consent required)

What race/ethnicity do you consider yourself? (please check one)

☐ Asian/Pacific Islander   ☐ Black/African American   ☐ Hispanic/Latino

☐ Native American/Alaskan Native   ☐ White/Caucasian   ☐ Other: _____

What SHONEN JUMP Graphic Novel did you purchase? (indicate title purchased)

_____

What other SHONEN JUMP Graphic Novels, if any, do you own? (indicate title(s) owned)

_____

_____

Reason for purchase: (check all that apply)

☐ Special offer   ☐ Favorite title   ☐ Gift

☐ Recommendation   ☐ Read in SHONEN JUMP Magazine

☐ Other_____

Where did you make your purchase? (please check one)

☐ Comic store   ☐ Bookstore   ☐ Mass/Grocery Store

☐ Newsstand   ☐ Video/Video Game Store   ☐ Other: _____

☐ Online (site: _____)

Do you read SHONEN JUMP Magazine?

- [ ] Yes
- [ ] No **(if no, skip the next two questions)**

Do you subscribe?

- [ ] Yes
- [ ] No

If you do not subscribe, how often do you purchase SHONEN JUMP Magazine?

- [ ] 1-3 issues a year
- [ ] 4-6 issues a year
- [ ] more than 7 issues a year

What genre of manga would you like to read as a SHONEN JUMP Graphic Novel?
(please check two)

- [ ] Adventure
- [ ] Comic Strip
- [ ] Science Fiction
- [ ] Fighting
- [ ] Horror
- [ ] Romance
- [ ] Fantasy
- [ ] Sports

Which do you prefer? (please check one)

- [ ] Reading right-to-left
- [ ] Reading left-to-right

Which do you prefer? (please check one)

- [ ] Sound effects in English
- [ ] Sound effects in Japanese with English captions
- [ ] Sound effects in Japanese only with a glossary at the back

THANK YOU! Please send the completed form to:

VIZ

VIZ Survey
42 Catharine St.
Poughkeepsie, NY 12601

All information provided will be used for internal purposes only. We promise not to sell or otherwise divulge your information.

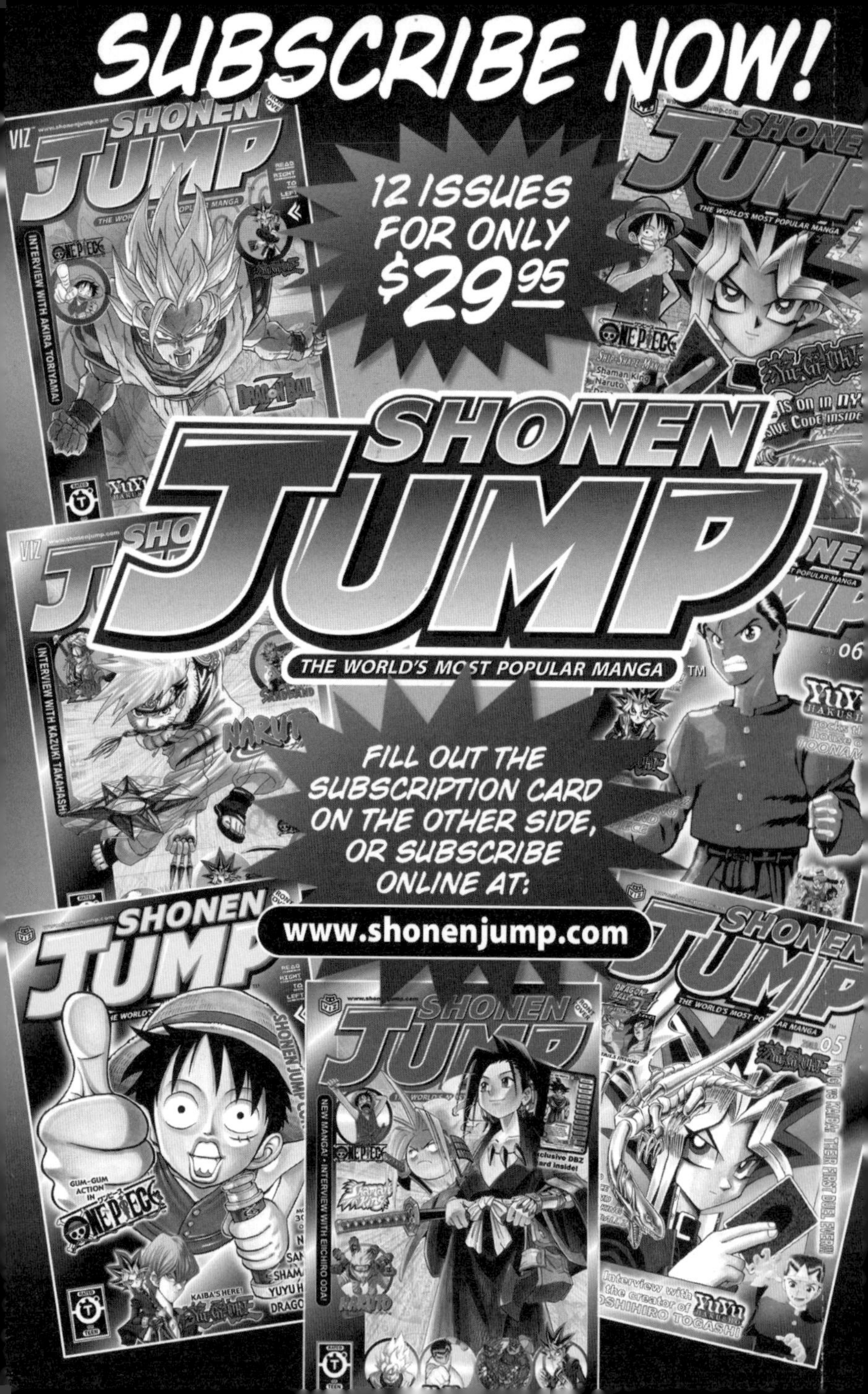
SUBSCRIBE NOW!
12 ISSUES FOR ONLY $29.95
SHONEN JUMP
THE WORLD'S MOST POPULAR MANGA™
FILL OUT THE SUBSCRIPTION CARD ON THE OTHER SIDE, OR SUBSCRIBE ONLINE AT:
www.shonenjump.com